The School Mathematics Project

When the SMP was founded in 1961, its main objective was to devise radically new secondary school mathematics courses to reflect, more adequately than did the traditional syllabuses, the up-to-date nature and usages of mathematics. The first texts produced embodied new courses for O-level and A-level, and SMP GCE examinations were set up, available to schools through any of the GCE examining boards.

Since its beginning the SMP has continued to develop new materials and approaches to the teaching of mathematics. Further series of texts have been produced to meet new needs, and the original books are revised or replaced in the light of changing circumstances and experience in the classroom.

The SMP A-level course is now covered by *Revised Advanced Mathematics Books 1, 2* and *3*. Five shorter texts cover the material of the various sections of the A-level examination *SMP Further Mathematics*. The SMP Additional Mathematics syllabus has been revised and a new text replaces the original two books at this level.

The six Units of *SMP 7–13*, designed for pupils in that age-range, provide a course which is widely used in primary schools, middle schools and the first two years of secondary schools. A useful preliminary to Unit 1 of *SMP 7–13* is *Pointers*, a booklet for teachers which offers suggestions for mathematical activities with young children.

There is now a range of SMP materials for the eleven to sixteen age-range. The SMP O-level course is covered by *Books 1, 2* and *New Books 3, 4, 5*. Books *A–G* and *X, Y, Z*, together with the booklets of the *SMP Calculator Series*, also cover the O-level course, while *Books A–H* provide a CSE course for which most CSE boards offer a suitable examination.

SMP 11–16, designed to cater for about the top 85% of the ability range, is the newest SMP secondary school course, providing varied materials which facilitate the provision of a differentiated curriculum to match the varying abilities of pupils. Publication of this course began in 1983 and will be complete in 1988.

Teacher's Guides accompany all these series.

The SMP has produced many other texts, and teachers are encouraged to obtain each year from Cambridge University Press, The Edinburgh Building, Shaftesbury Road, Cambridge CB2 2RU, the full list of SMP publications currently available. In the same way, help and advice may always be sought by teachers from the Executive Director at the SMP Office, Westfield College, Kidderpore Avenue, London NW3 7ST. SMP syllabuses and other information may be obtained from the same address.

The SMP is continually evaluating old work and preparing for new. The effectiveness of the SMP's work depends, as it always has done, on the comments and reactions received from a wide variety of teachers – and also from pupils – using SMP materials. Readers of the texts can, therefore, send their comments to the SMP in the knowledge that they will be valued and carefully studied.

THE SCHOOL MATHEMATICS PROJECT

New Book 5

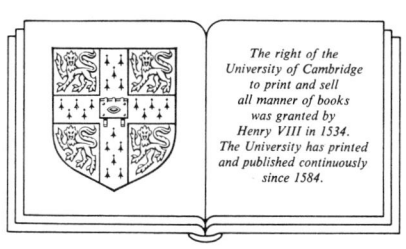

*The right of the
University of Cambridge
to print and sell
all manner of books
was granted by
Henry VIII in 1534.
The University has printed
and published continuously
since 1584.*

CAMBRIDGE UNIVERSITY PRESS

Cambridge
London   New York   New Rochelle
Melbourne   Sydney

Published by the Press Syndicate of the University of Cambridge
The Pitt Building, Trumpington Street, Cambridge CB2 1RP
32 East 57th Street, New York, NY 10022, USA
296 Beaconsfield Parade, Middle Park, Melbourne 3206, Australia

© Cambridge University Press 1983

First published 1983
Reprinted 1984

Printed in Great Britain by the
University Press, Cambridge

Library of Congress catalogue card number 82-1242

British Library cataloguing in publication data
School Mathematics Project
The School Mathematics Project
New Book 5
1. Mathematics–1961–
510   QA39.2
ISBN 0 521 27571 7

Contents

	Preface	*page* vii
1	Plans and elevations	1
2	Polynomials	25
3	Practical arithmetic	39
	Revision exercises 1–3	81
4	Mathematical models	83
5	Statistics	114
6	Structure	137
	Revision exercises 4–6	151
7	Equations, inequalities and graphs	155
8	Probability	176
9	Vectors applied	189
10	Geometry	214
	Revision papers	236
	Answers	245
	Index	253

Preface

SMP Books 1–5 were published in the early sixties and have remained as the basic SMP O-level course, unchanged except for metrication. The revision of *Books 3*, *4* and *5* draws on the experience of teaching with the original texts and incorporates other material developed by the SMP during the intervening years. While the mathematical content remains fundamentally unchanged the order of presentation of the material has been modified; the TEC Level I mathematics objectives have been borne in mind throughout the writing. The aim has been to make the texts accessible to a wider range of pupils, with clearer explanations and more carefully graded exercises, giving attention both to the practice of the necessary technical skills and to the use of the concepts in a variety of contexts. The electronic calculator is seen as the primary calculating aid throughout the books. Suggestions for ways in which pupils can use computers as an aid to learning mathematics are made at appropriate points in the latter half of the course. Most chapters conclude with a Summary exercise and a Miscellaneous exercise. Answers to about half the questions in exercises other than summary, miscellaneous and revision are provided at the end of each book; other answers are to be found in the accompanying *Teacher's Guides*.

The new books, like their predecessors, provide opportunities for the teacher to develop topics beyond the SMP O-level examination syllabuses, both of which are fully covered in the texts.

The 'two books per year' arrangement of the 'lettered' books has proved convenient and economical. It is hoped that presenting the last three years' work in five volumes rather than three will give schools the flexibility to allow for the different paces at which pupils work through the course. There is a range of SMP material designed for the first two years of the secondary school. Besides *Books 1* and *2*, *Books A–D*, *Cards I* and *II* and *Units 5* and *6* of *SMP 7–13* can be used. *SMP New Book 3* is written to follow from any of these alternatives; in addition it contains sufficient material for pupils who transfer to the SMP course at this stage.

The authors of the original books, on whose contributions this series is based, are named in *The School Mathematics Project: The First Ten Years*, published by Cambridge University Press.

SMP New Books 3, 4 and *5* have been produced by

    David Cundy   Timothy Lewis
    Giles Dickins   Charles Parker
    Colin Goldsmith   Alan Tammadge
    Katie Hairs   Nigel Webb
    John Hersee   Lynette Weekley

and edited by David Cundy.

The authors wish to express their thanks to those who have helped with advice and criticism, particularly the teachers and pupils who have tested the material in draft form, to Hilary Barton who typed the greater part of that draft, and to the Oxford and Cambridge Schools Examination Board for permission to reprint questions from SMP O-level papers.

1
Plans and elevations

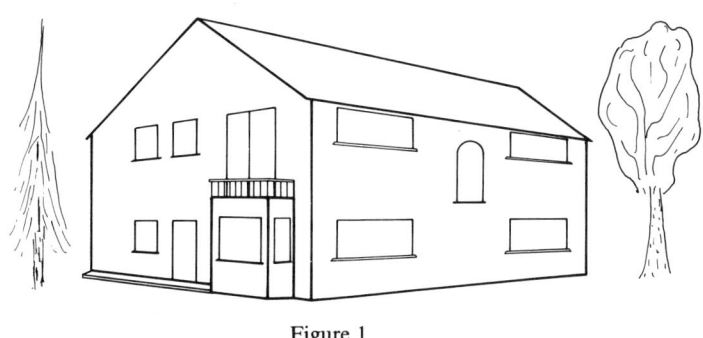

Figure 1

1. PLANS AND ELEVATIONS

One day you may have a house built for you. What will it look like? The sketch (Figure 1) shows one 'dream house', but the picture is not sufficient for the builder to work from. He will need exact measurements. Not only does the perspective sketch distort the part that it does show; it hides other information. Can you decide what the house would look like from a point of view on the other side of it?

Builders need a *plan* to set out the ground before they start to build. They also need *elevations*, or side views of the house, to get the walls right and the windows in the correct places, for example. Each of these drawings – plan, elevations – is made looking directly at the house from the appropriate direction. Figure 2 shows some drawings similar to those the architect would provide. (The usual conventions used by architects will be shown later in the chapter.)

You need to know a few 'conventions' to read these drawings. Doors are shown like this on the plan ═════╱═════ – indicating how they are hinged to open. Windows are shown like this: ▬▬▬ ═══ ▬▬▬
                                                                                                                     Wall   Window   Wall

2 Plans and elevations Ch. 1

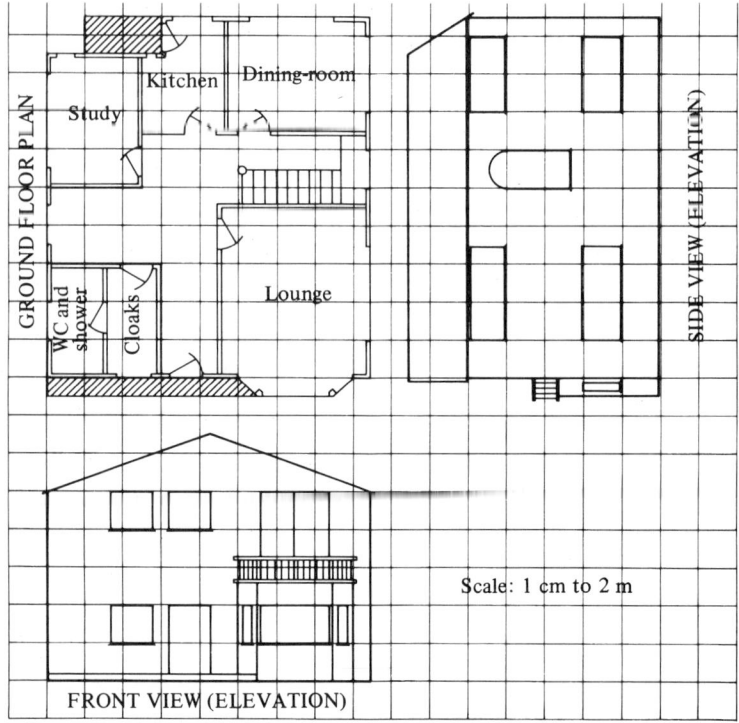

Figure 2

Exercise A

(You should do all of questions 1–7 at least.)

The plan

*1 What are the floor dimensions of (*a*) the lounge (including bay window), (*b*) the study, (*c*) the dining-room?
 2 How wide are the windows of (*a*) the dining-room, (*b*) the study?
 3 What are the dimensions of the tiled area outside the door into the kitchen from outside the house?

Elevations

The plan tells us the width of doors and windows, but it is the side views, or elevations, which tell us how high the windows are and how high up the walls they are positioned. The *side view* shown will help you to answer the next three questions.

*4 What is the height above ground level of the sill of the large window in the lounge?
 5 What is the height of the side windows of the bay window of the lounge?
 6 Why is the window with the circular top positioned at an intermediate height?
 7 Use the *front view* or elevation to answer the following:
   (*a*) What does the shaded section on the plan alongside the bay window represent?

(b) Why do the windows above the bay window not have the same sill level as the others on the first floor of the house?

(c) What is the distance from the 'ridge' (the highest point of the roof) to the gutter along the top of the walls?

Remember, the plan shows how the house is laid out on the ground, or on any horizontal level. So we could have a first floor plan as well, showing how the rooms are arranged at this level.

Elevations are not perspective views. They are drawn as if looking at the side of the house 'straight on'. So the walls, which are vertical, are drawn true; you could make a model by tracing from the elevations of the walls. But the same is not true of the roof. In question 7(c) above you found the sloping length of the roof. Compare this with the apparent measurement of the same distance on the side elevation. Because the roof slopes, the distance is apparently shortened in the side elevation.

8 Draw the other two elevations of the house, making sensible assumptions about the positions and heights of windows.

Look at the drawings carefully. The rooms on the first floor of the house are directly above those on the ground floor so that the walls carry on up through the house, except that there is one bedroom over the downstairs cloaks and WC and shower, so the dividing wall ends at ceiling level on the ground floor. The bathroom is over the kitchen.

9 Draw a first floor plan of the house. (You may find it helpful to use a tracing of the ground floor to start from.) What differences will there be from the ground floor plan? What happens at the staircase? What happens over the lounge?

2. HOW MANY DRAWINGS ARE NECESSARY?

Figure 3 shows the plan and one elevation of a bungalow. It is drawn to a scale of 1 centimetre to 2 metres and a half-centimetre grid is shown to help you with this piece of work.

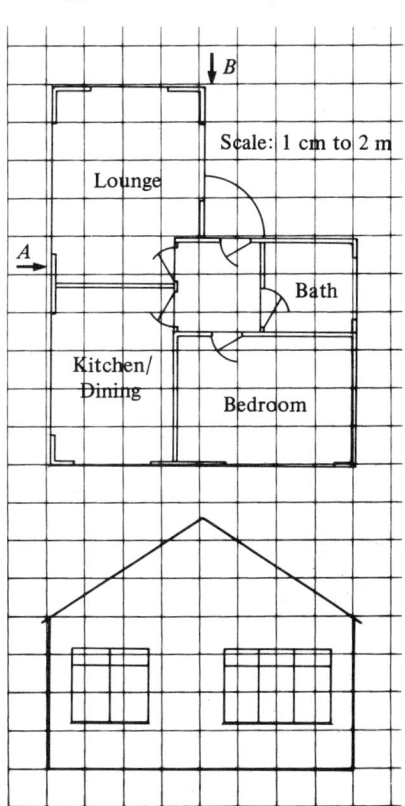

Figure 3

Exercise B

(You may find it helps to trace the plan and elevation given, but the Teacher's Guide includes a 'master' from which copies can be made.)

1. Assuming that window heights follow those on the elevation given, draw the elevation of this bungalow when viewed from the direction *A*. Start with the wall. Can you complete your drawing and be sure that it is correct?

   Since we are told that the building is a bungalow it is not difficult to draw the wall, but we cannot be certain about the roof. The elevation given in Figure 3 tells us that the *right*-hand edge of the roof should be drawn as in Figure 4(*a*). What would you need to add to the elevation shown in Figure 3 if, in fact, the drawing in Figure 4(*b*) were the correct one?

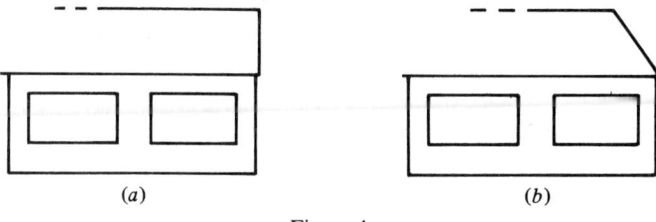

Figure 4

Even with that addition, we still would not know at what angle to draw the right-hand edge line of the roof; any one of the drawings in Figure 5 (and others!) could be correct. It is the elevation that you are drawing now that will tell the builder what he needs to know.

For the *left*-hand edge of the roof the drawings in Figure 3 tell us nothing, so that edge could be as the right-hand edge in Figure 4(*a*) or the mirror image of any of the ones in Figure 5.

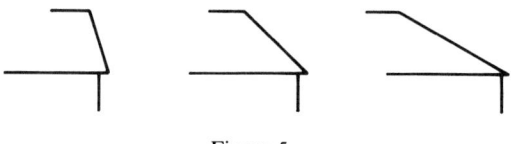

Figure 5

2. Assuming that no part of the roof has an end of the type shown in Figure 4(*b*) and that the door is 2 metres high, draw the elevation from the direction *B*.
3. What further information would the builder need that is not provided by the plan and the three elevations?
4. Although a perspective sketch can often suggest exactly what an object is like and, in other cases, only two drawings may be necessary, it is important that the drawings of any object, that is to be built or made, give complete information. In Figure 6 the drawings given are not sufficient to make definite the shape of the object. For each example, give as many objects as you can which the given drawings could partially represent. Give sketches to make your answers clear.

The Third Angle convention 5

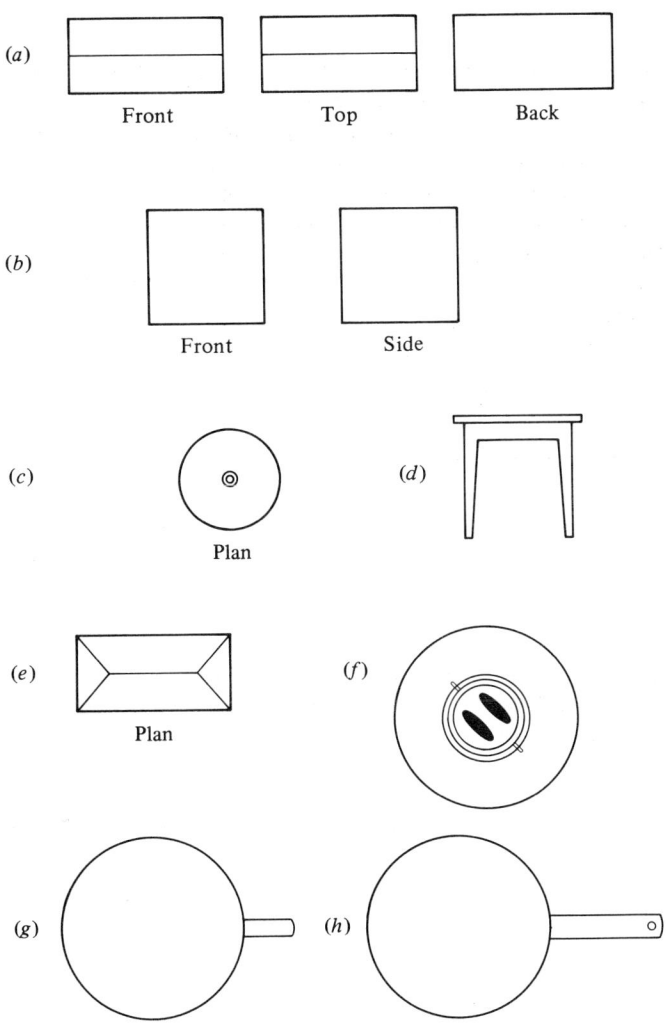

Figure 6

3. THE THIRD ANGLE CONVENTION

When working on the house and bungalow drawings you will have found it necessary to turn the page round from time to time. We now look at the conventional way of arranging the plan and elevations which avoids this difficulty. Another advantage of the standard convention is that, as drawings always have the same arrangement, interpretation becomes easier with practice. We shall work with a relatively simple object, shown in Figure 7.

Figure 8 shows how one view of the object is *projected onto a plane*. It is as if the view through a glass plate were to be etched onto the glass. Notice that the 'projectors' are *parallel* to each other and *perpendicular* to the plane of

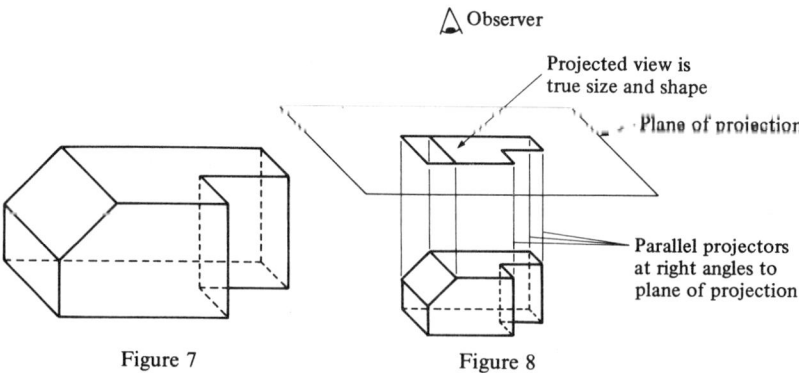

Figure 7 Figure 8

projection. The projected view is then the true shape and size, just as the elevations in the house and bungalow drawings are the true shape and size (to scale).

The standard planes of projection were first used by Gaspard Monge in a book published in 1795, and consist of a vertical plane (VP) intersected by a horizontal plane (HP), the line of intersection being called XY (see Figure 9). If necessary, other 'auxiliary' vertical planes (AVP) can be added at any angle to VP – most commonly at right angles. We shall return to this later.

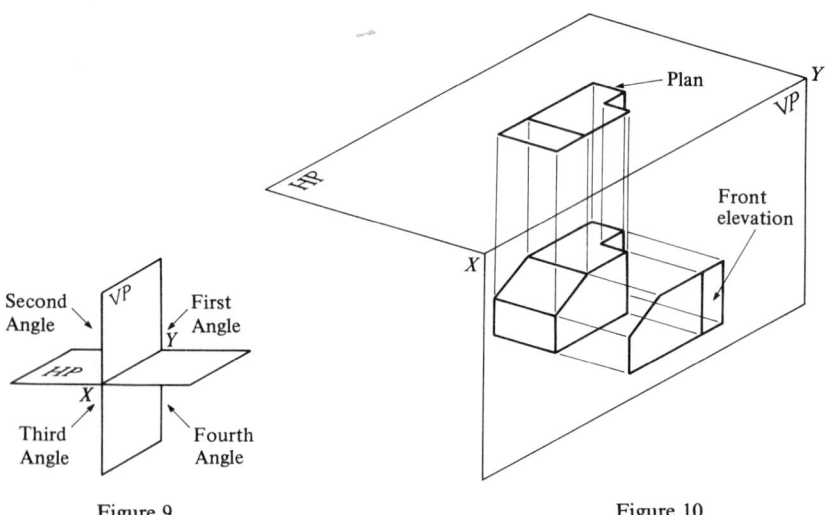

Figure 9 Figure 10

The angles between the planes are numbered First, Second, Third and Fourth, as shown. Figure 10 shows our object in the Third Angle, with the corresponding views projected onto HP and VP. So that the HP and VP views can be represented on a flat sheet of paper, we imagine HP to be rotated about XY until it is vertical (see Figure 11).

The Third Angle convention

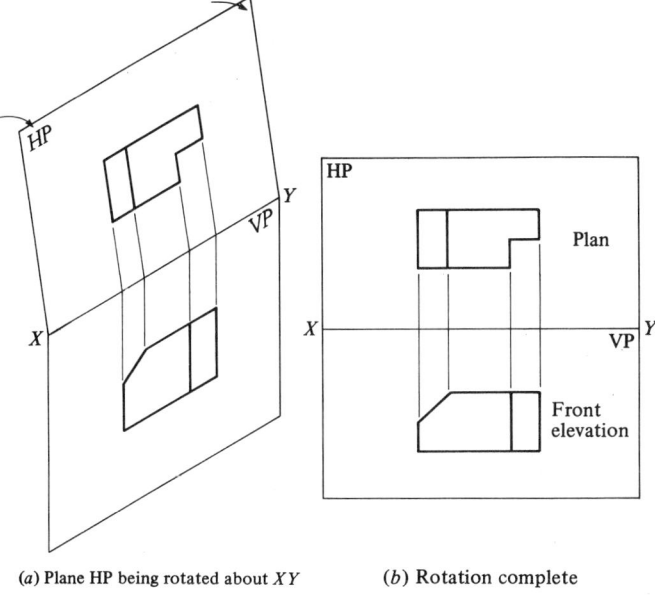

(a) Plane HP being rotated about XY   (b) Rotation complete

Figure 11

As with the drawings of the house, views projected onto horizontal planes are called plans, and views projected onto vertical planes are called elevations.

Two systems of arranging the projections are in use. The object may be placed in the First Angle or in the Third Angle. We shall use only the Third Angle method.

Figure 11(b) shows the final plan and elevation in this arrangement. The projection lines joining the two views are sometimes omitted and the abbreviations are omitted from the final drawing.

The same idea of rotating planes is used to show end or other side elevations. Some people find it helpful to imagine the object inside a glass box with hinged sides. The plan and elevations can then be imagined drawn on the sides of the box which is then opened out flat (see Figure 12). Figure 13 shows our simple object inside such a box.

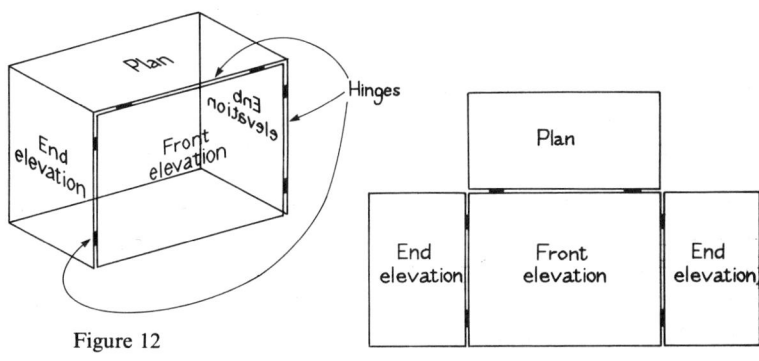

Figure 12

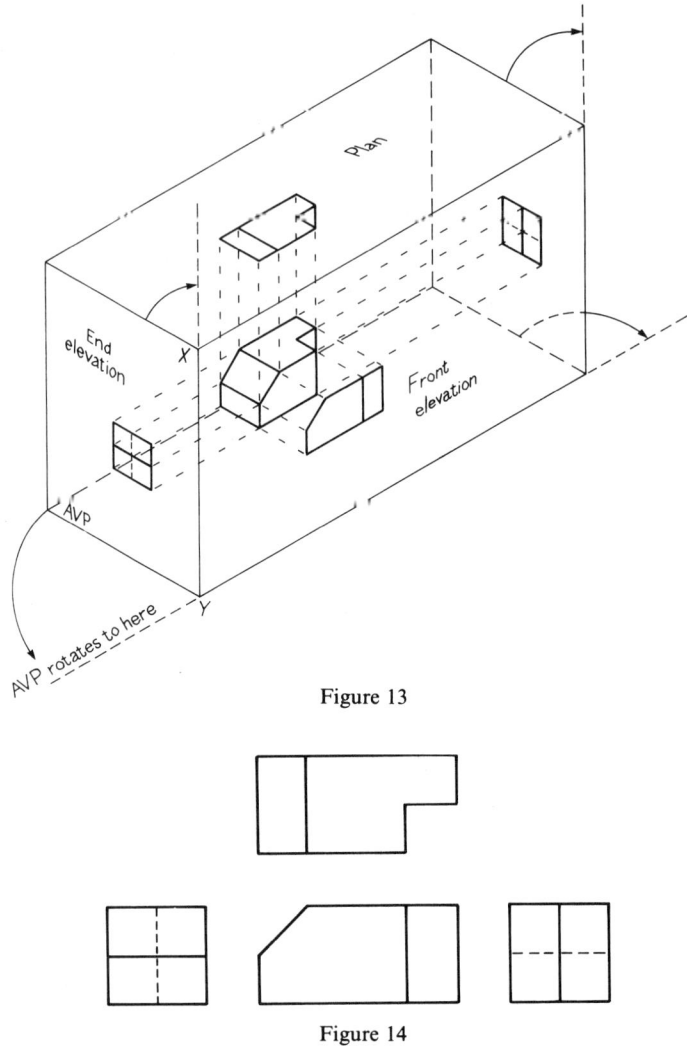

Figure 13

Figure 14

The final result when the box has been opened out is shown in Figure 14.

Notice the broken lines in the end elevations, each of which represents an edge that is hidden from view. In practice, for this solid, it would not be necessary to show both end elevations.

4. TWO METHODS OF DRAWING PLANS AND ELEVATIONS

In answering some of the questions in this chapter you have probably found your own methods for making extra drawings, but two methods that are commonly used lead to accurate drawings with the minimum of effort. Figure 15 shows the first applied to the solid we have been considering. The plan is drawn

Two methods of drawing plans and elevations

first, then the construction lines, including the line at 45° through the point of intersection of XY and $X_1 Y_1$, enable lengths to be transferred from the plan to the elevations. Study Figure 15 and note that some distances must be equal. Does the angled line have to be at 45°? Why?

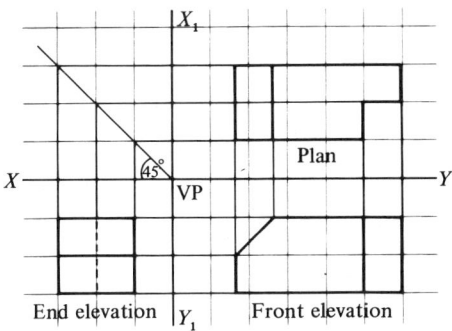

Figure 15

As Figure 15 shows, this method is easy to use with squared paper or graph paper and acceptable drawings can be produced in this way unless great accuracy is required.

The second standard method is similar, but uses compasses as shown in Figure 16.

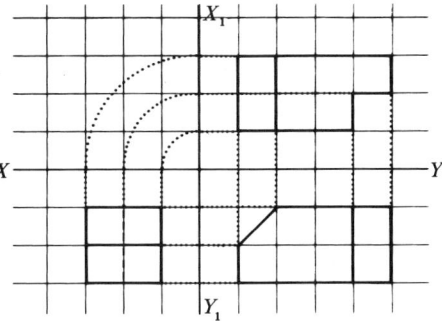

Figure 16

Exercise C

1 The drawings in Figure 17 show a Third Angle plan and elevation of a number of solids. Sketch or describe the object in each case, giving an 'every day' example where possible. (For example, (i) could be a roof.)

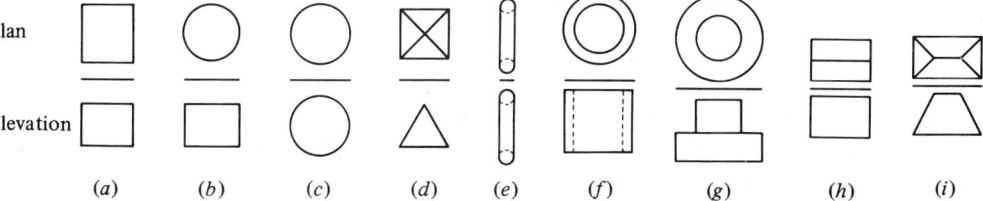

Figure 17

2 Figure 18 shows the ground floor and first floor plans for a holiday chalet and the outline of the south-facing elevation. Copy the drawings onto graph paper (the scale is 1 cm to 2 m) and complete the elevation, making sensible assumptions about window heights, etc. Draw also the east- and west-facing elevations.

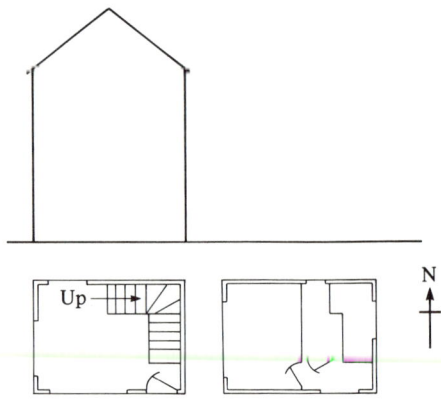

Figure 18

3 Figure 19 shows the plan and two elevations for a house, this time arranged as they would be presented by an architect. Copy the outline of the plan onto graph paper.
Draw the elevations looking from the directions *A* and *B*.
Draw also a first floor plan of the house, with the bathroom over the kitchen. You will find that it is difficult to fit in more than two bedrooms – why?

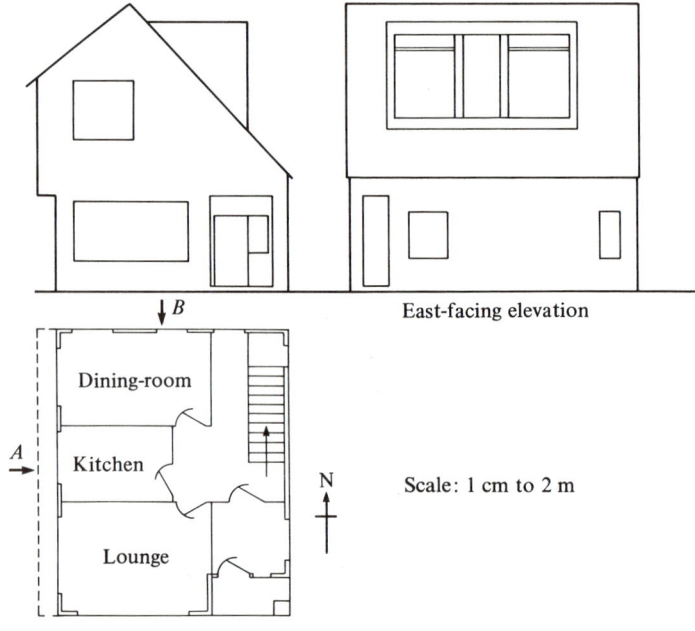

Figure 19

4 In Figure 20 one view out of three has in each case been omitted. Copy what is given and sketch in the missing view.

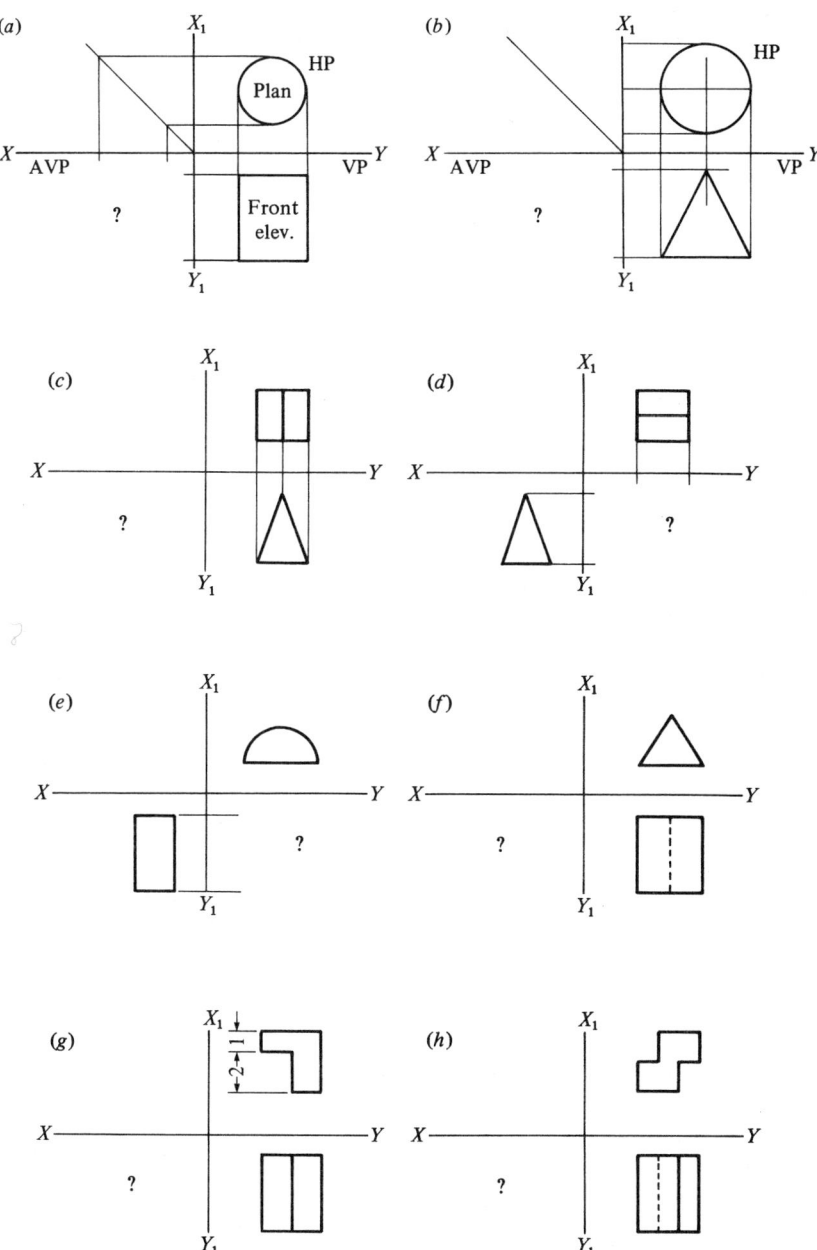

Figure 20(a–h)

12 Plans and elevations Ch. 1

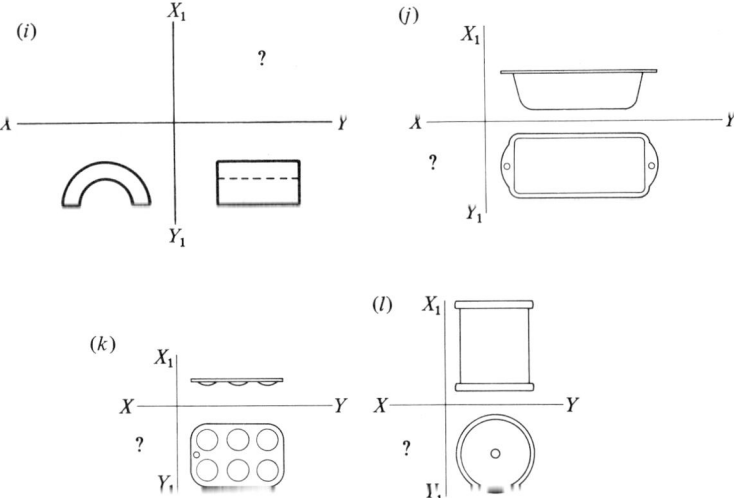

Figure 20(i–l)

5 In Figure 21 the end elevation is from the right instead of from the left, so AVP appears to the right of VP. Copy and complete each diagram. (a) is already completed as an example.

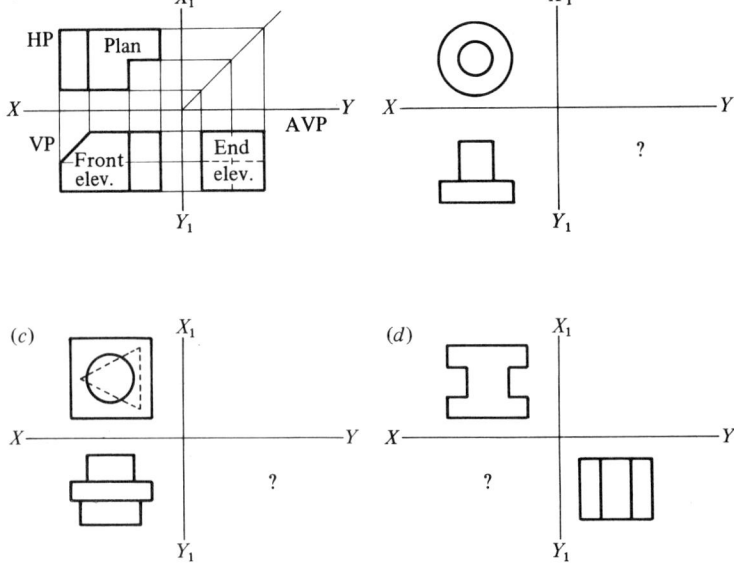

Figure 21(a–d)

Two methods of drawing plans and elevations 13

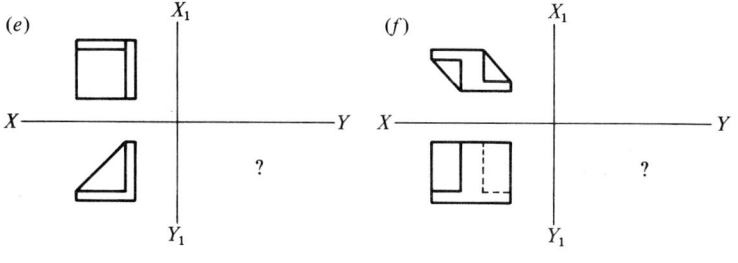

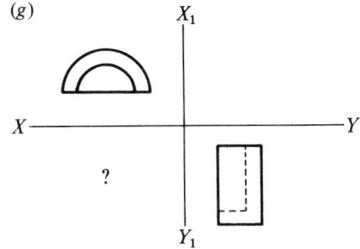

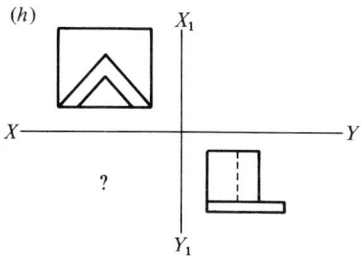

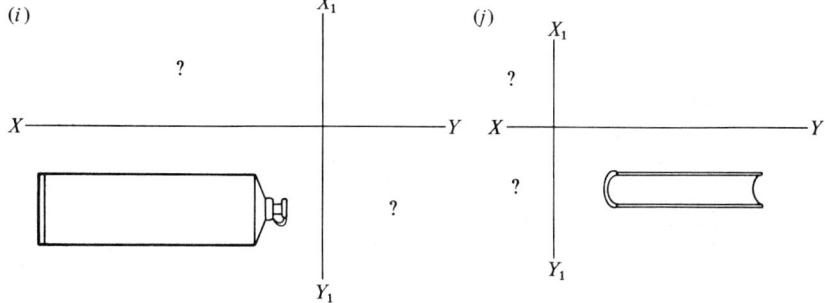

Figure 21 (*e–j*)

6 Draw a full size plan, side elevation (view from *A*) and front elevation (view from *B*) of the metal casting shown in Figure 22.

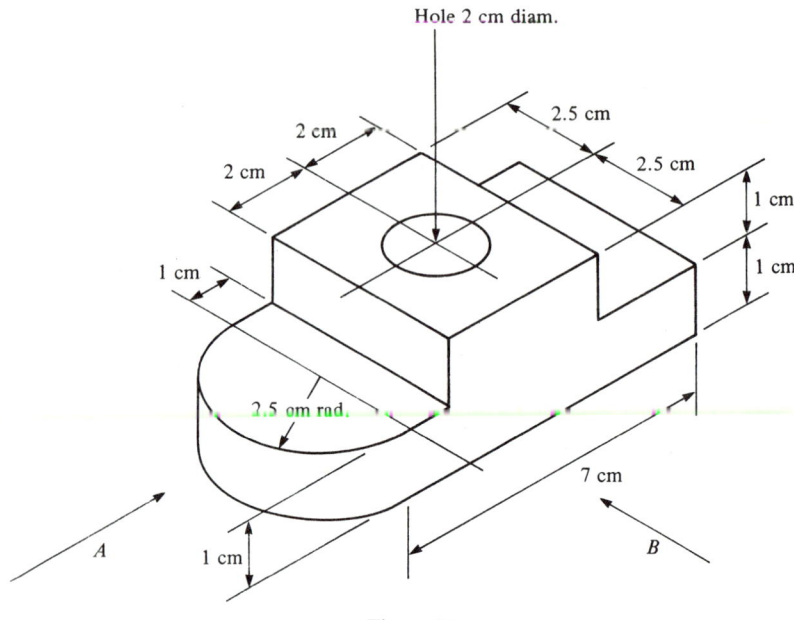

Figure 22

7 Draw a plan and two elevations (views from *A* and *B*) of the solid shown in Figure 23.

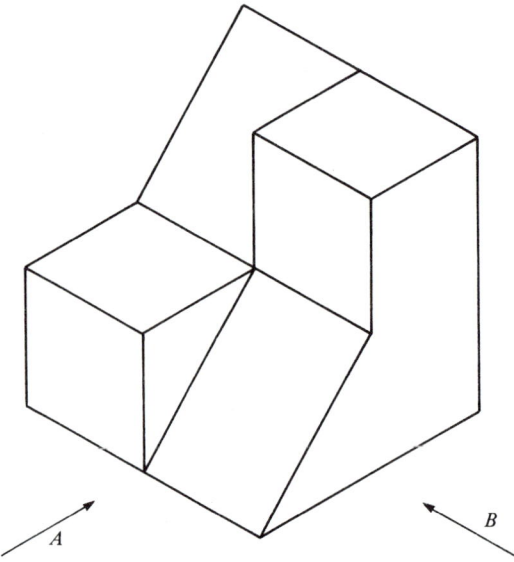

Figure 23

Two methods of drawing plans and elevations 15

*8 VABCD is a pyramid with a square base ABCD of side 8.0 cm. Its vertex V is vertically above O, the centre of its base, the distance VO being 8.5 cm. Taking the base of the pyramid parallel to HP and the edges of the base to be inclined at 45° to VP, draw a plan and elevation on a vertical plane parallel to AC. P and Q are points on CV, DV respectively, such that PV = QV = 3.5 cm. Find the length of PQ and the height of P above the base.

9 Figure 24 shows the net of a square-based pyramid. Find by drawing:
   (a) the height of the pyramid;
   (b) the angle between the edges VA and VC of the pyramid, where V is the vertex above the base ABCD.

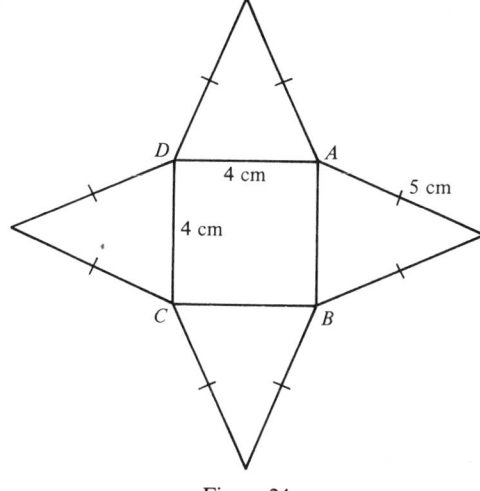

Figure 24

10 Figure 25 shows a plan and two elevations of a solid object. Carve such an object from wood or cork or some other suitable material.

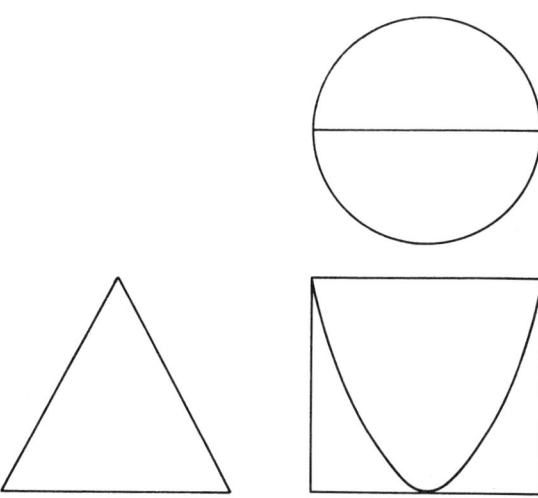

Figure 25

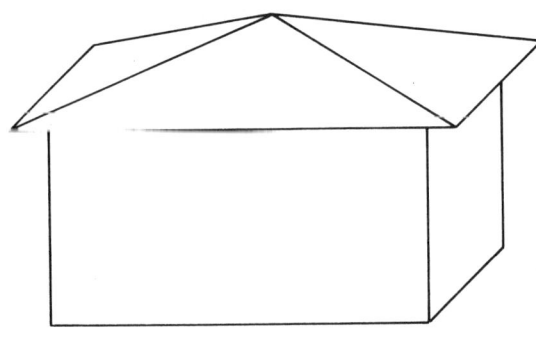

Figure 26

5. MEASUREMENTS IN THREE DIMENSIONS

An architect is designing a school. His plans include a rectangular tower surmounted by a roof in the form of a right pyramid (see Figure 26). (A *right* pyramid is one with its top vertex symmetrically placed relative to its base.)

The base of the pyramid is to be 8.0 m by 5.0 m. The sloping faces are to be covered with copper sheet (very expensive), so their area and hence the height of the pyramid must be kept to a minimum. The architect feels that for good looks the height of the pyramid should be 1.5 m; the question is, 'Will the slope of the faces then be sufficient to ensure efficient drainage of rainwater?'. (A slope of at least 15° is needed for this purpose.)

So he needs to know:
 (i) the slope of each face;
 (ii) the length of each sloping edge (because the lengths of the joists must be known);
 (iii) the area of each sloping face (to find the cost of the copper sheet).

All of the necessary measurements can be found by scale-drawing or by calculation. We shall demonstrate both approaches, but in practice only one of the two methods would be used.

Figure 27 shows the pyramid with its vertices labelled. Figure 28 shows the plan and two elevations. O is the centre of the base, M is the midpoint of BC and N is the midpoint of AB.

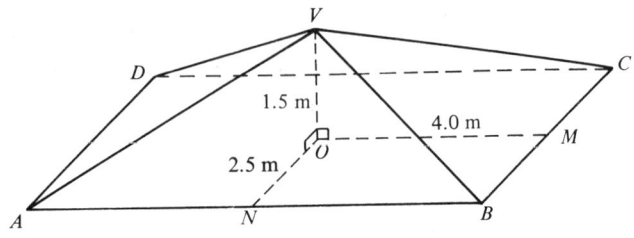

Figure 27

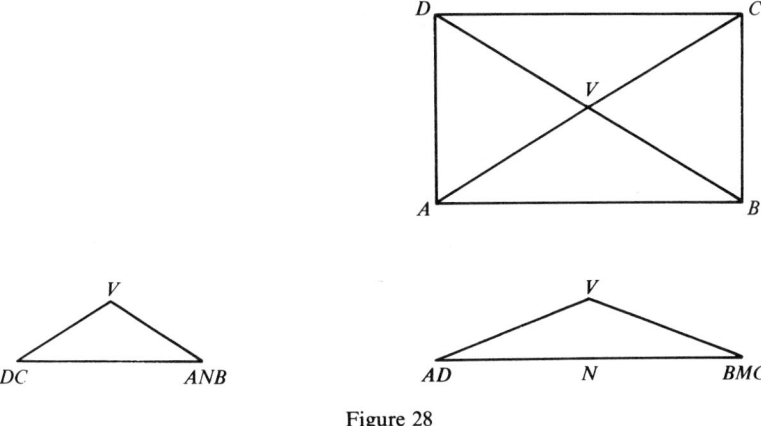

Figure 28

Scale-drawing

(a) The slope of the face VBC is the angle between plane VBC and the base $ABCD$, that is, the angle VMO. Similarly, angle VNO gives the slope of the face VAB.

By measurement from the front elevation shown in Figure 28,

$$\text{angle } VMO = 21°.$$

By measurement from the end elevation shown in Figure 28,

$$\text{angle } VNO = 31°.$$

(b) All the sloping edges (VA, VB, VC, VD) are of equal length, since V is vertically above O. A drawing of the isosceles triangle BVD (or half of it) will give the length of BV or DV. To draw this triangle we need to find the length of BD, which can be obtained from the plan in Figure 28. From the drawing of triangle BVD in Figure 29 we find that $VB = 5$ m.

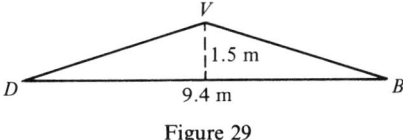

Figure 29

(c) From the elevations we can find the lengths of VM and VN. It is then a straightforward calculation to find the area of each sloping face.

By measurement $VM = 4.3$ m,

$$\begin{aligned}\text{so the area of triangle } VBC &= \tfrac{1}{2} \times \text{base} \times \text{height} \\ &= \tfrac{1}{2} \times 5 \times 4.3 \text{ m}^2 \\ &\approx 10.8 \text{ m}^2.\end{aligned}$$

By measurement $VN = 2.9$ m,

$$\begin{aligned}\text{so area of triangle } VAB &= \tfrac{1}{2} \times 8 \times 2.9 \text{ m}^2 \\ &\approx 11.6 \text{ m}^2.\end{aligned}$$

Therefore the total area of the roof
$$\approx 2\,(10.8 + 11.6)\ \text{m}^2$$
$$= 45\ \text{m}^2 \text{ to 2 s.f.}$$

Calculation

(Some of the explanation given under scale-drawing is still required here.)

(a) For example, we have $\tan \angle VMO = \dfrac{1.4}{4.0} = 0.375$ (see Figure 30)
$$\Leftarrow \angle VMO = 20.6°$$

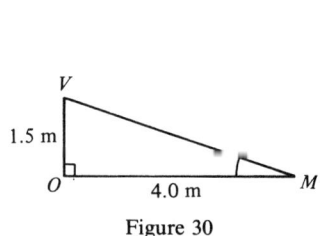

Figure 30

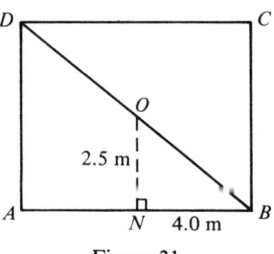

Figure 31

(b) By Pythagoras' theorem applied to triangle ONB,
$$BO^2 = (4.0^2 + 2.5^2)\ \text{m}^2 = 22.25\ \text{m}^2$$

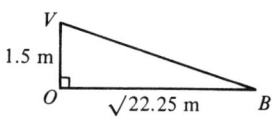

Figure 32

and, again, by Pythagoras' theorem in triangle BOV,
$$BV^2 = BO^2 + OV^2$$
$$= (22.25 + 2.25)\ \text{m}^2$$
$$= 24.5\ \text{m}^2.$$
So $BV = \sqrt{24.5}\ \text{m} = 4.95\ \text{m}$ to 3 s.f.
The length of each sloping edge is 5 metres.

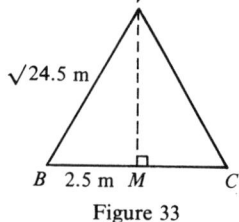

Figure 33

(c) For example, $MV^2 = BV^2 - BM^2$ (see Figure 33)
$$= (24.5 - 6.25)\ \text{m}^2$$
$$= 18.25\ \text{m}^2.$$
So $MV = \sqrt{18.25}\ \text{m} = 4.27\ \text{m}$ to 3 s.f.
and the area of triangle $VBC = \tfrac{1}{2} \times 5 \times 4.27\ \text{m}^2$
$$= 10.7\ \text{m}^2 \text{ to 3 s.f.}$$

In solving problems of this kind always (i) sketch the whole figure and (ii) sketch the relevant right-angled triangles separately. Notice, too, how later stages often depend on earlier results.

Measurements in three dimensions 19

Exercise D

Some of the following questions should be solved by drawing and some by calculation.

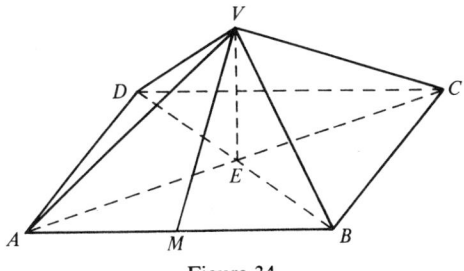

Figure 34

*1 Figure 34 shows a right pyramid with a rectangular base. $AB = 8.0$ cm, $BC = 6.0$ cm, $VE = 4.0$ cm, and M is the midpoint of AB.
  (a) Find AE and VA.
  (b) Find $\angle VME$.

2 O is the point $(0, 0, 0)$ and P is the point $(3, 4, 5)$.
  (a) Calculate the length OP.
  (b) Calculate the angle between OP and
    (i) the plane $x = 0$;
    (ii) the plane $y = 0$;
    (iii) the z-axis.

3 In Figure 35(a), TF represents a tower with two observation points A and B on the same level as F. If A is due west of F, B due south of F, the length of AB is 70 m, $\alpha = 45$, and the bearing of A from B is 330°, find the height of the tower.

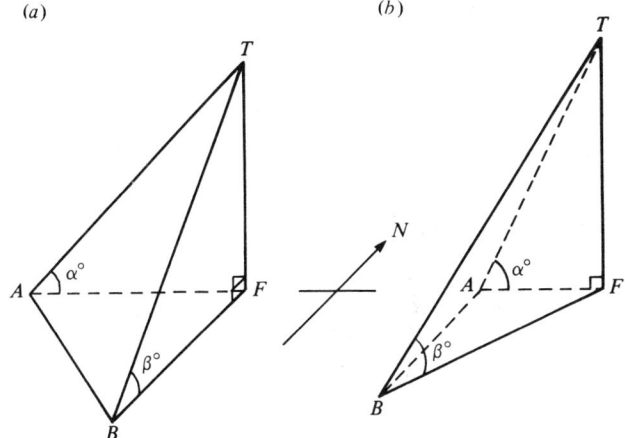

Figure 35

*4 If, in Figure 35(b), A is due west of F, $\tan \alpha° = \sqrt{3}$, B is 70 m due south of A, and the bearing of T from B is 060°, find β.

5 *VABCD*, in Figure 36, is a right pyramid, on a horizontal rectangular base, with dimensions shown. Find:
  (a) the length of *VO*;
  (b) the angle that the edge *CV* makes with the base;
  (c) the angle that the face *VAB* makes with the base.

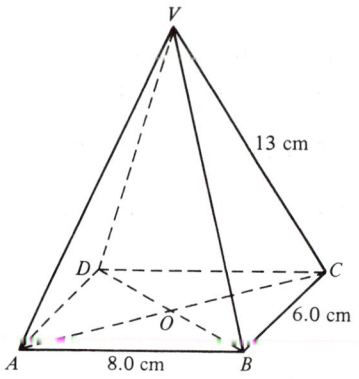

Figure 36

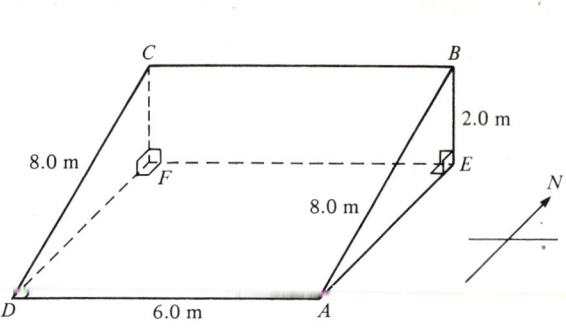

Figure 37

6 Using the dimensions given in Figure 37, find the slope of *DB* and the bearing of *B* from *D*.

*7 A rectangular gate is 2.0 m long and 1.0 m high. Calculate the angle between a diagonal in its final and original positions when the gate is opened through a right angle. Is it the same for both diagonals?

8 In the solid figure *ABCDEF*, shown in Figure 38, *CDEF* is a rectangle measured in centimetres. It is in a horizontal plane in which $CD = EF = 4$, $CF = DE = 6$; *AB* is a horizontal line, of length 4 cm, situated above the plane of the rectangle so that
$$AC = AD = BE = BF = 3.$$
Find:
  (a) the height of *AB* above the plane *CDEF*;
  (b) the angle the face *ACD* makes with the horizontal;
  (c) the angle the line *AC* makes with the horizontal.

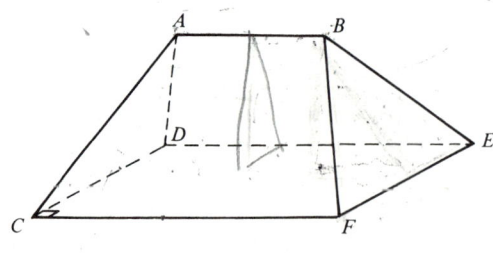

Figure 38

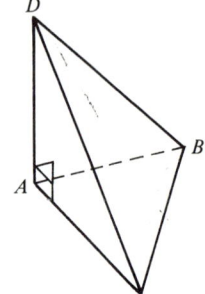

Figure 39

Measurements in three dimensions

9 Figure 39 shows a tetrahedron whose base *ABC* is an equilateral triangle of side 4.0 cm. *DA* is perpendicular to the base and 6.0 cm long.
   (a) Draw a 'net' which could be cut out and used to construct a model of *ABCD*.
   (b) Calculate angle *DBC*.
   (c) Find the length of the perpendicular from *A* to *BC*, and hence the volume of *ABCD*.

*10 A man zig-zags up a hill of slope 40°, his line of motion always making an angle of 30° to the line of greatest slope. Find the inclination of his path to the horizontal.

11 Figure 40 shows the net of a three-dimensional figure. *ABD* and *EBC* are straight lines.
   (a) If it were to be cut out and folded along *AB*, *BC* and *CA* what would the resulting figure be called?
   (b) How many edges will it have? What point(s) does *D* meet in the three-dimensional figure?
   (c) Calculate the lengths of *CD* and *AE*.
   (d) What must be the lengths of *AF* and *FC*?
   (e) What angle will *EB* make with the plane *ABC*?
   (f) Calculate angle *EAC* before and after folding.

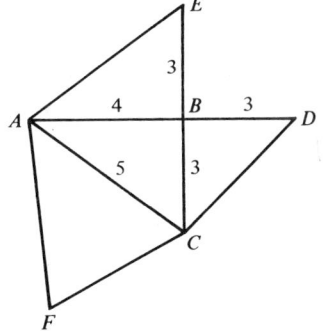

Figure 40

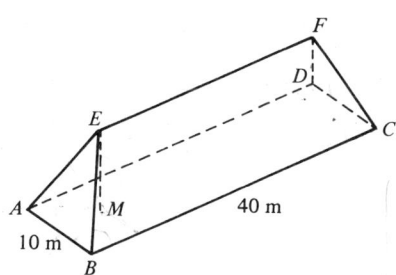

Figure 41

12 Figure 41 shows the roof of a barn which stands on a rectangular base 40 m by 10 m, all four planes of the roof being inclined at 60° to the horizontal base. *M* is the foot of the perpendicular from *E* onto the plane *ABCD*. Find the distance of *M* from *BC* and from *AB*; and find also the perpendicular distance of *E* from *BC*.
   It is required to tile the roof. Find its total area, and hence estimate the number of tiles required if each measures 40 cm by 30 cm and one third of its area overlaps another tile. (You may assume that tiles are bought by the thousand.)

13 An electric light shade consists of a hemispherical bowl of diameter 30 cm suspended by three equal chains from a hook in the ceiling to the edge of the shade so that the angle between each pair of chains is a right angle. Either by calculation or by drawing, find the length of each chain and the height of the hook above the bottom of the shade.

14 A vertical pole 20 m high stands on level ground. *P* is the top of the pole, *S* and *E* are two points on the ground, respectively due south and due east of the pole.

The distance *ES* is 24 m and the distance *PS* is 25 m. Either by calculation, or by drawing and measurement, find the length of *PE*.

Find also the angle of elevation (that is, the angle measured upwards from the horizontal) of the top of the pole from *E*.

SUMMARY

The plan of an object is its projection onto a horizontal plane.
An elevation of an object is a projection onto a vertical plane.

(Sections 1, 2)

In the Third Angle convention, the horizontal plane is placed above the object and a front elevation is drawn. An end elevation can also be drawn. The plan and elevations are then set out in a standard way. (Sections 3, 4)

Problems involving measurements in three dimensions can be solved using scale-drawing or calculation. Drawing the plan and elevations can help to obtain the necessary right-angled triangles. (Section 5)

Summary exercise

1   Draw a sketch to show the shape of the solid of which two elevations and a plan are given in Figure 42.

Mark in your sketch a line whose true length is represented by *XY* in the elevation.

(SMP O-level)

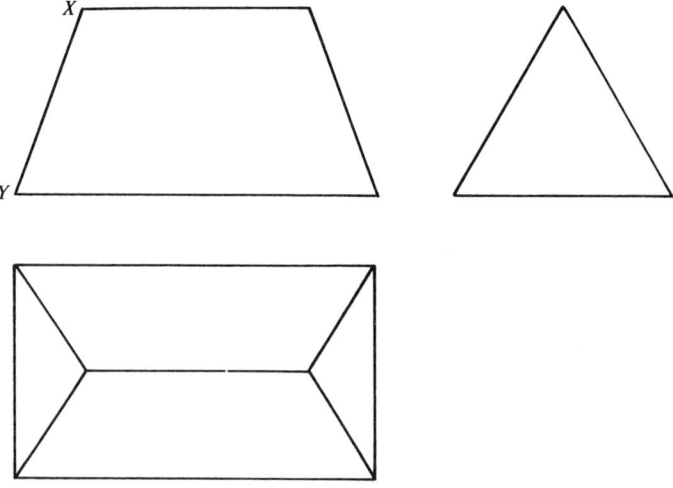

Figure 42

2   Figure 43(*b*) shows two elevations of the inside of an understairs cupboard, of which Figure 43(*a*) is a perspective view.

(*a*) Calculate the capacity of the cupboard in cubic metres, correct to one decimal place.

Summary 23

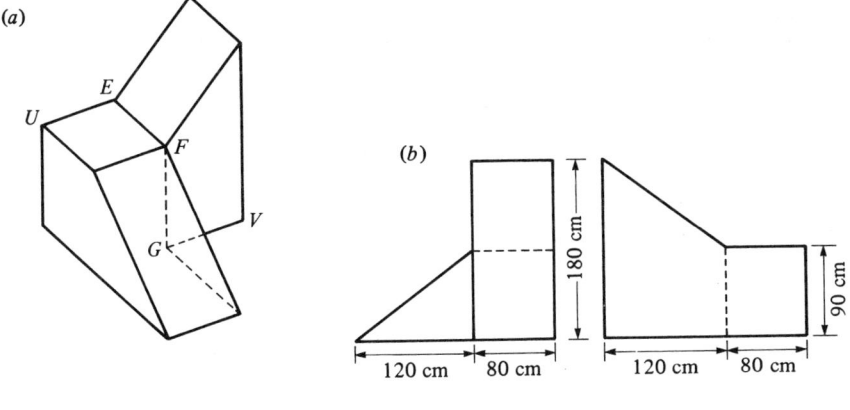

Figure 43

(b) An electric cable has to be run inside the cupboard from U to V. It must be run along the edges, but the edges EF and FG may not be used. Using wavy lines, show a possible route on a copy of both elevations. (SMP O-level)

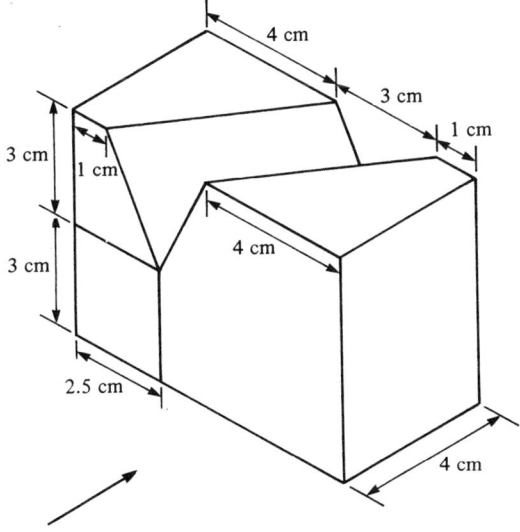

Figure 44

3 Figure 44 shows a rectangular block with an isosceles V-shaped groove of uniform width cut obliquely across the top.
   (a) Draw the plan of this object and its elevation when viewed in the direction of the arrow.
   (b) Name the geometrical transformation that could be applied to the *groove* to make it easier to find the volume of the whole object. Show the new position of the groove on your plan with dotted lines.
   (c) Calculate the volume of the object. (SMP O-level)

4   The base of a right pyramid is a regular hexagon *ABCDEF* of side 3.0 cm; *V* is the vertex; and the length of each sloping edge is 5.0 cm.
   (a) Find the height of the pyramid, and show by calculation that the size of angle *AVB* is about 35°.
   (b) Sketch the net for the *sloping faces* of the pyramid. (Do not include the base.)
   (c) Show on your sketch the shortest route for an ant to take from *A* to *D* over the sloping faces of the pyramid.
   (d) Calculate the length of this route, correct to two significant figures.

   (SMP O-level)

2
Polynomials

In this chapter we review our work on plotting graphs and finding solutions of the associated equations. We then examine in more detail the graphs of quadratic functions and the solution of quadratic equations.

1. FACTORS AND INEQUALITIES

Example 1
Plot a graph of $f(x) = (x+1)(x-5)$ for $^-3 \leqslant x \leqslant 7$. Hence write down the values of x for which:
  (a) $(x+1)(x-5) > 0$;
  (b) $(x+1)(x-5) < 0$.

The graph, drawn from the following table of values, is shown in Figure 1.

x	$^-3$	$^-2$	$^-1$	0	1	2	3	4	5	6	7
$x+1$	$^-2$	$^-1$	0	1	2	3	4	5	6	7	8
$x-5$	$^-8$	$^-7$	$^-6$	$^-5$	$^-4$	$^-3$	$^-2$	$^-1$	0	1	2
$f(x)$	16	7	0	$^-5$	$^-8$	$^-9$	$^-8$	$^-5$	0	7	16

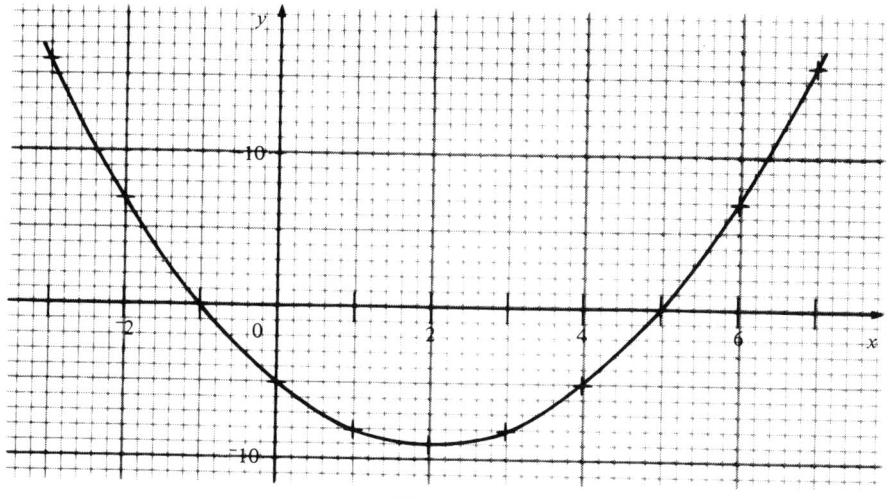

Figure 1

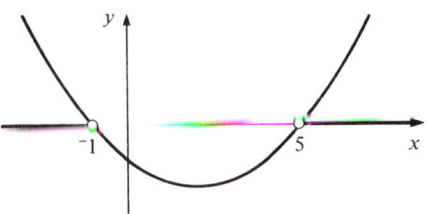

Figure 2

(a) From the graph we can see that $f(x) > 0$ when $x < {}^-1$ or $x > 5$, since for these values of x the graph is above the x-axis. (See Figure 2.) The solution set is therefore
$$\{x : x < {}^-1\} \cup \{x : x > 5\}.$$

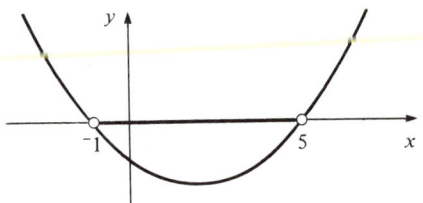

Figure 3

(b) Similarly we deduce that $f(x) < 0$ when ${}^-1 < x < 5$, since for these values of x the graph is below the x-axis. (See Figure 3.) The solution set is $\{x : {}^-1 < x < 5\}$.

Notice that $f(x) = 0$ when $x = {}^-1$ or $x = 5$, since
$$(x+1)(x-5) = 0 \Leftrightarrow (x+1) = 0 \quad \text{or} \quad (x-5) = 0$$
$$\Leftrightarrow x \quad\quad = {}^-1 \quad \text{or} \quad x \quad\quad = 5.$$

Example 2

Plot a graph of $f(x) = (2x+3)(x-1)(x-3)$ for ${}^-2 \leqslant x \leqslant 4$ and write down the set of values of x for which $f(x) \geqslant 0$.

First we note that
$$f(x) = 0 \Leftrightarrow 2x+3 = 0 \quad \text{or} \quad x-1 = 0 \quad \text{or} \quad x-3 = 0$$
$$\Leftrightarrow x \quad\quad = {}^-1.5 \quad \text{or} \quad x = 1 \quad \text{or} \quad x \quad\quad = 3.$$

The graph therefore crosses the x-axis at ${}^-1.5$, 1 and 3.

Using this, and the table of values below, the graph can be drawn as shown in Figure 4.

x	${}^-2$	${}^-1$	0	1	2	3	4
$2x+3$	${}^-1$	1	3	5	7	9	11
$x-1$	${}^-3$	${}^-2$	${}^-1$	0	1	2	3
$x-3$	${}^-5$	${}^-4$	${}^-3$	${}^-2$	${}^-1$	0	1
$f(x)$	${}^-15$	8	9	0	${}^-7$	0	33

Factors and inequalities 27

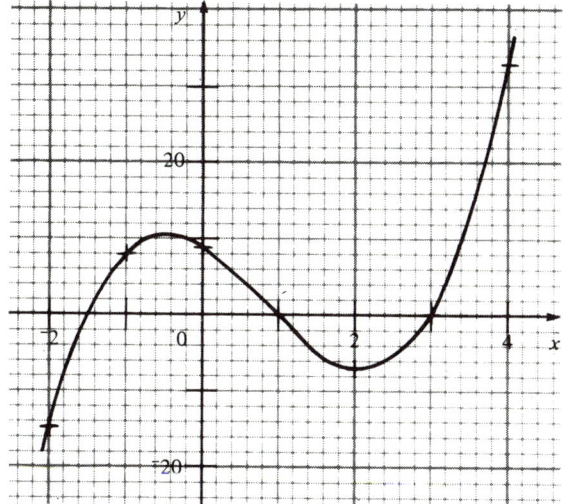

Figure 4

From the graph we see that $f(x) \geq 0 \Leftrightarrow {}^-1.5 \leq x \leq 1$ or $x \geq 3$. (See Figure 5.)

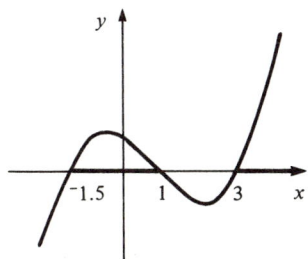

Figure 5

Exercise A

In all questions for which graphs are plotted, they should be drawn for $^-5 \leq x \leq 5$.

*1 Plot a graph of $f(x)$ and state the set of values of x satisfying the given inequalities for $f(x)$.
  (a) $f(x) = (x+2)(x-3)$; $f(x) > 0$.
  (b) $f(x) = (x+3)(x+1)$; $f(x) < 0$.
  (c) $f(x) = (4-x)(1-x)$; $f(x) \geq 0$.
  (d) $f(x) = (2+x)(3-x)$; $(2+x)(3-x) \leq 0$.
  (e) $f(x) = (2x-3)(x-4)$; $(2x-3)(x-4) > 0$.
  (f) $f(x) = (3x-5)(4x+9)$; $(5-3x)(4x+9) < 0$.

2 (a) Plot a graph of $y = (x+4)(2x-5)$ and hence state the smallest value of $(x+4)(2x-5)$.
  (b) Plot a graph of $y = (4-x)(5+2x)$ and hence state the largest value of $(4-x)(5+2x)$.

*3 Plot graphs of the following functions of x and state the values of x for which each function is positive.
   (a) $f(x) = (x+4)(x+3)(x-1)$;
   (b) $g(x) = (x+4)(x+3)(1-x)$;
   (c) $h(x) = (x+4)(x-3)(x-1)$;
   (d) $f(x) = (4+x)(3-x)(1-x)$;
   (e) $g(x) = (x-4)(x-3)(x-1)$;
   (f) $h(x) = (4-x)(3-x)(1-x)$.

4 State the solutions of $(x-7)(x+9) = 0$ and the set of values of x for which $(x-7)(x+9) \geq 0$. Hence sketch (do not plot) the graph of $f(x) = (x-7)(x+9)$.

5 State the solutions of $(x-2)(x+5)(x-8) = 0$ and the set of values of x for which $(x-2)(x+5)(x-8) \geq 0$. Hence sketch the graph of $f(x) = (x-2)(x+5)(x-8)$.

6 Sketch graphs of the following functions of t, indicating clearly the points at which the graph crosses the t-axis.
   (a) $f(t) = (t+6)(t+9)$;
   (b) $g(t) = (t-4)(t+5)$;
   (c) $h(t) = (2-t)(3-t)$;
   (d) $f(t) = (3+t)(7+t)$;
   (e) $g(t) = (t-3)(t+4)(t-5)$;
   (f) $h(t) = (t-1)(t-4)(t-7)$;
   (g) $f(t) = (2-t)(4+t)(6-t)$;
   (h) $g(t) = (t-1)(t-2)(t-5)$;
   (i) $h(t) = (4t+9)(2t-3)(6-t)$;
   (j) $f(t) = (t-1)(t+2)(t-3)(t+4)$.

2. POLYNOMIALS

An expression such as $2x^3 - 5x^2 - 6x + 9$ with non-negative integral powers of x is called a *polynomial* in x. This polynomial has *degree* 3, the highest power of x. The *coefficient* of x^2 is $^-5$. The *constant term* is 9. Polynomials of degree 3 are called *cubic* while those of degree 2 are called *quadratic*.

Example 3
Plot the quadratic $f(x) = x^2 - 4x - 5$ for $^-3 \leq x \leq 7$.

A table of values is shown below; the graph is shown in Figure 6.

x	-3	-2	-1	0	1	2	3	4	5	6	7
x^2	9	4	1	0	1	4	9	16	25	36	49
$-4x$	12	8	4	0	-4	-8	-12	-16	-20	-24	-28
-5	-5	-5	-5	-5	-5	-5	-5	-5	-5	-5	-5
$f(x)$	16	7	0	-5	-8	-9	-8	-5	0	7	16

Note that, if you are using a calculator with a memory, you do not need to draw up a table of values. For example, $x^2 - 4x - 5$ can be written as $x(x-4) - 5$ and calculated as follows:

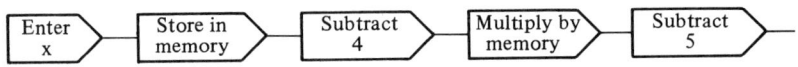

Polynomials

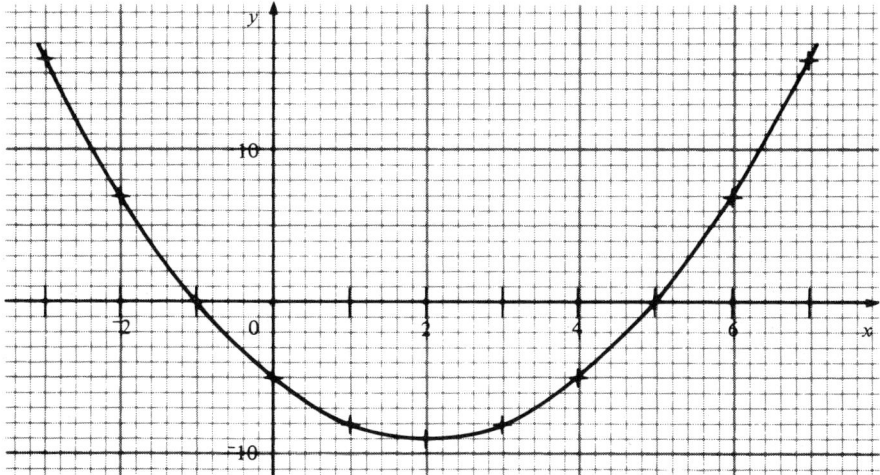

Figure 6

The graph in Figure 6 appears to be the same as that in Figure 1, suggesting that $x^2 - 4x - 5 = (x+1)(x-5)$. We can check this by using the distributive law.
$$(x+1)(x-5) = x(x-5) + 1(x-5)$$
$$= x^2 - 5x + x - 5$$
$$= x^2 - 4x - 5.$$

Example 4

Write $(2x+3)(x-1)(x-3)$ as a polynomial. What are:
(a) the degree of the polynomial;
(b) the coefficient of x^2?

$$(2x+3)(x-1)(x-3) = (2x+3)[x(x-3) - 1(x-3)]$$
$$= (2x+3)(x^2 - 3x - x + 3)$$
$$= (2x+3)(x^2 - 4x + 3)$$
$$= 2x(x^2 - 4x + 3) + 3(x^2 - 4x + 3)$$
$$= 2x^3 - 8x^2 + 6x + 3x^2 - 12x + 9$$
$$= 2x^3 - 5x^2 - 6x + 9.$$

(a) The degree of the polynomial is 3.
(b) The coefficient of x^2 is $^-5$.

Example 5

Plot the graph of $y = 2x^3 - 5x^2 - 6x + 7$ for $^-2 \leqslant x \leqslant 4$ and solve the equation $2x^3 - 5x^2 - 6x + 7 = 0$ to an accuracy of one decimal place.

When using a table of values, it is helpful to tabulate first the values of x^2 and x^3. (The calculation can also be carried out continuously on a calculator with a memory, using $2x^3 - 5x^2 - 6x + 7 = [(2x-5)x - 6]x + 7$.)

From the graph in Figure 7 we see that $y = 0$ when $x \approx ^-1.4$, $x \approx 0.8$ or $x \approx 3.2$.

Polynomials

x	$^-2$	$^-1$	0	1	2	3	4
x^2	4	1	0	1	4	9	16
x^3	$^-8$	$^-1$	0	1	8	27	64
$2x^3$	$^-16$	$^-2$	0	2	16	54	128
$^-5x^2$	$^-20$	$^-5$	0	$^-5$	$^-20$	$^-45$	$^-80$
^-6x	12	6	0	$^-6$	$^-12$	$^-18$	$^-24$
7	7	7	7	7	7	7	7
y	$^-17$	6	7	$^-2$	$^-9$	$^-2$	31

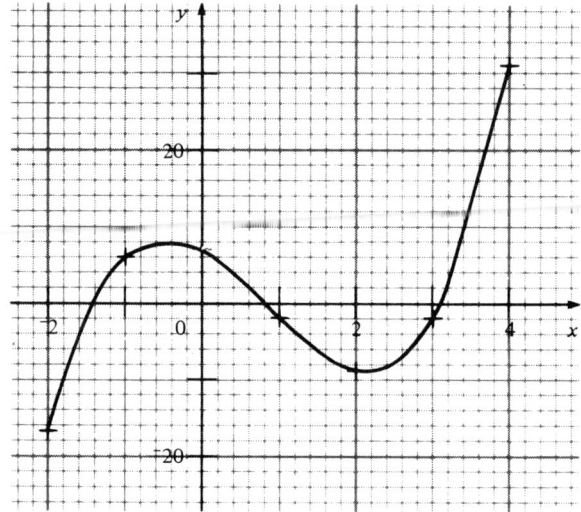

Figure 7

Further calculation gives, as a check,

$$x = {}^-1.4 \quad y = 0.112$$
$$x = {}^-1.5 \quad y = {}^-2$$
$$x = 0.7 \quad y = 1.036$$
$$x = 0.8 \quad y = 0.024$$
$$x = 3.1 \quad y = {}^-0.068$$
$$x = 3.2 \quad y = 2.136.$$

So, to one decimal place, the solutions are $x = {}^-1.4, 0.8$ and 3.1.

In Example 3, the graph crossed the x-axis at $^-1$ and 5, which corresponded to the factors $(x+1)$ and $(x-5)$. In Example 5, the points where the graph crosses the x-axis are not so convenient and there are no such simple factors.

Exercise B

*1 Express the following as polynomials:

(a) $(x+3)(x+7)$; (b) $(x+4)(x-8)$;
(c) $(x-4)(x-2)$; (d) $(x-6)(x+6)$;
(e) $(3+x)(7-x)$; (f) $(4+x)(8-x)$;

Symmetry   31

(g) $(4-x)(2-x)$;   (h) $(6-x)(6+x)$;
(i) $(2x+3)(4x+5)$;   (j) $(2x+3)(4x-5)$;
(k) $(2x-3)(4x+5)$;   (l) $(2x-3)(4x-5)$.

*2 Plot graphs of the following for $-5 \leqslant x \leqslant 5$. State the solutions of $f(x) = 0$, suggest factors of $f(x)$, and check by multiplication.
(a) $f(x) = x^2 + 4x + 3$;   (b) $f(x) = x^2 - x - 6$;
(c) $f(x) = x^2 - 5x + 4$;   (d) $f(x) = -x^2 + x + 6$;
(e) $f(x) = 2x^2 - 11x + 12$;   (f) $f(x) = 12x^2 + 7x - 45$.

3 The following expressions all have simple factors. Find them by trial and error, checking your answer in each case by multiplication.
(a) $x^2 + 5x + 6$;   (b) $x^2 + 6x + 5$;   (c) $x^2 - 8x + 15$;
(d) $x^2 - 8x + 12$;   (e) $x^2 + 2x - 15$;   (f) $x^2 + x - 12$;
(g) $x^2 - 9$;   (h) $25 - x^2$.

*4 Express the following as cubic polynomials:
(a) $(x+2)[(x+3)(x+7)]$;   (b) $[(x+2)(x+3)](x+7)$;
(c) $(x-2)[(x+4)(x-8)]$;   (d) $[(x-2)(x+4)](x-8)$;
(e) $(2x+3)(4x+5)(6x+7)$;   (f) $(2x-3)(4x+5)(6x+7)$;
(g) $(2x+3)(4x-5)(6x-7)$;   (h) $(2x+3)(2x-3)(x+1)$.

5 Plot graphs of the following cubics. State the values of x for which $y = 0$, suggest factors, and check by multiplication.
(a) $y = x^3 + 2x^2 - 11x - 12$;   (b) $y = x^3 - 3x^2 - 10x + 24$;
(c) $y = 2x^3 - 5x^2 - 21x + 36$;   (d) $y = 3x^3 - x^2 - 20x - 12$.

6 Plot graphs of the following functions. Give the solutions of $f(x) = 0$ to an accuracy of two significant figures. Check by substitution.
(a) $f(x) = x^2 + 3x - 5$;   (b) $f(x) = x^3 - 4x - 2$.

3. SYMMETRY

We now look more closely at quadratics and the particular property they have of being symmetrical.

Example 6
Plot the quadratic $y = (x-2)^2 - 9$ for $-3 \leqslant x \leqslant 7$. Hence find its axis of symmetry.

x	-3	-2	-1	0	1	2	3	4	5	6	7
$x-2$	-5	-4	-3	-2	-1	0	1	2	3	4	5
$(x-2)^2$	25	16	9	4	1	0	1	4	9	16	25
-9	-9	-9	-9	-9	-9	-9	-9	-9	-9	-9	-9
y	16	7	0	-5	-8	-9	-8	-5	0	7	16

The graph is plotted in Figure 8.
Observe that
$$y = (x-2)^2 - 9 = (x-2)(x-2) - 9$$
$$= (x^2 - 4x + 4) - 9$$
$$= x^2 - 4x - 5.$$
So this is the same graph as in Examples 1 and 3. But when the polynomial $x^2 - 4x - 5$ is written as $(x-2)^2 - 9$ we can really see all its symmetry. Look at

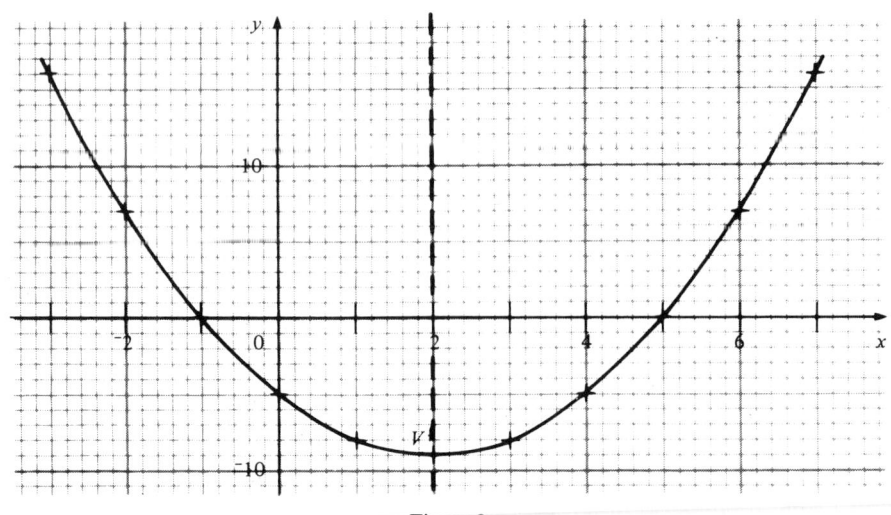

Figure 8

the table of values and the symmetry it has about $x = 2$. Indeed $x = 2$ is the axis of symmetry.

The point V on the axis of symmetry is called the *vertex*. Notice that $^-9$ is the ordinate of the vertex. $f(2) = ^-9$; V is the point $(2, ^-9)$.

Example 7

Express $f(x) = (x+1)(x+5)$ in symmetric form.

$f(x) = 0 \Leftrightarrow x = ^-1$ or $x = ^-5$. So the axis of symmetry is the line $x = ^-3$. Hence we start with $(x+3)^2$ which is x^2+6x+9. But
$$f(x) = (x+1)(x+5)$$
$$= x^2+6x+5$$
$$= (x^2+6x+9)-4$$
$$= (x+3)^2-4.$$

We can check with the vertex
$$f(^-3) = (^-3+1)(^-3+5) = ^-2 \times 2 = ^-4.$$

Notice that there are three distinct ways of expressing a quadratic: in factor form, in polynomial form and in symmetric form. For example:

$f(x) = (x+1)(x+5)$ is factor form
      $= x^2+6x+5$ is polynomial form
      $= (x+3)^2-4$ is symmetric form

each of which has its use.

Notice that the number 3 which appears in the symmetric form is the middle, or average, of the 1 and 5 which appear in the factor form and which give the 6 in the polynomial form. This suggests that we could go straight from polynomial to symmetric form by halving the coefficient of x, 6 in this case.

Example 8
Express $f(x) = x^2 + 10x + 13$ in symmetric form.

We start with $(x+5)^2$, obtained by halving 10 (the coefficient of x). This gives $x^2 + 10x + 25$.
So $f(x) = (x+5)^2 - 12$.

Exercise C

*1 Express the following in symmetric form and check with the vertex. Draw a sketch showing the points where the graph crosses the x-axis and the position of the vertex.
   (a) $(x+2)(x+6)$;   (b) $(x-3)(x-7)$;
   (c) $(x+4)(x-2)$;   (d) $(x-1)(x+5)$;
   (e) $(x+3)(x+6)$;   (f) $(x-2)(x-7)$;
   (g) $(x+5)(x-2)$;   (h) $(x-1)(x+6)$.

*2 Express the following in symmetric form and give the coordinates of the vertex:
   (a) $x^2 + 8x + 12$;   (b) $x^2 + 6x - 7$;
   (c) $x^2 - 4x - 12$;   (d) $x^2 - 6x + 8$;
   (e) $x^2 + 8x + 9$;   (f) $x^2 + 2x - 4$;
   (g) $x^2 + 3x - 4$;   (h) $x^2 - 5x + 6$.

3 Find the smallest value of:
   (a) $x^2 - 8x + 3$;   (b) $x^2 + 3x + 5$.

4 Express the following in symmetric form:
   (a) $(2-x)(6-x)$;   (b) $(3-x)(7+x)$;
   (c) $12 + 4t - t^2$;   (d) $7 - 6v - v^2$.

5 Find the greatest value of:
   (a) $6 + 5t - t^2$;   (b) $7 - 8t - t^2$.

4. QUADRATIC EQUATIONS

Once a quadratic polynomial $f(x)$ has been expressed in symmetric form, the solutions of $f(x) = 0$ can be found easily.

Example 9
Solve $x^2 - 4x - 5 = 0$.

$$x^2 - 4x - 5 = (x-2)^2 - 9$$

which is zero when $(x-2)^2 = 9$
that is $x - 2 = 3$ or $x - 2 = {}^-3$.
The solutions are $x = 5$ and $x = {}^-1$.
Check: $x = 5 \Rightarrow x^2 - 4x - 5 = 25 - 20 - 5 = 0$
$x = {}^-1 \Rightarrow x^2 - 4x - 5 = 1 - {}^-4 - 5 = 1 + 4 - 5 = 0$

The solutions will not generally be integers.

Example 10
Solve the equation $x^2 + 6x = {}^-4$.

$$x^2 + 6x + 4 = (x+3)^2 - 5$$
which is zero when $(x+3)^2 = 5$
$$x+3 = \sqrt{5} \quad \text{or} \quad x+3 = {}^-\sqrt{5}$$
$$x = {}^-3 + \sqrt{5} \quad \text{or} \quad x = {}^-3 - \sqrt{5}$$
$$x \approx {}^-0.8 \quad \text{or} \quad x \approx {}^-5.2$$

The solutions can still be found when the coefficient of x^2 is not 1.

Example 11

Solve $2x^2 - 6x + 1 = 0$.
$$2x^2 - 6x + 1 = 2(x^2 - 3x + 0.5)$$
We then solve $x^2 - 3x + 0.5 = 0$ as before.
$$x^2 - 3x + 0.5 = (x - 1.5)^2 - 1.75$$
So the solutions are given by
$$x - 1.5 = \sqrt{1.75} \quad \text{or} \quad x - 1.5 = {}^-\sqrt{1.75}$$
$$x = 1.5 \pm \sqrt{1.75}$$
$$\approx 2.82 \quad \text{or} \quad 0.18$$

The method of Example 11 can be used for any quadratic equation $ax^2 + bx + c = 0$. The solutions are found to be
$$x = \frac{{}^-b \pm \sqrt{(b^2 - 4ac)}}{2a}.$$

Example 12

Use the formula to find the solutions of $2x^2 - 6x + 1 = 0$.

Comparing $2x^2 - 6x + 1$ with $ax^2 + bx + c$, we have $a = 2$, $b = {}^-6$, $c = 1$.
$$\text{So} \quad x = \frac{{}^-b \pm \sqrt{(b^2 - 4ac)}}{2a}$$
$$= \frac{6 \pm \sqrt{(36 - 4 \times 2 \times 1)}}{4}$$
$$= \frac{6 \pm \sqrt{28}}{4}$$
$$\approx \frac{6 \pm 5.29}{4}$$
$$x \approx 2.82 \quad \text{or} \quad 0.18$$

Example 13

Solve the equation $3x^2 = 4x - 7$.

The equation can be re-written as $3x^2 - 4x + 7 = 0$.

Using the formula with $a = 3$, $b = {}^-4$ and $c = 7$, we have
$$x = \frac{{}^-b \pm \sqrt{(b^2 - 4ac)}}{2a}$$
$$= \frac{4 \pm \sqrt{(16 - 4 \times 3 \times 7)}}{6}$$
$$= \frac{4 \pm \sqrt{({}^-68)}}{6}.$$

But there is no real number which is $\sqrt{(^-68)}$. So the equation has no real solutions.

A graph of $y = 3x^2 - 4x + 7$ confirms that it does not meet the x-axis. (See Figure 9.)

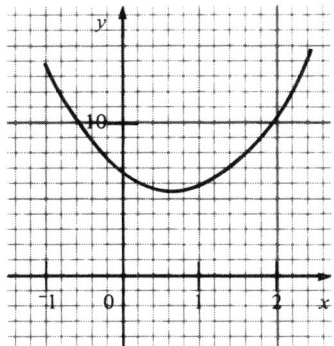

Figure 9

Exercise D

*1 Write the following expressions $f(x)$ in symmetric form, and hence solve $f(x) = 0$ in each case:
  (a) $x^2 + 4x - 5$; (b) $x^2 - 10x + 21$; (c) $x^2 + 2x - 3$;
  (d) $x^2 - 4x - 12$; (e) $x^2 + 5x - 6$; (f) $x^2 + 3x - 10$;
  (g) $x^2 - 9x + 14$; (h) $x^2 - 7x + 6$; (i) $x^2 + 6x + 4$;
  (j) $x^2 - 8x + 5$; (k) $x^2 - 3x - 4$; (l) $x^2 + 5x + 3$.

*2 Use symmetric form to solve the following equations:
  (a) $2x^2 + 8x - 3 = 0$; (b) $2x^2 - 7x + 3 = 0$;
  (c) $3x^2 + 2x = 1$; (d) $5x^2 - 6x = 7$.

3 Use the formula to find the solutions of the equations $f(x) = 0$ in question 1.

4 Use the formula to solve the equations given in question 2.

5 Solve the following equations:
  (a) $x^2 + 4x = 5$;
  (b) $x^2 - 9x = 14$;
  (c) $2x^2 - 3x = 4$.

*6 Find the solution sets for the following:
  (a) $x^2 + 4x > 5$;
  (b) $x^2 - 9x \leqslant 14$;
  (c) $2x^2 > 3x + 4$.

7 Find which of the following do not meet the x-axis:
  (a) $y = 5x^2 + 4x + 3$;
  (b) $y = 3x^2 - 5x + 2$;
  (c) $y = 2x^2 - 30x + 111$;
  (d) $y = x^2 + 19x + 99$.

8 Apply the method of Example 11 to the quadratic equation $ax^2 + bx + c = 0$ and establish the formula for its solutions.

9 For $f(x) = x^2 + 2px + q$, find the value of $f(^-p + \sqrt{(p^2 - q)})$.

10 For $f(x) = ax^2+bx+c$, find the value of $f(r)$ where
$$r = \frac{-b+\sqrt{(b^2-4ac)}}{2a}.$$

SUMMARY

A polynomial in x is a sum of multiples of non-negative integral powers of x. Its degree is its highest power of x. For example, $5x^3+7x^2-2x-6$ is a polynomial of degree 3.

The solutions of $f(x) = 0$ are the x-coordinates of the points where the graph of $y = f(x)$ crosses the x-axis.

$(x-a)$ is a factor of a polynomial $f(x)$ $\Leftrightarrow$ $f(a) = 0$.

Between two adjacent solutions of $f(x) = 0$, the graph of $y = f(x)$ is either entirely above or entirely below the x-axis.

A quadratic is a polynomial of degree two.

The graph of every quadratic function has an axis of symmetry. The axis of symmetry of the graph of $y = (x-p)^2+q$ is the line $x = p$. The vertex of the graph is (p, q). (Section 3)

The solutions of a quadratic equation $ax^2+bx+c = 0$ can be found by using symmetric form, or by using the formula
$$x = \frac{-b\pm\sqrt{(b^2-4ac)}}{2a}.$$ (Section 4)

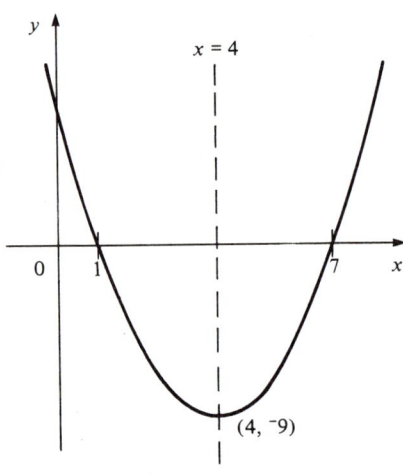

Figure 10

$$f(x) = x^2-8x+7 = (x-1)(x-7) = (x-4)^2-9$$

Summary exercise

1 $f(x) = (x+3)(x-4)$. Write down the solutions of $f(x) = 0$ and state the set of values of x for which $f(x) > 0$.

2 Sketch the graph of $y = (x+2)(x-3)(x+4)$, indicating clearly the points for which $y = 0$.
3 Express $(x+2)(x-3)(x+4)$ as a cubic polynomial.
4 Write $x^2 - 6x + 7$ in symmetric form. Hence write down the equation of the axis of symmetry of the graph of $y = x^2 - 6x + 7$ and the coordinates of its vertex.
5 Solve the equation $4x^2 = 3x + 5$, giving your answers correct to three significant figures.
6 Find the solution set for $3x^2 + 2 \geqslant 5x$.

Miscellaneous exercise

1 (In this question x belongs to the set of real numbers.) Which of the following statements are true and which are false?
   (a) $(x+1)(x-2) = 0 \Leftrightarrow x = {}^-1$ or $x = 2$.
   (b) $x = 3 \Rightarrow (x-3)(x+1) = 0$.
   (c) $x(x-3) < 0 \Rightarrow 0 < x < 3$.
   (d) $x^2 > 1 \Rightarrow x > 1$.

2 If
$$x + p + \frac{a}{x} = (x+a)\left(\frac{1}{x}+1\right),$$
express p in terms of a.

3 Which of the following statements about the expression $x^2 + 2x - 8$ are true, and which are false?
   (a) Its value is $^-11$ when $x = {}^-1$.
   (b) It may be written in the form $(x+1)^2 - 9$.
   (c) It is the product of $(x-4)$ and $(x+2)$.
   (d) It has the value 0 when $x = 2$.
   (e) It has the value 0 for some value of x other than $x = 2$.

4 If $A = \{x : x(x+2) = 0, x > {}^-1\}$, give a simpler expression for A.

5 If x belongs to the set of real numbers, which of the following statements are true and which are false?
   (a) $(x-2)(x+3) > 0 \Rightarrow x > 2$.
   (b) $x > 2 \Rightarrow (x-2)(x+3) > 0$.
   (c) $x > 2 \Rightarrow \dfrac{1}{x} > \dfrac{1}{2}$.
   (d) $x^2 > x \Rightarrow x > 1$.

6 (a) One factor of $x^2 + x - 2$ is $(x-1)$. State the other factor.
   (b) State the two possible values of x for which $x^2 + x - 2 = 0$.
   (c) State the value of x for which both $x^2 + x - 2 = 0$ and $x^2 + 5x + 6 = 0$.

7 The numbers p and q are so related that
$$(p-6)(q-6) = k,$$
where k is constant, and $p = 2$ when $q = {}^-3$.
   (a) Find the value of k and show that the equation may be put into the form $(p-6)q = 6p$.
   (b) L is the point $(p, 0)$, M is $(0, q)$. By using similar triangles or by some other argument, show that the line LM goes through the point $(6, 6)$.
   (c) Calculate the value of q if $p = 2q$.

8 Simplify $(x+4)(x-2) > x^2 + 2$.

9 (a) Taking $\mathscr{E} = \{\text{real numbers}\}$, give the solution sets of:

   (i) $\left(x - \dfrac{1}{x}\right)^2 = 0;$

   (ii) $\left(x - \dfrac{1}{x}\right)^2 < 0.$

   (b) Using the identity
   $$(x-y)^2 = x^2 - 2xy + y^2$$
   express $\left(x - \dfrac{1}{x}\right)^2$ in expanded form.

   (c) Use these results to show that
   $$x^2 + \left(\dfrac{1}{x^2}\right) \geqslant 2.$$
   What does this prove about the mean of a number and its reciprocal?

10 (a) State the solution set of the equation $(2x+5)(x^2-2) = 0$ when the universal set is (i) real numbers, (ii) rational numbers, (iii) integers.

   (b) State the solution sets of the inequality $x^2 - 2 \leqslant 0$ in the same universal sets (i), (ii) and (iii).

   (c) Make a table showing the sign of $(2x+5)(x^2-2)$ for $x = -3, -2, -1, 0, 1, 2$ and sketch the graph of $y = (2x+5)(x^2-2)$.

3
Practical arithmetic

Most of this chapter reviews the various arithmetic techniques that we have met so far, by means of a series of worked examples and summaries of important results. We conclude by extending our work on percentages to study two applications – mortgages and index numbers.

1. NUMBERS AND UNITS

Factors and primes

Example 1
Find the smallest number divisible by both 36 and 52.

The prime factors of 36 and 52 may be found as follows:

$$\begin{array}{c|c} 2 & 36 \\ \hline 2 & 18 \\ \hline 3 & 9 \\ \hline & 3 \end{array} \qquad \begin{array}{c|c} 2 & 52 \\ \hline 2 & 26 \\ \hline & 13 \end{array}$$

Thus $36 = 2^2 \times 3^2$ and $52 = 2^2 \times 13$.

The smallest number divisible by both (the *lowest common multiple*) must contain 2^2 and 3^2 and 13 as factors and so it is:
$$2^2 \times 3^2 \times 13 = 468.$$

Fractions and decimals

Example 2
$$\frac{3}{16} + \frac{7}{64} = \frac{12}{64} + \frac{7}{64} = \frac{19}{64}$$

Example 3
$$3\tfrac{1}{8} \div \frac{15}{32} = \frac{25}{8} \div \frac{15}{32} = \frac{25}{8} \times \frac{32}{15}$$
$$= \frac{25 \times 32}{8 \times 15} = \frac{\overset{5}{\cancel{25}} \times \overset{4}{\cancel{32}}}{\underset{1}{\cancel{8}} \times \underset{3}{\cancel{15}}} = \frac{5 \times 4}{1 \times 3} = \frac{20}{3} = 6\tfrac{2}{3}$$

(Be careful not to cross things out illegibly when you 'cancel'. Use the direction of the cancellation lines to indicate to the reader which pairs of numbers have been taken together when cancelling.)

When you 'cancel', as in this example, what you are really doing is dividing the top and bottom of the fraction by the same number, so obtaining an equivalent fraction.

Example 4

$$0.2 \times 0.3 = \frac{2}{10} \times \frac{3}{10} = \frac{6}{100} = 0.0\dot{6}.$$

Example 5

$$\frac{1}{0.02} = \frac{100}{2} = 50.$$

Scientific notation and metric units

$$
\begin{aligned}
10^5 &= 100\,000 \\
10^4 &= 10\,000 \\
10^3 &= 1000 \\
10^2 &= 100 \\
10^1 &= 10 \\
10^0 &= 1 \\
10^{-1} &= \frac{1}{10^1} = \frac{1}{10} = 0.1 \\
10^{-2} &= \frac{1}{10^2} = \frac{1}{100} = 0.01 \\
10^{-3} &= \frac{1}{10^3} = \frac{1}{1000} = 0.001 \\
10^{-4} &= \frac{1}{10^4} = \frac{1}{10\,000} = 0.0001 \quad \text{etc.}
\end{aligned}
$$

$10^a \times 10^b = 10^{(a+b)}$ and $10^a \div 10^b = 10^{(a-b)}$

$$10^{-a} = \frac{1}{10^a}$$

A number in *standard form* (or standard index form) is written as $A \times 10^n$ where n is an integer and $1 \leqslant A < 10$.

For example: $21\,000 = 2.1 \times 10^4$
$$0.0052 = 5.2 \times 10^{-3}$$

Rough estimates of the results of calculations, to an accuracy of one significant figure, can be made using standard form as a help.

Example 6

Estimate the value of $\dfrac{0.00621}{0.0287}$ to an accuracy of one significant figure.

$$\frac{0.00621}{0.0287} \approx \frac{6 \times 10^{-3}}{3 \times 10^{-2}} = \frac{6}{3} \times \frac{10^{-3}}{10^{-2}}$$

$$= 2 \times 10^{-3--2} = 2 \times 10^{-1} = 0.2$$

Here is a summary of important metric units:

Mass: 1 kg = 1000 g = 10^6 mg
1 g = 10^{-3} kg; 1 mg = 10^{-6} kg
1 tonne = 1000 kg

Length: 1 m = 100 cm = 1000 mm
1 cm = 10^{-2} m; 1 mm = 10^{-3} m
1 km = 1000 m

Area: 1 ha = 10^4 m²
1 km² = 100 ha

Volume: 1 dm³ = 1000 cm³
1 m³ = 1000 dm³; 1 cm³ = 10^{-3} dm³

Volume (fluid): 1 litre = 1 dm³ = 1000 cm³ or 1000 cc
1 litre = 100 cl = 1000 ml
1 ml = 10^{-3} litre

Example 7

Estimate the volume of water to be drained from 1 km of roadway of width 25 m when 5 cm of rain falls on it.

The volume of water is
1000 m × 25 m × 5 × 10^{-2} m = 1250 m³
$= 1.3 \times 10^3$ m³ to 2 s.f.

(An overestimate of, say, 1.5×10^3 m³ might be preferable for planning drainage.)

Exercise A

(Do not use a calculator in this exercise.)

1 In a school of 961 pupils, 88 boys and 69 girls are suffering from measles. How many pupils in the school are not measly?
   If, on average, a measly pupil has 120 spots, estimate the total number of spots to the nearest 100.

2 Unisex see-through Platinitex Jerkins are offered for sale by a mail-order company at £3.95 each including post and packing. How many can I buy for £12.00?
   Discovering that they are popular amongst my friends I ask for a quotation for a larger order and am offered them at £62.50 for 25. How much are they each?
   If I sell them to my friends at £3.75 each with a view to raising money for charity, how much will I have raised when all are sold?

3 In 1981 a school was successfully sued by the Music Publishers Association for photocopying about 15 000 sheets of music. The damages plus legal costs came to about £6000. The photocopying itself cost 4p per sheet. What was the total effective cost to the school per sheet of music?

4 Find the prime factors of 64 and 160.
   (*a*) What is the smallest number which each will divide into without remainder?
   (*b*) What is the largest number which will divide into each?

5 $\mathscr{E}$ = {positive integers less than 100}; T = {multiples of 2};
   H = {multiples of 3}; F = {multiples of 5}.
   (a) If $P = T \cap H$ and $Q = H \cap F$, list the elements of P and Q.
   (b) What is the smallest element of $P \cap F$? What are its prime factors?

In questions 6–10, state the letter corresponding to the correct answer.

6 In a machine used for stamping out shapes from sheet metal are two gear wheels. One of the wheels has 24 teeth, the other has 16 teeth, and the smaller wheel is used to drive the larger one. The machine stamps out a shape every time these two gear wheels are together in their original positions. If the smaller wheel completes one revolution every second then the time between successive cuts by the machine is:
   (a) 1 second;   (b) 3 seconds;   (c) 6 seconds;
   (d) 48 seconds.   (SMP O-level)

7 The fraction $\frac{7}{12}$ is equal to:
   (a) $\frac{2}{5}+\frac{5}{7}$; (b) $\frac{1}{3}\times\frac{1}{4}$; (c) $\frac{3}{8}$ of $1\frac{5}{9}$; (d) $\frac{6}{7}\div\frac{1}{2}$.   (SMP O-level)

8 Which of the following is the correct answer to $(\frac{1}{5}\times\frac{1}{3})+\frac{1}{6}$?
   (a) $\frac{3}{21}$; (b) $\frac{1}{10}$; (c) $\frac{7}{30}$; (d) $\frac{3}{10}$.   (SMP O-level)

9 The value of $\frac{3}{5}+\frac{7}{15}$ is
   (a) $\frac{1}{2}$; (b) $\frac{16}{15}$; (c) $\frac{16}{30}$; (d) $\frac{21}{75}$.   (SMP O-level)

10 (i) $(5\frac{7}{8}-3\frac{1}{4})\div 2$ is exactly
      (a) $4\frac{1}{4}$; (b) $1\frac{3}{4}$; (c) $1\frac{5}{16}$; (d) $\frac{3}{4}$.
   (ii) $\frac{3}{11}\times\frac{7}{9}$ equals
      (a) $\frac{10}{99}$; (b) $\frac{1}{2}$; (c) $\frac{7}{33}$; (d) $\frac{21}{20}$.   (SMP O-level)

11 If $\dfrac{1}{f}=\dfrac{1}{u}+\dfrac{1}{v}$, find the value of f when $u = 8$ and $v = {}^-10$.

12 Along with each of my seven brothers, I have been left by my grandmother a $\frac{1}{8}$ share in a family trust. The trust owns a $\frac{2}{9}$ share of property which has just been sold for £36 000. Before deduction of Estate Duty, Capital Gains Tax, Income Tax and any other forms of taxation which may apply, how much of the proceeds of sale does my share amount to?

13 I want a new mount cut to fit a picture and frame. A retired mount-cutter I know is a good craftsman but firmly prejudiced against metric units so I must give him measurements in inches to the nearest $\frac{1}{16}$ in.
   The external dimensions need to be $12\frac{1}{8}$ in. by $10\frac{1}{8}$ in. in order to fit the frame.

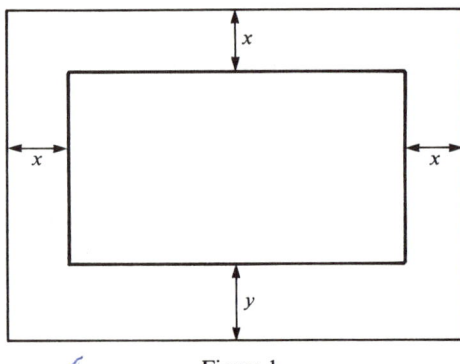

Figure 1

The opening in the mount needs to be $8\frac{1}{4}$ in. by $5\frac{7}{8}$ in. I want the sides and top of the mount to have the same width and the bottom to be slightly larger as in Figure 1. Is this possible? Draw a clearly labelled diagram showing all dimensions for the mount-cutter.

14 Express $\frac{1}{700}$ as a decimal correct to one significant figure.
15 (a) Subtract 5.2×10^{-5} from 8.546×10^{-3}.
    (b) How many significant figures are there in each of the following measured quantities?
    (i) 25.60 cm; (ii) 0.0038 m; (iii) 2.5×10^8 km; (iv) 2.09 g.
16 Write down the value of $(0.009)^2$ correct to one significant figure.
17 Write 0.040815 correct to two significant figures.
18 Write down the value of $\frac{(0.41)^2}{0.38}$ correct to one significant figure.
19 Estimate the value of
$$\frac{4.986 \times 7.83}{0.02},$$
giving the result to one significant figure.
20 (a) At 300 000 km/s, how long, to one significant figure, does it take light to travel from the sun to Saturn, a distance of 1.4×10^9 km?
    (b) An electron carries a charge of 1.6×10^{-19} coulomb. To one significant figure, how many electrons are required for a total charge of 1 coulomb?
21 Write 0.0046 in standard form. (SMP O-level)
22 (a) Express 0.000 004 in standard index form.
    (b) Calculate $\frac{0.000006}{0.002}$. (SMP O-level)
23 The surface of the earth is about 509 970 000 km². Express this in standard index form correct to two significant figures. (SMP O-level)
24 Assuming that 30 grains of sand placed in a line measure 1 cm and that the earth is a sphere of circumference 40 000 km, state, in standard index form, the number of grains required to form a line round the equator. (SMP O-level)
25 Express in standard index form
    (a) 0.097;
    (b) $(3 \times 10^5) \times (4 \times 10^{-1})$. (SMP O-level)
26 (a) $\frac{4700 \times 9.3}{6.2}$ and (b) $\frac{1}{2 \times 10^4}$ are put into standard index form $a \times 10^n$. Give the value of n in each case. (SMP O-level)
27 In a traditional story the inventor of chess claimed a prize of 2^{64} grains of rice. If 16 grains of rice weigh approximately 1 gram, use $2^{60} \approx 10^{18}$ to give the weight of the prize:
    (a) in grams;
    (b) in tonnes. (SMP O-level)
28 $x = 2 \times 10^{-2} - 4.9 \times 10^{-3}$. Which of the following are true and which are false?
    (a) $x = {}^-2.9 \times 10^{-5}$; (b) $x = {}^-2.9 \times 10^1$;
    (c) $x = 1.5 \times 10^{-2}$; (d) $x = 0.0151$. (SMP O-level)

2. CALCULATORS AND PERCENTAGES

Using a calculator

To remind yourself how best to use your calculator, experiment with easy numbers which allow you to forecast confidently the result of the type of calculation concerned. Make sure you know how your calculator deals with negative numbers.

If you have a calculator which does not display in 'exponent form' (for example, 5.2   06 meaning 5.2×10^6), you should use standard form to help you avoid entering very large or very small numbers.

Example 8
$$235\,000 \times 7\,960\,000 = 2.35 \times 10^5 \times 7.96 \times 10^6$$
$$= (2.35 \times 7.96) \times 10^{11}$$
– the part in brackets is then evaluated using the calculator.

Three methods of checking calculations performed on the calculator are recommended:
   (i) make an estimate, working to an accuracy of one significant figure;
  (ii) repeat the calculation, preferably in a different order;
 (iii) 'calculate back' from the answer to one of the original values.

Physical measurements are not exact; for example,
Time $= 2.3 \text{ s} \pm 0.2 \text{ s} \Rightarrow 2.1 \text{ s} \leqslant \text{Time} \leqslant 2.5 \text{ s}$
Length $= 4.6 \text{ m} \Rightarrow 4.55 \leqslant \text{Length} < 4.65 \text{ m}$

This last inequality assumes use of the convention, used throughout this course, that 4.55 is rounded up to 4.6 and 4.65 is rounded up to 4.7, etc., that is, always rounding upwards numbers ending in 5.

There is an alternative convention (British Standard 1957) by which, when rounding numbers ending in 5, you round either upwards or downwards, depending on which will make the final result end in an even number; for example, 19.55 would be rounded to 19.6 (even) rather than 19.5 (odd), but 19.45 would be rounded to 19.4 (even) rather than 19.5 (odd).

One convention for answers to calculations involving measurements is: give the answer to the same number of significant figures as the least accurate of the original measurements, if there is no good reason for doing otherwise.

Ratios and percentage

Ratios compare like quantities and can be multiplied or divided through by any number (except zero).

Thus, $2:3$, $4:6$, $\tfrac{2}{3}:1$, $1:1.5$ are all equivalent. When a ratio is written in the form $1:n$, n is called the *scale factor*.

Example 9

On an antique map (on which no scale is shown) the distance between Oakford and Stanton is 3.6 cm whereas in fact the distance as the crow flies is 19 km. It is required to express the scale in the form $1:n$ to an accuracy of two significant figures.

The ratio of distance on the map to true distance is
$3.6 : 19 \times 10^5$ (since 10^5 cm $= 1$ km)
$= 1 : \dfrac{19 \times 10^5}{3.6}$.
$= 1 : 5.3 \times 10^5$ to 2 s.f.

A percentage is a fraction whose denominator is 100. For example, $9\% = \frac{9}{100} = 0.09$.

Increasing a quantity by 9% is equivalent to multiplying it by a scale factor of 1.09. $(100+9 = 109)$.

For a decrease of 9% the scale factor is 0.91. $(100-9 = 91)$.

The effect of successive percentage changes can be found by multiplying together the corresponding scale factors.

Example 10

A dealer in second-hand cars buys a Marina in a car auction for £800, does £300 worth of work on it so that his total outlay is £1100 and offers it for sale with a 50% mark-up on £1100. Failing to sell it, he puts a notice on it saying 'SALE: 25% off all prices'. If he then sells it, what is

(*a*) his percentage profit; (*b*) his actual profit on £1100?

(*a*) The combined scale factor is $1.50 \times 0.75 = 1.125$ so he makes $12\frac{1}{2}\%$ profit.
(*b*) The actual profit is $12\frac{1}{2}\%$ of £1100 $= 0.125 \times £1100$
$= £137.50$.

The system of paying interest, in which, each year, the interest is added to the investment, is called *compound interest*.

Example 11

£300, invested for 6 years at 5% compound interest is then worth
£300 $\times 1.05^6 =$ £402 to the nearest pound.

Exercise B

1 Evaluate $\dfrac{2.44 \times 0.631}{0.0806}$ correct to two significant figures. (SMP O-level)

2 Evaluate $\dfrac{2.60 \times 3.25}{1.96}$ correct to two significant figures. (SMP O-level)

3 (*a*) Evaluate $\dfrac{61.3 \times \sqrt{9.3}}{2980}$ correct to one significant figure.

(*b*) State your answer to (*a*) in standard index form. (SMP O-level)

4 A calculator gives the area of a circle of radius 8.16 cm as 209.18482 cm². Round this off to an appropriate number of figures. (SMP O-level)

5 I bought $100 when the rate of exchange was $1.86 to £1. How much did I pay? (Answer to the nearest penny.) (SMP O-level)

6 The side of a square is measured as 121 mm. If the maximum possible error is 1 mm, calculate the smallest possible perimeter.

7 The sides of a rectangle are measured (correct to the nearest millimetre) as 21 mm and 37 mm. Which is nearest to the smallest possible true value of the area?
(a) 720 mm²;   (b) 748 mm²;   (c) 771 mm²;   (d) 777 mm². (SMP O-level)

8 The radius of a circle is given as 15 m correct to two significant figures. Estimate to one significant figure the maximum error in using this figure to calculate the circumference of the circle. (SMP O-level)

9 The standard gauge of railway track is 1.43 m. A model is to be made with gauge 11 mm. Calculate the scale in the form $1:n$, where $n > 1$. (SMP O-level)

10 The numbers p and r are in the ratio $5:2$. If $p = 2$, find r. (SMP O-level)

11 The rateable value of a house was £125. Rates were levied at 64p for each £1 of rateable value. The house has now been given a new rateable value of £200. At how many pence in the pound must the new rate be levied if the householder is to pay exactly the same amount as before? (SMP O-level)

12 Mathwaite village, shown in the plan, has nine houses (shown numbered) and a school. It is self-supporting, and the total cost of upkeep in 1978 is £10 000. The householders contribute the amounts shown in Figure 2 and they agree that, however the cost may vary from year to year, each will always contribute the same fraction of the total. For example, No. 1 will always pay $\frac{3}{10}$ of the total cost.

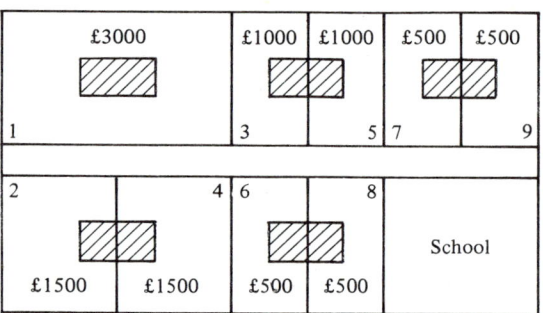

Figure 2

(The amount shown for each house is known as the Rateable Value (RV).)
(a) In 1984 the total cost drops to £5000. For the occupant of No. 5 calculate
    (i) the contribution paid;
    (ii) the number of pence paid for each pound of his RV.
(b) In 1990 inflation increases the total cost to 20% above that for 1984. Calculate the number of pence then paid by No. 6 for each pound of his RV.
(c) In 2001 each occupant pays 125p for each pound of his RV. Calculate the total cost for the village. (SMP O-level)

13 In 1974, public expenditure in the United Kingdom amounted to $£3.9 \times 10^{10}$, of which 12p in every pound was spent on education.
(a) Calculate the amount spent on education.

(b) The amount spent on other things was n times the amount spent on education. Calculate n, correct to the nearest whole number.

(c) Suppose the total expenditure had been the same but the amount spent on education had been increased by 10%. Express this increase as a percentage of the total expenditure. (SMP O-level)

14 In India, in a population of 600 million, there are estimated to be 370 million Hindus, 50 million Muslims, 11 million Christians and 8 million Sikhs. Express each of these figures as a percentage of the whole population.

15 The United States has 3.5 million children whose first language is not English. 70% of them are Spanish-speaking. How many of them are Spanish-speaking?

16 Excluding countries north of the Sahara, the population of Africa in the mid-1980s is estimated as 362 million, of which 21% live in Nigeria. Estimate the population of Nigeria then.

17 For the mid-1980s, it is estimated that
(i) in Britain, 23% of the population of 56 million are under the age of 15;
(ii) in Ethiopia, 45% of the population of 32 million are under the age of 15.
In which of these countries is there the greater number of children under 15?

18 The price of a kettle rises by 25%. Before the rise the price was £10. What is the price after the rise?

19 An electric toaster is offered in a sale at £15, after a reduction of 20%. What was the original price?

20 At an antiques sale, Ann bought a silver plated fruit basket together with a Britannia metal butter dish for £8.50. She later sold the fruit basket in another sale for £12.50 and the butter dish to an antique dealer for £10.00. Calculate her percentage profit on the whole operation.

21 Wheat is priced at £72 per tonne. There is to be a 20% increase in this price but a government subsidy will restrict the increase for the customer to 5%. How much will this subsidy be on one tonne of wheat? (SMP O-level)

22 In 1977, the expenditure of industrialised countries on defence was about 17 times their expenditure on aid to developing countries.
(a) If their defence bill could have been cut by 6%, and the savings transferred to aid to developing countries, what would have been the percentage increase in that aid?
(b) How does Britain's expenditure on defence now compare with her expenditure on aid?

23 A new car cost £2500. Each year its value decreased by 20% of its value at the beginning of that year.
What was its value after two years? (SMP O-level)

24 After a 20% devaluation of the £ it is worth $1.80.
Find the equivalent of £1 in dollars before this devaluation. (SMP O-level)

25 (a) Express $12\frac{1}{2}$% as a fraction in its lowest terms.
(b) (i) Find the total cost of a camera priced at '£39.60 + VAT at $12\frac{1}{2}$%'.
(ii) Calculate the percentage increase in this total cost if the rate of VAT is doubled.

26 The 'Acropolis' Greek restaurant advertises moussaka at £1.90; the price is inclusive of 15% VAT. The 'Taverna', in the next street, offers a very similar moussaka at £1.65, not including VAT.
At which restaurant is the moussaka cheaper?

27 In shop W the retail price (excluding VAT) of a freezer of capacity 0.38 m³ is £85.50. In shop X a freezer of capacity 0.43 m³ is on sale at £94.60 including VAT. VAT is added at the rate of 10% of the retail price.
  (a) Calculate the selling price, including VAT, of the freezer in shop W.
  (b) Calculate which is the 'better buy' in terms of m³ per £. (SMP O-level)

28 An auction room catalogue entry reads:
  '436 hand-coloured fashion prints (28 being double-page) and 58 uncoloured fashion prints, from the *Journal des Demoiselles* 1871–95'.
  A dealer purchases this collection for £1720. He reckons to be able to sell a double-page print at $1\frac{1}{2}$ times the price of one of the others and to have to spend a further £1.50 on each of the uncoloured prints to have them coloured.
  If the dealer allows himself about 100% profit and intends to have only two sale prices per print (normal and double-page), what should those prices be?

29 A normally expensive record shop has been doing rather badly lately and is having a clearance sale. From a rack labelled '75% off!', Bill selected 6 records for which he was charged a total of £10.10. What was the original total of the prices of these 6 records?

30 In 1980, Japan was the world's seventh most populous nation, the population being 114 million and increasing at 1.2% per annum, one of the lowest rates in the world.
  If the same growth rate continues, what will be its population in 1990?

31 A dealer in antiquarian maps is considering buying a lot at a sale consisting of five maps by John Speed (c. 1611). He expects to be able to sell them individually for £350, £300, £250, £250 and £150 respectively, and wants to make 50% profit on his total outlay. The auction room will charge him 10% 'buyer's premium' on the auction price. What should be his maximum bid to the nearest £10?

32 The bottom of Ngururu volcanic crater is approximately flat and circular with a diameter of about 12 km. At the end of the rainy season about a quarter of its surface area is flooded to an average depth of about 10 cm.
  (a) Estimate the area flooded in hectares and hence the volume of water in litres.
  (b) If the volume of water is originally V_0, then, after t days of evaporation without further rain the volume V is given by $V = V_0 \times 0.94^t$ (that is, a reduction of 6% per day). After how long will the volume of water be reduced to less than one hundredth of its original volume, a critical stage for the survival of the game in the crater?

33 An estimate in 1980 of the expected world population in 1985 put it at 4.4×10^9, with an annual birth rate of 28 per 1000 of the population and an annual death rate of 11 per 1000 of the population. On the basis of these estimates, calculate:
  (a) the annual increase in population per thousand of the population;
  (b) the annual percentage increase in the population;
  (c) the scale factor by which the population is multiplied annually;
  (d) the approximate population in the year 2000, assuming a constant rate of increase.
  Comment on the assumptions made.

34 The population of North America (USA and Canada) in the mid-1980s is estimated at 247 million with an annual growth rate of 0.7%. The comparable estimate of the population of the rest of America (that is, Latin America) is 360 million, with an annual growth rate of 2.6%.
  If these growth rates remain unchanged, by when would you expect the population of Latin America to be double that of North America?

3. MENSURATION

Here are the main results you have met earlier in the course:
Area of parallelogram = (length of base) × (perpendicular height)
Area of triangle = ½ (length of base) × (perpendicular height)
Area of trapezium = ½ (sum of parallel sides) × (distance between parallels)
Circumference of a circle (radius r), $C = 2\pi r$
Area enclosed by circle, $A = \pi r^2$
Area of sector is $\frac{\theta}{360}$ × area enclosed by circle ($\theta°$ is the angle of the sector)
Area of curved surface of cylinder (height h), $A = 2\pi rh$
Area of curved surface of sphere (radius r), $A = 4\pi r^2$
Volume of prism = (area of base) × (perpendicular height)
Volume of cylinder = $\pi r^2 h$
Volume of pyramid = ⅓ (area of base) × (perpendicular height)
Volume of circular cone = $\tfrac{1}{3}\pi r^2 h$
Volume of sphere = $\tfrac{4}{3}\pi r^3$

Example 12

Calculate the area shaded in Figure 3.

The area of the sector OAB, which includes the triangle OAB and the shaded area, is

$$\frac{50}{360} \times \text{area of circle} = \frac{50}{360} \times \pi \times 2.5^2 \text{ cm}^2$$
$$= 2.7271 \text{ cm}^2 \text{ to 5 s.f.}$$

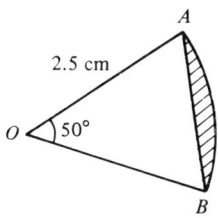

Figure 3

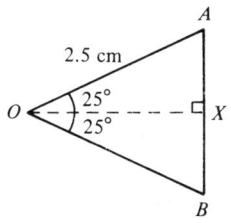

Figure 4

The area of the triangle OAB may be found, as illustrated in Figure 4, by treating AB as base and OX, the perpendicular from O to AB, as height.

Then the area of OAB is

½(length of base) × perpendicular height
$= \tfrac{1}{2}AB \times OX = AX \times OX = (2.5 \sin 25°) \times (2.5 \cos 25°) \text{ cm}^2$
$= 2.3939 \text{ cm}^2 \text{ to 5 s.f.}$

The area of the shaded segment is therefore the area of the sector minus the area of the triangle = $(2.7271 - 2.3939) \text{ cm}^2$
$= 0.33 \text{ cm}^2$ to 2 s.f.

(Was it in fact necessary to retain five significant figures in the intermediate results? Could we have been sure of this at the beginning of the calculations?)

Example 13

Calculate the area of the quadrilateral having vertices at $A(1,1)$, $B(2, 4)$, $C(4, 5)$, $D(6, 3)$.

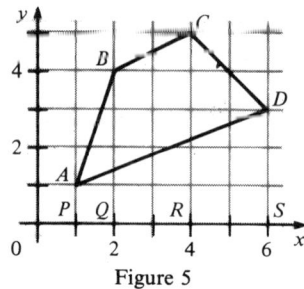

Figure 5

The quadrilateral is drawn in Figure 5.
The area of the quadrilateral can be calculated as
(area of $ABCDSP$ − area of $ADSP$)
$$= \text{area } ABQP + \text{area } BCRQ + \text{area } CDSR - \text{area } ADSP.$$
All these are trapezia, the areas of which may be calculated as
$\frac{1}{2}$ (sum of parallel sides) × (distance between parallels).
So the area required is
area $ABQP$ + area $BCRQ$ + area $CDSR$ − area $ADSP$
$= \frac{1}{2}(1+4) \times 1 + \frac{1}{2}(4+5) \times 2 + \frac{1}{2}(5+3) \times 2 - \frac{1}{2}(1+3) \times 5$
$= \frac{5}{2} + 9 + 8 - 10$ square units $= 9\frac{1}{2}$ square units.

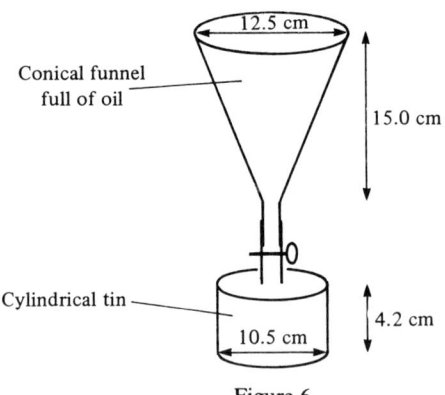

Figure 6

Example 14

Adrian proposes to allow the rather dirty oil from the sump of a motorcar to flow from its temporary position in a funnel into an old tin he has found. (See Figure 6.)

What volume of oil will be left in the funnel when the tin is full of oil?

Neglecting the volume of oil in the tube, etc., the volume of oil is approximately that of a cone radius $\dfrac{12.5}{2}$ cm and height 15.0 cm.

Volume of oil is $\frac{1}{3}\pi \times \left(\frac{12.5}{2}\right)^2 \times 15.0$ cm³ $= 614$ cm³ to 3 s.f.

Volume of cylindrical can is $\pi \times \left(\frac{10.5}{2}\right)^2 \times 4.2$ cm³ $= 364$ cm³ to 3 s.f.

The volume of oil remaining will therefore be about $(614 - 364)$ cm³ $= 250$ cm³ or 0.25 litre to 2 s.f.

Do you think that the intermediate results have been recorded to sufficient accuracy?

Similarity

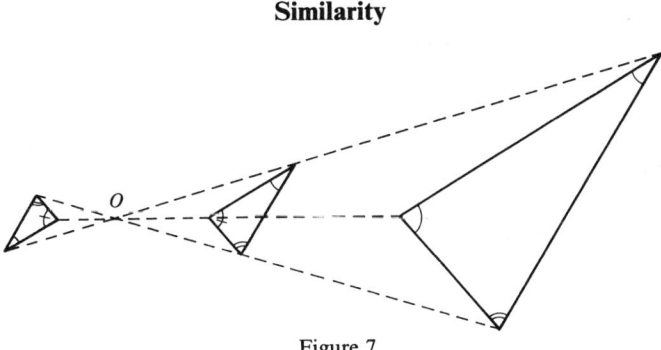

Figure 7

The three triangles illustrated in Figure 7 may be mapped onto each other by enlargement, centre O. These triangles are *similar* to each other, that is, they contain the same angles at their vertices and are the same shape, although different in size.

Similar shapes can always be mapped onto each other by a combination of enlargement and rotation and/or reflection, as illustrated in Figure 8, in which all the triangles shown are similar to each other.

Triangles ABC and $A_1 B_1 C_1$ are congruent to each other; so also are triangles $A_2 B_2 C_2$ and $A_3 B_3 C_3$.

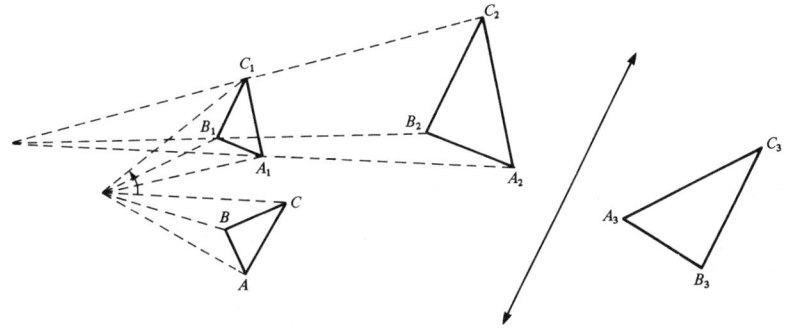

Figure 8

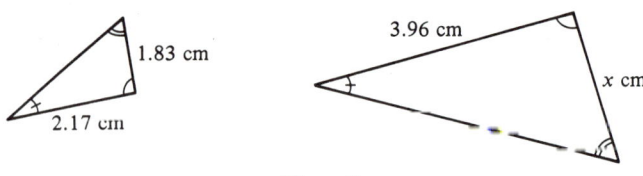

Figure 9

Example 15

In Figure 9, if we know the two triangles to be similar, we can calculate the scale factor of the enlargement involved by comparing lengths of corresponding sides.

Looking at sides opposite angles marked ◁, we see that the scale factor of the enlargement involved in mapping the smaller triangle onto the larger is $\frac{3.96}{2.17}$.

That is, $3.96 = 2.17 \times \frac{3.96}{2.17}$.

Side in large triangle = side in small triangle × scale factor

so that in Figure 9, $x = 1.83 \times \frac{3.96}{2.17}$

$x = 3.34$ to 3 s.f.

Area and volume scale factors

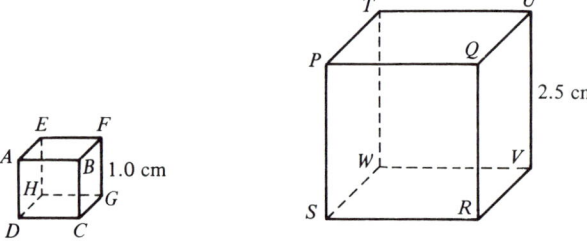

Figure 10

Any length in the larger cube in Figure 10 is 2.5 times the corresponding length in the smaller cube. For example, $PV = AG \times 2.5$. The length scale factor is 2.5.

The area of a face of the smaller cube is 1 cm × 1 cm = 1 cm², while the area of a face of the larger is

$$2.5 \text{ cm} \times 2.5 \text{ cm} = 2.5^2 \text{ cm}^2 = 6.25 \text{ cm}^2.$$

The area scale factor is 2.5^2, that is (the length scale factor)².

For example, the area of triangle PUV is the area of triangle $AFG \times 2.5^2$.

The volume of the smaller cube is 1 cm × 1 cm × 1 cm = 1 cm³ while the volume of the larger is

$$2.5 \text{ cm} \times 2.5 \text{ cm} \times 2.5 \text{ cm} = 2.5^3 \text{ cm}^3 \approx 15.6 \text{ cm}^3.$$

The volume scale factor is 2.5³, that is (the length scale factor)³.

For example, a large cylindrical can of soup, similar in shape but 2.5 times the height and diameter of a smaller one will hold 2.5³ times, that is, 15.6 times as much soup.

Example 16

On an architect's plan of a house, the total floor area is 676 cm². If the scale of the drawing is 1:50, find the actual floor area of the house.

The length scale factor is 50 so the area scale factor is 50². The floor area is
$$676 \times 50^2 \text{ cm}^2 = 1\,690\,000 \text{ cm}^2 = 169 \text{ m}^2.$$

Example 17

The Government Tourist Cooperative of Amnesia proposes to make 50 000 scale models of the famous statue of the Queen's prize yak to sell to tourists. The statue is known to weigh 3600 kg and the models, which will be cast from the same type of metal alloy, will be 2.5 cm high instead of 135 cm. It is required to estimate the mass of alloy needed for the models.

The length scale factor, mapping the statue onto a model of it, is $\frac{2.5}{135}$. The volume scale factor is therefore $\left(\frac{2.5}{135}\right)^3$.

Since both model and statue are made of the same material and mass is proportional to volume, the mass of a model yak will be $3600 \times \left(\frac{2.5}{135}\right)^3$ kg.

The mass of alloy needed for 50 000 such models is therefore
$$3600 \times \left(\frac{2.5}{135}\right)^3 \times 50\,000 \text{ kg} = 1140 \text{ kg to 3 s.f.}$$

Exercise C

1 Figure 11 represents the cross-section of a river.

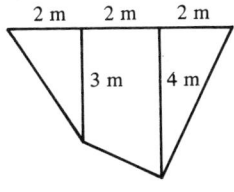

Figure 11

(*a*) Find the area of the cross-section.

(*b*) If the river flows uniformly at $\frac{1}{6}$ m/s, find the volume of water passing each minute. (SMP O-level)

2 In Figure 12, the area of the rectangle *R* is equal to the shaded area between the two squares. Calculate the value of *l*. (SMP O-level)

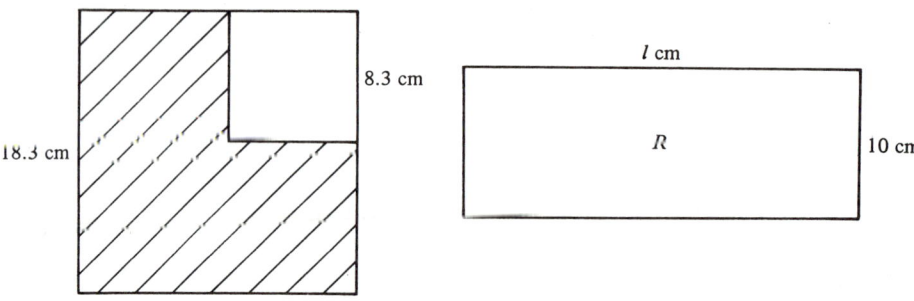

Figure 12

3 Figure 13 shows the mainsail of a yacht. Calculate the area of the sail.

(SMP O-level)

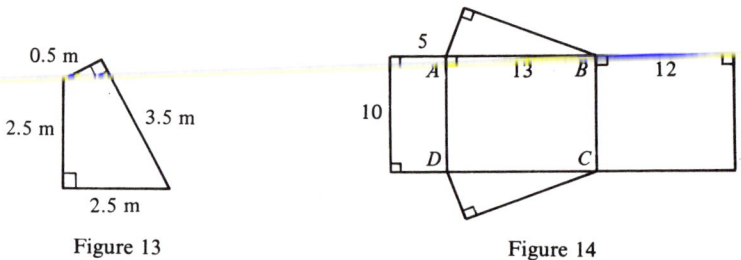

Figure 13   Figure 14

4 Figure 14 is the net of a solid. Dimensions are given in cm.
Which of the following statements are true and which are false?
(a) The solid is a pyramid.
(b) The area of face $ABCD$ is 130 cm².
(c) The surface area of the solid is 350 cm².
(d) The volume of the solid is 300 cm³.   (SMP O-level)

5 A triangle has vertices at the points $(0,0)$, $(3,4)$, $(^-4,3)$.
Which of the following statements are true and which are false?
(a) The triangle is equilateral.
(b) The triangle is acute angled.
(c) The triangle has an axis of symmetry which divides it into two triangles which are similar to the original triangle.
(d) The triangle has an area of $12\frac{1}{2}$ square units.   (SMP O-level)

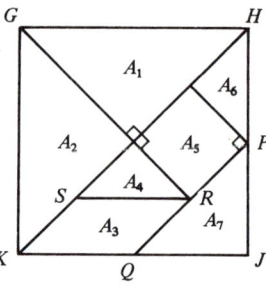

Figure 15

6 In Figure 15, $A_1, A_2, ..., A_7$ represent the areas of the parts of the square $GHJK$ shown in the diagram. $HP = PJ$, $KQ = QJ$ and RS is parallel to JK.
Which of the following statements are true and which are false?
(a) $2A_5 = A_1$.
(b) The region labelled A_5 can be transformed into the region labelled A_3 by a shear.
(c) $A_3 + A_4 + A_6 = A_1$.
(d) The regions labelled A_3, A_4 and A_5 can be rearranged to form a rectangle.
(SMP O-level)

7 Figure 16 shows a square pyramid whose triangular faces are equilateral. The edges are each 2 units long.
Which of the following statements are true and which are false?
(a) The angle between AB and the base is 60°.
(b) The angle between the faces ABC and ABE is greater than 90°.
(c) The height of the pyramid is 3 units.
(d) The volume of the pyramid is between 1.5 and 2 units³.
(SMP O-level)

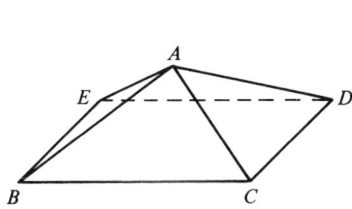

Figure 16

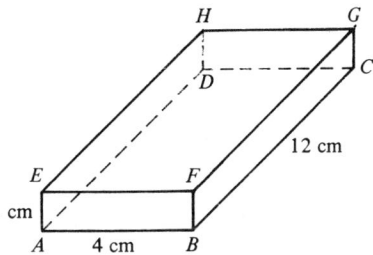

Figure 17

8 The cuboid in Figure 17 stands on a horizontal base $ABCD$.
Which of the following statements are true and which are false?
(a) A thin straight stick 12.8 cm long could go inside a box with these interior measurements.
(b) Area of rectangle $CDEF > 48$ cm².
(c) BH is more steeply inclined to the horizontal than AH.
(d) Volume of pyramid $GABC = 24$ cm³.
(SMP O-level)

9 The shaded area in Figure 18 represents a semi-circular garden path, of width 0.6 m, which is to be covered with tarmac. Tarmac costs £50 per tonne, and is sold in 25 kg bags. Each bag contains sufficient tarmac to cover one square metre. Calculate the number of bags required, and their total cost.
(1 tonne = 1000 kg)
(SMP O-level)

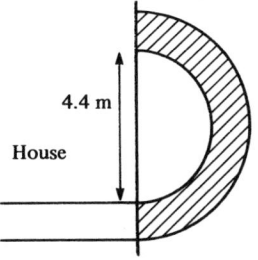

Figure 18

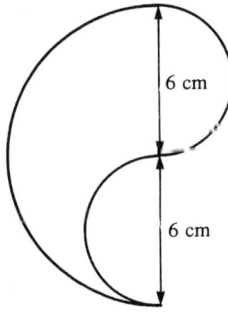

Figure 19

10 The boundary of the shape in Figure 19 consists of three semi-circular arcs. Write down its area as a multiple of π. (SMP O-level)

11 The boundary of the shaded region in Figure 20 consists of four circular quadrants, each of radius r. Write down a formula for the area of the shaded region. (SMP O-level)

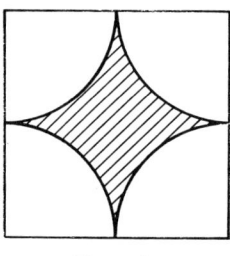

Figure 20

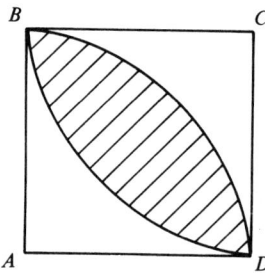

Figure 21

12 In Figure 21, $ABCD$ represents a square of side 1 cm. The arcs shown have centres at A and C. Find the shaded area. (SMP O-level)

13 C is the centre of a circle of radius 4 cm; $\angle PCR = 90°$.
Leaving π in your answers, find the area of:
 (a) the sector $CPQR$;
 (b) the segment PQR. (SMP O-level)

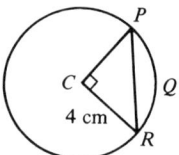

Figure 22

14 A drilling machine operator needs to drill an alloy for which the recommended cutting speed is given as 350 feet per minute. This is the speed at which a point on the circumference of the circular steel drill-bit should be moving. At what speed, in revolutions per minute to the nearest 10 rpm, should a $\tfrac{3}{8}$ inch diameter drill be rotated, ideally? (12 inches = 1 foot.)

Mensuration 57

15 Figure 23 shows a right circular cylinder whose circumference is 16 cm and whose height is 15 cm. *AB* is a diameter of the base and *C* is vertically above *B*. What is the length of the shortest piece of string which will join *A* to *C* when pulled tightly round the surface of the cylinder? (SMP O-level)

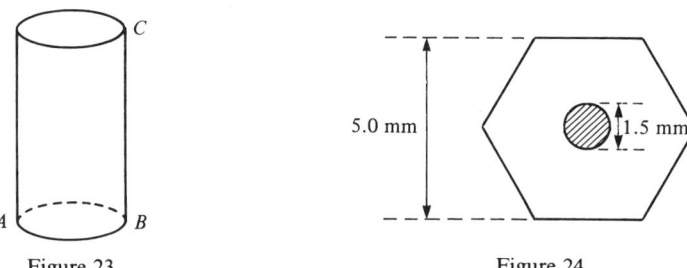

Figure 23   Figure 24

16 The cross-section of a pencil is a regular hexagon of width, between the opposite faces, 5.0 mm (see Figure 24). The 'lead' has diameter 1.5 mm. Calculate the ratio volume of 'lead': volume of wood for the pencil (when unsharpened) in the form $1:n$.

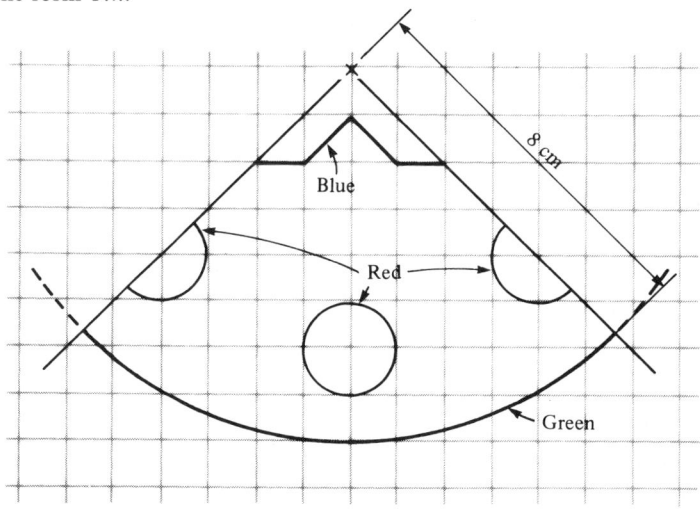

Figure 25

17 The following instructions are taken from an embroidery pattern for a circular table mat. (See Figure 25.)

'The drawing gives part of the design, the centre being marked by a cross. To complete the design, repeat this part three times around the centre point.'

(*a*) On squared paper draw the complete design full-size.
(*b*) Describe the symmetries of the complete design.
(*c*) The circumference of the large (outer) circle is 50 cm, and it is found that 125 cm of green thread are required to embroider this. On this basis calculate how much red thread is required for the small circles.
(*d*) Find also the total length of blue thread required for the central motif.
(All measurements in parts (*c*) and (*d*) are to the nearest centimetre.)

(SMP O-level)

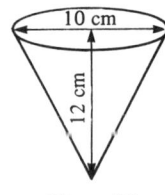

Figure 26

18 The dimensions of a hollow, right circular cone are given in Figure 26.
   (a) What is the volume of the cone?
   (b) The cone is part of a sugar dispenser and is to be filled with sugar. If 1000 cm³ of sugar weighs 900 g, what weight of sugar will the cone hold?
   (SMP O-level)

19 A lampshade has a metal frame consisting of two circular hoops of radii p cm and q cm joined together by four straight struts each of length h cm. The total length of metal is T cm.
   (a) (i) Find T when $p = 21$, $q = 24.5$, $h = 27$.
       (ii) Find an expression for T in terms of p, q, h.
   (b) The area of the material covering the frame is A cm², where $A = h(p+q)$. Find an expression for p in terms of A, h, q. (SMP O-level)

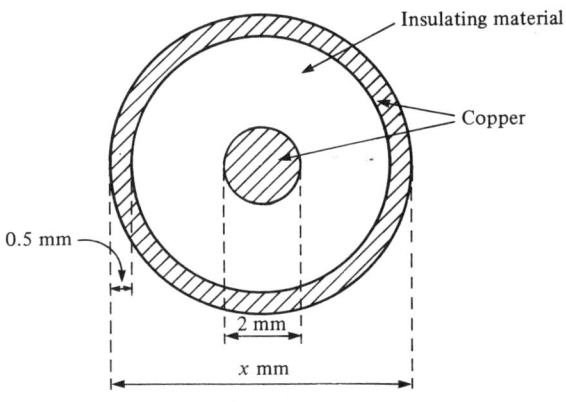

Figure 27

20 An electrical cable of diameter x mm is made with a copper inner conductor diameter 2 mm and a copper outer case of thickness 0.5 mm separated by insulating material. (See Figure 27.)
   The specification states that
   (i) the insulation must be at least 4 mm thick;
   (ii) the mass per metre length of copper in the cable must not exceed 0.2 kg.
   It is given that 1000 mm³ of copper has a mass of 0.008 kg.
   (a) Find in terms of x the total area of copper in the cross-section and hence show that the volume of copper in 1 m of cable is $250\pi(3+2x)$ mm³.

(b) Express the two conditions of the specification in terms of x.
(c) Find the values of x which satisfy the conditions. (SMP O-level)

21 A rug, 80 cm by 75 cm, covering the rectangle $ABCD$, is to be replaced by a new semi-circular rug.
  (a) One suggestion is that the new rug should be large enough to cover completely the rectangle $ABCD$, as shown in Figure 28. Calculate the radius of such a rug.
  (b) It is decided instead that the new rug should have the same area as the rectangular rug. Show that the radius of the rug in this case will be $\sqrt{\left(\dfrac{12000}{\pi}\right)}$ cm, and evaluate this quantity. (SMP O-level)

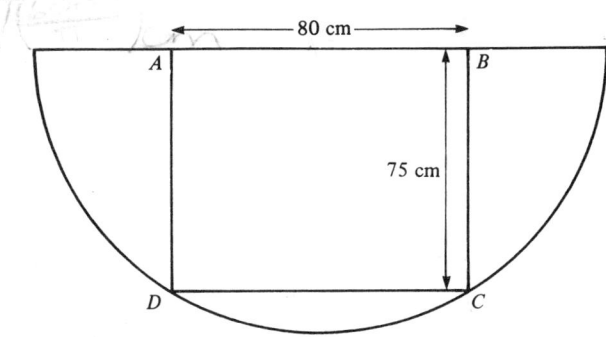

Figure 28

22 A water engineer uses the circular cone illustrated in Figure 29 as an approximation to the shape of a reservoir. When full, the reservoir has a maximum depth of 100 m and holds 3.6×10^7 m³ of water.
  Use the same approximation to answer the following questions.
  (a) Calculate the area of the water surface when the reservoir is full. (There is no need to find the radius.)
  (b) A fall in the water level reduces the diameter of the surface of the water to one-third of its value when full. Calculate the area of the water surface now.
  (c) When the water level is 50 m above the lowest point, the engineer estimates that he has ten weeks' supply remaining. How many weeks' supply has he when the reservoir is completely full?
  (d) In a drought the engineer decides that he will ration the water when he has only five weeks' supply remaining in the reservoir. What will be the height of the water level above the lowest point at this moment? (SMP O-level)

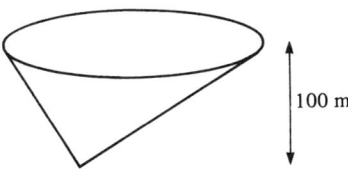

Figure 29

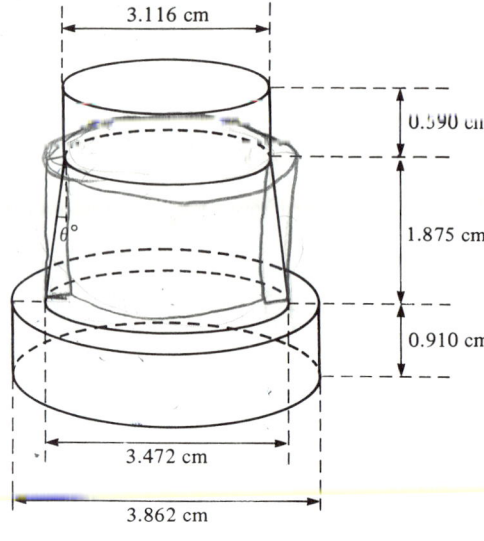

Figure 30

23 An engineering component is partly tapered to form a truncated cone with a cylinder at each end as shown in Figure 30. With the dimensions given, calculate the angle of taper, $\theta°$, and the volume of the whole component, assuming that it is solid.

24 The angle of taper of a conically tapered hole (see Figure 31) is discovered as follows:
A sphere of diameter d_1 is dropped into the hole and the depth, h_1, of the top of the sphere below the top of the hole is measured.

This sphere is then replaced by another, of diameter d_2, and the depth of its top, h_2, is measured.

Find a formula for the angle of taper, $\theta°$, in terms of d_1, d_2, h_1 and h_2.

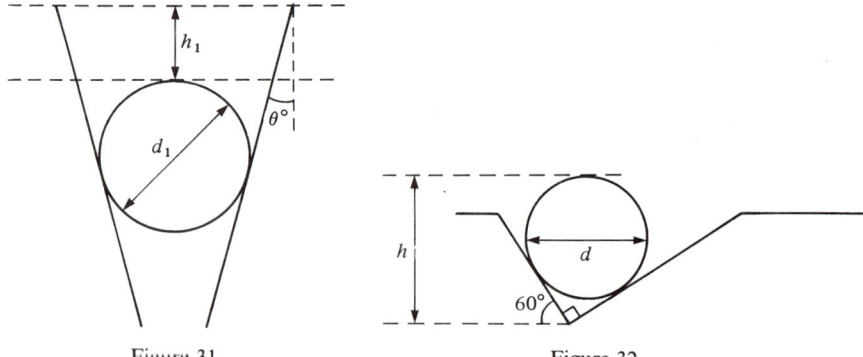

Figure 31   Figure 32

25 A cylinder of diameter d rests in a V-shaped groove, the angle of the V being 90° as shown in Figure 32.

Find a formula, in terms of d, for the height, h, of the top of the cylinder above the bottom of the groove.

26 A tall mirror is to be fixed on a wall with the top x m from the floor. A girl, 1.5 m tall, whose eyes are 1.4 m from the floor, needs to see the top of her head in the mirror when she stands 1 m away.
   What is the smallest possible value of x? (SMP O-level)

27 In Figure 33, BC and DE are parallel.
   (a) If $AB = 3$ cm, $AD = 4$ cm and $BC = 2.4$ cm, calculate DE.
   (b) If $AB = 2.8$ cm, $BD = 1.1$ cm and $BC = 2.5$ cm, calculate DE.
   (c) If $AB = 3.1$ cm, $BD = 0.9$ cm and $DE = 3.2$ cm, calculate BC.

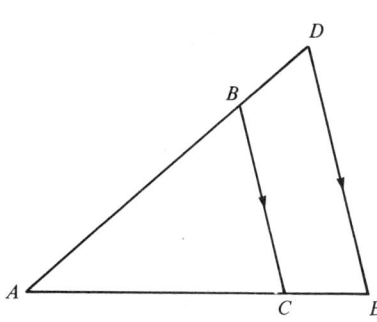
Figure 33

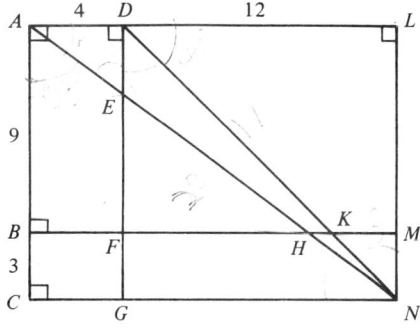
Figure 34

28 Figure 34 is not to scale. Distances are given in centimetres.
   Which of the following statements are true and which are false?
   (a) $DE = 3$ cm.
   (b) $\triangle ABH$ is an enlargement of $\triangle NMH$.
   (c) $\triangle HMN$ can be mapped onto $\triangle NGE$ by a translation followed by an enlargement.
   (d) $\triangle HMN$ can be mapped onto $\triangle ALN$ by an enlargement with scale factor 3. (SMP O-level)

29 In Figure 35, $AP = 2PB$ and $AP' = 2P'B$; the images of P, B, under reflection in m are P', B'; and AP is parallel to $P'B'$.
   (a) **E** is the enlargement with centre C which maps P onto B'. Name with reasons the images under **E** of (i) P', (ii) AP, (iii) CA.
   (b) Explain why $AP = 2P'B'$ and state the scale factor of **E**.
   (c) (i) Express the lengths of CP' and CB as multiples of CA.
       (ii) If $AB = 12$ cm, find the lengths of CB and CP.
   (d) If A, B are fixed points 12 cm apart and P varies so that $AP = 2PB$, what is the locus of P? (SMP O-level)

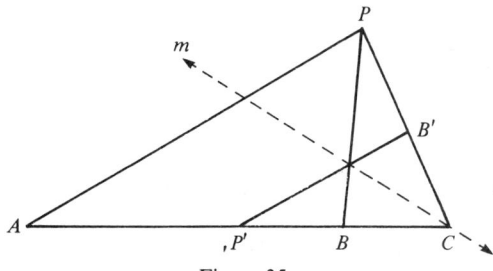
Figure 35

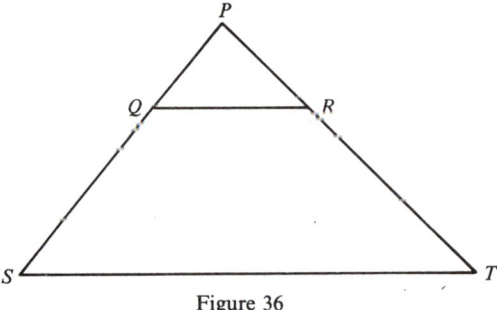

Figure 36

30 In Figure 36, △PST is an enlargement of △PQR, centre P.
  (a) If RT = 2PR, what is the scale factor of the enlargement?
  (b) Express the ratio   area PQR:area PST   in the form 1:n.
  (c) Express the ratio   area PQR:area QRTS   in the form 1:n.

31 In Figure 37, △JMK is an enlargement of △LNK. JK = 2.1 cm and KL = 3.5 cm.
  (a) Where is the centre of enlargement? What is the scale factor of the enlargement?
  (b) Express the ratio MK:KN in the form 1:n and hence the ratio MK:MN in the form 1:n.

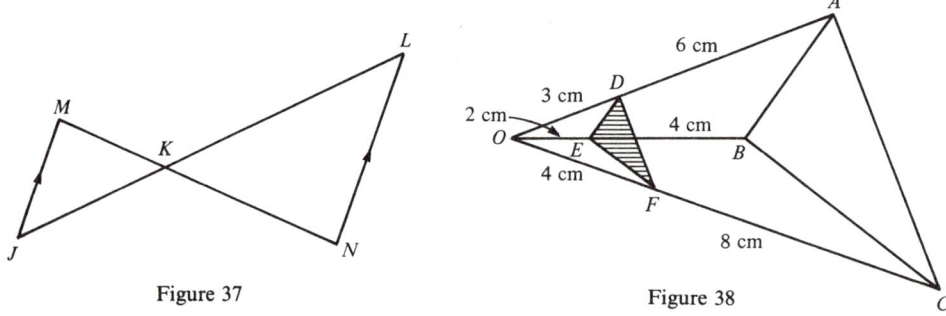

Figure 37   Figure 38

32 In Figure 38, distances between the lettered points are shown and triangle ABC has area 18 cm².
  Calculate the area of the shaded triangle DEF.   (SMP O-level)

33 Quadrilateral A'B'C'D' is an enlargement of quadrilateral ABCD by a scale factor of three. Which of the following statements are true and which false?
  (a) $A'B' = \frac{1}{3}AB$.
  (b) The area of the larger quadrilateral is six times that of the smaller.
  (c) The perimeter of the larger quadrilateral is three times that of the smaller.
  (d) Angle A'B'D' = 3 × angle ABD.   (SMP O-level)

34 Objects A, B and C are exactly the same shape.
  (a) If A is twice as long as B, give the ratio of their volumes.
  (b) If A has 16 times the surface area of C, give the ratio of their lengths.
          (SMP O-level)

35 Two full tins of coffee contain 125 g and 1 kg respectively. The two tins are geometrically similar and the smaller is 8 cm high. How high is the larger tin?
          (SMP O-level)

36 The height of the sculpture in Figure 39 is 2 m. A scale model 20 cm high has a volume $\frac{1}{x}$ of the volume of the sculpture. Find x. (SMP O-level)

Figure 39   Figure 40

37 The shape in heavy outline in Figure 40 is an enlargement of the shaded shape, and has an area of 18 square units.
    Find the area of the shaded shape. (SMP O-level)

38 (a) On a map drawn to a scale of 1:50 000 the distance from Dolgoed to the top of the mountain Waun-oer is 7 cm. Calculate the horizontal distance, in kilometres, between the two points.
    (b) The height above sea-level of Dolgoed is 198 m and of Waun-oer is 670 m. Calculate the average gradient of a straight footpath between the two in the form $1:n$, giving n correct to two significant figures.
    (c) From Waun-oer the horizontal distance to Lake Hendre-ddu is estimated to be 2.5 km, on a bearing of 150°. What will be the distance and bearing on the map?
    (d) On the map the area of the lake is 1 cm². Calculate the true surface area in hectares. (1 ha = 10 000 m².)
    (e) From Waun-oer the angle of depression of the lake is 7°. Calculate the height above sea-level of the surface of the lake. (SMP O-level)

39 The fixed cone OAB is transformed into the cone $OA'B'$ by an enlargement, centre O and variable positive scale factor k. The cone $OA'B'$ has volume V, surface area S and the circumference of its base is C. (See Figure 41.) Which of the following statements are true and which are false?
    (a) $AA' = kOA$. (b) $C \propto k^2$. (c) $V \propto k^3$. (d) $\frac{S}{V} \propto k$. (SMP O-level)

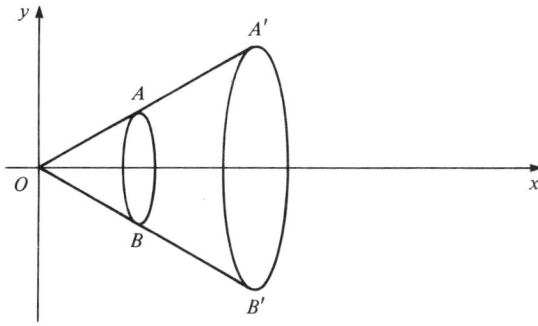

Figure 41

40 A factory makes model cars which are to a scale 1:100. The real car is 4.2 m long and costs £1436.80. The windscreen of the model is a rectangle with area approximately 1.73 cm². The cost of the model is also scaled (to the nearest penny) to $\frac{1}{100}$th of the cost of the real car.

Which of the following statements are true and which are false?

(a) The length of the model is 4.2 cm.
(b) The area of the real windscreen is approximately 17.3 m².
(c) The volume of the storage boot of the real car is 1000 times that of the model.
(d) The model costs £14.37. (SMP O-level)

4. INDEX NUMBERS

The Zambanian Minister of Agriculture wants to compare the progress in hic bean production with the progress of the Forestry Department's yuk-fruit tree planting programme.

He has the following sets of figures:

Year	Hic bean production (tonnes)	Number of yuk-fruit trees planted
1980	1750	724
1981	2170	812
1982	2490	995
1983	2660	1280
1984	2900	1610

The two sets of figures are in different units and although it is clear that both are increasing, it is not easy to see how their growth rates compare.

If we take, as 'base period', the year 1980, we can work out a hic bean 'index' (to three significant figures) as follows:

Call the hic bean index for 1980 (the base period), 100

Then the hic bean index for 1981 is $\frac{2170}{1750} \times 100 = 124$

the hic bean index for 1982 is $\frac{2490}{1750} \times 100 \approx 142$

the hic bean index for 1983 is $\frac{2660}{1750} \times 100 = 152$

the hic bean index for 1984 is $\frac{2900}{1750} \times 100 \approx 166$.

Check some of these calculations.

Similarly, a yuk-fruit index can be obtained, again taking 1980 as the base period, so that:

the yuk-fruit index for 1980 = 100

for 1981 is $\frac{812}{724} \times 100 = 112$

etc.

Index numbers

The full results are given in the table below; check the remaining yuk-fruit index calculations.

Year	Hic bean index	Yuk-fruit index
1980	100	100
1981	124	112
1982	142	137
1983	152	177
1984	166	222

The figures are now much more easily comparable and a graphical display shows the comparison very clearly. (See Figure 42.)

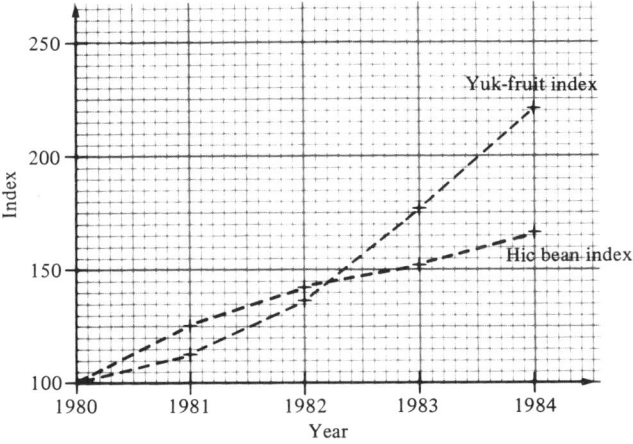

Figure 42

Over the five years the increase in hic bean production has tended to fall although in the final year there seems to have been a slight upturn. Yuk-fruit tree planting, however, has gone ahead better and better.

Of course the actual values of each index give more precise (but not necessarily more useful) information. For instance, the hic bean index in 1984 is 166 which tells us that there has been a 66% increase in hic bean production over the five-year period. Between 1982 and 1983 hic bean production increased by a scale factor

$$\frac{152}{142} \approx 1.07, \text{ that is by } 7\%$$

between 1983 and 1984, it increased by a factor

$$\frac{166}{152} \approx 1.09, \text{ that is by } 9\%$$

– a little better.

Exercise D

1 The Dow-Jones Index measures the performance of American shares on the Wall Street exchange. In the autumn of 1982 it rose from 776.9 to 925.1. What percentage increase was this?

2 The Financial Times (FT) All-Share Index is based on the prices of 750 selected shares on the stock market. If the FT Index increases from 340.1 to 353.5, by what percentage does it increase? If it falls from 353.5 to 329.8, by what percentage does it fall?

3 The price of bottles of Fizzango has fluctuated as shown in the table below.

Year	Price (pence)
1980	$12\frac{1}{2}$
1981	16
1982	$19\frac{1}{2}$
1983	21
1984	$24\frac{1}{2}$

Work out a Fizzango price index with 1980 as the base period. By what percentage has Fizzango increased in price during these five years? By what percentage did it increase from 1980 to 1981?

4 From the population figures given in Table 1, calculate
   (a) an index of population of England and Wales;
   (b) an index of population of Scotland.
In each case, take 1901 as base period.

(Thus, for example, the 1851 index of population of Scotland will be $\frac{2889}{4472} \times 100$.)

Compare the changes of population in Scotland with the changes in England and Wales over this period and suggest possible explanations.

Year	Population of England and Wales (million)	Population of Scotland (million)
1801	8.893	1.608
1851	17.928	2.889
1901	32.528	4.472
1951	43.758	5.096
1981	49.011	5.117

Table 1

(Based on figures from the *Annual Abstract of Statistics 1982*, HMSO.)

5 The figures given below describe the consumptions of beer and wine in Britain in the years indicated.

Year	Beer (million litres)	Wine (million litres)
1970	5637	161
1972	5998	226
1974	6399	299
1976	6653	316
1978	6780	362
1980	6549	402

Calculate a beer index and a wine index taking 1970 as base period in each case. Display the two indices on the same graph.

Compare the ways the consumptions of beer and wine have changed over this period and suggest some possible explanations.

(Based on figures taken from the *Annual Abstract of Statistics 1982*, HMSO.)

6 In the next section we shall show how an index such as the Retail Price Index is constructed: for the moment take it to be simply a measure of average prices of goods in shops, etc.

In January 1974, the Retail Price Index was taken to be 100. By December 1977 it was 188.4; by December 1978 it was 204.2 and by December 1979 it had reached 239.4. By what percentage did the Retail Price Index increase

(a) between January 1974 and December 1977;

(b) between January 1974 and December 1979?

What was the annual inflation rate, that is, the percentage change in the Retail Price Index, between December 1978 and December 1979?

5. WEIGHTED INDEX NUMBERS

Suppose that Zambian peasants grow or make nearly everything they need for living and have only three items of expenditure: salt, beads and copper wire. Prices are shown in the table below for the years 1980 and 1981, and a 1981 index is calculated for each item – for instance, for salt, this is

$$\frac{13.20}{11.50} \times 100 = 115 \text{ to 3 s.f.}$$

	Price in Zambian dollars		1981 index (1980 as base year)
	1980	1981	
Salt (per kilogram)	11.50	13.20	115
Beads (per hundred)	35.10	27.30	78
Wire (per kilogram)	242.70	261.20	108

In order to calculate a 'cost of living index' for the Zambian peasant, some estimate (based on a survey) needs to be made of the relative amount of income spent on each of these items.

Suppose that, on average, 70% of total expenditure is spent on salt, 10% on beads, and 20% on wire. Then a *weighted index* can be calculated as follows:

Weighted
index   = salt index × salt weighting + beads index × beads weighting + wire index × wire weighting
        = 115 × 0.70   + 78 × 0.10   + 108 × 0.20
        = 110 to 3 s.f.

So the Zambian cost of living has increased by 10%.

In our own society the construction of a national index, such as the Retail Price Index or the Index of Industrial Production, is much more complicated and has to be based on a large number of different items. Changes in fashion need to be taken into account and also changes in technology; for example, an index calculated in 1960 would not have taken into account production or price of calculators.

In any case, it is important to remember that any index is based on averages: the Retail Price Index takes account of the price of cigarettes and petrol, for instance, but some families do not smoke and do not own a car, so that they are not affected by changes in tobacco prices and are only indirectly affected by changes in petrol prices.

Exercise E

1   As a by-product of their plastic wrapped kipper fillets, a company manufactures a savoury chewing gum from kipper tails.

To help the manager who is trying to decide what price to charge for this product, you are asked to combine into a single total cost index the average hourly wages of the employees and the processing cost index, given in the table below.

Year	Average hourly wages (£)	Processing cost index
1980	2.65	100
1981	2.98	112.3
1982	3.15	137.5
1983	3.32	149.1
1984	3.57	160.0

(*a*) Calculate a wage index with 1980 as base period.
(*b*) Assuming that the total cost is made up of 65% wages and 35% processing, work out a suitable total cost index with 1980 as the base period.

Weighted index numbers

2 Curiosa Imports plc deals mainly in three commodities, recent prices of which are displayed in the table below.

	Price (£)		
	1981	1982	1983
Bees' knees from Brunei (per gram)	130	94	76
Down of the humpy duck from Australia (per kg)	7.55	8.20	12.48
Scrap television tubes from the USA	185	207	241

The company spends 62% of its budget on bees' knees, 27% on humpy duck down and the rest on TV tubes.

(a) Taking 1981 as base period in each case, calculate price indices for each of the commodities separately.

(b) Calculate a weighted price index using the budget percentages given in conjunction with your answers to (a).

3 In a certain manufacturing process the cost of manufacture depends on the cost of materials used, lead and pig iron, and on the cost of labour. The table below shows price indices for these, with year 1 as base period.

	Year 1	Year 2	Year 3	Year 4
Lead	100	121	185	226
Pig iron	100	106	147	262
Labour	100	104	113	127

Assuming that the weightings appropriate to the calculation of a total cost index are:

Lead cost 4%
Pig iron cost 58%
Labour cost 38%

calculate a total cost index for the four years, taking Year 1 as base year.

4 The table below shows the value per tonne of the two commonest sea fish from 1977 to 1980, together with the landed weights of each in 1977.

Type of fish	Value per tonne (£)				Landed weight 1977 (thousand tonnes)
	1977	1978	1979	1980	
Cod	522	535	584	562	146.5
Haddock	390	478	494	402	122.9

Work out a fish price index as follows:

(a) Taking 1977 as base period, work out a cod value index (100 in 1977) and a haddock value index (100 in 1977).

(b) Find what percentage of the total landed weight of cod and haddock consists of (i) cod and (ii) haddock.

(c) Use the percentages calculated in (b) as weightings to calculate a fish price index from your results in (a).
(d) Comment on the figures you have obtained.
(Based on figures taken from the *Annual Abstract of Statistics 1982*, HMSO.)

5 Figure 43 below is typical of the sort of diagrams often published in the financial sections of newspapers. The date scale starts in May 1979 when there was a General Election. Criticise the diagram.

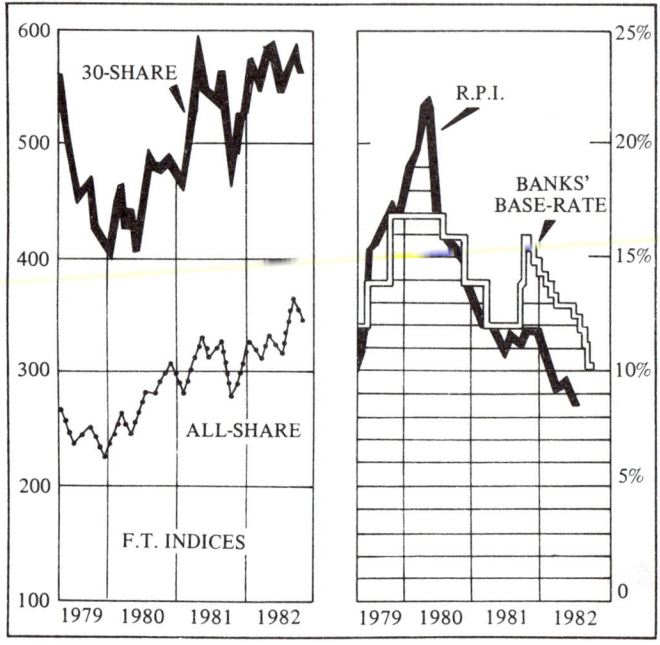

Figure 43

The 30-Share FT Index is based on the price of 30 selected shares, mainly of large industrial concerns.
The All-Share FT Index is based on 750 selected shares, covering a wide range of companies.
Compare the performance of these two indices, as follows:
(a) Make a table of values of each of these indices, estimated from the diagram, for about 10 dates in the period concerned, choosing values which seem to represent the main trend, but including the main peaks and troughs.
(b) Calculate values of a 'New 30-Share Index' and a 'New All-Share Index', each with a base period May 1979, so that each starts at 100 then.
(c) Plot both your new indices on one graph and compare them.
(d) During 1980, inflation (as measured by the percentage increase in the Retail Price Index) averaged about 16% whilst, during 1981 it averaged about 12%. In general, did the price of shares, as measured by the All-Share Index, keep pace with inflation during this two-year period?

6. REGULAR SAVINGS

When Colin was 7 years old, his grandfather decided to pay £10 into Colin's savings account at a local bank each year on Colin's birthday. The bank has (unusually) paid the same interest, 8%, each year and Colin has never taken any money out of the account. We can see how the amount in the account has been mounting up by following the flow chart below, using a calculator, and plotting the results on a graph. (See Figure 44.)

Colin's age	7	8	9	10	11	12	13	14	15	16
Amount in account (£)	10	20.80	32.46	45.06	58.66	73.35	89.22	106.36	124.87	144.86

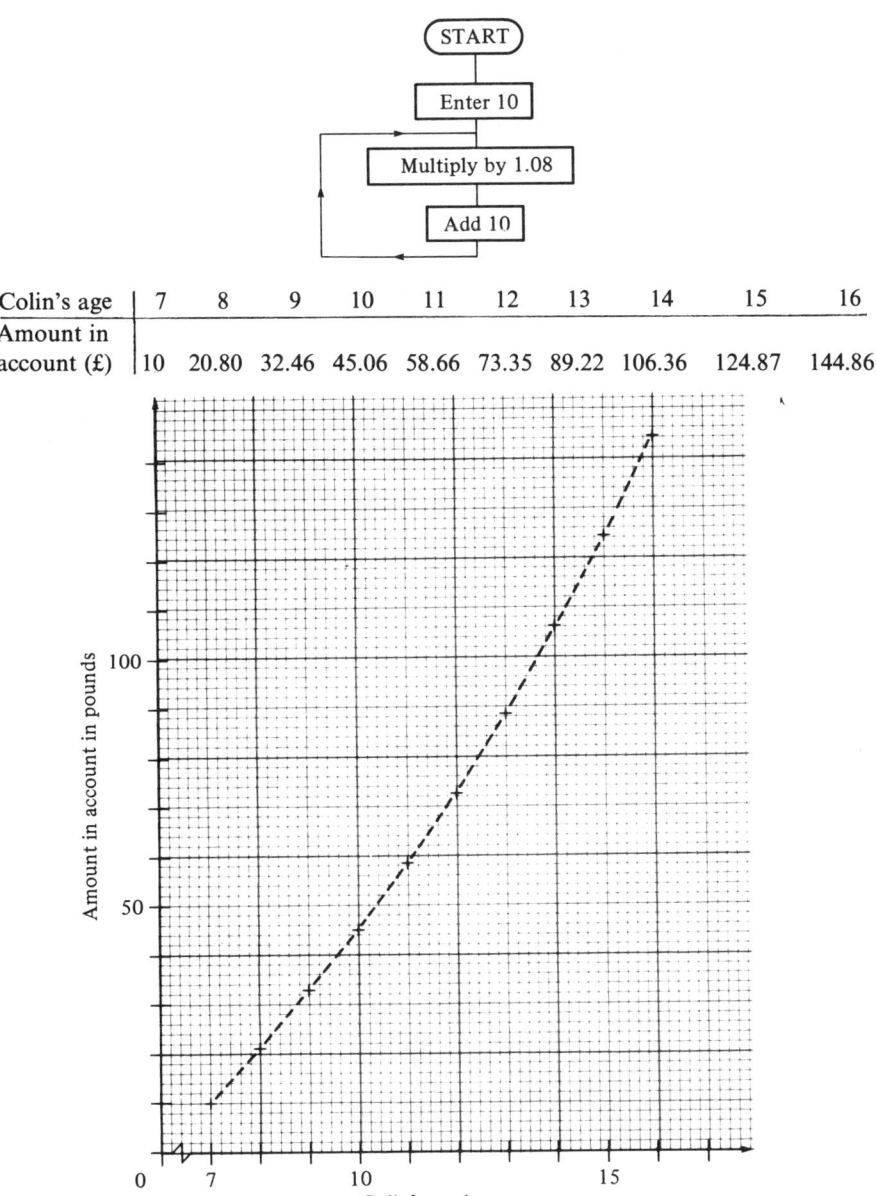

Figure 44

Exercise F

1 £7 is placed in a bank account on 1st January each year and earns interest at 9% per year. How much is in the account just after the fifth payment has been made?

2 If the amount placed in the account each year is £75 and the rate of interest is 9.5% per year, how much is in the account just after the seventh payment has been made?

Whilst the method you have been using to calculate the final sum after several years is quite quick, it is helpful to develop a formula for this sum. To do this, we will look at question 1 of Exercise F in another way.

Just after the fifth payment has been made, there is:

the £7 which has just been paid in	£7.00
the £7 which was paid in a year before (the fourth payment) which, with interest, is now £7 × 1.09	£7.63
the £7 which was paid in a year before (the third payment) which, with interest, is now £7 × 1.09^2	£8.32
the £7 which was paid in a year before (the second payment) which, with interest, is now £7 × 1.09^3	£9.07
the £7 which was paid in a year before (the first payment) which, with interest, is now £7 × 1.09^4	£9.88
making a total sum, S	£41.90

(In this calculation, all the figures have been rounded to the nearest penny (as does indeed happen in banks) so that it would be reasonable to expect this method to produce a slightly different answer to the other – in fact, in this case the difference is only 1p.)

We could write out this sum, S, like this:
$$S = 7 + 7 \times 1.09 + 7 \times 1.09^2 + 7 \times 1.09^3 + 7 \times 1.09^4.$$

If we now multiply this equation by 1.09 (for reasons which will become clear shortly) and then write down the line above once again, we obtain:
$$1.09S = 7 \times 1.09 + 7 \times 1.09^2 + 7 \times 1.09^3 + 7 \times 1.09^4 + 7 \times 1.09^5$$
while
$$S = 7 + 7 \times 1.09 + 7 \times 1.09^2 + 7 \times 1.09^3 + 7 \times 1.09^4.$$
Subtracting: $1.09S - S = -7 + 7 \times 1.09^5$
$$(1.09 - 1)S = 7(1.09^5 - 1)$$
$$S = \frac{7(1.09^5 - 1)}{(1.09 - 1)} = 41.89$$

If, instead, £75 were placed in an account each year for 7 years with an interest rate of 9.5%, as in Exercise F, question 2, the final amount is
$$£\frac{75(1.095^7 - 1)}{(1.095 - 1)} = £700.70.$$
Does this agree with your answer to this question?

In general, if there are n payments of £P each, and interest is added at a rate of r%, then the final amount is
$$£\frac{P(R^n - 1)}{R - 1} \quad \text{with} \quad R = 1 + \frac{r}{100}$$

Regular repayment and mortgages

Exercise G
Find the final sum in these accounts just after the last payment has been made.
1 £5 a year for 10 years, rate of interest 5% per year.
2 £5 a year for 10 years, rate of interest 7% per year.
3 £20 a year for 5 years, rate of interest 7% per year.
4 £2 a year for 50 years, rate of interest 7% per year.
5 £12 a year for 10 years, rate of interest 6% per year.
6 £1 a month for 10 years, rate of interest $\frac{1}{2}$% per month.

7. REGULAR REPAYMENT AND MORTGAGES

If you borrow money from a bank the interest you will be charged is at a rather higher rate than the interest you would obtain by investing in a savings account: this is one source of profit for the bank.

Suppose you borrow £500 at an interest rate of 12% and agree to repay it at a rate of £100 per year; at the end of each year you will be charged interest on the amount still owing during that year. We can see how the debt progresses by following the flow chart below, using a calculator, and plotting the results on a graph.

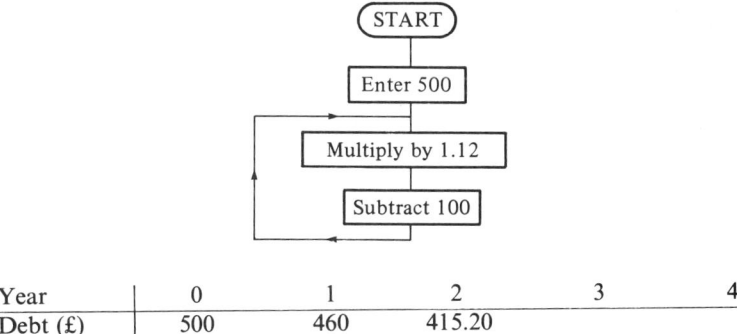

Year	0	1	2	3	4
Debt (£)	500	460	415.20		

Copy and continue the table above, up to the time when the whole debt has been repaid and plot the results on a graph.
After how many years has the debt been repaid?
Altogether how much is paid to the bank?

Exercise H

1 How long does it take to pay off a bank loan of £750, borrowed at an interest rate of 10%, if £150 is paid back each year?
2 How long does it take to pay off a bank loan of £1000, borrowed at an interest rate of 12$\frac{1}{2}$%, if £200 is paid back each year? Experiment with different annual repayments in order to find one which will result in the whole debt being paid off by the end of the fifth year (but not earlier).
   Try, now, to find the annual repayment which will result in the fifth payment of this amount exactly completing repayment of the debt.

When Mr Smith bought his house in 1960 he paid for it partly from savings and partly by borrowing £5000 from the Sumpfield Building Society. He agreed to repay the loan over the course of 25 years together with interest of $8\frac{1}{2}\%$. This method of borrowing money is called a repayment mortgage. Each year Mr Smith pays the same amount and Mr Smith's annual payment has to be chosen so that at the end of the 25th year he has exactly paid back the loan. Since the amount of money on loan to Mr Smith from the Building Society is decreasing every year, he has to pay less interest each year: in the 1960s most of his payment is for interest, in the 1980s most goes towards reducing the loan.

Although Mr Smith pays monthly, the calculations are carried out as if he paid at the end of each year, and, working in £, begin as follows:

Year 1: Amount owed = 5000
Amount plus interest = 5000×1.085
Repayment = A

Year 2: Amount owed = $5000 \times 1.085 - A$
Amount plus interest = $(5000 \times 1.085 - A) \times 1.085$
$= 5000 \times 1.085^2 - A \times 1.085$
Repayment = A

Year 3: Amount owed = $5000 \times 1.085^2 - A \times 1.085 - A$
Amount plus interest = $(5000 \times 1.085^2 - A \times 1.085 - A) \times 1.085$
$= 5000 \times 1.085^3 - A \times 1.085^2 - A \times 1.085$
Repayment = A

Year 4: Amount owed = $5000 \times 1.085^3 - A \times 1.085^2 - A \times 1.085 - A$

You should be able to see the pattern building up, so that the following are the amounts owed:

Year 5: $5000 \times 1.085^4 - A \times 1.085^3 - \ldots - A \times 1.085 - A$
Year 10: $5000 \times 1.085^9 - A \times 1.085^8 - \ldots - A \times 1.085 - A$
Year 20: $5000 \times 1.085^{19} - A \times 1.085^{18} - \ldots - A \times 1.085 - A$.

The end of the 25th year must see the loan completely repaid. The amount at the start of the 26th year must therefore be zero:

$5000 \times 1.085^{25} - A \times 1.085^{24} - A \times 1.085^{23} - \ldots - A \times 1.085 - A = 0$

So
$$5000 \times 1.085^{25} = A(1.085^{24} + 1.085^{23} + 1.085^{22} + \ldots + 1.085 + 1)$$
$$5000 \times 1.085^{25} = \frac{A(1.085^{25} - 1)}{1.085 - 1} \quad \text{(see page 72)}$$
$$38\,433.8 = A \times 78.6678$$
$$A = 488.56.$$

Mr Smith's annual payment is £488.56.

The table and Figures 45 and 46 show how the £5000 loan decreases during the 25 years and the proportions of interest and repayment in his yearly payment change.

Regular repayment and mortgages

		Total £488.56	
Year	Outstanding loan	Interest payment ($8\frac{1}{2}\%$ of loan)	Loan repayment
1	£5000	£425	£63.56
2	£4936.44	£419.60	£68.96
3	£4867.48	£413.74	£74.82
...	...	...	...
23	£1247.80	£106.06	£382.50
24	£865.30	£73.55	£415.01
25	£450.29	£38.27	£450.29

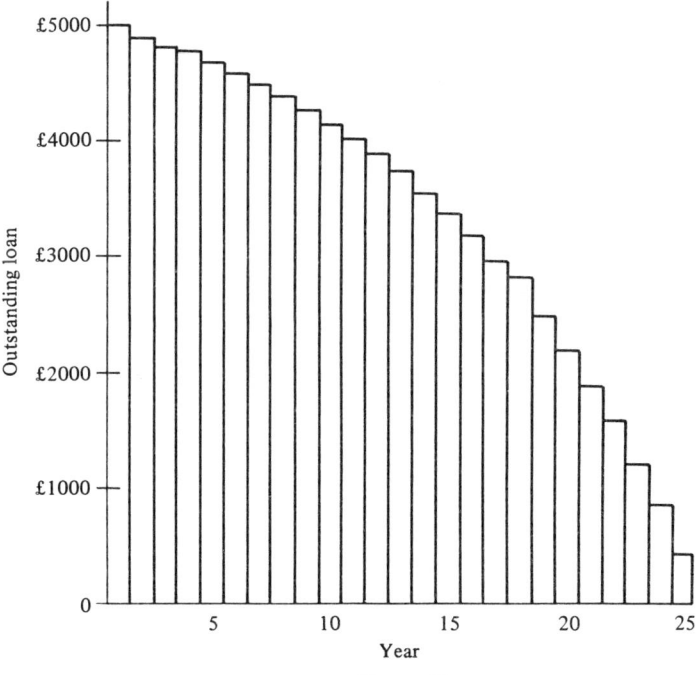

Figure 45

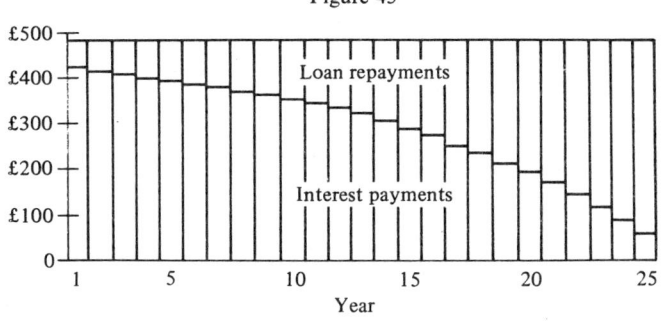

Figure 46

Exercise I

1. Construct a similar table and diagram for a repayment mortgage of £8000 for 20 years at an interest rate of $10\frac{1}{2}\%$.
2. Calculate the monthly repayments ($\frac{1}{12}$ of the annual repayments) for the following mortgages:
   - (a) £10 000 for 20 years at 10% interest;
   - (b) £5000 for 10 years at 10% interest;
   - (c) £1250 for 15 years at $11\frac{1}{4}\%$ interest.
3. Building Societies publish mortgage tables from which you can read off the monthly repayment ($\frac{1}{12}$ of the annual repayment) for a mortgage and current interest rates. A typical table is illustrated below.

Houses less than 50 years old
    Maximum term   25 years
    Normal advance   80%
    Maximum advance   95% with approved additional security
    Interest rates – repayment mortgage

Advance not exceeding £15 000	13.00%
Exceeding £15 000 but not exceeding £20 000	13.50%
Exceeding £20 000 but not exceeding £25 000	14.00%
Exceeding £25 000 but not exceeding £35 000	14.50%
Exceeding £35 000	15.00%

Houses over 50 years old
    Maximum term   20 years
    Normal advance   80%
    Maximum advance   90% with approved additional security

The rate of interest on a repayment mortgage is 0.50% above that which would apply to a house or bungalow less than 50 years old, subject to a maximum of 15.00%.

Repayment table
Monthly payments

	20 years				
Advance £	13.00% £p	13.50% £p	14.00% £p	14.50% £p	15.00% £p
100	1.19	1.22	1.26	1.29	1.33
200	2.37	2.44	2.52	2.59	2.66
300	3.56	3.67	3.77	3.88	3.99
400	4.75	4.89	5.03	5.18	5.33
500	5.93	6.11	6.29	6.47	6.66
1000	11.86	12.22	12.58	12.95	13.31

Regular payments – hire purchase 77

	25 years				
Advance £	13.00% £p	13.50% £p	14.00% £p	14.50% £p	15.00% £p
100	1.14	1.17	1.21	1.25	1.29
200	2.27	2.35	2.43	2.50	2.58
300	3.41	3.52	3.64	3.75	3.87
400	4.55	4.70	4.85	5.00	5.16
500	5.68	5.87	6.06	6.25	6.45
1000	11.37	11.75	12.12	12.51	12.89

If I buy a house built in 1875, with the approval of the Building Society, which costs £17000, what is the maximum advance (that is, the maximum I can borrow) from the Building Society? What will be my monthly repayment for a 20 year mortgage?

4 Using the mortgage tables in question 3, find the monthly repayment for a normal (80%) advance on a house costing £32000 repayable over 25 years.

5 Check the method of calculation described before this exercise against the result obtained from the tables in question 3 or 4.

8. REGULAR PAYMENTS – HIRE PURCHASE

If you read the small print at the bottom of the advertisement in Figure 47, you will find that if you were to use the loan scheme to buy the super de luxe open-top sports car you would have to:

(1) pay a deposit of at least $\frac{1}{3} \times £2307 = £769$

and (2) pay the balance (£1538) together with 6% interest within two years.

With the minimum deposit and the maximum loan repayment period, a buyer would pay $2 \times 0.06 \times £1538 = £184.56$ in interest and the repayments each month would be

$$(£1538 + £184.56) \div 24 = £71.77.$$

Notice that this system of borrowing money is different from a mortgage. On a mortgage, interest is paid on the loan outstanding at any time; in this case, interest is paid on the original loan as if it were borrowed for the whole two years, although, in fact, the amount on loan is reduced each month until it is finally zero. For this reason the rate of interest is called a 'flat' rate. The 'true rate' of interest, mentioned at the foot of the advertisement, is the rate which you are really paying on the loan, taking into account the fact that each monthly payment reduces the amount on loan until it is finally zero, as with a Building Society loan.

It is not easy to calculate the true rate of interest without more advanced mathematical techniques, and firms operating hire purchase schemes usually have tables from which the figure can be read. Using the method from the previous section on mortgages, a trial and error approach could be as follows:

(a) £1538 borrowed at 1% per month and repaid in 24 monthly instalments of £M would require M to be given by

$$M \frac{1.01^{24} - 1}{1.01 - 1} = 1.01^{24} \times 1538$$
$$\Rightarrow \quad 26.9735 M = 1952.85$$
$$\Rightarrow \quad M = 72.40,$$

so 1% per month is slightly too high a rate of interest.

For one month only you can buy our new super de luxe sports car at a special low interest rate of 6%.*

This superb car seats two in the front, with space for two more on the special bench seat behind. The boot loads up with masses of luggage.

There is an overhead cam drive and twin carburetters. The car accelerates from 0 to 60 mph in 11.3 seconds yet it does 27 miles to the gallon.

Our special warranty scheme covers the car against all major defects for two years.

The price is £2307 for the open top and £2777 for the hard top version.

Prices are correct at time of going to press, and include car tax, VAT and front seat belts, but exclude delivery charges and number plates.

*6% per annum flat is equivalent to a true rate of interest of 11.7% for a 2 year agreement. Loan is subject to the approval of the applicant's credit worthiness. The maximum loan repayment period for cars purchased under this scheme is 2 years, the minimum deposit being one third.

Figure 47

Regular payments – hire purchase

(b) £1538 borrowed at 0.9% per month and repaid in 24 monthly instalments of £M would require M to be given by

$$M\frac{1.009^{24}-1}{1.009-1} = 1.009^{24} \times 1538$$

$$\Rightarrow \quad 26.6560M = 1906.97$$
$$\Rightarrow \quad\quad\quad M = 71.54,$$

so 0.9% is slightly too low a rate of interest.

Continuing by trial and error, we can arrive at:

(c) £1538 borrowed at 0.927% per month and repaid in 24 monthly instalments of £M would require M to be given by

$$M\frac{1.00927^{24}-1}{1.00927-1} = 1.00927^{24} \times 1538$$

$$\Rightarrow \quad 26.7412M = 1919.26$$
$$\Rightarrow \quad\quad\quad M = 71.77$$

Since $1.00927^{12} = 1.11709$, the equivalent true interest rate is 11.7% approximately.

For periods of time up to about three years, an estimate of the true rate of interest can be obtained by simply doubling the flat rate of interest. (This is equivalent to imagining that half the original sum borrowed is on loan for the whole period on a simple interest basis.)

It is often difficult to make sensible decisions about whether or not to enter into hire purchase agreements: here are some of the factors which might be taken into account when deciding whether to buy a car now, on hire purchase, or whether to save up for it for two years (say) and then buy it outright.

(1) Against buying it now, on HP:
   (a) If you buy now on HP you will have the extra cost of interest on the HP loan.
   (b) If you buy now on HP the car you will own in two years' time will no longer be new; its value will have depreciated.
   (c) If you buy now on HP and then suffer some misfortune which makes it difficult to continue payments, you could lose the car as well as a lot of money.
   (d) If you save up for the car, you will have not only the actual sum saved but also the interest on it if you invest it sensibly.

(2) In favour of buying now on HP:
   (a) If you buy now on HP you will have immediate use of the car, for the next two years.
   (b) If you wait for two years, the price of the car (or the equivalent model) may well have gone up substantially because of inflation or for other reasons.

Other matters which may be relevant are the costs of alternative forms of transport, the cost of licensing, insuring, servicing etc.

Exercise J

1. Find the monthly payments for the following hire purchase agreements:
    (*a*) cash price £60, or, on hire purchase: deposit £10, three years to pay, with a flat interest rate of 8%;
    (*b*) cash price £150, or, on hire purchase: deposit 25%, two years to pay, flat interest rate 10%.

2. What would be the monthly repayment on a loan of £60 at a true rate of interest of 1½% per month, if the loan is to be paid off over a period of two years? How much, in total, is paid in interest? What is the equivalent 'flat rate' of interest?

3. Repeat question 2 with the period of repayment as three years.

4. Which is the cheaper way of borrowing £90:
    (*a*) a hire purchase agreement for 15 months at 12% per year flat rate, or
    (*b*) regular payments of £6 a month, interest free for the first month but, after that, plus 2% per month interest on the outstanding loan, to a credit card company? (Make a table showing, for each month, the interest, the amount repaid and the outstanding loan.)

SUMMARY

Section 1: Factors and primes
Calculations with fractions
Scientific notation (standard form)
Units
Section 2: Using a calculator
Accuracy of measurements
Ratio
Percentages
Section 3: Areas and volumes
Similarity
Section 4: Index numbers
Section 5: Weighted index numbers
Section 6: Regular savings
Section 7: Mortgages
Section 8: Hire purchase

Revision exercises

REVISION EXERCISE 1

1. If $g: x \to 3x^2 - 1$, write down: (a) $g(5)$; (b) $g(-2)$.
2. A sequence is defined by $t_1 = 3$, $t_{n+1} = 2t_n - 1$. Find t_6 and t_7.
3. One pint (568 ml) of water is poured into a cylindrical jar. If the depth of water is 141 mm, what is the radius of the inside of the jar?
4. Write without brackets, simplifying if possible:
   (a) $(3x+4y)(3x-4y)$; (b) $(5p-3q)^2$.
5. Using ruler and compasses only, construct a triangle ABC with $BC = 7.0$ cm, $AB = 5.0$ cm and $AC = 4.0$ cm.
   Construct the loci
   $$m = \{P: PA = PC\} \quad \text{and} \quad n = \{P: PB = PC\}.$$
   $m \cap n$ consists of a single point Z. Mark this point and draw the circle centre Z and radius ZA. Explain why this circle should pass through A, B and C.
6. Solve the equation $\frac{1}{2}(3x-2) + \frac{1}{3}(2x+5) = x+3$.
7. Make t the subject of the formula $p = \frac{1}{2}(q-rt)$.
8. In the nineteenth century the population of a village increased from 625 to 1125. What percentage increase is this?

REVISION EXERCISE 2

1. If $f: x \to \dfrac{4}{3-x}$, find $f^{-1}(x)$ and solve $f(x) = 5$.
2. Solve the simultaneous equations:
   $$3p - 4q = 5$$
   $$p + 2q = 0$$
3. A line passes through the points (2, 7) and (8, 4). Find its gradient and its equation.
4. A ladder is leaning against a vertical wall. If the top of the ladder is 5.7 m above the (level) ground and the angle between the ladder and the wall is 27°, what is the length of the ladder?
5. If $\mathbf{A} = \begin{bmatrix} 3 & -1 & 2 \\ 4 & 5 & -7 \end{bmatrix}$ and $\mathbf{B} = \begin{bmatrix} 1 & -3 \\ 5 & 1 \\ 1 & -1 \end{bmatrix}$ find $\mathbf{AB}$ and $\mathbf{BA}$.
6. The heights of nine children in metres are:
   1.3, 1.2, 1.3, 1.3, 1.5, 1.4, 1.5, 1.4, 1.6.
   (a) Write down the mode and the median of this set of data.
   (b) Another child joins the group and the mean height of the ten children is now 1.4 m. What is the height of this child? (SMP O-level)
7. The matrix $\mathbf{P}$ represents a rotation of 90° about the origin, and the matrix $\mathbf{Q} = \begin{bmatrix} 1 & 0 \\ 0 & -1 \end{bmatrix}$.
   (a) What transformation does $\mathbf{Q}$ represent?
   (b) Write down the matrix $\mathbf{P}$.
   (c) Evaluate the matrix product $\mathbf{PQ}$. (SMP O-level)
8. Show on graph paper (shading out the region not required) the region given by the inequalities
   $$y < 2x, \quad x + 2y < 10 \quad \text{and} \quad y > 0.$$

REVISION EXERCISE 3

1. If $f: x \to 2x+5$ and $g: x \to x^2$, find: (a) $gf(-1)$; (b) $fg(z)$.
2. Draw the graphs of $y = 50 \cos x°$ and $y = x$ on the same diagram, with values of x from 0 to 90. Deduce a solution of the equation $x = 50 \cos x°$, to the nearest 5. Use decimal search to find this solution to the nearest integer.
3. Use the iteration $x_{new} = 50 \cos x°$, starting with $x = 30$, to find a solution of the equation $x = 50 \cos x°$ to the nearest integer. Write down each value of x_{new} that you obtain.
4. Calculate the volume of a cone of base radius 53 mm and height 237 mm. Give your answer:
   (a) in cubic millimetres; (b) using standard form, in cubic metres.
5. (a) Find the cartesian coordinates of the point with polar coordinates (12, 21°).
   (b) Find the polar coordinates of the point with cartesian coordinates (−8, 15).
6. If $y \propto x^2$ and $y = 5$ when $x = 2$, find y when $x = 3$.
7. The diameter of a circle is measured as 2.8 m. Calculate the upper and lower bounds for the area of the circle (to an accuracy of three significant figures).
8. Find the coordinates of the centre of the rotation which maps $A(7, 4)$ to $A'(3, 6)$ and $B(7, -1)$ to $B'(7, 3)$. What is the angle of rotation?

4

Mathematical models

When, as mathematicians, we speak of 'modelling' a real-life situation, we may mean anything from a sketch or drawing describing the situation to a set of algebraic equations representing it. In this chapter we concentrate mainly on relations of proportionality and their discovery and use. But we also consider more general formulae and the less precise relationship described by scatter diagrams.

1. SIMPLIFICATION AND APPROXIMATION

The essence of modelling lies in making simplifications and approximations which will enable us to extricate what, for us, are the most important, basic features of the situation from the rest.

In the design of a Choc-gunge factory, the food technologist's model may consist of a set of chemical equations and quality control statistics representing the process for manufacturing Choc-gunge; for the engineer, the modelling process may consist of arriving, with the aid of tables, standard formulae, equations and some computer programs, at a design specification for the plant and a set of drawings; the marketing manager's model may consist of a series of computer programs and diagrams representing movement of Choc-gunge salesmen, movement of Choc-gunge from factory to distributors, etc. The jobs of all these people would be impossible without extensive simplification and approximation, and concentration on that part of the total picture of special interest to them. On the other hand, they must not lose sight of the dangers of over-simplification and must allow for errors which may result from approximation.

Consider the following problem.

The police are asking for help from motorists who passed through High Wycombe between 11.00 p.m. and 11.15 p.m. on a certain night. A man knows that he left London at 10.00 p.m. and arrived in Oxford at midnight having driven through High Wycombe, and he knows that this town is about half-way along his route. He did not stop and unfortunately did not note the time while travelling. Should he offer his help?

He reasons like this. 'I assume that my journey was made roughly at a steady speed and so I should have covered half the distance in about half the time. I expect that I was in High Wycombe at about 11.0 p.m. and so I will telephone the police to see how I can help.'

How has he made a mathematical model? Consider some of the facts that he has left out of account.

What are the actual distances involved? For which parts of the journey is speed restricted? Was he held up at all by traffic lights, roundabouts, heavy vehicles, etc? Did he increase speed considerably on the sections with dual carriageway? Where is 'London'? How long is his car?

Since he has assumed steady speed and treated London, Oxford and his car as having no dimensions, it is easy to see that his mathematical model consists of a point which travels at a steady speed between two fixed points, and hence passes through the midpoint at half-time. Assuming that he was not unduly held up in London and did not break the speed limit as soon as he was through High Wycombe, this model will fit the facts reasonably accurately.

It may become important later, however, to try to fix the time more precisely. The distance from London to Oxford according to the *AA Handbook* is 92 km, while from London to High Wycombe it is 50 km. He might try to take speed restrictions in built-up areas into account. His average speed, however, is less than 50 km/h so that there is not likely to have been any very great difference between his speeds in restricted and unrestricted areas. He might therefore retain the assumption of steady speed but use $\frac{50}{92}$ of two hours as his estimate of the time taken. This would put his time of arrival at about 11.05 p.m. His calculations could become more complicated as he tried to take into account more facts.

This example indicates three basic questions which must be answered when solving a problem using a mathematical model.
 (i) Which factors should be taken into consideration and which should be omitted?
 (ii) Are the omitted factors so important that leaving them out makes nonsense of the solution?
 (iii) Is the solution obtained physically likely?

In any problem in which you have to set up mathematical equations you are effectively using a mathematical model.

Exercise A

1   Figure 1 shows a ladder, inclined at 60° to the horizontal, leaning against a wall. What sort of assumptions are normally made, in modelling a real situation of this sort – assumptions, for example, about the wall, the ground, the ladder, the weather? Supposing we wish to find how far up the wall the ladder will reach; to what accuracy is it reasonable to wish to know the length of the ladder? To what accuracy is the answer likely to be reliable in practice? Make up a suitable ladder length and state how far its foot will be from the wall.

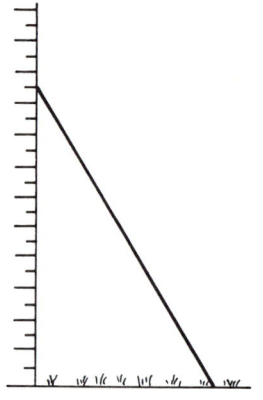

Figure 1

Using scale factors and multipliers

2 What sort of assumptions would you have to make in order to answer the following question? 'A plane flies 350 km on a bearing 030°, followed by 200 km on a bearing 140°. Give the distance and bearing of the shortest route back to the starting point.' Making these assumptions, answer the question.

3 I wish to estimate how much petrol I will use on a journey from Oakham to Cambridge and back which appears, from the map, to be 80 km each way. I expect to average about 100 km/h and my car averages about 15 km per litre of petrol.
What are the main simplifications of the real situation inherent in the data given and in the calculation involved in making the estimate? Make the estimate: what sort of margin of error do you expect there to be? Give reasons for your answer.

4 'Assuming the earth to be a sphere of radius 4000 miles...'. To what extent is this a reasonable assumption?

5 A cookery book gives the roasting time for poultry as 25 minutes per kilogram plus 15 minutes extra. What variables have not been taken into account which might substantially affect the final result of cooking by these instructions?

2. USING SCALE FACTORS AND MULTIPLIERS

Sometimes real-life situations can be simplified, without too much loss of accuracy, to a simple proportionality relationship between two variables. In such cases, just one known pair of values of the two variables enables us to use scale factors or multipliers to solve problems.

Example 1

The distance moved by a car after the brakes are applied may be taken to be proportional to the square of its initial speed.

If it takes 12.5 m to stop when initially travelling at 50 km/h, how far will it travel when initially travelling at 120 km/h?

The data can be set out in a table:

Initial speed s (km/h)	50	120
s^2	2500	14400
Stopping distance d (m)	12.5	?

The solution using the scale factor is:

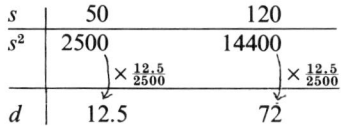

The solution using multipliers is:

s	50	$\xrightarrow{\times \frac{12}{5}}$ 120
s^2	2500	$\xrightarrow{\times \frac{144}{25}}$ 14400
d	12.5	$\xrightarrow{\times \frac{144}{25}}$ 72

so the stopping distance for 120 km/h is 72 m.

Alternatively we may write

$$d \propto s^2 \quad \Rightarrow \quad d = ks^2 \quad \Rightarrow \quad \frac{d}{s^2} = k,$$

so that, for the two pairs of values (s_1, d_1) and (s_2, d_2),

$$\frac{d_2}{s_2^2} = \frac{d_1}{s_1^2}$$

and, in this case,

$$\frac{d_2}{120^2} = \frac{12.5}{50^2}$$

$$\Rightarrow \quad d_2 = \frac{12.5}{50^2} \times 120^2 = 72.$$

Exercise B

These questions can be solved using any of the three approaches illustrated in Example 1. It is suggested that, for the first few questions, all methods are used – one acts as a check on another – in order to increase understanding and efficiency.

*1 A shell fired from a gun experiences resistance to motion, due to air friction, proportional to the square of its speed. If the resistance is 100 N when the speed is 300 m/s, find:
(a) the air resistance when the speed is 600 m/s;
(b) the speed for which the air resistance is 200 N.

2 The time of oscillation of the pendulum of a clock is proportional to the square root of the (adjustable) distance between two marks on it. The pendulum is designed to make one complete oscillation every two seconds but is found to take 64 minutes 35 seconds to rotate the hands through one hour when the distance between marks is 99.5 cm. By how much should the distance between marks be changed?

3 The electrical resistance of a given length of wire is inversely proportional to the square of the diameter. For 100 cm of wire of diameter 1.25 mm made of a particular alloy, the resistance is 1.5 ohm. What will be the resistance of 100 cm of wire made of the same alloy but having double the diameter? What information was unnecessary?

4 The cost of 26 tweengirdles is £5.72. What is the cost of 14 tweengirdles at the same price per unit? How many tweengirdles can be bought for £10? Incomplete tweengirdles are useless: how much change will I get from £10 if I buy as many as possible?

*5 The wavelength of a sound vibration is inversely proportional to the frequency.

Middle C has a frequency of 256 Hz and a wavelength 1.29 m. What is the wavelength of concert A (frequency 440 Hz)? What is the frequency of a note of wavelength 1.00 m?

6   At a time when £1.00 buys fr. 9.52, what is the value in £ of fr. 100? What is the equivalent price in £, approximately, of a house in Normandy priced at fr. 450000?

7   The mass of 100 cm³ of gold is 1920 g. What is the volume of 1.00 kg of gold?

8   A car travels 45 km in 23 minutes. How far will it travel at the same speed in 10 minutes? How long will it take to travel 100 km at the same speed?

*9 A marshmallow, falling off a marshmallow tree on the planet Hesion from a height of 24 hesiometres, takes 35 hesioseconds to reach the ground. Assuming that the time taken is proportional to the square root of the height, find how long it would take a marshmallow to reach the ground if dropped from the top of the Peoples' Palace tower, a height of 239 hesiometres.

10 An old map has a scale of ½ inch : 1 mile. (1 mile = 5280 feet; 1 foot = 12 inches.) What distance is represented by 1 foot on the map? What distance on the map corresponds to 17 miles? A reservoir is shown on the map and is roughly a circle of diameter 1 inch. It is stated to be 22 feet deep on average. Approximately what volume of water, in cubic feet, will the reservoir hold?

*11 It is found that 10.5 g of iron combines with 6.0 g of sulphur, forming iron sulphide. How much sulphur will be required to combine fully with 25.0 g of iron?

12 The rate at which enmeshed gearwheels turn is inversely proportional to the number of teeth. If a gear with 48 teeth, rotating at 1400 rpm, is enmeshed with a gear having 18 teeth, what is the speed of rotation of the smaller gearwheel?

13 At constant temperature, the pressure of a given mass of gas is inversely proportional to its volume.

   At constant pressure, the volume of a given mass of gas is proportional to its absolute temperature.

   (*a*) If the volume occupied by a given mass of gas is doubled,
       (i) what will be the effect on the temperature if the pressure is kept constant;
       (ii) what will be the effect on the pressure if the temperature is kept constant?
   (*b*) If the absolute temperature is changed from 273 K to 373 K at constant pressure, by what percentage is the volume changed?

*14 A spaceship travelling at a steady speed of 2.3×10^7 hesiometres per hesiohour covers the distance from Hesion Spacelab 215 to Hesion Moon 17 in 32.7 hesiohours. How long will it take to do the same journey at 3.5×10^7 hesiometres per hesiohour? At this latter speed, how far can it get away from Hesion, starting from the Peoples' Palace launch-pad, in 20 hesiohours (in the event of a nuclear attack by the Splods)?

15 If $y \propto x^2$ and $y = 4$ when $x = 3$, find the value of y when $x = 6$.

3. FORMING AN ALGEBRAIC MODEL

Scientists may approach something which they wish to understand better from two different standpoints: (i) they may do a number of experiments, perhaps displaying the results graphically, and then try to fit an equation or equations to their findings, and (ii) they may make some simplifying assumptions, form a theory probably involving some mathematical equations and then test the theory experimentally, attempting to revise it if the experimental results do not fit closely enough. Usually, these two different approaches are combined.

Quite often, in science, variables are connected by simple relations, so that it is helpful to be aware of the shapes of graphs of those relations occurring most commonly.

(1) $y \propto x$, that is, $y = kx$ where k is a constant, is a straight line passing through the origin (see Figure 2).

More generally, $y = mx + c$ is a straight line of gradient m, passing through the point $(0, c)$ (see Figure 3).

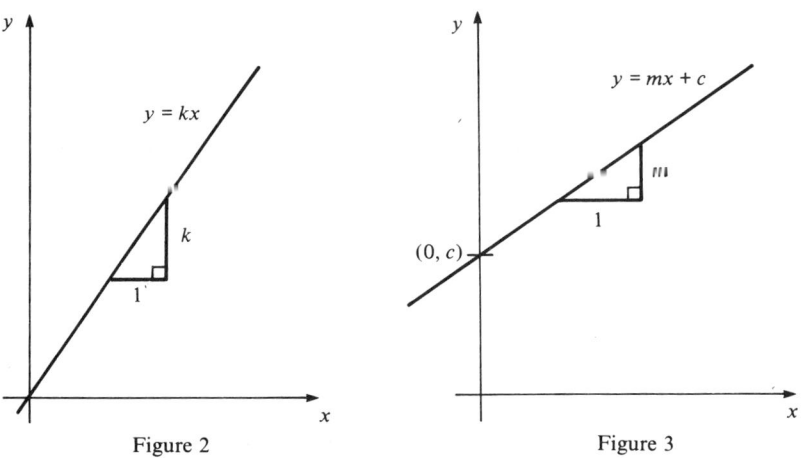

Figure 2   Figure 3

Figures 4 and 5 show graphs of relations of the type $y = mx + c$.

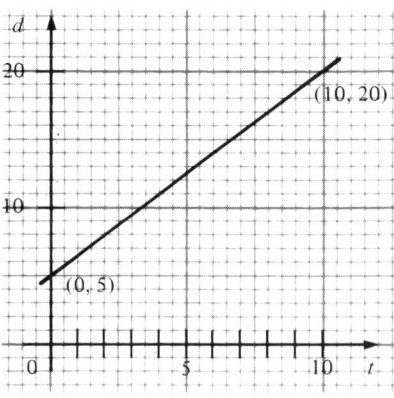

Figure 4   Figure 5

Gradient is $\dfrac{20-5}{10-0} = 1.5$.

Equation is $d = 1.5t + 5$.

Gradient is $\dfrac{-13.5}{7.6} \approx -1.78$.

Equation is $p = -1.78v + 13.5$.

(2) $y \propto x^2$, that is, $y = kx^2$, where k is a constant, is a parabola passing through the origin (see Figure 6).

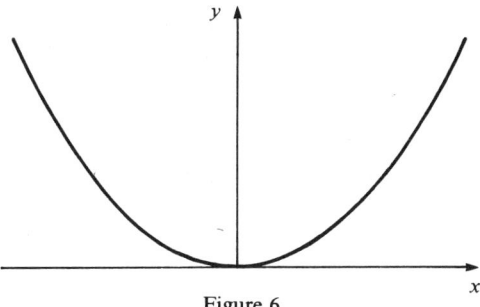

Figure 6

Often, since many measurable quantities cannot be negative, we are only concerned with the 'right-hand side' of this graph.

Confirmation that data fit a curve of this sort, rather than some other similarly shaped curve, is achieved by plotting y against x^2 which, if straight, shows that $y \propto x^2$. The gradient is then the value of k. An example is illustrated by Figure 7(a) and (b).

Data:	d	0	5	20	46	79	125
	t	0	1	2	3	4	5
Calculated values of t^2		0	1	4	9	16	25

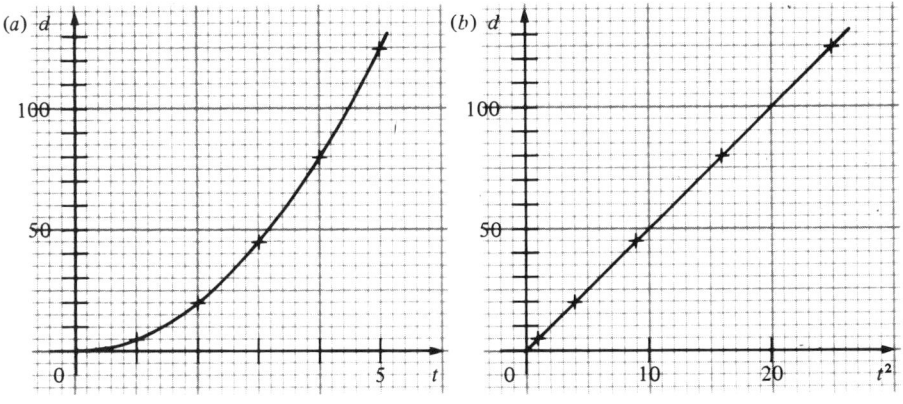

Figure 7

The gradient of the straight line in Figure 7(b) is $\dfrac{125}{25} = 5$ so the relation is $d = 5t^2$.

(3) $y \propto \sqrt{x}$, that is, $y = k\sqrt{x}$, where k is a constant, is also half a parabola (because $y = k\sqrt{x} \Rightarrow y^2 = k^2 x$, that is, $x \propto y^2$). See Figure 8.

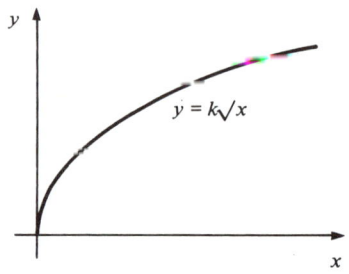

Figure 8

The value of k is found by plotting y against $\sqrt{x}$ which is a straight line of gradient k if $y = k\sqrt{x}$ fits the data.

(4) $y \propto \dfrac{1}{x}$, that is, $y = k \times \dfrac{1}{x} = \dfrac{k}{x}$ or $xy = k$ is a rectangular hyperbola (see Figure 9)

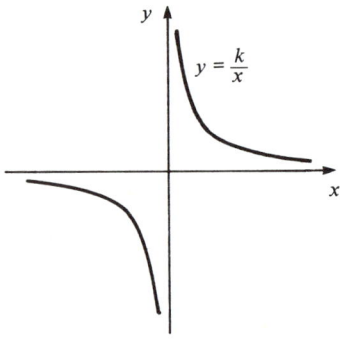

Figure 9

This curve has half-turn symmetry about the origin and is also symmetrical about the line $y = x$. Often, we are only concerned with the 'top right hand' section of it, that is, for x and y positive.

The value of k is found by plotting y against $\dfrac{1}{x}$ which is a straight line of gradient k if $y = k \times \dfrac{1}{x}$.

(5) $y \propto \dfrac{1}{x^2}$, that is, $y = k \times \dfrac{1}{x^2} = \dfrac{k}{x^2}$ is as in Figure 10.

The value of k is the gradient of a graph of y against $\dfrac{1}{x^2}$.

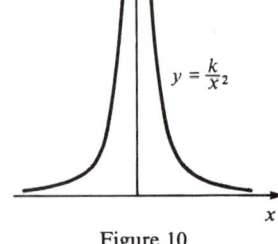

Figure 10

Forming an algebraic model

Example 2

Assuming that $y \propto x$, complete the table of values below:

x	1	2	3	4	5	10
y		5				50

Approach (1)

$y \propto x \Rightarrow y = kx$ and the value of k, the 'scale factor' or 'constant of proportionality', can be found from the pair of given values.

$$x = 2, y = 5 \quad \Rightarrow \quad 5 = 2k \quad \Rightarrow \quad k = \tfrac{5}{2}$$

So values of y may be obtained by multiplying values of x by $\tfrac{5}{2}$.

The table now becomes

x	1	2	3	4	5	10
y	2.5	5	7.5	10	12.5	25	50

(each multiplied by $\times \tfrac{5}{2}$)

Similarly, we can obtain values of x from values of y by dividing by $\tfrac{5}{2}$, or multiplying by $\tfrac{2}{5}$. So, finally we deduce that $y = 50 \Rightarrow x = 50 \times \tfrac{2}{5} = 20$.

Approach (2)

As an alternative, we can use multipliers working along the table as follows:

x	1	2	3	4	5	10	20
y	2.5	5	7.5	10	12.5	25	50

with multipliers $\times \tfrac{1}{2}$, $\times \tfrac{3}{2}$, $\times \tfrac{4}{3}$, $\times \tfrac{5}{4}$, $\times 2$, $\times 2$ along both rows.

Example 3

Assuming that $y \propto \dfrac{1}{x^2}$, complete the table of values below:

x	-2	-1	1	2	3	4
y				90		

Approach (1)

$$y \propto \frac{1}{x^2} \Rightarrow y = k \times \frac{1}{x^2} \Rightarrow y = \frac{k}{x^2} \Rightarrow k = x^2 y.$$

Using the pair of values $(2, 90)$, $k = 2^2 \times 90 = 360$.

The table may be rewritten as:

x	-2	-1	1	2	3	4
x^2	4	1	1	4	9	16
$\tfrac{1}{x^2}$	$\tfrac{1}{4}$	1	1	$\tfrac{1}{4}$	$\tfrac{1}{9}$	$\tfrac{1}{16}$
y				90		

(with $\times 360$ linking $\tfrac{1}{x^2}$ to y)

and hence completed as follows:

x	-2	-1	1	2	3	4
x^2	4	1	1	4	9	16
$\frac{1}{x^2}$	$\frac{1}{4}$	1	1	$\frac{1}{4}$	$\frac{1}{9}$	$\frac{1}{16}$
y	90	360	360	90	40	22.5

(arrows indicating ×360 between each $\frac{1}{x^2}$ and y)

Approach (2)

To use multipliers, we notice that if $y \propto \dfrac{1}{x^2}$, and x is multiplied by some number c, y will be multiplied by $\dfrac{1}{c^2}$.

x	-2	-1	1	2	3	4
y	90	360	360	90	40	22.5

(arrows: x: ×2, ×⁻1, ×½, ×⅔, ×¾; y: ×(½)², ×(⁻1)², ×2², ×(³⁄₂)², ×(⁴⁄₃)²)

Example 4

The table of values below from a science experiment corresponds fairly closely to a relation of one of the forms

$$t = kl, \quad t = kl^2, \quad t = \frac{k}{l}, \quad t = \frac{k}{l^2}.$$

It is required to discover which of these relations fits best and to find the constant of proportionality, k.

l	2.18	3.75	4.47	6.31	8.59
t	2.38	1.34	1.19	0.80	0.57

First we notice that as l goes up in value, t goes down and the shape of the graph is very roughly as in Figure 11. This suggests $t = \dfrac{k}{l}$ or $t = \dfrac{k}{l^2}$.

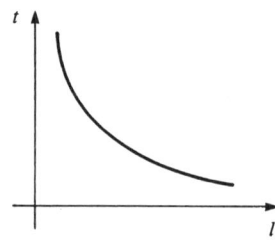

Figure 11

Approach (1)

$$t = \frac{k}{l} \Rightarrow k = tl \quad \text{and} \quad t = \frac{k}{l^2} \Rightarrow k = tl^2.$$

So we will work out tl and tl^2 for each pair of values:

l	2.18	3.75	4.47	6.31	8.59
t	2.38	1.34	1.19	0.80	0.57
tl	5.19	5.03	5.32	5.05	4.90
tl^2	11.31	18.84	23.78	...we need go no further	

Clearly tl is quite nearly constant and tl^2 is not; and so the required relation is $t = \dfrac{k}{l}$.

To obtain a value for k we could average the values of tl; this comes to 5.1 to 2 s.f.

Approach (2)

If $t = \dfrac{k}{l}$, the multiplier for t is the reciprocal of the multiplier for l. For the first pair of values in the table, the multiplier for l is $\dfrac{3.75}{2.18} = 1.72$; the multiplier for t is $\dfrac{1.34}{2.38} = 0.563$. The reciprocal of 1.72 is $\dfrac{1}{1.72} = 0.58$, which is quite close. So it looks as though it may be correct that $t = \dfrac{k}{l}$, and we could check other multipliers from the table.

If we had tested $t = \dfrac{k}{l^2}$, we would have expected the multiplier for t to be the reciprocal of the square of the multiplier for l. But $\dfrac{1}{1.72^2} = 0.34$, which is not so close to 0.563.

We now plot the graph of t against $\dfrac{1}{l}$, drawing the 'best' straight line through the points plotted and measuring its gradient which is the value of k. It is easy to see if any particular points are a long way out of place, possibly due to experimental error or miscalculation.

The table of values to be plotted is as follows:

l	2.18	3.75	4.47	6.31	8.59
$\dfrac{1}{l}$	0.459	0.267	0.224	0.158	0.116
t	2.38	1.34	1.19	0.80	0.57

The graph is shown in Figure 12.

As $\dfrac{1}{l}$ increases from 0 to 0.4 (to choose a convenient value), t increases from 0 to 2.05, so the gradient is $\dfrac{2.05}{0.4} = 5.1$ to 2 s.f., and $t = \dfrac{5.1}{l}$.

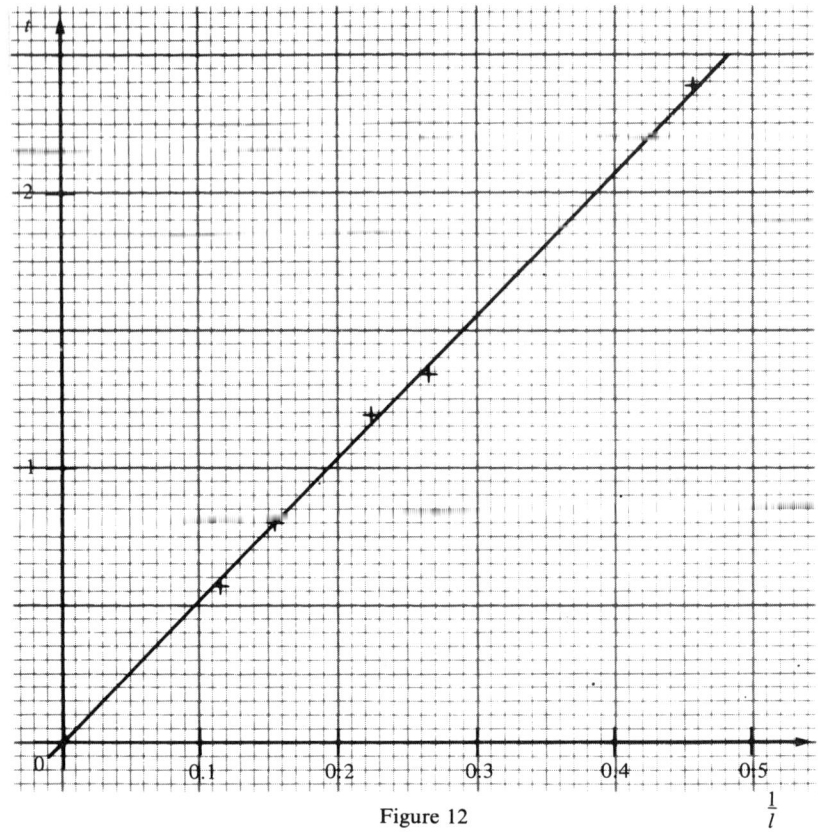

Figure 12

Exercise C

In questions 1–6, make tables of values of x and y, using values of x as shown, in this form:

x	-3	-2	-1	0	1	2	3
y							

Then draw graphs of the relations, using the values from the tables you have made, putting parts (*a*), (*b*) and (*c*) of each question all on the same diagram. If there is no value of y for any particular value of x, say so, giving reasons.

1 (*a*) $y = 2x$; (*b*) $y = 2x + 1$; (*c*) $y = -\tfrac{1}{2}x + \tfrac{1}{2}$.
2 (*a*) $y = x^2$; (*b*) $y = 2x^2$; (*c*) $y = \tfrac{1}{2}x^2 - 1$.
3 (*a*) $y = \sqrt{x}$; (*b*) $y = 2.5\sqrt{x}$; (*c*) $y = \sqrt{(6.25x)}$.
   Explain the relationship between graphs (*b*) and (*c*).
4 (*a*) $y = \dfrac{1}{x}$; (*b*) $y = \dfrac{6}{x}$; (*c*) $y = \dfrac{-1.8}{x}$.
5 (*a*) $y = \dfrac{1}{x^2}$; (*b*) $y = \dfrac{2.35}{x^2}$; (*c*) $y = 1 - \dfrac{1}{x^2}$.
6 (*a*) $y = x^0$; (*b*) $y = x^3$; (*c*) $y = \dfrac{1}{x^3}$.

In questions 7–14, each of the given tables of values exactly fits one and only one of the following types of equations:

(a) $y = kx$; (b) $y = kx^2$; (c) $y = k\sqrt{x}$;
(d) $y = \dfrac{k}{x}$; (e) $y = \dfrac{k}{x^2}$.

Find the right equation and state the value of k.

*7

x	-2	-1	0	1	2	3
y	12	3	0	3	12	27

8

x	1	2	3	4	5
y	60	30	20	15	12

9

x	-2	-1	0	1	2	3
y	-6	-3	0	3	6	9

10

x	-3	-2	-1	1	2	3
y	-4	-6	-12	12	6	4

*11

x	0	1	4	9	16
y	0	2	4	6	8

12

x	-3	-2	-1	1	2	3
y	4	9	36	36	9	4

13

x	-3	-2	-1	0	1	2
y	1.5	1	0.5	0	-0.5	-1

14

x	1	10	100	1000	10000
y	100	10	1	0.1	0.01

In questions 15–19, complete the given tables of values, assuming the given relations to hold true.

*15 $y \propto x$:

x	-1.5	0	1	2		
y				3	7.5	100

Without drawing the graph of $x \to y$, state its gradient.

16 $y \propto x^2$:

x	0		0.5	1	2	
y		1	2			100

$y \propto x^2 \Rightarrow y = kx^2$, where k is a constant; find the value of k. Plot a graph of $x^2 \to y$ (not $x \to y$) for $0 \leq x \leq 2$ and state its gradient.

*17 $T \propto \sqrt{n}$:

n	0	1	2		
T		3.14		7.02	31.4

(n is an integer; T is given to an accuracy of 3 s.f.) Without plotting it, describe as fully as possible the graph of $\sqrt{n} \to T$ (not the graph of $n \to T$).

18 $wf = k$, where k is a constant:

w		150	250		
f	2000			600	500

Rewrite the given relation in the form $f \propto \ldots$

With values of f on the 'vertical' axis, what values would you plot on the 'horizontal' axis so as to obtain a straight line of gradient k?

19 $y \propto \dfrac{1}{x^2}$:

x	2.64	3.97	5.84
y	0.267	0.238	0.100

(values of x and y accurate to 3 s.f.)

$y \propto \dfrac{1}{x^2} \rightarrow y = \dfrac{k}{x^2}$ or $x^2 y = k$. Find the value of k.

Without plotting it, describe as fully as possible the graph of $\dfrac{1}{x^2} \rightarrow y$.

In questions 20–25, each table of values corresponds reasonably closely to a relation of the form $y \propto x^n$ where $n = -2, -1, \tfrac{1}{2}, 1$ or 2: that is, the possibilities are

$$y \propto \dfrac{1}{x^2}, \quad y \propto \dfrac{1}{x}, \quad y \propto \sqrt{x}, \quad y \propto x, \quad y \propto x^2.$$

For each question,
(a) identify the value of n;
(b) write the relation in the form $y = kx^n$ where k is a constant which should be stated to whatever accuracy seems reasonable.

*20

x	0	1	2	3	4
y	0	0.90	1.27	1.56	1.80

21

x	0.035	0.047	0.069	0.081
y	13.7	10.0	6.9	5.9

22

x	2.5	5.0	7.5	10.0	12.5
y	3.5	7.0	10.4	14.1	17.5

*23

x	1	2	3	4	5
y	1000	250	110	60	40

24

x	1.96	3.24	4.84	5.19	7.01
y	5.50	7.16	8.61	9.01	10.48

25

x	24	39	65	82	100
y	29	76	210	341	498

26 The table shows values of x and y which satisfy a relation between them.

x	0	$\tfrac{1}{2}$	1
y	0	p	1

Which of the following statements are consistent with this statement and which are not?
(a) If $p = 2$ then x is a linear function of y.
(b) If $p = \tfrac{1}{4}$ then y is a square function of x.
(c) If $p = \tfrac{1}{2}$ then y is a linear function of x.
(d) If $p = \dfrac{1}{\sqrt{2}}$ then x is a square function of y. (SMP O-level)

*27 The points $(-2, -1), (0, 0), (2, 1)$ lie on the graph of a function f. Which may be true and which must be false? (k is a constant.)

(a) $f: x \rightarrow kx$; (b) $f: x \rightarrow kx^2$; (c) $f: x \rightarrow kx^3$; (d) $f: x \rightarrow \dfrac{k}{x}$. (SMP O-level)

Forming an algebraic model 97

28 The table shows three results obtained in an experiment set up to find if there is any relationship between the quantities s and t.

s	2	5	6
t	0.8	5	7.2

Which of the following statements is consistent with these values?
(a) $t \propto s^2$. (b) The function $f:s \to t$ is an exponential function.
(c) $s \propto t^2$. (d) None of them. (SMP O-level)

29

x	3	6
y	4	1

Which are possible forms and which are not possible forms of the relation between x and y?
(a) $y = mx + c$. (b) $y = px^2 + 5$. (c) xy is constant. (d) $y \propto \dfrac{1}{x^2}$.

(SMP O-level)

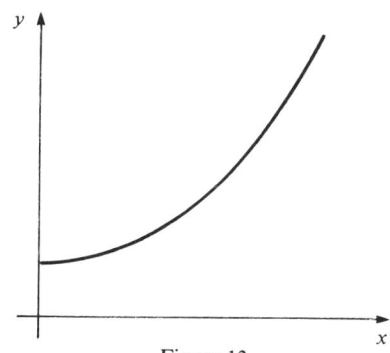

Figure 13

30 Figure 13, which is not drawn to scale, shows a sketch of part of the graph of a function $x \to y$. Which of the following statements can be consistent with this sketch?
(a) $y \propto x^2$. (b) $y \propto x^{-2}$. (c) $y = 2x^2 + 3$. (d) $xy = 60$. (SMP O-level)

***31** The time (t seconds) for ten oscillations of a coiled spring supporting a mass (m kg) is given below:

m (kg)	1.000	1.500	2.000	2.500	3.000
t (s)	23.2	28.8	33.0	37.0	40.2

(a) Plot a graph of $m \to t$.
(b) Plot a suitable graph so that the points lie very nearly on a straight line and hence deduce a simple relation between t and m which fits the data well.

32 The 'maximum safe working load' of a particular type of artificial fibre 'rope' is given as follows:

Diameter when unstretched in millimetres	(d)	5	10	15	20	25
Safe working load in newtons	(L)	400	1600	3500	6500	10000

Plot a suitable graph so that the points lie very nearly on a straight line and state a simple relation between the safe working load and the diameter (unstretched) which fits the data well.

The price per metre of the rope depends on the diameter as follows:

Diameter when unstretched in millimetres	(d)	5	10	15	20	25
Price per metre length in pence	(P)	10	22	42	70	100

Plot a graph of $d^2 \to P$ and deduce a simple equation for P in terms of d.

33 A zoologist notes that as a Webble's Warbler grows, the frequency of its warble is reduced. A series of observations produces the following results:

Age of Warbler in days	(a)	5	10	15	20	25
Mean warble frequency, in cycles per minute	(f)	126	58	39	31	23

Plot a suitable graph so that the points lie very nearly on a straight line and state a simple equation which fits the data well.

34 Leo Newtrix (a Martian scientist) decided to investigate the relationship between the strength of the stink of an adult male Martian skunk and the distance between his nose and the skunk. Choosing a windless day, he fitted a stinkmeter to the end of his nose and made a number of observations. Some of these were unprintable, but the others are given below:

Distance from skunk d (marmetres)	5.0	6.0	7.0	8.0	9.0	10.0
Stinkmeter reading s (marsnuffs)	9.5	6.6	4.8	3.8	2.9	2.5

Investigate the relationship between stink strength and distance. From a suitable graph, on which the points lie quite nearly in a straight line, deduce the constant of proportionality.

Newtrix defines stink strength as follows: One marsnuff is the strength of stink at a distance of n marmetres from an adult male Martian skunk. What is the value of n, as given by the experiment described?

35 The mass of magnesium sulphate which will dissolve in 100 g of water at various temperatures is shown below:

Temp. θ (°C)	10	20	30	40	50	60	70	80	90
Mass m (g)	31.4	36.3	40.7	45.8	50.3	54.9	59.8	64.0	69.1

Plot a graph of $\theta \to m$ and deduce an equation for m in terms of θ.

4. SOME OTHER COMMON MODELS

Growth and decay functions (see Figure 14) and wave functions (see Figure 15) also occur commonly in connection with science and engineering.

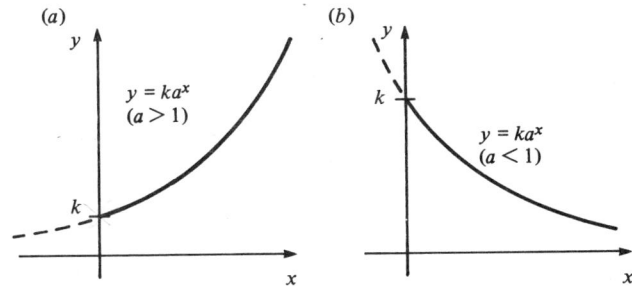

Figure 14

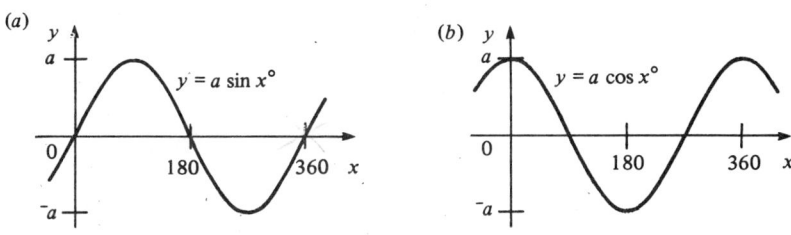

Figure 15

The scale factor and multiplier methods appropriate to proportionality models do not apply here. Trial and error methods, using a calculator, provide the simplest approach.

Exercise D

In questions 1–3, make tables of values of x and y, using values of x as shown, in this form:

x	-3	-2	-1	0	1	2	3
y							

Then draw graphs of the relations, using the values from the tables you have made, plotting parts (a), (b) and (c) on the same graph.

*1 (a) $y = x^2$; (b) $y = 2^x$; (c) $y = 2.5^x$.

2 (a) $y = \dfrac{1}{x^2}$; (b) $y = 0.5^x$; (c) $y = 0.9^x$.

3 (a) $y = \sin(120x)°$; (b) $y = 2\sin(60x)°$; (c) $y = \tfrac{1}{2}\cos(120x)°$.

In questions 4–6, each of the given tables of values fits one and only one of the following types of equation:

(a) $y = kx^2$; (b) $y = \dfrac{k}{x^2}$; (c) $y = a^x$.

Find the correct equation and state the value of k or a.

*4

x	-2	-1	0	1	2	3
y	0.25	0.5	1	2	4	8

5

x	-3	-2	-1	0	1	2	3
y	27	9	3	1	$\frac{1}{3}$	$\frac{1}{9}$	$\frac{1}{27}$

6

x	-2	-1	1	2	3
y	0.5	2	2	0.5	0.25

*7

x	-1	0	1
f(x)	1	2	3

Which are consistent and which are not consistent with the data?
(a) $f: x \to x+2$. (b) $f: x \to 2x^2 - x + 2$. (c) $f: x \to x^3 + 2$. (d) $f: x \to 2^x + 1$.
(SMP O-level)

8

x	1	2
y	1	4

The table shows two pairs of corresponding values for x and y. Which may be true and which must be false?
(a) $f: x \to y$ is linear. (b) $y \propto x^2$. (c) $y = 2^x$. (d) $y = 2x - 1$. (SMP O-level)

9   For the values

z	10	100	1000
w	1	2	3

which may be true and which must be false?
(a) w is a linear function of z.
(b) z is a linear function of w.
(c) w is an exponential function of z.
(d) z is an exponential function of w. (SMP O-level)

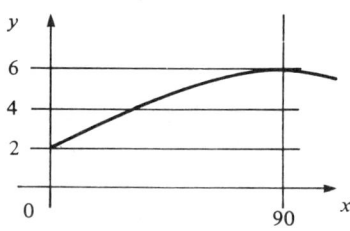

Figure 16

10 Figure 16 shows part of the graph of $y = A \sin x° + k$. State the values of (a) k, and (b) A. (SMP O-level)

11 On the planet Hesion there are seas of treacle, and the height of the treacle tide above the top of the foundation stone of the Peoples' Palace at Sucari is observed to fluctuate as shown in the table below, with one high tide every nine hesiodays:

Number of hesiodays (n)	0	1	2	3	4	5	6	7	8	9
Midday height in hesiospans (h)	19.6	34.7	42.7	40.0	27.6	11.6	0.8	−3.5	4.5	19.6

Plot a graph of $n \to h$ and suggest a suitable equation connecting h and n.

There are 10 hesiohours in a hesioday: for how many hours will the top of the foundation stone be exposed when the tide is down?

12 In an electrical circuit, the alternating current is oscillating with frequency 50 Hz and amplitude 6.5 A. Assuming that the relation between the current I amperes and the time t seconds can be written in the form $I = I_0 \cos kt°$, find the values of I_0 and k.

13 As the sun rises one day on a captive colony of Marbled White butterflies, just about to emerge from their pupae, the numbers which have emerged t minutes after 9 a.m. are observed to be as follows:

Time after 9 a.m. (t minutes)	0	10	20	30	40	50	60
Number (n)	2	4	6	12	21	38	68

Assuming that the relation between n and t is approximately of the type $n = 2 a^{(t/10)}$, experiment with various possible values of a, using your calculator, until you find one which fits the data reasonably well. What percentage increase, every ten minutes, does this value of a represent? What is the percentage increase per hour?

14 The temperature of a cooling liquid is measured every minute with the following results:

Time (t minutes)	0	1	2	3	4	5	6	7	8	9	10
Temp. (θ°C)	85	72	61	52	44	38	32	27	23	20	17

Assuming that these observations are approximately consistent with an equation of the type $\theta = ka^t$, find possible values for k and a with the aid of a calculator. What percentage decrease in temperature per minute does your value represent?

5. APPROPRIATE RELATIONS AND CURVE FITTING

When attempting to fit an appropriate relation to a set of data, it is important to look for good reasons for expecting a particular type of relation. Given a particular set of points it is usually possible to fit several sorts of curves to them fairly convincingly: for example, see Figure 17.

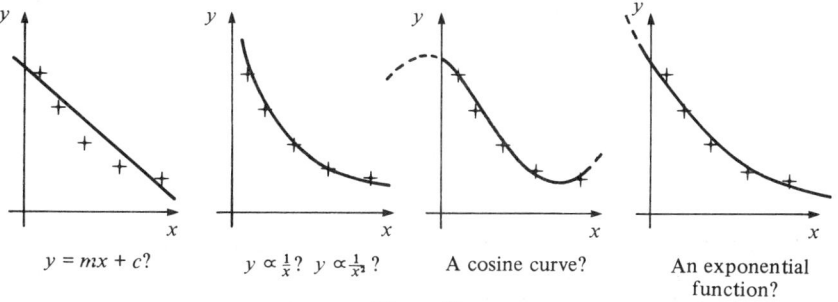

$y = mx + c$? $y \propto \frac{1}{x}$? $y \propto \frac{1}{x^2}$?   A cosine curve?   An exponential function?

Figure 17

In some cases, two variables are measured independently and then one is plotted against the other, on what is known as a *scatter diagram*, to help discover any possible relation between the two variables.

Ten students in a class each sat two tests, one in Mathematics and one in English. Here are the marks they obtained out of 100.

Student	Mathematics mark	English mark
Tom	93	64
Helen	75	54
Peter	40	23
Aziz	64	70
Anne	80	32
Simon	63	50
Chandra	94	80
Michael	33	23
Paul	40	32
Julie	55	45

A scatter diagram displaying this information is shown in Figure 18, in which each cross corresponds to the pair of marks for one person. It can be seen that most of the students who did well in the English test also did well in the Mathematics test. Anne stands out as being an exception to this general rule.

It would probably be valid to say that 'most people who score high marks on the Mathematics test also score high marks on the English test' and, ignoring Anne, we could attempt to fit a 'best straight line' to the remaining points such that the sum of the distances from the points to this line was as small as possible. This could then be used, for example, to suggest an appropriate English mark for someone who missed that test, but took the Mathematics test.

We must, however, beware of making unjustified assumptions that relations between variables exist at all. For example, a graph showing tobacco sales against road maintenance expenditure for a particular ten years proved to be very close to a straight line but we would hesitate to suggest that these figures are in fact related in any way.

Bearing this danger in mind, however, we can use computer library programs very effectively to help with the problem of curve fitting.

Just as there is a unique straight line, with equation of the type $y = ax+b$, through two known points, so there is just one parabola, $y = ax^2+bx+c$, through three known points, and one cubic, $y = ax^3+bx^2+cx+d$, through four known points, and one quartic, $y = ax^4+bx^3+cx^2+dx+e$, through five known points, etc.

There exist library programs which may be used to find the coefficients a, b, c, etc. for the relevant equation fitting any (reasonable) given number of points.

Appropriate relations and curve fitting

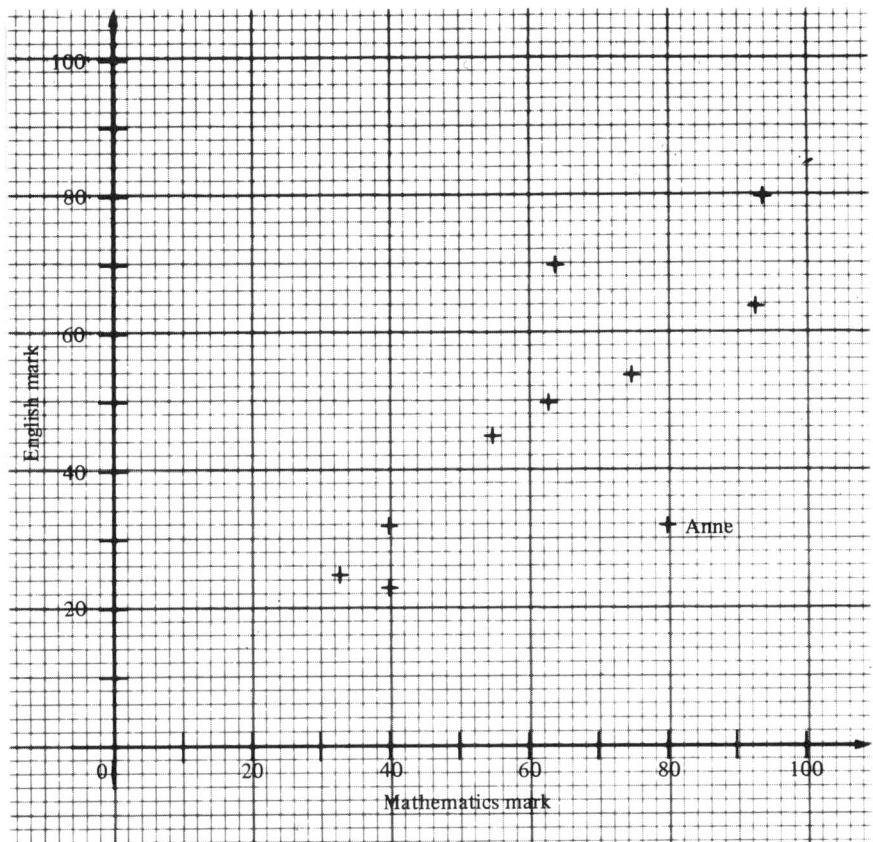

Figure 18

Also, if we have good theoretical reasons for expecting a particular type of curve, for example, a parabola, then there are library programs which enable us to find the 'best fit' parabola for the data we have, and to measure the goodness of fit.

Exercise E

1 Ten students were given two tests, one in Physics and the other in Mathematics. The percentages they obtained are given below. Show the information on a scatter diagram and comment on the pattern of the information.

Student	A	B	C	D	E	F	G	H	I	J
Physics	34	45	63	52	35	63	44	35	58	30
Mathematics	27	30	70	64	77	68	31	26	60	27

2   The table below shows the noon temperatures on 15 October 1982, and the latitude north of the Equator, of thirty towns. Draw a scatter diagram to show this information. Do you notice any pattern?

Town	Latitude	Temperature in °C	Town	Latitude	Temperature in °C
Algiers	37	23	Luxembourg	49.5	8
Athens	38	25	Mexico City	19.5	16
Berlin	52.5	13	Moscow	55.5	13
Birmingham	52.5	11	New York	40.5	19
Boston	42.5	19	Paris	49	13
Bristol	51.5	12	Peking	40	19
Cairo	30	31	Reykjavik	64	3
Casablanca	33.5	20	Riyadh	24.5	21
Dublin	53.5	11	Tangier	36	20
Geneva	46	11	Tel Aviv	32	28
Helsinki	60	6	Tokyo	35.5	24
Hong Kong	22	29	Toronto	43.5	13
Inverness	57.5	10	Vienna	48	14
Lisbon	38.5	17	Washington	39	22
London	51.5	12	Zurich	47.5	9

3   The table below shows the scores in ten football matches. Show the information on a scatter diagram and describe the pattern.

Match	1	2	3	4	5	6	7	8	9	10
Goals scored by home side	3	4	0	0	1	2	2	3	2	1
Goals scored by away side	0	1	2	3	2	2	0	0	5	3

4   Eight people were chosen at random and asked to state their age, weight and height. Here is the information obtained.

Person	A	B	C	D	E	F	G	H
Age in years	28	32	42	40	53	50	36	70
Height in metres	2.0	1.6	1.7	1.5	1.9	1.9	2.1	1.8
Weight in kilograms	74	59	59	50	62	68	71	56

Draw two separate scatter diagrams. On the first, show the age and weight information, and on the second show the height and weight information. Comment on any patterns you see from the diagrams.

5   Twelve people were chosen at random and invited to attempt to solve a word puzzle. Each person was timed (to the nearest minute) for the completion of the task. The age (to the nearest year) of each person was also noted. The information obtained is shown below.

Person	A	B	C	D	E	F	G	H	I	J	K	L
Age	14	45	18	74	60	23	21	56	20	39	30	40
Time	20	12	12	23	15	6	5	18	6	11	7	10

Draw a scatter diagram and comment on the pattern.

6   For each of the following situations, state with reasons whether or not you would expect there to be a relationship between the two variables. In those cases where you do expect a relationship, suggest an appropriate one in the form of an English sentence and also as a mathematical sentence, using the symbol '$\propto$'.
   (a) The mass of a cube of side one centimetre and the density of the material of which it is made.
   (b) The diameter of a steel wire and the tension which will cause it to break.
   (c) The length of a steel wire and the tension which will cause it to break.
   (d) The rate of heat generated by an electric fire element and the current flowing in it.
   (e) The acceleration of a solid metal sphere rolling down an incline of 30° and the temperature of the metal.
   (f) The average air pressure and the number of artificial satellites in orbit.
   (g) The volume of petrol used by a car and the distance travelled at approximately constant speed.
   (h) The rate of inflation and the price of a particular model of computer.
   (i) The time taken to run 100 m and the average speed of running.
   (j) The time taken to play Beethoven's ninth symphony and the number of people in the orchestra and choir.
   (k) The height of a cylinder of fixed volume and its diameter.
7   If you have access to computer library programs for curve fitting, experiment with them using a selection of questions from Exercise C.

6. MODELLING WITH FORMULAE

There is no essential difference between a formula and an equation. When several variables are related by an equation, we tend to describe the relation as a formula.

Formulae may often be transposed (that is, rearranged), so as to express any one of the variables in terms of all the others, using the same algebraic techniques as we apply in solving equations algebraically.

The extent to which formulae are useful as models of real-life situations depends on how much simplification of the real situation is involved.

Example 5
   Model, with a formula, the volume of metal required to make 100 disc-shaped gold coins, all of the same size.

   Each coin may be regarded as approximately a cylinder of height t (the thickness of the coin) and diameter d.
   The radius is therefore $\tfrac{1}{2}d$ and the base area of the cylinder is $\pi(\tfrac{1}{2}d)^2 = \tfrac{1}{4}\pi d^2$. So the volume of a coin is $\tfrac{1}{4}\pi d^2 \times t$ and the volume of gold required for 100 of them is
$$100 \times \tfrac{1}{4}\pi d^2 t = 25\pi d^2 t.$$

Example 6
Rearrange the formula obtained in Example 5, so as to obtain an expression for d in terms of t and the volume, V, of the gold used. Hence find the diameter

of each coin if they are each of thickness 1.8 mm and 88 cm³ of gold was required to make 100 of them.

$$V = 25\pi d^2 t \Rightarrow \frac{V}{25\pi t} = d^2$$

$$\Rightarrow d = \sqrt{\left(\frac{V}{25\pi t}\right)}$$

(This could also be written as $d = \frac{1}{5}\sqrt{\left(\frac{V}{\pi t}\right)}$ but this does not make evaluation easier so there is little point in doing so.)

With the given values, $d = \sqrt{\left(\frac{88}{25\pi \times 0.18}\right)} = 2.5$ to 2 s.f.

The diameter should be about 2.5 cm.

The accuracy of our result is likely to depend a good deal on how 'thickness' was measured. Consider the problem of measuring the 'thickness' of a 2p coin.

Example 7

A particle, travelling at initial speed u m/s, is given an acceleration a m/s² while it covers a distance s m. Its speed is then v m/s, given by the formula
$$v^2 = u^2 + 2as.$$
(a) Find v (assumed positive) if $u = 3$, $a = 4$ and $s = 5$.
(b) Find u if $v = 8.5 \times 10^{-6}$, $a = 2.1 \times 10^{-3}$ and $s = 9.3 \times 10^{-9}$, assuming $u > 0$.
(c) Rearrange the formula to make a the subject.

(a) $v^2 = u^2 + 2as \Rightarrow v^2 = 3^2 + 2 \times 4 \times 5$
$= 9 + 40 = 49$
So $v = 7$.

(b) Substituting in the formula,
$(8.5 \times 10^{-6})^2 = u^2 + 2 \times 2.1 \times 10^{-3} \times 9.3 \times 10^{-9}$
$\Rightarrow 72.25 \times 10^{-12} = u^2 + 39.06 \times 10^{-12}$
$\Rightarrow \qquad u^2 = 33.19 \times 10^{-12}$
So $u = 5.8 \times 10^{-6}$ to 2 s.f.

(c) $v^2 = u^2 + 2as \Rightarrow v^2 - u^2 = 2as$
$$\Rightarrow a = \frac{v^2 - u^2}{2s}$$

Exercise F

*1 Model, with a formula, the volume of an orange of diameter D cm. If it is assumed that the thickness of the peel of the orange is t cm, give a formula for the volume of the orange without its peel. Assuming that an orange without its peel has density d kg/m³, give a formula for the mass m kg of n such peeled oranges.

Rearrange your formula to make n the subject, and use it to calculate the number of oranges required for marmalade making if 5 kg of peeled oranges are required, and the oranges available have diameter about 11 cm and peel thickness about 0.5 cm. Assume the density of a peeled orange is much the same as water, 1000 kg/m³.

Would a marmalade maker really work it out this way?! What sort of model would an experienced marmalade maker use to decide how many oranges to buy?

2 To calculate the exposure time (t seconds) when using a photographic paper the instructions are: 'Divide the distance in centimetres between the lens and the paper by 10, square, and add 5.'
   (a) Copy and complete the flow diagram below, where d cm is the distance between the lens and the paper.

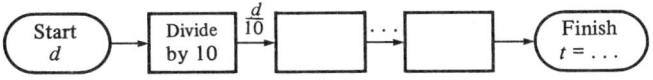

   (b) Find the exposure time required when $d = 36$.
   (c) 'For good results the exposure time should not be less than 9 seconds.' Find the value of d when $t = 9$. (SMP O-level)

3 The total cost of a printing job is made up of three parts: labour, materials, and a miscellaneous charge. For printing a certain poster the labour costs are £4 an hour, the materials cost 3p per poster, and the miscellaneous charge is calculated as £1.20 for every hundred posters, plus £13. It takes three hours to set up the presses, after which the posters are printed at the rate of 500 per hour.
   (a) How many hours will it take to set up and print 1000 posters?
      Calculate the total cost of printing 1000 posters.
   (b) Write down an expression for the total cost (£ C) of printing n thousand posters, and show that it simplifies to
   $$C = 25(2n+1).$$
   (c) Rearrange this formula to make n the subject, and find how many posters may be printed for a total cost of £150. (SMP O-level)

4 A reel of recording tape has a radius of r cm and contains n turns of tape. The tape has a thickness of t cm and a total length of d m. These quantities are connected by the equations
$$100d = \pi n(r+3)$$
$$nt = r - 3.$$
   (a) Express t in terms of n and r.
   (b) Find, correct to two significant figures, the values of n and t when $d = 540$ and $r = 8.4$. (SMP O-level)

*5 The formula $K = \dfrac{\alpha h^2}{c^2}$ arises in connection with modelling heat-flow. Transpose this formula,
   (a) making α the subject;
   (b) making h the subject;
   (c) making c the subject.

6 Two measurements, p and q, are to be multiplied together, giving a product pq. The measurements are not very accurate and the true values are P and Q, respectively, where $P = p + \alpha$ and $Q = q + \beta$.
   The error, e, in the final result is therefore, $PQ - pq$. Express e in terms of p, q, α and β, in as simple a formula as possible.

7 Which of the following is a correct rearrangement of the formula $p = q(1+rx)$?
   (a) $x = \dfrac{p}{qr} - 1$.
   (b) $x = 1 - \dfrac{p}{qr}$.
   (c) $x = \dfrac{p}{qr} - \dfrac{1}{r}$.
   (d) $x = \dfrac{1}{r}\left(1 - \dfrac{p}{q}\right)$.   (SMP O-level)

8 $P(x-3) = 2x - r$.
   Which must be true and which may be false?
   (a) If $r = 8$ and $x \neq 3$, then $P = 2$.
   (b) If $2x = r$, then $P = 0$.
   (c) If $P = 0$ and $x \neq 3$, then $r = 3$.
   (d) If $P \neq 2$, then $x = \dfrac{3P - r}{P - 2}$.   (SMP O-level)

9 If $6 - y = 2$ and $x + py = 5$, find y.
   Hence find p when $x = 3$.   (SMP O-level)

10 $T = 2\pi\sqrt{\left(\dfrac{l}{g}\right)}$.
   Which expression for g is correct?
   (a) $2\pi\sqrt{\left(\dfrac{l}{T}\right)}$;
   (b) $\dfrac{2\pi l}{T^2}$;
   (c) $\dfrac{T^2}{4\pi^2 l^2}$;
   (d) $\left(\dfrac{2\pi}{T}\right)^2 l$.   (SMP O-level)

*11 A home brewer uses the rule that, if he puts in x gram of sugar per litre, the percentage of alcohol in his beer will be $A\%$, where
$$A = \dfrac{x}{16} - 1,$$
provided that $20 \leq x \leq 208$.
   (a) Write down a formula for x in terms of A.
   (b) State the greatest value of A for which your formula applies.   (SMP O-level)

12 For a motorist who travels n km in a year the cost per kilometre is C pence, where
$$C = \dfrac{20\,000}{n} + 3.$$
   (a) What is the exact cost per kilometre if the car travels 16 000 km?
   (b) Rearrange the formula to express n in terms of C.
   (c) Find the number of kilometres travelled when the cost per kilometre is 5.5 pence.   (SMP O-level)

13 (a) $f : x \to \dfrac{360}{x}$,
   $g : x \to 180 - x$,
   $h : x \to 180 - \dfrac{360}{x}$.

Write down
(i) h in terms of f and g,
(ii) f^{-1} in the form $f^{-1}: x \to \ldots$
and g^{-1} in a similar form,
(iii) h^{-1} in the form $h^{-1}: x \to \ldots$

(b) The interior angle $q°$ of a regular polygon of n sides is given by the formula
$$q = 180 - \frac{360}{n}.$$
(i) Find the value of q when $n = 18$.
(ii) Make n the subject of the formula.
(iii) Part of a text-book question reads '…a regular polygon with interior angles of 1■5° has N sides…' but it is not clear whether ■ is 5 or 6. State which value is not possible, and explain why. Calculate N for the other value. (SMP O-level)

*14 Make C the subject of the formula $D = \sqrt{(C^2 + T^2)}$.

15 A particle travelling at initial speed u m/s, given a constant acceleration a m/s² for a time t s, is finally travelling at speed v m/s.
This situation is represented by the formula $v = u + at$.
(a) Find v if $u = 2$, $a = 3$, $t = 4$.
(b) Find u if $v = 8.5 \times 10^{-6}$, $a = 2.1 \times 10^{-3}$, $t = 2.0 \times 10^{-3}$.
(c) Rearrange the formula to make a the subject.

16 Rearrange the formula $\sin \theta = \dfrac{r_1 - r_2}{h_1 - h_2}$,
(a) to make r_1 the subject;
(b) to make h_2 the subject.

17 Transpose the formula $\theta = 90(\alpha + \beta)$,
(a) making α the subject;
(b) making β the subject.

18 A formula used in optics is $\dfrac{1}{z} = \dfrac{1}{(x+y)} + \dfrac{1}{(x-y)}$.
(a) Simplify $(x+y)(x-y)$ by multiplying out the brackets.
(b) Express the right-hand side of the given formula as a single fraction.
(c) Hence show that the formula may be written
$$z = \frac{x^2 - y^2}{2x} \quad \text{if} \quad x \neq 0.$$
(d) Transpose the formula to make y the subject.
(e) Rearrange the formula as a quadratic equation in x and hence use the fact that
$$ax^2 + bx + c = 0 \Rightarrow x = \frac{-b \pm \sqrt{(b^2 - 4ac)}}{2a}$$
to help you write down a formula for x in terms of y and z.

7. SETTING UP EQUATIONS AND INEQUALITIES

Mathematical modelling often involves setting up and attempting to solve equations and inequalities. Consider these examples:

Example 8

A spy in an instant soup factory discovers that the cost of the raw materials in 10 kg of 'beef and tomato soup' powder is £20.30 and that it is made up of 'beef soup' powder which costs £2.60 per kg, and 'tomato soup' powder, which costs £1.65 per kg.

Wishing to find the proportions in the mixture without indulging in chemical analysis, he proceeds as follows:

Suppose there are b kg of 'beef soup' in 10 kg of mixture.
There are then $(10-b)$ kg of 'tomato soup'.
Cost of 'beef soup' in the mixture is $b \times £2.60 = £2.60b$.
Cost of 'tomato soup' in the mixture is
$$(10-b) \times £1.65 = £1.65(10-b).$$
So $\qquad 2.60b + 1.65(10-b) = 20.30.$

He can now find the value of b by solving the equation and we expect, as our answer, a number between 0 and 10. We say that the domain of the solution is $\{b : 0 \leqslant b \leqslant 10\}$.

What, in fact, is the value of b? In what proportions are the two basic soup powders mixed?

Example 9

'Two free oranges for every purchase over £1', it says on the market stall. I want to take advantage of this offer and come away with an equal number of oranges at 12p each and best home grown apples at 5p each, but I want to spend as little over £1 as possible.

Suppose I buy a apples at a cost of $5a$ pence. Then to get a oranges, including 2 free ones, I will have to pay for $(a-2)$ oranges at 12p each, that is, $12(a-2)$ pence altogether.

My inequality is $5a + 12(a-2) > 100$.

In this case the domain of my solution is {positive integers}. Values of a which are not positive integers are meaningless in the context of this problem.

How many apples will I get?

Example 10

Becoming tired of being asked, by her Aunt Jemima, how old she is, Jill replies: 'I'm three years older than Jack, and if you multiply our ages together you get 154.'

Aunt Jemima thinks, '$n(n-3) = 154$'. (Where did she get that equation from? What has she defined n to be?)

She deduces that n might be 14 or $^-11$. (Do you agree? Check these values in the equation.) She replies: 'Then either you're 14 or you'll be born in 11 years time'.

Given that Jill has, in fact, been born, the domain for the solution of this equation is {positive numbers} or perhaps {positive integers} since ages are usually given, as here, to the nearest previous birthday.

Exercise G

*1 What are appropriate domains for solutions in the following cases?
  (a) An equation in p, where p is the probability of an event.
  (b) An equation in t, where t seconds is the average time taken for some schoolchildren to eat lunch.
  (c) An equation in θ, where θ kelvin is the temperature of water in a kettle.
  (d) An equation in θ, where θ kelvin is any possible temperature.
  (e) An equation in r, where r is the ratio boys:girls in a school.
  (f) An equation in d, where d is the number of shopping days to Christmas.
  (g) A pair of simultaneous equations in n and N, where n is the number of girls, in a school of 1500, who eat ice-cream at least twice per week, and N is the number of times per week one of these girls eats ice-cream.
  (h) A pair of simultaneous equations in m and f, where m is the mean number of birds' eggs in a population of nests and f is the frequency of a particular number of eggs.

2 A number is multiplied by 3 and 11 is then added. The result is 38. Write down an equation from which you can find the number: solve it.

3 The sum of two consecutive numbers is 257. Write down an equation to enable you to find the numbers and solve it.

4 Can £72 be shared between Albert, Barry and Cedric so that Albert has £12 more than Barry and Barry has £6 more than Cedric? How? Can you find another sum of money less than £100 which could be shared in the same way, so that each ends up with a whole number of pounds?

*5 Albert, Barry and Cedric share £100 so that Albert has twice as much as Barry who has three times as much as Cedric. How much does Albert have?

6 What quantity of kosi nuts at £1 per kilogram must I buy in order that I can give away 10 kg as Christmas presents to old age pensioners, having sold the rest at £1.20 per kilogram, and still end up with £10 profit?

*7 Sue's garden is a rectangle three times as long as it is wide. An old footpath, 2.0 m wide, runs along a short side and along one long side (outside the garden). If the area of the footpath is 120 m², what is the area of the garden?

8 Dan cannot remember how much he spent at the greengrocers, but he only bought oranges and peaches, and he knows that each peach cost twice as much as each orange; he bought four peaches and ten oranges and the oranges came to 16p more than the peaches. How much were the oranges, each? How much did he spend altogether?

9 In a small game park, containing only ostriches and giraffes, the warden counts heads while his son counts feet. There appear to be 92 heads and 290 feet (humans not included). How many giraffes are there?

10 A 5-kilogram bag of Gro-Hy fertilizer, selling wholesale at £6.20, is made up of chemical P costing 55p per kilogram and chemical Q costing 80p per kilogram. Allowing £1 for mixing and bagging and £2 profit margin, calculate the amount of each chemical in the bag.

SUMMARY

Making a mathematical model involves making simplifications and approximations which enable us to extract the most important features of a situation. A solution obtained from a model should be checked to see if it is physically likely or appropriate. (Sections 1, 7)

Proportionality relations can be investigated using either scale factors or multipliers. Such relations can also be found to fit experimental data by drawing appropriate graphs.

For other relations trial and error methods may be necessary.
(Sections 2, 3, 4)

A scatter diagram can be used to help discover a possible relation between two variables. (Section 5)

When several variables are related by an equation, that equation is called a formula. It may be useful to rearrange a formula to make a particular variable the subject of the formula. (Section 6)

Summary exercise

1 It is found that 36 g of calcium combines fully with 64 g of chlorine. What mass of chlorine will combine fully with 100 g of calcium?

2 Complete the following table if $y \propto x^2$ and $z \propto \dfrac{1}{x}$.

x	2	3	4	5	6	10	12
y	2						
z	60						

3 The cost (£C) of a Gomango 7-day package holiday varies with the distance (d km) from London. Some examples are given in the table below.

Destination	Paris	Hamburg	Lisbon	Athens
Distance in kilometres (d)	325	730	1520	2400
Cost in £ (C)	35.20	38.80	43.60	47.60
$x = \sqrt{d}$	18			

(a) Copy and complete the table above.

(b) Draw axes to show values of x from 0 to 60 using a scale of 1 cm for 5 units and values of C from 20 to 50, using a scale of 1 cm to 2 units. (Place the x-axis across the page.) Plot the four ordered pairs (x, C) given by the table, and join up the points with a straight line.

(c) If the equation of this line is $C = mx + k$, estimate from your graph the values of k and m (correct to one decimal place). Hence write down a formula for C in terms of k, m and d.

(d) Find the distance to a destination for which the cost is £40.00.

(SMP O-level)

4 The cooking time (t minutes) for a joint of meat is given by
$$t = \frac{2000(4W+3)}{H}$$
where W kg is the weight of meat and H °C is the cooking temperature.
   (a) Calculate the cooking time for a joint weighing 2 kg at a temperature of 160 °C.
   (b) Rearrange the formula to give
       (i) H in terms of W and t;
       (ii) W in terms of H and t. (SMP O-level)

5 Celia bought some remaindered copies of a special limited edition of *The History of Dutch Flea-markets* from a London bookshop for £40, kept one for her grandmother's Christmas present and one for herself, and then sold the rest to her local bookshop, at £1 profit per book, for a total of £40. How many copies did she originally buy?

5
Statistics

As you watch television or read the newspapers you must have noticed how often you are given information in the form of statistics. In this chapter we review methods of presenting such information and of calculating and using averages and measures of spread.

1. REPRESENTATION OF DATA

There are several types of pictorial representation of numbers. We will remind you by illustrating the following data in three ways.

Country of manufacture of cars seen on the way to school one morning	Number of cars seen
United Kingdom	32
France	15
Germany	7
Japan	10
Italy	1
	65

Bar chart (Figure 1)

Each quantity being represented has a column of appropriate length on a stated scale. The columns are all of the same width; sometimes they are just straight lines. We draw a bar chart when (*a*) one axis cannot have a numerical scale (as in this example) or (*b*) when no physical meaning can be attached to intermediate points on a numerical axis.

Pictogram (Figure 2)

This is an attractive and striking method of displaying data, but less informative, since it is impossible to read the scale with any degree of accuracy if fractions of the unit are involved.

Representation of data 115

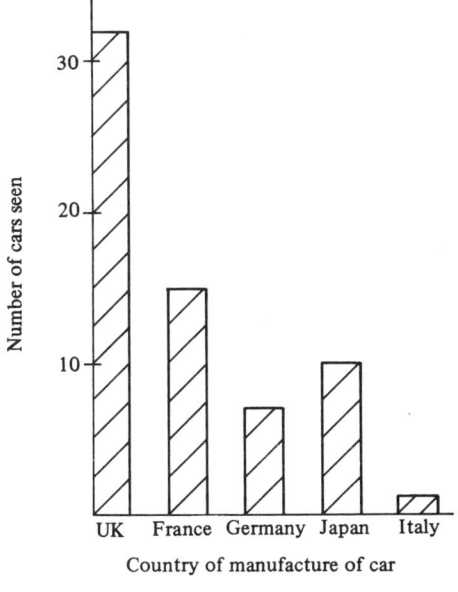

Figure 1

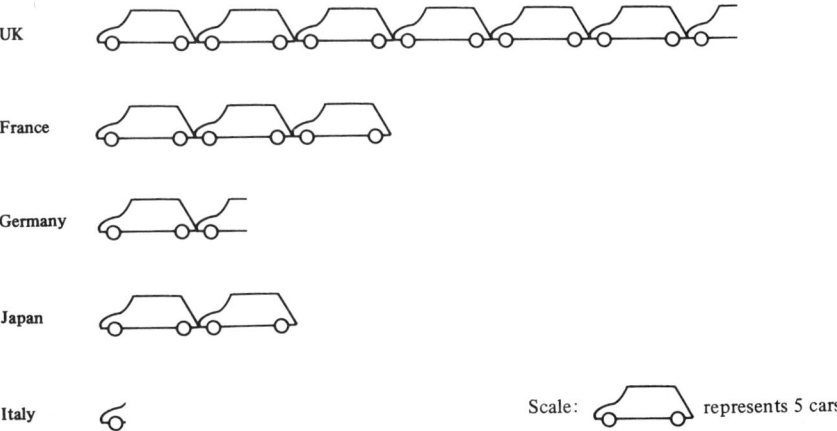

Figure 2

Pie chart (Figure 3)

The circular 'pie' is divided so that the areas of the 'slices' are proportional to the numbers involved. This means that the angles at the centre must also be proportional to them. The table below shows the calculation. The total number of cars (65) must be represented by the full turn (360°). Hence the multiplier for number of cars → number of degrees is $\frac{360}{65}$. Use a calculator and work to the nearest degree.

Country of manufacture of cars seen on the way to school one morning	Number of cars seen		Angle in degrees of sector of pie chart
United Kingdom	32	→	177
France	15	→	83
Germany	7	→	39
Japan	10	→	55
Italy	1	→	6
Total	65	$\times \frac{360}{65}$ →	360

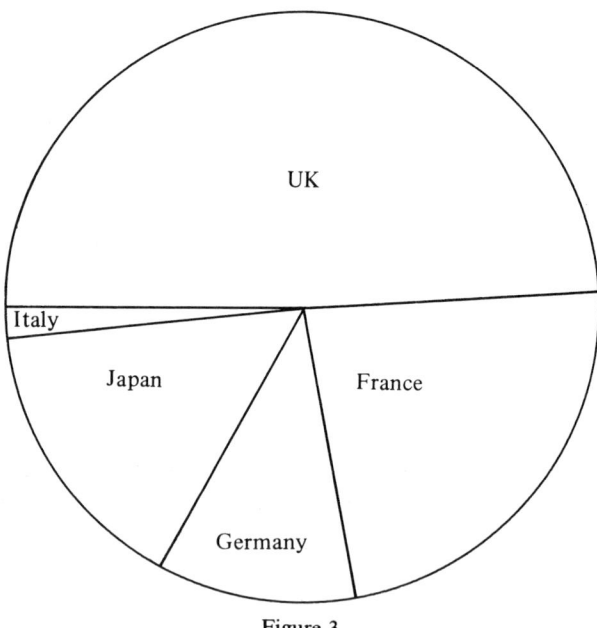

Figure 3

It will sometimes happen that the number of degrees obtained will not add up to 360°, but to 359° or 361° because of rounding errors. This need not bother you since a high degree of accuracy is neither possible nor needed.

Line graph

The following table shows the shade temperature in a garden at 2-hourly intervals during an afternoon and evening.

Number of hours after noon	0	2	4	6	8	10
Shade temperature in °C	22.5	23	22.5	21	18.5	15

None of the previous methods is satisfactory for illustrating this information. The temperature varies continuously between the measured times. We do not expect any sudden variations. It is logical to join the points with a smooth curve and to use this to estimate temperatures between the readings. Figure 4 shows the result.

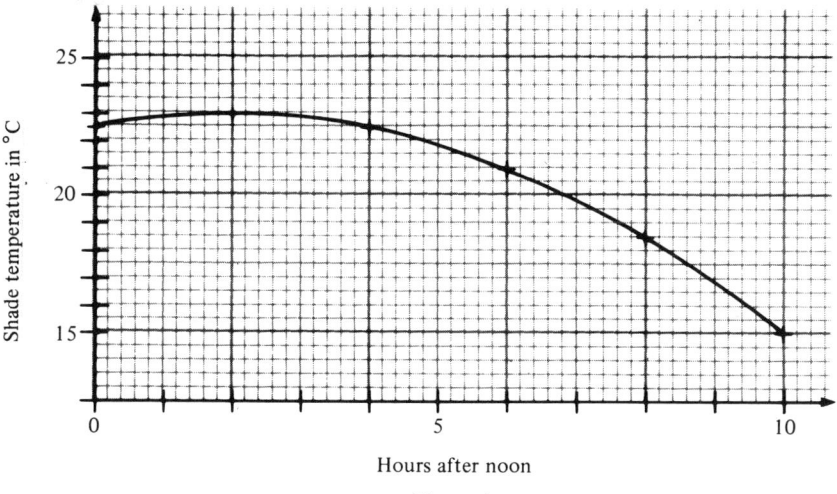

Figure 4

If we are uncertain what happens between the values given in a table we can (a) leave the marked points unjoined, (b) join them with straight line segments (in which case it is usual to use a broken line) or (c) adopt a different form of graph, perhaps a bar chart.

Exercise A

1   The expenses of a small printing firm are as follows:

Printing costs	£5000
Wages and salaries	£10000
Maintenance of capital	£3000
Miscellaneous	£2000

(a) Illustrate these figures on a pie chart of radius 5 cm.
(b) In the following year printing costs go down by 20% and wages and salaries go up by 10%. What should be the area of the new pie chart, compared with the old one, if it is to represent the proportional change in costs?
(c) What should the size of the angle of the new sector devoted to salaries and wages be?

2 The diagram (Figure 5) shows the breakdown of £1 paid to a certain county in rates.
(a) Which service costs the most?
(b) If the total sum raised is £5m, how much is spent on (i) the police, (ii) highways and transportation?
(c) What extra percentage could be spent on social services if a 1% cut is made in education?
(d) What effect does a 20% increase in Fire costs have on the total sum that the county needs to raise?

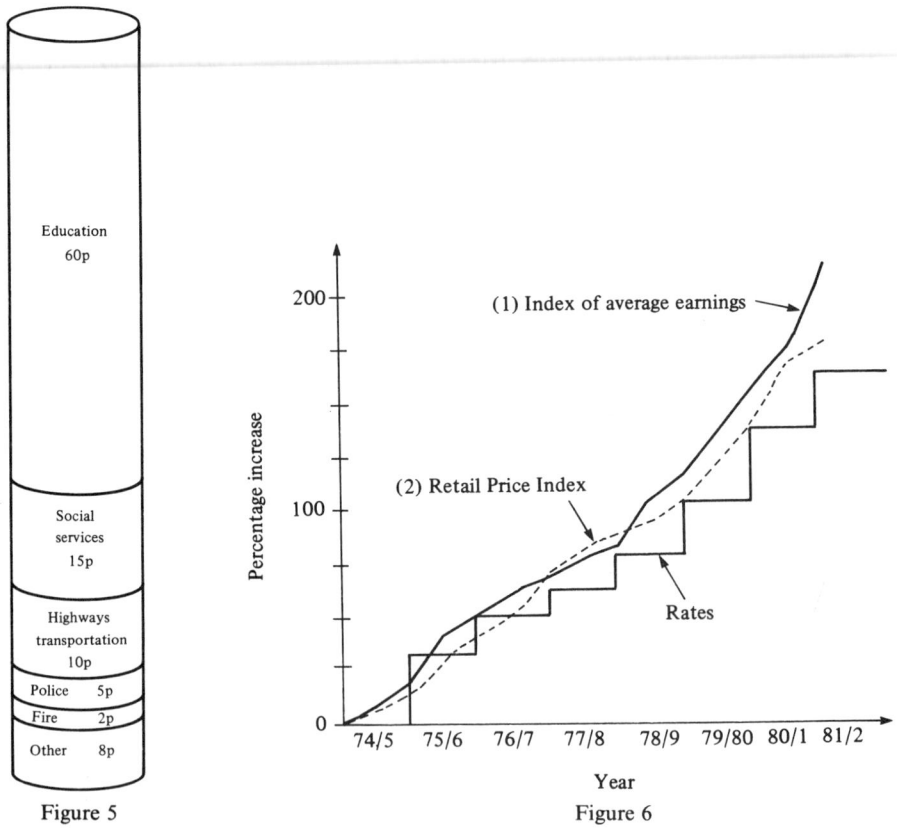

Figure 5   Figure 6

3 The graph (Figure 6) shows the percentage increase in the rates for a county compared with indexes representing (1) average earnings, (2) retail prices.
(a) Why is the rate graph stepped while the others are not?
(b) Make a general statement about the relation between the three graphs.

(c) Between which years did (i) the rates, (ii) the Retail Price Index, increase the fastest?
(d) Between which years did (i) the Retail Price Index, (ii) average earnings, increase faster than the rates?

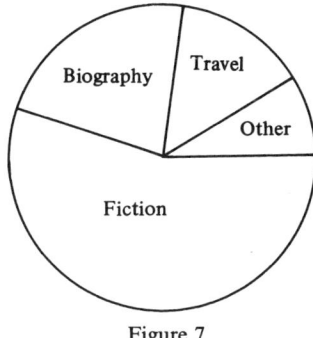

Figure 7

4   Figure 7 shows the pie chart representing books borrowed from a library during a certain month. Measure the appropriate angles. Complete the following table if the total number of books borrowed was 18 000.

Type of book	Angle representing number of books borrowed	Actual number of books borrowed
Fiction		
Biography		
Travel		
Other		
Total		18 000

5   Draw charts to illustrate the following information:

Year	1965	1975
No. of cars up to 1300 cc observed passing a certain house between 0900 and 1200 on the first Sunday in August	465	191
No. of the above which were of British manufacture	381	104
No. of Japanese manufacture	28	27

(a) What governed your choice of type of chart?
(b) What information is easily read from the charts?
(c) What information is not easily read, or cannot be seen at all?
(d) Do the charts enable you to make any predictions for 1985? If so, what?

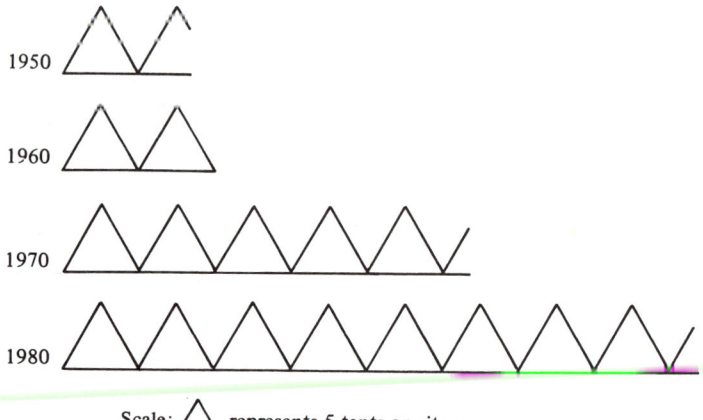

Figure 8

6 Figure 8 is a pictogram showing the number of tents on licensed Old Forest sites during August of the years given.
   (a) Estimate the number of tents in August 1950.
   (b) How many more tents used the sites in August 1980 than in August 1960?
   (c) Estimate the percentage increase between 1970 and 1980.
   (d) Does the rate of increase appear to be increasing or decreasing?
   (e) List the merits and drawbacks of this form of representation of data.

7 A pie chart is drawn to show how a family spends its income. The total is £90 per week and the sector representing 'Food and drink' has an angle of 110°. Find the actual amount spent on this item.

8 The annual numbers of inland telephone calls made in the United Kingdom (in millions) were as follows:

1969	1971	1973	1975	1977
8627	10747	13539	15836	16092

Plot this information and estimate the number of calls for 1979 and 1981. What suppositions do you have to make, and what events could make nonsense of your predictions? Can you use the figures to find the figure for 1976?

I tried to memorise the number of million calls in 1967. I know the answer contained a 2, a 3, a 7 and an 8. What do you think the answer was?

2. FREQUENCY AND GROUPING OF DATA

Descriptive statistics is concerned with summarising concisely a large number of individual numbers. To show some of its main ideas, we shall take one example, and show how the various collections of numbers may be presented in a brief, meaningful way.

Frequency and grouping of data 121

The example has been worked through in full detail, but you are recommended to check every step in the working yourself, so that you are aware of everything that is involved. It is very easy to forget small but important steps in the calculation.

A scientist in a developing country has produced a new strain of maize which has a larger number of grains per ear than those currently being grown in the rather difficult conditions. In order to convince the farmers that the new strain really is better, he wants to be able to make some clear statements about it. How can this be done?

The most obvious idea is to say something about the number of grains per ear. This will have to be some form of average, since we would not expect all ears to be exactly the same. It is impossible to count the grains on all the ears, so the most sensible thing to do is to take a sample of reasonable size, and count the number of grains. He decides to take a sample of 80 ears, and writes down the results thus:

47	97	45	68	75	80	63	75	68	71
61	88	55	83	55	66	70	68	64	42
139	85	53	85	54	86	107	59	61	79
84	104	76	79	54	48	92	99	36	116
67	114	52	92	106	71	70	112	41	107
129	62	107	60	89	96	107	124	77	61
70	83	31	79	91	65	84	50	55	35
76	47	89	57	61	80	72	60	47	92

Table 1. Number of grains on each of 80 ears of maize

What information can he get out of these numbers? As they stand, they convey very little, since there is no order in them. One thing we might do is to write them out again in order:

31	35	36	41	42	45	47	47	47	48
50	52	53	54	54	55	55	55	57	59
60	60	61	61	61	61	62	63	64	65
66	67	68	68	68	70	70	70	71	71
72	75	75	76	76	77	79	79	79	80
80	83	83	84	84	85	85	86	88	89
89	91	92	92	92	96	97	99	104	106
107	107	107	107	112	114	116	124	129	139

Table 2. Number of grains on each of 80 ears of maize arranged in order

This is more useful, since we can see that they extend from 31 to 139 grains, and most are between 50 and 100.

Figure 9 illustrates the results on a *frequency diagram*. Because there are so many columns to be drawn over such a large range it is more convenient to use straight lines to represent frequency, rather than columns of definite thickness.

This gives us some idea of his results, but there are far too many lines to pick

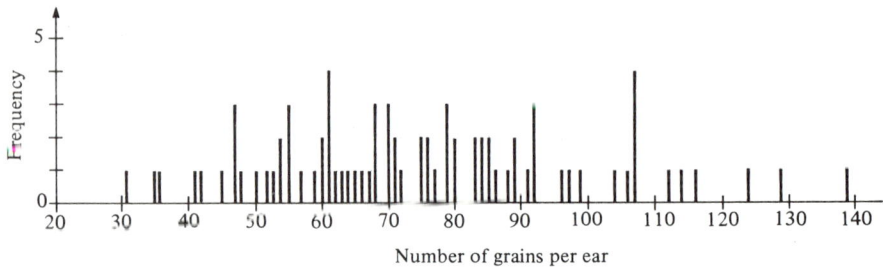

Figure 9

out the main idea quickly, and they are very irregular in height. In order to obtain a clearer picture it is sensible to place the individual values into small classes and to draw a frequency diagram for the classes. The new diagram cannot convey all the information which is contained in Figure 9.

What size of group is best? Try taking classes of 5, 10, 15, and 20, and graph their frequency functions. Table 3 and Figure 10 show this for classes of size 10, but you do not need to group the numbers the same way.

Warning: When drawing these frequency diagrams it is not easy to put the columns in the right place. Consider Table 3. Since the class intervals cover all the range from 30 to 139, we would expect the frequency diagram to cover all this, without any gaps between the columns. And since each class represents 10 grains we would expect the columns to be 10 units wide.

If the third column started exactly at 50, it would finish exactly at 60, although it does not include any of the ears with 60 grains. For this reason, the column should start at 49.5, and finish at 59.5.

Class interval	Frequency (f)
30–39	3
40–49	7
50–59	10
60–69	15
70–79	14
80–89	12
90–99	7
100–109	6
110–119	3
120–129	2
130–139	1
	80

Table 3

Grouping the data in this way we lose some of the detail of the original data, but we obtain a better overall picture. Choosing a larger group size would mean losing more detail, so we want to choose a group size which gives a clear picture

Frequency and grouping of data 123

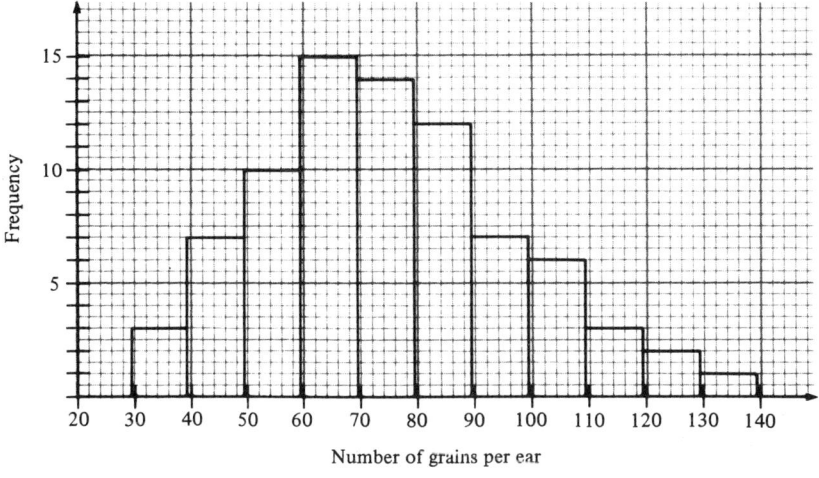

Figure 10

without losing too much information. A good working rule is to have about 10 columns, but the actual number will depend on the measurements. A class interval of 10 seems to suit these figures well.

Exercise B

1 Group the following numbers into classes of 5, where the first class is from 3 to 7:

26	17	42	28	23	17	39	3	38	10	44	25	4	10	33
38	31	38	23	42	29	40	37	18	6	22	15	15	32	32
15	12	37	38	37	12	29	12	18	27	30	30	12	40	45
4	26	24	22	33	17	8	3	7	42	39	6	41	20	11

2 You are asked to group the following lengths, measured to the nearest millimetre, into (*a*) five, (*b*) eight, groups. List your boundary values and say why you chose them.

251	246	264	249	253
238	252	260	255	271
246	251	241	250	262
254	255	248	261	260
259	257	255	239	264

3 The masses of 25 packets of corn flakes are measured to the nearest gram and recorded as follows:

401	403	403	399	404
400	402	403	405	398
404	401	402	400	401
405	407	402	403	401
400	399	402	403	401

Construct a frequency table and draw a frequency diagram.

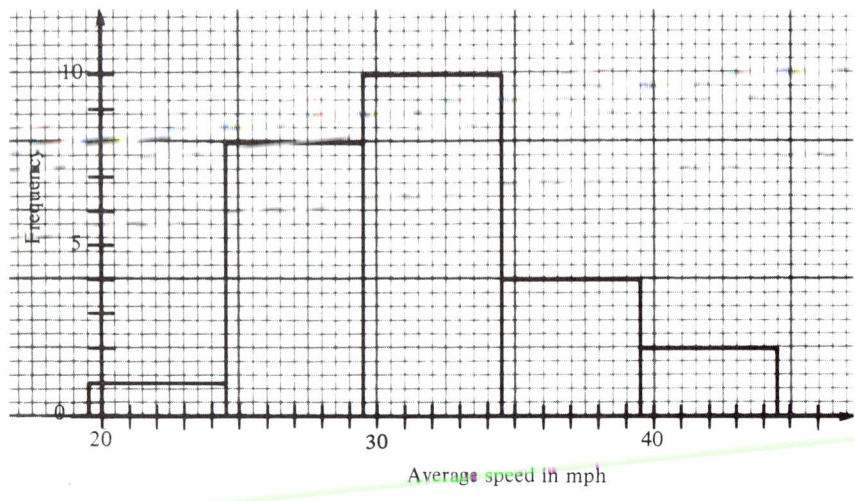

Figure 11

4 Cars were timed over a 200-yard stretch of straight road and their average speeds estimated. The frequency distribution is shown in Figure 11.
   (a) Estimate the number of cars which were breaking the speed limit (30 mph).
   (b) If the metric speed limit used in France (60 km/h or about 37 mph) were to be adopted, how many would satisfy the new speed limit but not the old one?

5 Thirty pupils were asked to estimate the length of a certain piece of string and to record their results in centimetres to the nearest centimetre. The resulting frequency table was as follows:

Length in cm	31–34	34–37	37–40	40–43	43–46	46–49	49–52
Frequency	1	3	2	7	9	6	2

With this method of grouping explain what the pupils should have done with an estimate of 40 cm. Graph the information. What do you think the true length was likely to have been?

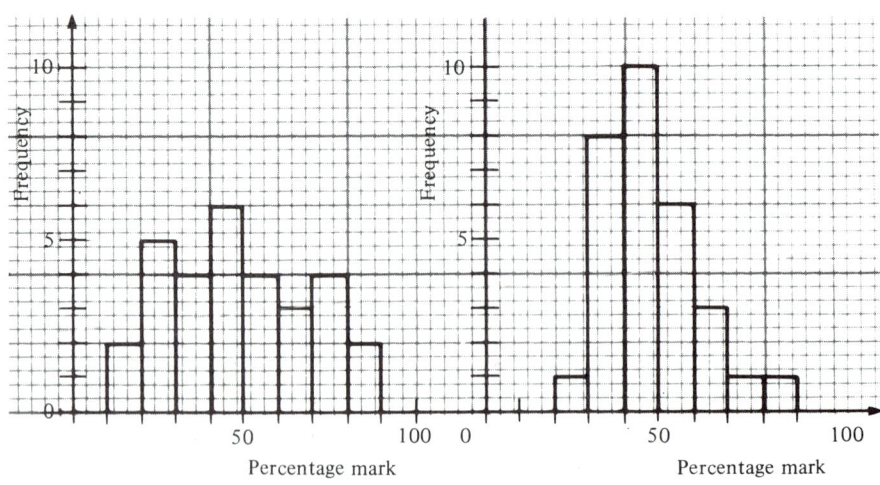

Figure 12

6 The graphs in Figure 12 show the performance of thirty fifth-formers in each of two schools on the same test.
   (a) Comment on the performance of the two classes.
   (b) Estimate the number of passes in each school (45% pass mark).
   (c) Can you say which is the 'better' class?

3. AVERAGES

The *average* of a set of numbers or quantities is a 'middle' value that represents the whole set. We talk about an average man who has the virtues, interests, physical characteristics of the group he belongs to. If your class get an average mark of 50% in a test you can feel that the standard was about right for the class. If another class got 60% on the same test you can make a rough and ready comparison between the classes.

If you want to compare the height of boys of age 15 with girls of the same age you would measure individuals in two representative groups (not necessarily the same number of boys and girls) and calculate the average of each. You have met three averages in the course so far and you would want to choose the one that is most revealing.

Median

If you have the boys and girls at your beck and call the easiest thing to do is to ask each group to stand in order, tallest on the right, shortest on the left, and measure the height of the middle one. This is called the *median height*.

If you have an odd number in the group, say 9, the person to measure is the 5th: xxxx(x)xxxx Note that $5 = \frac{1}{2}(9+1)$.

If you have an even number, say 10, the measurement to give is half-way between the 5th and the 6th: xxxxx(x)xxxxx Note that $5\frac{1}{2} = \frac{1}{2}(10+1)$.

If you have n in the group, the middle one will be the $\frac{1}{2}(n+1)$th. This is quite an easy formula to remember.

Arithmetic mean

The method which probably came into your mind was to measure the heights of all the boys, add them and divide by the number present and then do the same thing for the girls. This would give you the *arithmetic mean* of the heights of each group.

Mode

If you had a large enough number of boys and girls in each group you could measure all their heights, group the data into (say) 3 cm class intervals (160 cm but less than 163 cm, 163 cm but less than 166 cm, etc). You could then take the class interval with most members as the *modal class interval* and the middle value of the interval (161.5, 164.5, or whichever one it is) as mode.

Let us now return to the scientist and his maize. Looking again at Table 2 on page 121, it can be seen that the middle ear of maize is half-way between the 40th and the 41st (or remember that the middle is the $\frac{1}{2}(80+1)$th). The 40th number of grains in an ear is 71, the 41st is 72. Thus the median number of grains is 71.5.

If the scientist wants to use the arithmetic mean he adds up all the numbers in Table 2 (or Table 1, of course), getting 6005 and divides by 80. This gives him 75.1 to one decimal place. It is usual to give an arithmetic mean to one more significant figure than the data.

Thirdly he could look at the grouped data in Table 3. He would see that the class interval with most members is 60–69 with 15 members. This is the modal class.

He has now found three averages: Arithmetic mean   75.1
　　　　　　　　　　　　　　　　　Median   71.5
　　　　　　　　　　　　　　　　　Modal class   60–69

Which of these three quite different averages is the scientist to take? There is no fixed answer to this question. Part of the art of using statistics is being able to choose the one which gives the clearest summary of the original numbers. In this case, since having a crop with about the same number of grains per ear is agriculturally desirable, the median is possibly the best. If we were interested in the wages of employees of a firm then the mode might be best, since the other two are more affected by the very high wages of a few senior employees. For the average mark in an exam the mean is probably best.

When the frequency diagram is more symmetrical than this one, the three averages are closer to each other.

Arithmetic mean from grouped data

With eighty values it is not difficult to add them all up. It there had been eight hundred or eight thousand it would have been better to group the data and work out the arithmetic mean from this. Table 4 shows the maize distribution with the midvalues of the class intervals. We assume that the ten ears in the third

Class interval	Frequency (f)	Class mid-mark (x)	fx
30–39	3	34.5	103.5
40–49	7	44.5	311.5
50–59	10	54.5	545
60–69	15	64.5	967.5
70–79	14	74.5	1043
80–89	12	84.5	1014
90–99	7	94.5	661.5
100–109	6	104.5	627
110–119	3	114.5	343.5
120–129	2	124.5	249
130	1	134.5	134.5
	80		6000

Table 4

class, say, have themselves a mean of 54.5, giving a total of 545. This may or may not be true, but usually any mistakes made by underestimating will be balanced by those which overestimate.

The mean by this method comes to 6000 (the total of the fx column) divided by 80 (the total of the f column) giving 75.0. The true mean of the eighty numbers was 75.1. Thus this method produces an error of 0.1 which is a very small percentage error.

Median from grouped data

As we have already seen, the median of the maize distribution is 71.5, from the actual count.

It is possible to make a rough estimate from the grouped data in Table 4. We are looking for the $40\frac{1}{2}$th value.

Counting down the frequency column we get:
$$3+7+10+15 = 35$$
$$3+7+10+15+14 = 49$$

We see that the $40\frac{1}{2}$th value lies in the fifth class interval, that is $70-79$.

Now $40\frac{1}{2} - 35 = 5\frac{1}{2}$ so that we expect the median to lie about $\frac{5\frac{1}{2}}{14}$ of the way from 70 to 79.

So estimated median $= 70 + \frac{5\frac{1}{2}}{14} \times 10$ (since 10 is the class interval)

≈ 73.9.

As you see, this is some way from the true median and it is interesting to see why. The actual numbers in the interval (from Table 2) are:

70 70 70 71 71 72 75 75 76 76 77 79 79 79.

They are not, in fact, evenly spread and the $5\frac{1}{2}$th number is close to the start of the interval, not $5\frac{1}{2}/14$th of the way through. When we assume regularity we must expect to introduce some errors. With the median there is no way by which underestimates can balance overestimates as in the case of the calculation of the arithmetic mean from grouped data.

In the next section we shall look at the drawing method, but this has the same 'built-in' error.

Exercise C

*1 Find the mean of:
    (a) {2, 3, 4, 5, 6};
    (b) {4, 5, 6, 7, 8, 9};
    (c) {1, 6, 7, 9, 12};
    (d) {105, 109, 112, 113, 117, 120};
    (e) {1.6, 2.3, 5.2, 7.6, 8.5};
    (f) {3145, 3151, 3143, 3148, 3141};
    (g) $\{1\frac{1}{2}, 5\frac{3}{4}, 6\frac{2}{3}, 7\frac{1}{8}\}$;
    (h) {⁻8, ⁻5, 2, 6, 7, 10};
    (i) {⁻5, 8, 11, 0, ⁻9};
    (j) {⁻1.7, ⁻0.4, 0.8, 1.2, 7.6}.

2 Give examples, each of a set of five elements, in which the mean is:
(a) greater than 7;   (b) less than 0;
(c) greater than ⁻3;   (d) 1.5;   (e) ⁻4.

3 (a) Calculate the mean height of the members of a racing eight whose heights are: 1.74 m, 1.89 m, 1.88 m, 2.07 m, 2.04 m, 1.91 m, 1.98 m, 1.92 m.
(b) The height of the cox was 1.46 m. Make an educated guess of the difference made by including him in the average height of the crew.
(c) Check your answer to (b) by actual calculation.

4 The results of 29 rugby club matches on a Saturday were as follows:

Aberavon	23	Llanelli	13
Abertillery	7	Pontypool	21
Bradford	29	Hartlepool R.	10
Bath	9	Newport	3
Birkenhead P.	6	Middlesborough	4
Bridgend	15	Rosslyn Pk.	9
Bristol	21	Harlequins	0
Cardiff	40	Bedford	12
Coventry	30	Rugby	6
Cross Keys	4	Maesteg	28
Ebbw Vale	12	Newbridge	16
Exeter	28	Cheltenham	12
Halifax	25	Manchester	3
Harrogate	21	Davenport	6
London Irish	33	Birmingham	13
L. Welsh	12	Swansea	26
Met. Police	9	Broughton Pk.	16
Morley	18	Malone	9
Neath	16	Richmond	3
N. Brighton	3	Liverpool	9
Northampton	35	Headingley	0
Nottingham	15	Wasps	16
Orrell	22	Otley	10
Penarth	24	S. Wales Police	14
Plymouth Alb.	30	Glam Wand	31
Pontypridd	22	Saracens	6
US Portsmouth	11	Black	6
Vale of Lune	36	Widnes	6
Waterloo	21	St Helens	7

The first match was won by a margin of 10 points. Calculate the average winning margin.

*5 For the following frequency tables find the mean, mode, and median:

(a) x	f	(b) x	f	(c) x	f	(d) x	f
1	3	2	4	54	4	40	6
2	6	5	7	57	7	60	3
3	8	6	8	59	8	80	12
4	7	9	5	61	5	100	20
5	6	11	6	68	6	120	9

6 For the following grouped frequency tables estimate the mean, mode, and median:

(a) x	f	(b) x	f	(c) x	f	(d) x	f
3–5	3	1–10	6	0–10	6	1–15	7
6–8	7	11–20	9	10–20	9	16–30	10
9–11	8	21–30	13	20–30	13	31–45	15
12–14	6	31–40	12	30–40	12	46–60	12
15–17	6	41–50	10	40–50	10	61–90	9

7 Write out ordered sets with the following properties:

	Number of elements	Mean	Median	Mode
(a)	5	3	—	—
(b)	5	3	4	—
(c)	5	—	2	3
(d)	5	7	—	5
(e)	4	—	6	—
(f)	7	4	5	6
(g)	6	5.2	—	—
(h)	5	3.7	2.6	—

8 The following are the number of hours of sunshine (to the nearest hour) per day for the month of May at a certain school:

3   1   4   8   11   12   9   7   5   3   4   9   8   4   7   9
11   12   1   8   7   4   5   6   6   6   5   7   6   9   8

(a) Find the mean number of hours of sunshine per day.
(b) Classes work outside on sufficiently sunny days: in this case one-quarter of the days of the month. How many hours of sunlight are necessary for the class to work outside?
It rains on three-quarters of those days which have four hours of sunshine or less. It rains on one-third of all other days.
(c) Estimate the number of days on which it rained.
(d) Estimate the number of days on which the class got wet.

4. SPREAD AND CUMULATIVE FREQUENCY DIAGRAMS

Range

A farmer wants a good uniform crop. It is not enough to say that this particular strain produces a median number of grains of 71.5 per ear. So the scientist must devise some measure of the reliability of the strain. The first, and the most obvious, way to measure the spread of the yield is to find the difference in the number of grains between the ear with the best yield and the one with the worst. In this case, the difference is $139 - 31 = 108$. This figure is known as the *range*.

It is a useful method of making a quick estimate of the spread of the figures. But it has one important disadvantage. One particularly unusual result can make the range too large to represent the real spread. Thus, if there had been one very small ear in the sample which had produced only 4 grains, then the range will be increased by 17, although the numbers themselves have altered very little indeed. No farmer is going to mind if one or two plants are unsuccessful, provided that most are satisfactory. We need to use a measure which does not take too much account of extreme values. We shall deal here only with the simplest measure, and leave more complicated ones to another course.

Inter-quartile range

This measure of spread is related to the median. The median divides the population, arranged in order of magnitude or 'ranked', into two halves. We could equally well divide it into four quarters. The dividing lines are known as the *lower quartile*, the median (*middle quartile*) and the *upper quartile*. Thus, in our example, the lower quartile will be just after the twentieth number, which is between 59 and 60. Since the twentieth number is 59, and the 21st number is 60, the lower quartile, which is the $\frac{1}{4}(80+1)$th or $20\frac{1}{4}$th number, will be 59.25.

In general, for n numbers ranked in order the lower quartile is at the $\frac{1}{4}(n+1)$th rank, and the upper quartile is at the $\frac{3}{4}(n+1)$th rank.

In this case, the upper quartile is at rank $60\frac{3}{4}$. Since both 60th and 61st numbers are 89 then the upper quartile is also 89. So the middle half of the population lies between 59.25 and 89. We say that its *inter-quartile range* is 29.75. Remember that this tells us nothing about the occasional exceptional ear. If another strain has a median of 71.5 and an inter-quartile range of only 10, then we might reasonably suspect that it had fewer ears with a very large number of grains or with a very small number, but we would have no proof of this.

Cumulative frequency

Very often, however, we do not have the original numbers, but only have a grouped frequency distribution. A reliable way of estimating the median and quartiles is to draw a *cumulative frequency* graph. This is done in Table 5, and Figure 13.

From Table 5 we see that 20 of the ears had fewer than 60 grains, so we can estimate that the lower quartile is 60. 49 ears had fewer than 80 grains and 61 ears had fewer than 90 grains so the 60th ear had approximately

$$80 + \frac{11}{12} \times 10 \text{ grains} \approx 89 \text{ grains}.$$

(Compare the calculation for the median on page 127. Note that, since we do not require a high degree of accuracy, we have not used cumulative frequencies of $20\frac{1}{4}$ and $60\frac{3}{4}$.)

The quartiles and median can also be read directly from the graph (see Figure 13).

Spread and cumulative frequency diagrams

Class interval	Frequency	Cumulative frequency	Number of ears represented by cumulative frequency
		0	Less than 30
30–39	3	3	Less than 40
40–49	7	10	Less than 50
50–59	10	20	Less than 60
60–69	15	35	Less than 70
70–79	14	49	Less than 80
80–89	12	61	Less than 90
90–99	7	68	Less than 100
100–109	6	74	Less than 110
110–119	3	77	Less than 120
120–129	2	79	Less than 130
130–139	1	80	Less than 140

Table 5

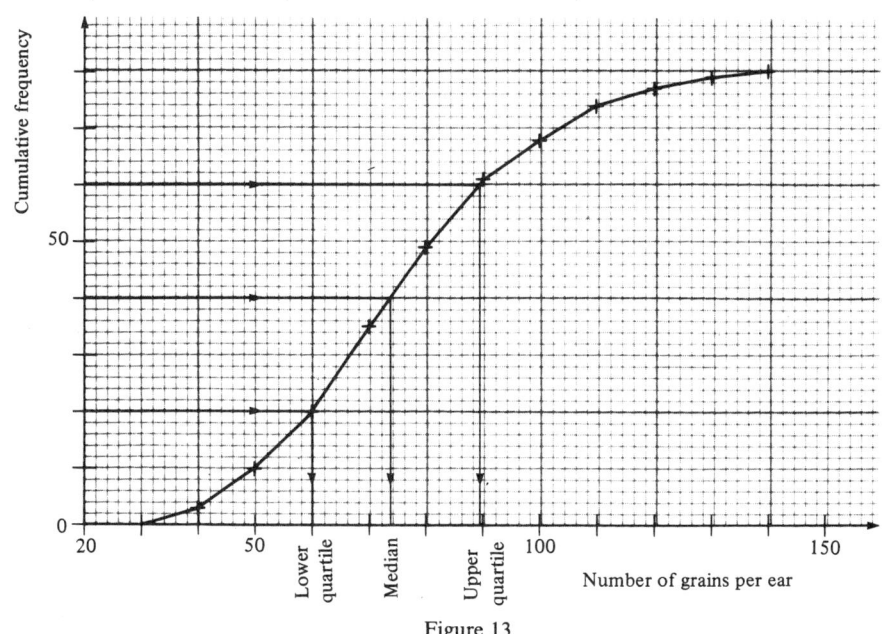

Figure 13

One-quarter (20) of the ears have fewer than 60 grains so the lower quartile is 60.

Half (40) of the ears have fewer than 74 grains so the median is 74.

Three-quarters (60) of the ears have fewer than 89 grains so the upper quartile is 89.

Exercise D

*1 Each member of a class was asked to telephone a friend at two stated times of day and count the number of rings before an answer was obtained. The results were as follows:

Number of rings	Frequency Time *A*	Frequency Time *B*
0–2	1	0
3–5	0	4
6–8	2	7
9–11	8	5
12–14	9	3
15–17	3	4
18–20	2	2

From a cumulative frequency diagram find the median number of rings at each time, and the inter-quartile range. Give possible reasons for the differences between the patterns.

2 Calculate the median and quartiles of the following distribution of weekly pocket money for a group of 100 fifth-formers.

Pocket money in pence	Frequency
20–39	1
40–59	11
60–79	10
80–99	9
100–119	41
120–139	6
140–159	15
160–179	3
180–199	1
200	3

(*a*) Account for the somewhat unusual distribution.

(*b*) There are about 700 pupils in the school. Make an estimate of the total amount received weekly in pocket money, noting any assumptions you have to make and any important reservations.

*3 (*a*) The marks out of 30 obtained by a fifth-form set on its half-term test were as follows:

```
        17  17  12   9  12   9   7  18  17   7  17  15
        10  11  17   6   6  17  14  12   9  10  13
```

Find (i) the median mark, (ii) the mean mark. Explain why, in general, the mean and the median will be different.

Under what circumstances will they be the same?

(b) The marks obtained by a parallel set B were as follows:

```
12  12   7  14  18  29  21  14  13   8   6   6  10
11  11  16  18  12  21  25          11  11  17  15
```

(i) Find the mean and median marks for set B. Which one will be more useful for making a rough comparison of the abilities of the two sets?

(ii) Group the information for each set separately taking intervals 6–8, 9–11, 12–14, etc. Hence draw cumulative graphs and comment on the differences between them.

4 A small set of pupils took weekly mathematics tests with the following results.

Pupil	A	B	C	D	E	F	G	H	I	J
Test 1	4	5	8	2	5	4	1	5	6	5
Test 2	5	5	9	4	6	3	0	7	4	6
Test 3	8	9	10	6	9	7	5	9	10	7
Test 4	3	4	6	2	4	4	2	5	4	4

(a) Find the range of marks for each test. What does the range tell you? Which test was the best at distinguishing the best pupil from the worst?

(b) Find the range of marks for each pupil. Does this tell you anything?

(c) Find the average mark for each test and the average mark for each pupil.

(d) Arrange the pupils in order of merit. Does it follow that a good pupil has a large mean and/or a large range, or vice versa?

5 A test of authorship is to select one of a number of known key words and count how many times it occurs in blocks of 100 words taken from different authors' writings. One such word (a so-called 'marker' word) is BOTH. The table shows the frequency distribution of this word for two authors in 15 groups of 100 words. (This is too few for actual diagnosis but will do to show the method.)

Times the word BOTH occurred in each group of 100 words	Frequency	
	Author A	Author B
0	4	1
1	5	3
2	3	1
3	1	6
4	2	3
5	0	1

(a) Draw a cumulative frequency graph for each author and find the median and inter-quartile range.
(b) Is the difference well marked?
(c) Carry out the experiment for yourself, or with a group. Other marker words are ENOUGH, WHICH, ALSO. Select fifteen groups of 100 words from different parts of the authors' works. Do the results seem to be consistent?

Summary Exercise

1 In an orchard containing 100 young apple trees, half of the trees were treated with a special chemical JXS. The yields from these trees are summarised in the frequency table below:

Yield (apples per tree)	0–4	5–9	10–14	15–19	20–24
Frequency (number of trees)	0	0	0	1	2
Yield (apples per tree)	25–29	30–34	35–39	40–44	45–49
Frequency (number of trees)	7	21	15	3	1

Table 1

The other 50 trees received no special treatment, and their individual yields were

27	18	30	13	17	36	24	42	15	22
26	28	43	21	2	11	28	25	34	14
8	30	19	30	23	25	32	16	23	26
20	33	24	17	13	38	6	20	19	39
13	19	27	16	32	25	48	10	24	29

(a) Calculate from Table 1 the mean yield of the treated trees.
(b) Compile a Table 2, with the same classes as Table 1, for the frequency of yields from the untreated trees.
(c) Illustrate the data of Tables 1 and 2 by frequency diagrams.
(d) Comment briefly on ways in which JXS appears to have had an effect. (The mean for Table 2 is 23.5 apples per tree.) (SMP O-level)

2 In an examination the candidates took two papers each marked out of 100. Figure 14 shows the cumulative frequency curves for the results of each paper.
(a) Estimate the median mark for each paper.
(b) Estimate the inter-quartile range for each paper.
(c) State with a reason which paper the candidates found more difficult.
(d) A candidate obtained 52 marks for Paper I but missed Paper II.
  (i) What percentage of candidates did no better than him on Paper I?
  (ii) Suggest what mark he could reasonably be given for Paper II.
(SMP O-Level)

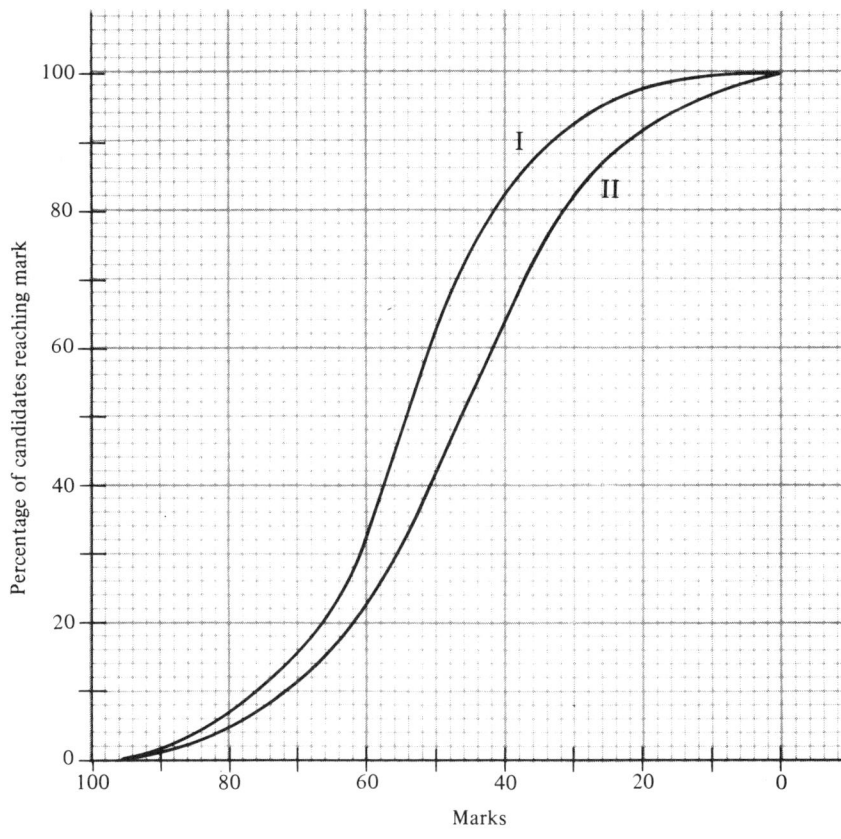

Figure 14

SUMMARY

The scientist and his new strain of maize

The aim of the scientist was to convince farmers in the developing country that they should sow his new strain.

He started by showing them the results of his experiment which consisted of counting the number of grains in 80 ears. He knew that he would need to illustrate his data (Section 1) and also simplify and organise it. This is what he did.

(a) He grouped his data in 10s (Section 2, Table 3).

(b) He drew a frequency diagram (Section 2, Figure 10). This he could compare with a similar diagram for the old strain of maize.

(c) He calculated three averages for his sample: median, arithmetic mean and mode (Section 3). These could be compared with the corresponding figures for the old strain.

(d) He calculated two measures of spread: range and inter-quartile range (Section 4). These also he could compare.

(*e*) He doubtless now asserted higher yield and more consistency.

His next step would certainly have been to find some measure of significance for the differences he found. 'Higher' and 'more' are vague terms. He would then have to repeat his experiment with further samples of 80. This would lead him to study theories of sampling and significance which are too complex for the present course.

6
Structure

1. ALGEBRAS

We have used letters to stand for numbers in ordinary algebra. At other times, letters have stood for transformations, matrices, functions, sets or vectors. Two transformations can be combined to make a third transformation; matrices can sometimes be added or multiplied; sets can be combined by the operations of union and intersection. So we have the ingredients of several algebras besides the familiar algebra based on the arithmetic of numbers. In this chapter we investigate these algebras – their differences and their similarities.

Exercise A

*1 If **Q** is the rotation of 90° about a point A, write down the single transformations equivalent to:
   (a) $\mathbf{Q}^4$; (b) $\mathbf{Q}^5$; (c) $\mathbf{Q}^{60}$; (d) $\mathbf{Q}^{89}$.

2 If $f(x) = 1 - \dfrac{1}{x}$, calculate:
   (a) $f(5)$; (b) $ff(5)$; (c) $fff(5)$.
   Hence write down the values of: (d) $f^{60}(5)$; (e) $f^{89}(5)$.

*3 If $\mathbf{M} = \begin{bmatrix} 3 & -2 \\ 5 & -3 \end{bmatrix}$, calculate:
   (a) $\mathbf{M}^2$; (b) $\mathbf{M}^3$; (c) $\mathbf{M}^4$; (d) $\mathbf{M}^5$.
   Hence write down the single matrices equivalent to:
   (e) $\mathbf{M}^{60}$; (f) $\mathbf{M}^{89}$.

4 Repeat question 3 for:
   (a) $\mathbf{M} = \begin{bmatrix} 2 & 1 \\ -7 & -3 \end{bmatrix}$; (b) $\mathbf{M} = \begin{bmatrix} -5 & -6 \\ 4 & 5 \end{bmatrix}$; (c) $\mathbf{M} = \begin{bmatrix} -2 & 1 \\ -7 & 3 \end{bmatrix}$;
   (d) $\mathbf{M} = \begin{bmatrix} 1 & 2 \\ 0 & 1 \end{bmatrix}$; (e) $\mathbf{M} = \begin{bmatrix} 0 & 2 \\ -2 & 2 \end{bmatrix}$.
   (In part (e), leave powers of 2 in your answers.)

*5 For the functions $f: x \to 2x - 2$ and $g: x \to 5x - 8$, find:
   (a) $fg(3)$; (b) $gf(3)$; (c) $fg(4)$; (d) $gf(4)$;
   (e) $fg(x)$; (f) $gf(x)$.

6 Repeat question 5 for the functions $f: x \to x - 5$ and $g: x \to x^2$.

*7 If $\mathbf{A} = \begin{bmatrix} 2 & 3 \\ 4 & 5 \end{bmatrix}$, $\mathbf{B} = \begin{bmatrix} 1 & 6 \\ 8 & 7 \end{bmatrix}$ and $\mathbf{C} = \begin{bmatrix} -1 & 4 \\ 6 & 2 \end{bmatrix}$, calculate:
   (a) **AB**; (b) **BA**; (c) **AC**; (d) **CA**; (e) **BC**; (f) **CB**.

2. COMBINATION TABLES

When the set we are considering has a fairly small number of members, it is convenient to show all the possible combinations of those elements in a table. For example, Tables 1 and 2 are the combination tables for addition and subtraction in arithmetic modulo 7. (Arithmetic in this system is carried out on a seven-hour clock, as shown in Figure 1, so that, for example, $5+4 = 2$ because 2 is four places round the 'clock' from 5.)

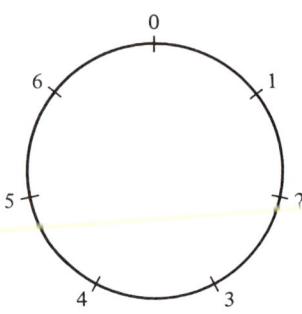

Figure 1

+ mod 7	0	1	2	3	4	5	6
0	0	1	2	3	4	5	6
1	1	2	3	4	5	6	0
2	2	3	4	5	6	0	1
3	3	4	5	6	0	1	2
4	4	5	6	0	1	2	3
5	5	6	0	1	2	3	4
6	6	0	1	2	3	4	5

Table 1

− mod 7	0	1	2	3	4	5	6
0	0	6	5	4	3	2	1
1	1	0	6	5	4	3	2
2	2	1	0	6	5	④	3
3	3	2	1	0	6	5	4
4	4	3	2	1	0	6	5
5	5	4	3	2	1	0	6
6	6	5	4	3	2	1	0

Table 2

Notice that the first element determines which row of the table to look at; the second element fixes the column. So the relation $2-5 = 4$ is shown by the ringed element in Table 2. This is important because the order in which we subtract two elements matters:
$$2-5 = 4 \quad \text{but} \quad 5-2 = 3.$$
For addition, the order does not matter. For example:
$$5+4 = 2 \quad \text{and} \quad 4+5 = 2.$$
For every pair of numbers a and b in Table 1, $a+b = b+a$. We say that addition modulo 7 is *commutative*.

Example 1

Solve, in arithmetic modulo 7, the equations: (*a*) $x+5 = 2$; (*b*) $3-x = 4$.

(a) By searching down the '5' column in Table 1, we find that $4+5 = 2$, so $x = 4$.

(b) By searching along the '3' row in Table 2, we find that $3-6 = 4$, so $x = 6$.

Exercise B

(Combination tables compiled in this exercise should be kept for use in Exercise C.)

*1 Copy and complete the following table for multiplication modulo 7. Is this multiplication commutative?

× mod 7	1	2	3	4	5	6
1					5	
2					3	
3	3	6	2	5	1	4
4					6	
5					4	
6					2	

Solve (a) $2x = 3$, (b) $3x = 2$, in arithmetic modulo 7.

2 If $x = 12$ and $y = 29$, calculate:
  (a) $x+y$; (b) $y+x$; (c) $x-y$; (d) $y-x$;
  (e) xy; (f) yx; (g) $x \div y$; (h) $y \div x$.
  Which of the operations, $+$, $-$, $\times$, $\div$, when used with numbers, are commutative? Which are not commutative?

*3 **X** = reflection in the *x*-axis,
  Y = reflection in the *y*-axis,
  H = rotation of 180° about (0, 0), and
  I = rotation of 360° about (0, 0).
  (a) Find the single transformations equivalent to:
    (i) **XY**; (ii) **YX**; (iii) **XH**; (iv) **HX**.
  (b) Compile a complete combination table for {**X, Y, H, I**}.
  (c) Solve, for **Q**, the equation **HQ** = **X**.

4 Compile a combination table for the following four isometries:
  Q = rotation of 90° about a point *A*,
  H = rotation of 180° about *A*,
  T = rotation of 270° about *A*, and
  W = rotation of 360° about *A*.
  Is combining these transformations a commutative operation?

*5 Copy and complete the following tables for intersection and union of sets:

∩	∅	{a}	{b}	{a, b}
∅				
{a}			{a}	
{b}				
{a, b}				

∪	∅	{a}	{b}	{a, b}
∅				
{a}				{a, b}
{b}				
{a, b}				

Are both operations commutative?

6 A penny and a 10p-piece are placed, heads up, side by side on a table. Four operations on them are defined as follows:
  I = leave them as they are,
  P = turn the penny over,
  T = turn the 10p-piece over, and
  B = turn both coins over.
  (a) What single operation is equivalent to **P** followed by **B**?
  (b) Compile a combination table for {I, P, T, B}.
  (c) Is combining these operations on the coins commutative?
  (d) Solve for **X**: **PX** = **T**.

*7 Anne, Bill and Catherine are standing in a line with Anne at the front, and Catherine at the back. Six rearrangements of this 'queue' are possible:
  P = interchange the front two people,
  Q = interchange the back two people,
  R = interchange the front person with the last person,
  S = move the last person to the front,
  T = move the front person to the back, and
  U = leave the order unchanged.
  (a) Which rearrangement is equivalent to the combination '**P** follows **R**'? Is this the same as '**R** follows **P**'?
  (b) Compile a table for the operation 'follows' on the set {P, Q, R, S, T, U}. Is the operation commutative?
  (c) Solve: '**Q** follows **X**' = **T**.

8 Compile a combination table for multiplication of the following four matrices:
$$\mathbf{I} = \begin{bmatrix} 1 & 0 \\ 0 & 1 \end{bmatrix}; \quad \mathbf{X} = \begin{bmatrix} 1 & 0 \\ 0 & -1 \end{bmatrix}; \quad \mathbf{Y} = \begin{bmatrix} -1 & 0 \\ 0 & 1 \end{bmatrix}; \quad \mathbf{H} = \begin{bmatrix} -1 & 0 \\ 0 & -1 \end{bmatrix}.$$
Is multiplication of these matrices commutative?

9 Compile a combination table for multiplication of the following eight matrices:
$$\mathbf{I} = \begin{bmatrix} 1 & 0 \\ 0 & 1 \end{bmatrix}; \quad \mathbf{X} = \begin{bmatrix} 1 & 0 \\ 0 & -1 \end{bmatrix}; \quad \mathbf{Y} = \begin{bmatrix} -1 & 0 \\ 0 & 1 \end{bmatrix}; \quad \mathbf{H} = \begin{bmatrix} -1 & 0 \\ 0 & -1 \end{bmatrix};$$
$$\mathbf{Q} = \begin{bmatrix} 0 & -1 \\ 1 & 0 \end{bmatrix}; \quad \mathbf{T} = \begin{bmatrix} 0 & 1 \\ -1 & 0 \end{bmatrix}; \quad \mathbf{M} = \begin{bmatrix} 0 & 1 \\ 1 & 0 \end{bmatrix}; \quad \mathbf{N} = \begin{bmatrix} 0 & -1 \\ -1 & 0 \end{bmatrix}.$$
Is multiplication of these matrices commutative?

10 (a) If $f(x) = 4x - 6$ and $g(x) = 3x - 4$, show that $fg(x) = gf(x)$.
   (b) If also $h(x) = 2x - 3$, show that $fh(x) \neq hf(x)$.

3. IDENTITY AND INVERSE

In addition modulo 7, adding 0 makes no difference. Multiplying a (2 row, 2 column) matrix **M** by $\begin{bmatrix} 1 & 0 \\ 0 & 1 \end{bmatrix}$ leaves the matrix **M** unchanged. Combining any transformation **T** and a rotation of 360° is equivalent to **T**. These three elements – 0, $\begin{bmatrix} 1 & 0 \\ 0 & 1 \end{bmatrix}$, rotation of 360° – are all examples of *identity elements*. Combining any element with the identity leaves the element unchanged.

Comparison of Tables 1 and 2 on page 138 shows that there is a special relationship between the numbers 2 and 5: the column for 2 in one table is the same as the column for 5 in the other table. This is because $5 + 2 = 2 + 5 = 0$

Identity and inverse   141

(mod 7), which means that adding 5 and then adding 2 (in either order) is equivalent to adding 0, that is, leaving every element unchanged. Adding 5 is therefore equivalent to subtracting 2, and vice versa.

A pair such as 5 and 2 which combine to give the identity for a particular operation is called an *inverse pair*: 5 is the inverse of 2, and 2 is the inverse of 5.

Example 2
For the operation of addition of (2 row, 2 column) matrices:
(a) write down the identity;
(b) find the inverse of $\begin{bmatrix} 1 & -3 \\ 2 & 4 \end{bmatrix}$.

(a) We require a matrix **Z** such that $\mathbf{Z}+\mathbf{M}=\mathbf{M}$ for any matrix **M**. Clearly
$$\mathbf{Z} = \begin{bmatrix} 0 & 0 \\ 0 & 0 \end{bmatrix}.$$
(b) We must find a matrix **M** such that
$$\mathbf{M} + \begin{bmatrix} 1 & -3 \\ 2 & 4 \end{bmatrix} = \begin{bmatrix} 1 & -3 \\ 2 & 4 \end{bmatrix} + \mathbf{M} = \begin{bmatrix} 0 & 0 \\ 0 & 0 \end{bmatrix}$$
from which we deduce that $\mathbf{M} = \begin{bmatrix} -1 & 3 \\ -2 & -4 \end{bmatrix}$.

Example 3
Find f^{-1} if (a) $f:x \to 2x+3$;   (b) $f:x \to 6-x$.

(a) f can be represented by the flow chart

x —[Multiply by 2]— $2x$ —[Add 3]— $2x+3$

The inverse function is given by the flow chart

x —[Subtract 3]— $x-3$ —[Divide by 2]— $\dfrac{x-3}{2}$

since combining these two is equivalent to the identity function. So $f^{-1}: x \to \dfrac{x-3}{2}$.

(b) In this case f can be represented by the flow chart

x —[Change sign]— ^-x —[Add 6]— $^-x+6 = 6-x$

(Remember that 'change sign' is equivalent to 'multiply by $^-1$'.)
f^{-1} is therefore given by the flow chart

x —[Subtract 6]— $x-6$ —[Change sign]— $^-(x-6)$

So $f^{-1}(x) = {^-}(x-6) = {^-}x+6 = 6-x$.
In this case f^{-1} is the same as f, so f is said to be *self-inverse*.

Inverses are particularly useful when solving equations. For example, to solve the equation $x+5 = 1 \pmod 7$ we can add 2 to both sides, since adding 2 is the same as subtracting 5:
$$\begin{aligned} & x+5 = 1 && \pmod 7 \\ \Rightarrow\; & x+5+2 = 1+2 && \pmod 7 \\ \Rightarrow\; & x+0 = 3 && \pmod 7 \\ \Rightarrow\; & x = 3 && \pmod 7 \end{aligned}$$

Example 4

Solve the matrix equation $\begin{bmatrix} 3 & 1 \\ 7 & 4 \end{bmatrix} \mathbf{X} = \begin{bmatrix} 5 & -4 \\ 10 & -1 \end{bmatrix}$.

The inverse (for multiplication) of the matrix $\begin{bmatrix} 3 & 1 \\ 7 & 4 \end{bmatrix}$ is $\begin{bmatrix} 0.8 & -0.2 \\ -1.4 & 0.6 \end{bmatrix}$, so we multiply both sides of the equation by this matrix:
$$\begin{bmatrix} 0.8 & -0.2 \\ -1.4 & 0.6 \end{bmatrix} \begin{bmatrix} 3 & 1 \\ 7 & 4 \end{bmatrix} \mathbf{X} = \begin{bmatrix} 0.8 & -0.2 \\ -1.4 & 0.6 \end{bmatrix} \begin{bmatrix} 5 & -4 \\ 10 & -1 \end{bmatrix}$$
$$\begin{bmatrix} 1 & 0 \\ 0 & 1 \end{bmatrix} \mathbf{X} = \begin{bmatrix} 2 & -3 \\ -1 & 5 \end{bmatrix}$$
$$\mathbf{X} = \begin{bmatrix} 2 & -3 \\ -1 & 5 \end{bmatrix}$$

Exercise C

*1 Use your table from Exercise B, question 1, to write down the identity and all the inverse pairs for multiplication modulo 7. Does every element have an inverse?

2 Compile a combination table for $\{2, 4, 6, 8\}$ under multiplication modulo 10. What is the identity? What is the inverse of 8?

3–9 Write down the identity and list each element and its inverse for the sets and operations described in Exercise B, questions 3–9.

10 Solve the equations
    (a) $4x = 3 \pmod 7$, (b) $2x = 5 \pmod 7$,
    (i) by inspection of the table compiled in Exercise B, question 1;
    (ii) by using inverses.

11 In the set $\{P, Q, R, S, T, U\}$ described in Exercise B, question 7, solve the following equations for X:
    (a) 'P follows X' = S;
    (b) 'X follows P' = S.

*12 If $f(x) = 3x+2$ and $g(x) = x-5$,
    (a) find $fg(x)$ and $(fg)^{-1}(x)$;
    (b) find $f^{-1}(x)$, $g^{-1}(x)$, $f^{-1}g^{-1}(x)$, and $g^{-1}f^{-1}(x)$;
    (c) is $(fg)^{-1}$ the same as $f^{-1}g^{-1}$ or $g^{-1}f^{-1}$, or neither? Is this always the case?

13 (a) If $g(x) = 3x-7$, find $g^{-1}(x)$ and $g^{-1}(6x+2)$.
    (b) If also $gf(x) = 6x+2$, find $f(x)$.

*14 If $\mathbf{A} = \begin{bmatrix} 2 & 3 \\ 4 & 5 \end{bmatrix}$ and $\mathbf{B} = \begin{bmatrix} 5 & 2 \\ -3 & -1 \end{bmatrix}$, calculate:
    (a) $\mathbf{AB}$; (b) $\mathbf{BA}$; (c) $\mathbf{A}^{-1}$; (d) $\mathbf{B}^{-1}$; (e) $(\mathbf{AB})^{-1}$; (f) $(\mathbf{BA})^{-1}$; (g) $\mathbf{A}^{-1}\mathbf{B}^{-1}$; (h) $\mathbf{B}^{-1}\mathbf{A}^{-1}$.
Which two pairs are equal? Is this always the case?

15 Solve the equations:

(a) $\begin{bmatrix} 2 & 1 \\ 5 & 3 \end{bmatrix} \mathbf{X} = \begin{bmatrix} -2 & 8 \\ -7 & 21 \end{bmatrix}$; (b) $\mathbf{Y} \begin{bmatrix} 2 & 1 \\ 5 & 3 \end{bmatrix} = \begin{bmatrix} -2 & 8 \\ -7 & 21 \end{bmatrix}$.

16 What happens if you try to solve $\begin{bmatrix} 2 & 3 \\ 4 & 6 \end{bmatrix} \mathbf{X} = \begin{bmatrix} 1 & 7 \\ 5 & 9 \end{bmatrix}$?

4. GROUPS

Table 3 is a combination table for an (imaginary) operation $*$ on the set $\{a, b, c, d, e, f\}$. You will notice that the operation is commutative, that e is the identity, and that every element is self-inverse, except for the inverse pair (c, d).

$*$	a	b	c	d	e	f
a	e	c	d	f	a	b
b	c	e	f	a	b	d
c	d	f	b	e	c	a
d	f	a	e	b	d	c
e	a	b	c	d	e	f
f	b	d	a	c	f	e

Table 3

Suppose that we try to solve the equation $d * x = a$. The inverse of d is c, so we 'multiply' both sides on the left by c.

$$d * x = a$$
$$c * d * x = c * a$$
$$e * x = d$$
$$x = d$$

But if we check this, we discover that
$$x = d \Rightarrow d * x = d * d = b,$$
so $x = d$ is not the solution to the equation. Examination of the table shows that $d * b = a$, so the solution is $x = b$. What has gone wrong?

There is one hidden assumption in our method: that the operation $*$ is *associative*. We started by 'multiplying' both sides by c, thus obtaining, on the left-hand side $c * (d * x)$. We then assumed that this was the same as $(c * d) * x = e * x$.
But
$$c * (d * b) = c * a = d$$
and
$$(c * d) * b = e * b = b$$
so we cannot assume that, in general, $c * (d * x) = (c * d) * x$.

If, for every choice of elements a, b and c,
$$a * (b * c) = (a * b) * c$$
then the operation $*$ is said to be *associative*. Many of the operations we have been using (addition of numbers, combining functions, multiplying matrices, for example) are associative, but the operation $*$ in Table 3 is not associative.

For our method of equation-solving to work properly, we need the following properties:

(1) the operation is associative;
(2) there is an identity;
(3) each element has an inverse.

It is not necessary for the operation to be commutative. There is, however, one last property we have assumed:

(4) the set is *closed* under the operation.

This means that whenever we combine two elements of the set we obtain another element of the set. For example, the set {positive integers} is closed under addition and multiplication but not under subtraction or division. ($2-5$, and $2 \div 5$ are not positive integers, for example.)

If a set and an operation have all of these four properties then the set is called a *group* under the operation. In a group all equations of the form $a * x = b$ have unique solutions.

Exercise D

*1 $a \sim b$ means 'the positive difference between a and b' (so that, for example, $3 \sim 8 = 5$).
   (a) Is {positive integers} closed under $\sim$?
   (b) Is $\sim$ commutative?
   (c) Is $\sim$ associative?

2 If a and b are whole numbers, let $a * b$ mean 'the average of a and b'.
   (a) Is {whole numbers} closed under the operation $*$?
   (b) Is the operation commutative?
   (c) Is the operation associative?

3 If a and b are whole numbers, let $a * b$ mean 'the highest common factor of a and b'.
   (a) Calculate: (i) $30 * 42$; (ii) $(30 * 42) * 70$; (iii) $30 * (42 * 70)$.
   (b) Is $*$ (i) commutative; (ii) associative? Can you prove your assertions?

*4 Investigate whether the following sets of transformations are closed under the operation 'followed by':
    (a) {translations}; (b) {reflections}; (c) {rotations}.
    For which sets is the operation: (i) commutative; (ii) associative?

5 If $x = 60$, $y = 30$ and $z = 6$, find:
   (a) $x+(y+z)$; (b) $(x+y)+z$; (c) $x-(y-x)$; (d) $(x-y)-z$;
   (e) $x \times (y \times z)$; (f) $(x \times y) \times z$; (g) $x \div (y \div z)$; (h) $(x \div y) \div z$.
   Comment on your answers.

6 If $P = \{2, 4, 6, 8, 10\}$, $Q = \{1, 2, 3, 6, 12\}$ and $R = \{2, 3, 6, 10\}$, find:
   (a) $P \cap (Q \cap R)$; (b) $(P \cap Q) \cap R$; (c) $P \cup (Q \cup R)$; (d) $(P \cup Q) \cup R$.
   Comment on your answers.

7 If $L = \begin{bmatrix} 1 & 2 \\ 3 & 4 \end{bmatrix}$, $M = \begin{bmatrix} 5 & 0 \\ -2 & 2 \end{bmatrix}$, and $N = \begin{bmatrix} 6 & -1 \\ 3 & 3 \end{bmatrix}$, find:
   (a) $L+(M+N)$; (b) $(L+M)+N$; (c) $L(MN)$; (d) $(LM)N$.
   Comment on your answers.

5. TWO OPERATIONS

When two operations are defined on a set, we need to agree about their priority, and investigate how they interact. In the case of addition and multiplication of numbers, the convention is that

$$2+3 \times 4 \text{ means } 2+(3 \times 4) = 14$$

and that

$$2 \times 3+4 \text{ means } (2 \times 3)+4 = 10,$$

that is, we give priority to multiplication. (Does your calculator agree?)

There is no comparable convention for $P \cup Q \cap R$, so brackets have to be used to make it clear whether we are talking about $P \cup (Q \cap R)$ or $(P \cup Q) \cap R$.

We also notice that

$$2 \times (3+4) = (2 \times 3)+(2 \times 4) \quad \text{and} \quad (3+4) \times 2 = (3 \times 2)+(4 \times 2)$$

or, in general,

$$a \times (b+c) = (a \times b)+(a \times c) \quad \text{and} \quad (b+c) \times a = (b \times a)+(c \times a)$$

for any numbers a, b and c.

We say that multiplication is *distributive* over addition. This property of this pair of operations enables us to 'multiply out' algebraic expressions. Other properties enable us to simplify the resulting expression.

$$\begin{align}
(2a+3)(5a+1) &= (2a+3)\,5a+(2a+3)\,1 \tag{1}\\
&= (2a+3)\,5a+(2a+3) \tag{2}\\
&= (2a \times 5a+3 \times 5a)+(2a+3) \tag{3}\\
&= (10a^2+15a)+(2a+3) \tag{4}\\
&= 10a^2+(15a+2a)+3 \tag{5}\\
&= 10a^2+17a+3 \tag{6}
\end{align}$$

In step (1) we have used the distributive law,
in step (2) the fact that 1 is the identity for multiplication,
in step (3) the distributive law,
in step (4) the commutative and associative laws for multiplication,
in step (5) the associative law for addition, and
in step (6) the distributive law 'in reverse':

$$15a+2a = (15+2)\,a = 17a.$$

Exercise E

*1 Without using a calculator, and showing intermediate steps, find:
   (a) $2 \times (37-19)$; (b) $(2 \times 37)-(2 \times 19)$;
   (c) $(37-19) \times 2$; (d) $(37 \times 2)-(19 \times 2)$.
   Comment on your answers.

2 If $P = \{2, 4, 6, 8, 10\}$, $Q = \{1, 2, 3, 6, 12\}$ and $R = \{2, 3, 6, 10\}$ list the following sets:
   (a) $Q \cup R$; (b) $P \cap (Q \cup R)$; (c) $P \cap Q$; (d) $P \cap R$;
   (e) $(P \cap Q) \cup (P \cap R)$.
   Comment on your answers.

3 For the sets given in question 2, find:
   (a) $Q \cap R$; (b) $P \cup (Q \cap R)$; (c) $P \cup Q$; (d) $P \cup R$;
   (e) $(P \cup Q) \cap (P \cup R)$.
   Comment on your answers.

4 If $x = 20$, $y = 25$ and $z = 5$, calculate:

(a) $\dfrac{x+y}{z}$; (b) $\dfrac{x}{z} + \dfrac{y}{z}$; (c) $\dfrac{z}{x+y}$; (d) $\dfrac{z}{x} + \dfrac{z}{y}$.

Is it true or false that: (i) $(x+y) \div z = (x \div z) + (y \div z)$;
(ii) $z : (x+y) = (z \div x) + (z \div y)$?

*5 If $L = \begin{bmatrix} 1 & 2 \\ 3 & 4 \end{bmatrix}$, $M = \begin{bmatrix} 5 & 0 \\ -2 & 2 \end{bmatrix}$ and $N = \begin{bmatrix} 6 & -1 \\ 6 & 3 \end{bmatrix}$, find:

(a) $M+N$; (b) $L(M+N)$; (c) LM; (d) LN; (e) $LM+LN$.
Comment on your answers.

6 For the matrices of question 5, find:

(a) $L+M$; (b) $(L+M)N$; (c) MN; (d) $LN+MN$.
Comment on your answers.

7 (a) Multiply out $(a+b)(a-b)$.

(b) If $A = \begin{bmatrix} 1 & 2 \\ 3 & 4 \end{bmatrix}$ and $B = \begin{bmatrix} 3 & 0 \\ 2 & -1 \end{bmatrix}$, find:

(i) $A+B$; (ii) $A-B$; (iii) $(A+B)(A-B)$;
(iv) A^2; (v) B^2; (vi) $A^2 - B^2$.

The answers to (iii) and (vi) are different because matrix operations do not have one property. Which property?

6. SETS OF NUMBERS

If we start with the *natural numbers* $\mathbb{N} = \{1, 2, 3, 4, ...\}$ then different extensions of this set ensure that different types of equations always have solutions.

The equation $x+5 = 8$ has a solution in $\mathbb{N}$, but $x+8 = 5$ does not. If we extend $\mathbb{N}$ to the *integers*, $\mathbb{Z} = \{0, 1, ^-1, 2, ^-2, 3, ^-3, ...\}$, then every equation of the form $x+a = b$, where a and b are integers, has a solution in $\mathbb{Z}$.

The equation $2x = ^-10$ has a solution in $\mathbb{Z}$, but $^-10x = 2$ does not. Extending $\mathbb{Z}$ to the *rationals*, $\mathbb{Q} = \{0, 1, ^-1, 2, ^-2, \frac{1}{2}, ^-\frac{1}{2}, 3, ^-3, \frac{1}{3}, ^-\frac{1}{3}, \frac{2}{3}, ^-\frac{2}{3}, ...\}$, enables us to solve all equations of the form $ax = b$, with $a, b \in \mathbb{Q}$ and $a \neq 0$, since a always has an inverse under multiplication. In fact, all equations $ax+b = c$ ($a, b, c \in \mathbb{Q}$, $a \neq 0$) have a solution in $\mathbb{Q}$.

Between any two rational numbers, such as $\frac{3}{4}$ and $2\frac{1}{2}$, there is always their mean ($1\frac{5}{8}$ in this case). However close two rational numbers may be, there are thus always many other rationals between them. So the whole of the number line is packed with rational numbers. Yet it can be shown that numbers such as $\sqrt{2}$ are not rational (see Miscellaneous exercise, question 6). Also, somewhere between 3.1 and 3.2 there is another number π which is also irrational. So there must be a few 'gaps' between the rational numbers, although it is hard to imagine how there can be. Just a few gaps? Well, infinitely many – and infinitely many more gaps than there are rational numbers!

Extending $\mathbb{Q}$ to 'all decimals', to include numbers such as $\sqrt{2}$ and π, gives us $\mathbb{R}$, the *real numbers*, represented by the number line. But some relatively simple equations, such as $x^2 = ^-1$ still have no solution in $\mathbb{R}$, so we need to extend again. The next extension gives us *complex numbers*, which need a plane, rather than just a line, to represent them.

Will the process ever stop? From the point of view of equation-solving, we need to go no further, since every polynomial equation has a solution in complex numbers.

Exercise F

*1 Solve the following equations (i) in $\mathbb{N}$; (ii) in $\mathbb{Q}$; (iii) in arithmetic modulo 7.
(a) $2x = 6$; (b) $2x = 3$; (c) $(2x+3)(x-3) = 0$;
(d) $x^2 = 4$; (e) $4x^2 = 1$; (f) $x^2 = 2$.

2 If $a \sim b$ means 'the positive difference between a and b', solve the following equations (i) in $\mathbb{N}$; (ii) in $\mathbb{Z}$; (iii) in arithmetic modulo 7.
(a) $x \sim 2 = 1$; (b) $x \sim 3 = 5$.

SUMMARY

A set of elements $S = \{a, b, c, ...\}$ combined by some operation $*$ may have the following useful properties:

Commutative: $a * b = b * a$ for all $a, b \in S$
Identity: an element I such that
                   $a * I = I * a = a$ for all $a \in S$
Inverses: b is the inverse of $a \Leftrightarrow a * b = b * a = I$
Associative: $a * (b * c) = (a * b) * c$ for all $a, b, c * S$
Closure: $a * b \in S$ for all $a, b \in S$ (Sections 2, 3, 4)

If the operation $*$ is associative, the set S is closed under $*$, there is an identity, and every element has an inverse, then S is a group.

In a group, the equation $a * x = b$ has a unique solution, obtained by 'multiplying' both sides by the inverse of a.   (Section 3, 4)

When there are two operations defined on S, one operation may be distributive over the other. For example, multiplication is distributive over addition:
$$a(b+c) = ab+ac \quad \text{and} \quad (b+c)a = ba+ca.$$
(Section 5)

Sets of numbers:
Natural numbers $\mathbb{N} = \{1, 2, 3, 4, 5, ...\}$
Integers $\mathbb{Z} = \{0, 1, {}^-1, 2, {}^-2, ...\}$
Rational numbers $\mathbb{Q} = \{0, 1, {}^-1, \frac{1}{2}, \frac{-1}{2}, 2, {}^-2, \frac{1}{3}, \frac{-1}{3}, \frac{2}{3}, \frac{-2}{3}, ...\}$
Real numbers $\mathbb{R} = \{\text{all decimals}\}$

(Section 6)

Set	Operation	Commutative?	Associative?	Identity	Inverses	Distributive?
Numbers	+	Yes	Yes	0	Yes; ^-a is the inverse of a	$\times$ is distributive over +
	$\times$	Yes	Yes	1	Yes, for non-zero numbers; $\frac{1}{a}$ is the inverse of a	
Matrices $\begin{bmatrix} a & b \\ c & d \end{bmatrix}$	+	Yes	Yes	$\begin{bmatrix} 0 & 0 \\ 0 & 0 \end{bmatrix}$	Yes; $\begin{bmatrix} ^-a & ^-c \\ ^-b & ^-d \end{bmatrix}$	$\cdot$ is distributive over +
	$\cdot$	No	Yes	$\begin{bmatrix} 1 & 0 \\ 0 & 1 \end{bmatrix}$	Only if $ad-bc \neq 0$	
Sets	$\cup$	Yes	Yes	$\emptyset$	No	$\cup$ is distributive over $\cap$
	$\cap$	Yes	Yes	$\mathscr{E}$	No	$\cap$ is distributive over $\cup$
Transformations	'follows'	No	Yes	I	Yes	—
Functions	'follows'	No	Yes	$x \to x$	For some	—

Summary exercise

1 $a * b$ denotes the remainder when the product $a \times b$ is divided by 11.
   (a) Evaluate $4 * 5$.
   (b) Find an integer y such that $8 * y = 1$. (SMP O-level)

2 The operation **P** applied to a square of card $ABCD$ (lettered as shown in Figure 2) means 'rotate through 90° *clockwise* about the centre'. The operation **Q** means 'turn over about whichever diagonal is running from bottom left to top right'. The results of **P** and **Q** are shown in Figure 2. **PQ** means 'do **Q**, then **P**'.

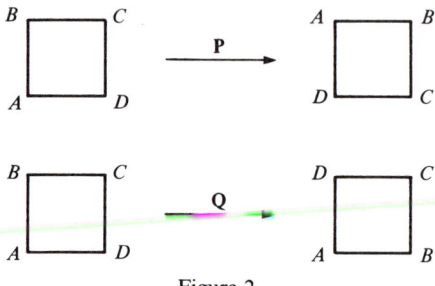

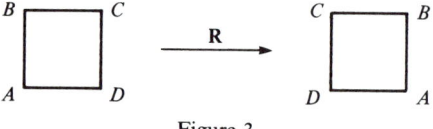

Figure 2

   (a) Draw similar pairs of diagrams to illustrate the effect of **P²**, **PQ**.
   (b) What is the lowest positive integer k for which $\mathbf{P}^k = \mathbf{I}$, where **I** is the identity operation which leaves $ABCD$ unchanged?
   (c) Show that $\mathbf{P^2Q} = \mathbf{QP^2}$.
   (d) The result of a third operation **R** is as shown in Figure 3. Express **R** in terms of **P** and **Q**. (SMP O-level)

Figure 3

3 The combination table for a set of four elements $\{a, b, c, d\}$ under the operation $*$ is given in Table 4.

*	a	b	c	d
a	b	c	a	d
b	c	d	b	a
c	a	b	c	d
d	d	a	d	c

Table 4

   (a) State the identity element.
   (b) State the inverses of a and of d.
   (c) Is the operation commutative?
   (d) By considering $a * b * d$ show that the set is *not* associative under $*$.
   (SMP O-level)

Summary

4 In this question '$\frac{1}{3} \oplus \frac{1}{4}$ of a cake' means 'the fraction of a cake formed by taking $\frac{1}{3}$ of a cake and then $\frac{1}{4}$ of what is left'.
  Thus $\frac{1}{3} \oplus \frac{1}{4} = \frac{1}{3} + (\frac{1}{4}$ of $\frac{2}{3}) = \frac{1}{2}$.
  (a) Simplify $\frac{1}{4} \oplus \frac{1}{3}$ of a cake.
  (b) Evaluate (i) $\frac{1}{2} \oplus \frac{1}{5}$, (ii) $\frac{1}{5} \oplus \frac{1}{2}$.
  (c) Use your answers to (a) and (b) to suggest a property of the operation $\oplus$.
  (d) Evaluate (i) $\frac{1}{2} \oplus (\frac{1}{3} \oplus \frac{1}{4})$, (ii) $(\frac{1}{2} \oplus \frac{1}{3}) \oplus \frac{1}{4}$, and comment on your answers.
  (e) Evaluate $\frac{1}{p} \oplus \frac{1}{q}$. (SMP O-level)

Miscellaneous exercise

1 Compile combination tables for the following:
  (a) {1, 2, 3, 4} under multiplication mod 5;
  (b) {1, 3, 7, 9} under multiplication mod 10;
  (c) {0, 1, 2, 3} under addition mod 4.
  Compare the patterns of the tables in (a) and (b). Can you change the order of the elements in (c) to produce the same pattern?

2 There are six symmetry operations on an equilateral triangle as illustrated in Figure 4. Construct a combination table for these transformations under 'follows'; compare with the table for Exercise B, question 7.

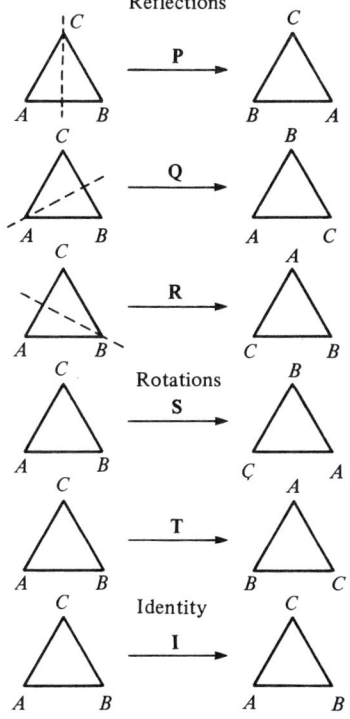

Figure 4

3 (a) By denoting Sunday by 1, Monday by 2, etc., explain how the question 'If it will be Monday in four days' time, what day is it today?' can be replaced by the equation $x+4 = 2 \pmod 7$. Solve the equation and answer the question.
   (b) If the day after three days before yesterday is Saturday, what day of the week is it today?
   (c) January 1st 1900 was a Monday. What day of the week was:
   (i) January 1st 1901;
   (ii) January 1st 1904;
   (iii) February 29th 1904;
   (iv) January 1st 1940;
   (v) the birthday of Albert Einstein, March 14th, 1879;
   (vi) your birthday?
   (1900 was not a leap year.)

4 (a) Calculate $x^7 \pmod 7$ for $x = 1, 2, 3, 4, 5, 6$. What do you notice?
   (b) Calculate $x^6 \pmod 6$ for $x = 1, 2, 3, 4, 5$.
   (c) Read Program 1 and explain what is being calculated. Run the program for a variety of values of N and comment on your results.

```
 10    INPUT N
 20    FOR X = 1 TO N-1
 30        LET A = X
 40        FOR I = 2 TO N
 50            LET A = A*X
 60            IF A<N THEN GOTO 90
 70            LET A = A - N
 80            GOTO 60
 90        NEXT I
100        PRINT X, A
110    NEXT X
120    END
```
Program 1

5 (a) Explain why $10^n = 1 \pmod 9$ for any positive integer n.
   (b) Use your answer to (a) to explain the test for divisibility for 9: a number is divisible by 9 if and only if the sum of its digits is divisible by 9.

6 Suppose that there are integers p, q such that $p^2 = 2q^2$. Consider the prime factorisations of p and q.
   (a) If $p = 2^a \times 3^b \times \ldots$ and $q = 2^A \times 3^B \times \ldots$, show that $2a = 2A+1$.
   (b) Explain why it is impossible that such integers a and A should exist. Deduce that integers p and q with $p^2 = 2q^2$ cannot exist.
   (c) Deduce that $\sqrt 2$ is irrational (that is, there is no fraction equal to $\sqrt 2$).
   (d) Can you adapt this proof to show which natural numbers have rational square roots?

REVISION EXERCISE 4

1. Write down the inverse of the matrix $\begin{bmatrix} 3 & -4 \\ 5 & -7 \end{bmatrix}$ and hence solve the equations
$$3x - 4y = 7$$
$$5x - 7y = 11.$$

2. Consider the sequence $(1), (3+5), (7+9+11), \ldots$
   (a) State the numbers in the next bracket.
   (b) For the second bracket $3+5 = 8$, for the third bracket $7+9+11 = 27$, and so on. State the total of the numbers in the tenth bracket. (SMP O-level)

3. Find the single transformation equivalent to reflection in the line $y = x - 1$ followed by reflection in the line $x = 3$. (Consider the image of a simple figure, or use a general property of reflections.)

4. Find the distance between the points (in three-dimensional space) with coordinates $(1, -4, 7)$ and $(3, 6, -4)$.

5. There are 13 girls and 14 boys in form 5Z. If two pupils are chosen at random from the form, what is the probability that they are of different sexes?

6. AB is one side of a regular polygon drawn with its vertices on a circle centre O. X is another vertex of the polygon. If $\angle AXB = 12°$, what is the size of $\angle AOB$? How many sides does the polygon have?

7. Figure 1 shows a speed–time graph for the motion of a train. How far did it travel in the first 8 minutes?

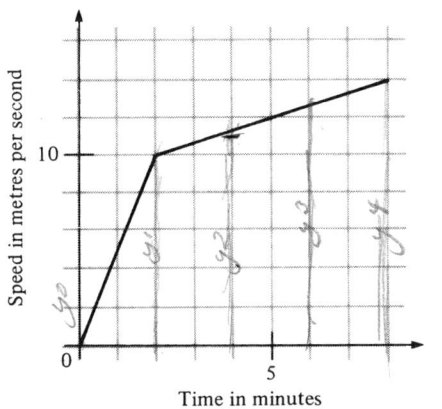

Figure 1

8. Kuching, Sarawak, is at latitude 3° N and longitude 110° E; Leticia, Colombia, is at latitude 3° S and longitude 70° W; Cape Cod, Massachusetts, is at latitude 42° N and longitude 70° W. Taking the earth to be a sphere and the length of the equator to be 40 000 km, find in kilometres the shortest distance on the earth's surface
   (a) between Kuching and Leticia;
   (b) between Kuching and Cape Cod. (SMP O-level)

REVISION EXERCISE 5

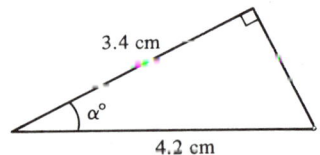

Figure 2

1. Calculate the angle $\alpha°$ marked in Figure 2.
2. Each angle of a regular polygon is 160°. How many sides does the polygon have?

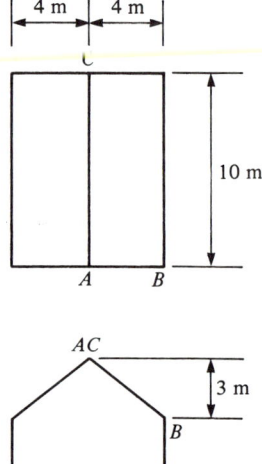

Figure 3

3. For the house in the plan and elevation shown in Figure 3, calculate:
   (a) the distance from A to B;
   (b) the angle ABC;
   (c) the distance from B to C. (SMP O-level)
4. The transformations **M** and **T** are defined by:
$$\mathbf{M}: \begin{bmatrix} x \\ y \end{bmatrix} \rightarrow \begin{bmatrix} 0 & 1 \\ 1 & 0 \end{bmatrix}\begin{bmatrix} x \\ y \end{bmatrix} \quad \mathbf{T}: \begin{bmatrix} x \\ y \end{bmatrix} \rightarrow \begin{bmatrix} x \\ y \end{bmatrix} + \begin{bmatrix} -2 \\ 2 \end{bmatrix}$$
   (a) Find the images of $A(3, 5)$ and $B(4, 0)$ under **TM**.
   (b) **TM** is equivalent to reflection in a line l. Find the equation of l.
5. Which is more probable: a total score of 9 when two dice are thrown, or three 'heads' when tossing a coin three times? Why?

6 Draw a network with route matrix

$$\begin{array}{c} \begin{array}{ccc} P & Q & R \end{array} \\ \begin{array}{c} P \\ Q \\ R \end{array}\left[\begin{array}{ccc} 0 & 1 & 2 \\ 1 & 2 & 0 \\ 2 & 0 & 2 \end{array}\right]. \end{array}$$

7 Which of the following statements are implied by the statement 'All Fridays are holidays' and which are not?
    (a) All Fridays are not holidays.
    (b) All holidays are Fridays.
    (c) Not all holidays are Fridays.
    (d) A day that is not a holiday is not a Friday.   (SMP O-level)

8 If x is a real number, which of the following are true and which are false?
    (a) $x = 1 \Rightarrow (x+1)(x-1) = 0$.
    (b) $(x+1)(x-1) = 0 \Rightarrow x = 1$.
    (c) $x > 3 \Rightarrow x^2 > 9$.
    (d) $(x+1)(x-1) < 0 \Rightarrow x < {}^-1$ or $x > 1$.

REVISION EXERCISE 6

1 Figure 4 shows a cuboid of height 1.2 m whose base is a rectangle of length 3.0 m and width 2.0 m. Calculate:
    (a) the length of the diagonal AG;
    (b) the angle between AG and the face $BCGF$.

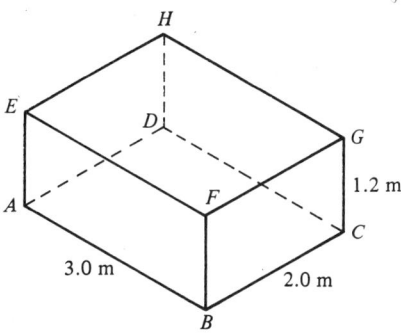

Figure 4

2 Find all numbers x between 0 and 360 for which $5 \sin x° = 3$. (Give your answers to the nearest integer.)

3 If t is inversely proportional to v and $t = 12$ when $v = 30$, find t when $v = 18$. Find an equation connecting t and v.

4 A pigeon flies from a hill at grid reference 341157 to a dovecote at 672913. How far has it flown (in a straight line), and on what bearing?
    (A grid reference of 341157 is equivalent to cartesian coordinates (34.1, 15.7), the units being kilometres. Bearings are measured clockwise from north.)

5 The number of frogs in the marshes of Palusia is increasing at the rate of 8% per year.

(a) By what percentage does the frog population increase in five years?
(b) If there were 10 000 frogs in the marshes in 1980, when will there first be more than 20 000 frogs there?

6 Sketch the graph of $y = (x+2)(x-3)$. For what values of x is $(x+2)(x-3) < 0$?
7 Write down the matrices representing the transformations illustrated in Figure 5.

(a)
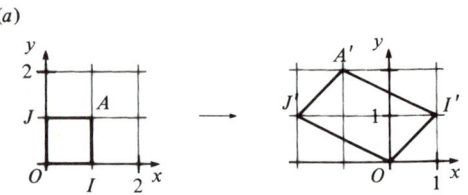

(b)
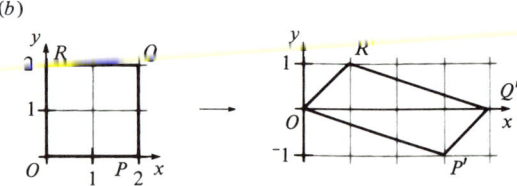

Figure 5

8 Solve the equation $(x+5)^2 = (x-3)^2$.

7

Equations, inequalities and graphs

In this chapter we review graphical and iterative methods of solving equations, and then extend the graphical ideas to consider solutions of simultaneous inequalities and their applications.

1. GRAPHICAL SOLUTIONS TO EQUATIONS

Equations in one or two unknowns may be solved graphically as illustrated in the examples below. Graphs can also often provide additional information about the model, as will be seen.

Example 1

An agricultural officer of the Ukosi tribe has carried out some experiments on growing ornamental gourds. The variety concerned produces gourds of several different colours including a golden gourd which fetches a particularly high price on the export market. If the plants are placed too close together, most of the gourds turn out green, however, and she states that the yield of golden gourds per hectare (g) is approximately related to the number of (evenly spaced) plants per hectare (p) by the equation:

$$g = \frac{p^2}{25} - \frac{p^3}{60000} \quad \text{(for } g > 0 \text{ and } p > 0\text{).}$$

Using this model, find (a) the possible numbers of plants per hectare which should produce 20 000 golden gourds per hectare (which matches up with the current demand of the exporters), (b) the maximum number of golden gourds per hectare which can be produced, and the appropriate density of gourd plants to achieve this.

A graph of $g = \dfrac{p^2}{25} - \dfrac{p^3}{60000}$ is shown in Figure 1.

(a) The possible numbers of plants per hectare which should produce 20 000 golden gourds per hectare, that is, the solution of the equation

$$\frac{p^2}{25} - \frac{p^3}{60000} = 20000,$$

is read off from the graph as 870 or 2130 (to the nearest 10) plants per hectare.

(The smaller number would obviously be preferred if it were not for the fact that green gourds are not worthless and compressed dried gourd leaves have a sale value as a fuel.)

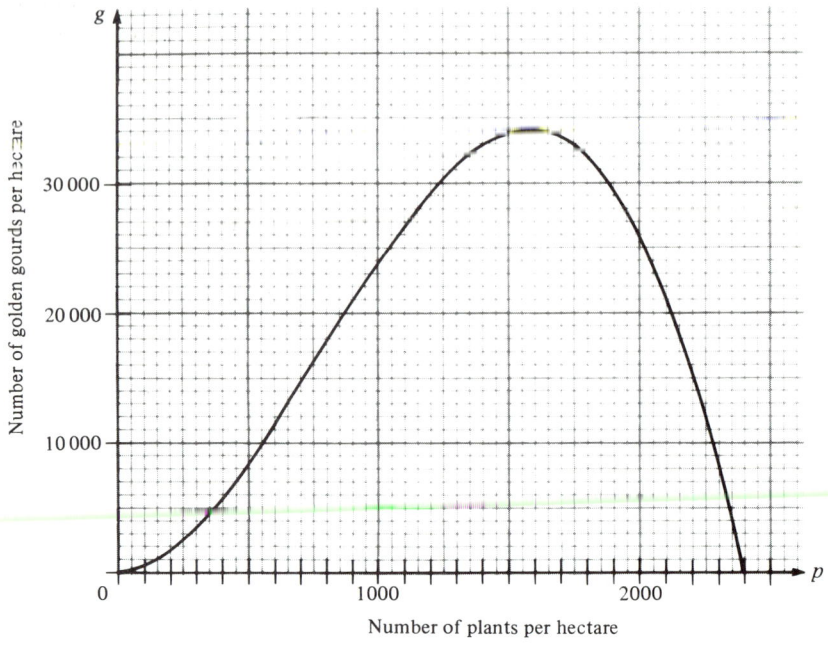

Figure 1

(*b*) The maximum number of golden gourds per hectare is read from the graphs as 34 100, which should be achieved with 1600 plants per hectare.

It will probably have occurred to you to wonder why the agricultural officer bothered with a mathematical model in the form of an equation in the first place when all she had to do was to graph her experimental results and then take readings from the graph. The sad truth is that the long rains never came; she never completed her experiments and she obtained the equation from a textbook on ornamental gourd growing written by another agricultural officer in a different country: we should therefore be extremely pessimistic about the reliability of the conclusions.

Example 2

An ornamental gourd-seller offers tourists gourds by the dozen as follows: 3 golden gourds plus 9 green ones for 54 cents or 6 golden gourds plus 6 green gourds for 72 cents.

Assuming that he is allowing the same price per golden gourd or price per green gourd in calculating the price of each collection, find these prices of individual gourds.

Let the price of a golden gourd be x cents and the price of a green gourd be y cents.

Then we have the equations $3x+9y = 54$
and $6x+6y = 72$.

These can be solved by various algebraic methods but we can also use a graphical method. Both equations give straight lines, so we need only find two points on each to plot them. We also find a third point on each, as a check.

$3x+9y = 54$ $\quad x = 0 \Rightarrow 9y = 54 \Rightarrow y = 6$ $\quad$ (0, 6) is on the line;
$\quad\quad\quad\quad\quad y = 0 \Rightarrow 3x = 54 \Rightarrow x = 18$ $\quad$ (18, 0) is on the line;
$\quad\quad\quad\quad\quad x = 6 \Rightarrow 18+9y = 54 \Rightarrow y = 4$ $\quad$ (6, 4) is on the line.

$6x+6y = 72$ $\quad x = 0 \Rightarrow 6y = 72 \Rightarrow y = 12$ $\quad$ (0, 12) is on the line;
$\quad\quad\quad\quad\quad y = 0 \Rightarrow 6x = 72 \Rightarrow x = 12$ $\quad$ (12, 0) is on the line;
$\quad\quad\quad\quad\quad x = 6 \Rightarrow 36+6y = 72 \Rightarrow y = 6$ $\quad$ (6, 6) is on the line.

The graphs are therefore as in Figure 2. The lines meet at (9, 3), so $x = 9$ and $y = 3$ satisfy both equations. The price of a golden gourd is 9 cents, and the price of a green gourd is 3 cents.

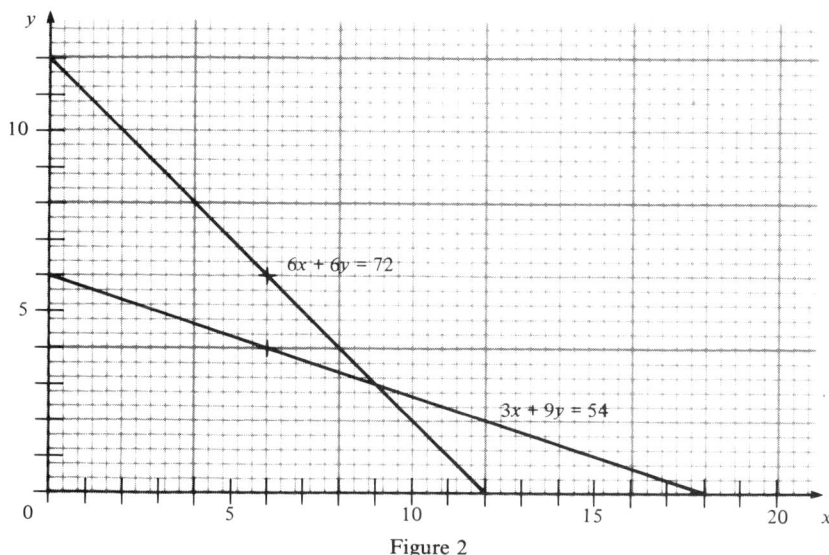

Figure 2

Exercise A

*1   Plot the graph of $y = 5x - x^2$ for $0 \leqslant x \leqslant 5$. Hence write down the solutions of the equations:
    (a) $5x - x^2 = 0$;
    (b) $5x - x^2 = 5$.

2   Plot the graph of $y = x^3 - 7x + 6$ for $-3 \leqslant x \leqslant 3$. Hence write down the solutions of the equations:
    (a) $x^3 - 7x + 6 = 0$;
    (b) $x^3 - 7x = -1$.

*3   Plot the graph of $y = 2.9x - x^2 - 1.9$ for $0 \leqslant x \leqslant 3$. Estimate, from your graph, solutions to the equation $x^2 + 1.9 = 2.9x$.

4   Plot the graph of $y = x^3 - 0.6x^2 - 1.2x + 0.3$ for $-2 \leqslant x \leqslant 3$, taking values of x at intervals of 0.5.
    (a) Estimate the solutions of the equation $x^3 - 0.6x^2 - 1.2x + 0.3 = 0$.
    (b) Estimate the maximum value of y between the two lower roots, and both values of x which give this value of y.

*5 Solve, graphically, the simultaneous equations $2x+3y = 7$; $3x+2y = 8$. Check your solutions by an algebraic method.

6 On the same diagram, draw the graphs of $y = 0.4x+1.2$ and $y = -2.5x+3.6$ for $-1 \leqslant x \leqslant 3$.
Estimate, from your graph, the solution of the simultaneous equations $y = 0.4x+1.2$; $y = -2.5x+3.6$. How accurate do you expect your solution to be? Check your estimate by substituting the values of x and y into both sides of both equations.

*7 Solve, graphically, the simultaneous equations $2x+3y = 7$; $xy = 1$.

8 (a) Sketch, roughly, the graphs of $y = 2x$ and $y = \dfrac{2}{x}$.

(b) Solve, by substitution, the simultaneous equations $y = 2x$, $y = \dfrac{2}{x}$, and show that your sketch graph agrees with the solution.

(c) By drawing, accurately, the relevant part of the graphs of $y = 2.1x+0.1$ and $y = \dfrac{1.9}{x+0.1}$, find the positive value of x for which they meet and hence state the positive solution of the equation $(2.1x+0.1)(x+0.1) = 1.9$.

2. TRIAL AND ERROR METHODS AND ITERATION

Decimal search or an iterative method of solution, using a calculator or computer, are appropriate for all equations where no exact solution can be found by a simple algebraic method. Such numerical methods of solution can of course be used for all equations but in simple cases an algebraic solution will often provide an exact solution, or a solution to whatever accuracy is needed, more quickly than a numerical method.

Example 3
Consider the equation $x^2 - 5x + 2 = 0$.
(a) Algebraically, we can in fact solve this:
$$ax^2+bx+c = 0 \Rightarrow x = \frac{-b \pm \sqrt{(b^2-4ac)}}{2a}$$
so $\quad x^2-5x+2 = 0 \Rightarrow x = \dfrac{5 \pm \sqrt{(25-8)}}{2}$
$$\Rightarrow x = \frac{5 \pm \sqrt{17}}{2} = 4.56 \quad \text{or} \quad 0.44 \quad \text{to 2 d.p.}$$

(b) Graphically, we can tabulate some values:

x	0	1	2	3	4	5
x^2-5x+2	2	-2	-4	-4	-2	2

A sketch graph therefore gives Figure 3.
This confirms our algebraic solution, showing solutions at about $\frac{1}{2}$ and $4\frac{1}{2}$.

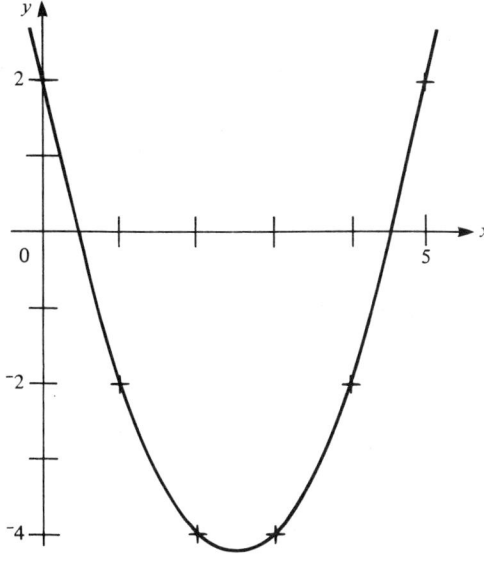

Figure 3

(c) A more accurate tabulation of values around $x = \frac{1}{2}$ and $4\frac{1}{2}$, using a 'decimal search' approach, but omitting unnecessary steps, might produce something like this:

(i)
x	$x^2 - 5x + 2$
0.5	⁻0.25
0.4	0.16
⋮	
0.43	0.0349
0.44	⁻6.4 × 10⁻³
⋮	
0.438	1.844 × 10⁻³
	etc.

(ii)
x	$x^2 - 5x + 2$
4.5	⁻0.25
4.6	0.16
⋮	
4.56	⁻6.4 × 10⁻³
4.451	⁻2.279 × 10⁻³
4.562	1.844 × 10⁻³
	etc.

and we could continue as far as accuracy demanded.

(d) Alternatively, we may try various rearrangements of the equation with a view to producing an inductive definition of a sequence which will converge on one or other solution, given a suitable first term. We have

$$x^2 - 5x + 2 = 0 \Rightarrow 5x = x^2 + 2 \Rightarrow x = \frac{x^2 + 2}{5}, \qquad \text{(i)}$$

or $x^2 - 5x + 2 = 0 \Rightarrow x(x-5) + 2 = 0 \Rightarrow x(x-5) = {}^-2$

$$\Rightarrow x = \frac{-2}{x-5}, \qquad \text{(ii)}$$

or $x^2 - 5x + 2 = 0 \Rightarrow x(x-5) + 2 = 0 \Rightarrow x(x-5) = {}^-2$

$$\Rightarrow x-5 = \frac{-2}{x} \Rightarrow x = 5 - \frac{2}{x}, \qquad \text{(iii)}$$

or $x^2 - 5x + 2 = 0 \Rightarrow x^2 = 5x - 2 \Rightarrow x = \pm\sqrt{(5x-2)}.$ (iv)

Possible inductive definitions therefore include

(1) $x_{n+1} = \frac{x_n^2 + 2}{5},$ (ii) $x_{n+1} = \frac{2}{x_n - 5},$

(iii) $x_{n+1} = 5 - \frac{2}{x_n},$ (iv) $x_{n+1} = \sqrt{(5x_n - 2)}.$

A simple computer program may then be written to tabulate terms in each of these sequences for various different first terms. Here are some computer print-outs for $x_1 = 6$, that is, a value above the largest root:

```
( X * X  +  2 ) / 5    - 2 / ( X - 5 )    5  -  2 / X    SQR ( 5 * X - 2 )
6                      6                  6              6
7 . 6                  - 2                4 . 666667     5 . 291503
11 . 952               . 2857143          4 . 571429     4 . 945454
28 . 97006             . 4242424          4 . 5625       4 . 767313
168 . 2529             . 4370861          4 . 561644     4 . 672961
5662 . 207             . 4383164          4 . 561562     4 . 622208
6 . 412119E+6          . 4383346          4 . 561554     4 . 594675
8 . 223053E+12         . 438446           4 . 561553     4 . 57967
1 . 352372E+25         . 4384471          4 . 561553     4 . 571471
```

We notice that sequence (i) fails to converge on either root; sequence (ii), after jumping initially to a negative value for x_2, then approaches the lower root from below; sequences (iii) and (iv) both converge, from above, on the higher root but sequence (iii) converges much more quickly.

Example 4

As a result of a chemical experiment to determine an 'equilibrium constant', it is known that the constant, x, which must be between 0 and 1, is a solution of the equation

$$56.24 = \frac{x^4(8.762 - x)}{160(1-x)^5}.$$

(a) In this case, an algebraic solution is out of the question as the equation is too complicated.
(b) An approximate graphical solution is not going to be particularly helpful since we already know that the solution lies between 0 and 1; in any case the graph will not be easy to plot.
(c) A trial and error solution, based on decimal search, is the obvious method to use.
  Here, it can save time to estimate the approximate size of x first, as follows:
  (i) Since we know x is between 0 and 1, $(8.762 - x)$ is nearly 8.

Roughly then, $55 \approx \dfrac{8x^4}{160(1-x)^5} \Rightarrow 1100 \approx \dfrac{x^4}{(1-x)^5}.$

Tabulating values using a calculator:

x	$\dfrac{x^4}{(1-x)^5}$	
0.9	65610	
0.8	1280	suggesting that x is just below 0.8
0.7	99	

(ii) In the original equation

x	$\dfrac{x^4(8.762-x)}{160(1-x)^5}$
0.80	63.7
0.79	47.5
0.795	54.94
0.796	56.57
0.7955	55.75

So $x = 0.796$ to 3 s.f.

The approximation in (i) is of course unnecessary; one can start immediately with the method of (ii) but the working in (i) perhaps makes it easier to choose an initial guess for x in (ii).

(d) One could attempt to rearrange the equation in order to suggest an inductive definition for a sequence which might converge on the root. In view of the complication of the equation, however, little seems likely to be gained by this.

Exercise B

1 In Example 3, the two roots of the equation $x^2 - 5x + 2 = 0$ were found by use of iterations based on one or another of the rearrangements:

(i) $x = \dfrac{x^2+2}{5}$, (ii) $x = \dfrac{-2}{x-5}$, (iii) $x = 5 - \dfrac{2}{x}$, (iv) $x = \sqrt{(5x-2)}$.

The roots turned out to be 4.56 and 0.44 to two decimal places and we were able to find both of them when starting with $x_1 = 6$.

(a) With the aid of a calculator or computer, investigate the effects of each iteration for a value of x_1 which lies between the two roots.

(b) Investigate the effect of each iteration for a value of x_1 less than the smaller root.

Are there values of x_1 for which any of the iterations are impossible to use?

2 A mathematician is asked to set up a series of equations to model the running costs of an ocean liner. He comes to the conclusion that the speed, V knots (nautical miles per hour), which will make the cost of fuel for a certain trip as small as possible, is the solution of the equation

$$1 + \frac{V}{30} - \frac{450}{V^2} = 0.$$

Show that this equation may be rearranged in the form
$$V = \sqrt{\left(\frac{450}{1+V/30}\right)}$$
and hence solve it to an accuracy of three significant figures by iteration.

3 Tabulate values of $f(x) = x^3 + 2.1x^2 - 0.9x - 1.9$ for $x = -2, -1, 0, 1, 2, 3$, and hence draw a graph of the function for $-2 \leqslant x \leqslant 3$.

From your graph, estimate the roots of the equation.

The positive root of the equation is required to an accuracy of three decimal places. Show that the equation can be rearranged in the form $x^2(x+2.1) = 0.9x + 1.9$ and hence in the form $x = \pm\sqrt{\left(\frac{ax+b}{cx+d}\right)}$ where a, b, c, d are known.

Use this rearrangement as the basis of an iteration to find the positive root to the required accuracy.

Investigate an iteration based on another possible rearrangement.

4 In a wire-drawing operation where the cross-sectional area is reduced from A_1 to A_2, the ratio R (where $R = A_1/A_2$) is found to satisfy the equation
$$R^3 - 2R^2 + 1.17 = 0.$$
Find R by trial and error, or otherwise, and so find the radius which may be obtained from an initial radius of 5 mm.

5 After treatment with a new fertiliser the yield of golden gourds per hectare (g) in Ukosaland is approximately related to the number of (evenly spaced) plants per hectare (p) by the equation
$$g = \frac{p^2}{20} - \frac{p^3}{48\,000}.$$
Find, by trial and error, the value of p (to the nearest 100), which makes g a maximum. What is then the yield?

If the demand for golden gourds is such that a yield of 30 000 gourds per hectare will satisfy it, find by trial and error the least number of plants per hectare necessary.

6 It can be shown that, under certain conditions, an estimate of the load, M kg, just sufficient to cause a vertical steel column to buckle, depends upon the solution of the equation
$$\tan\left(\frac{180\lambda}{\pi}\right)^\circ = \lambda.$$
Solve this equation, by trial and error, to an accuracy of three significant figures and hence calculate M for a particular column given that, for Figure 4,
$$M = 1.75 \times \frac{10^9 \lambda^2 b d^3}{l^2}$$
where $b = 2.5 \times 10^{-2}$, $d = 2.5 \times 10^{-3}$ and $l = 1.0$.

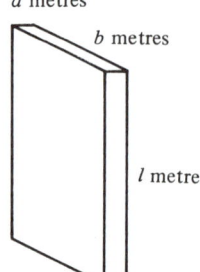

Figure 4

3. LINEAR PROGRAMMING

Commercial and industrial problems often involve inequalities, rather than equations, in a considerable number of unknowns. When a model can be based on linear inequalities the methods of finding a solution set are known as *linear programming* techniques. The process of attempting to find a *best* solution (for example, maximum profit or minimum cost) is called *optimisation*. Usually such problems are solved by numerical methods on a computer but we can illustrate the techniques effectively by looking at graphical solutions in simple cases with only two unknowns.

Example 5

A haulage contractor has 7 six-tonne lorries and 4 ten-tonne lorries. He has 9 drivers, each of whom stays with the same lorry once it has been allocated to him. The six-tonne lorries can make 8 journeys a day, but the ten-tonne lorries can make only 6 journeys a day. He has contracted to move at least 360 tonnes of coal from a pit-head to a power station each day. What numbers of lorries can the contractor use?

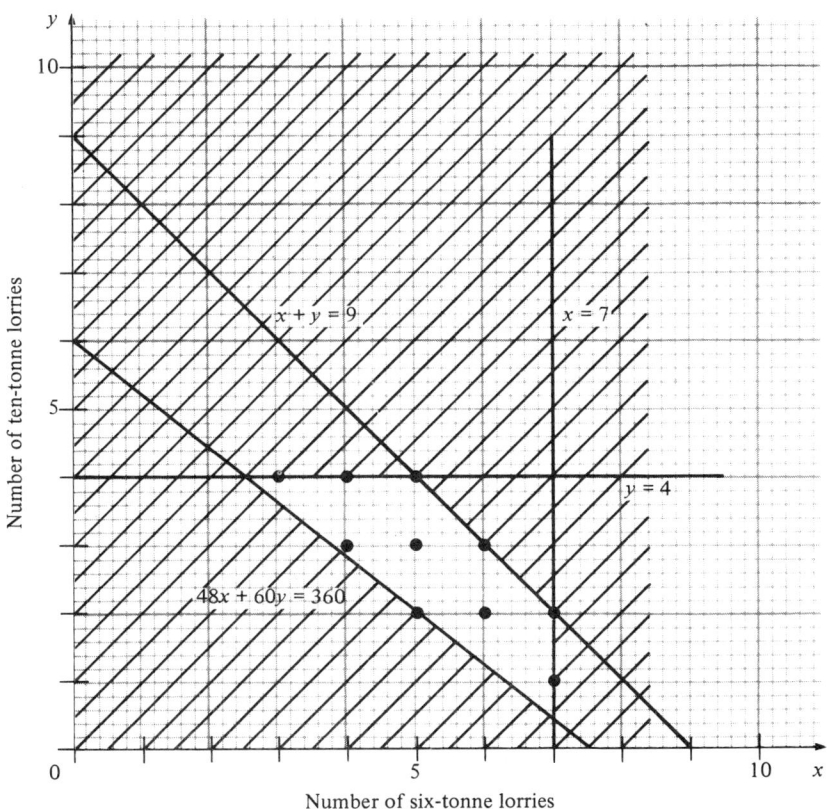

Figure 5

If x is the number of six-tonne lorries, and y is the number of ten-tonne lorries, then the various conditions give us the following inequalities:

$x \leqslant 7$ (no more than 7 six-tonne lorries are available)
$y \leqslant 4$ (no more than 4 ten-tonne lorries are available)
$x + y \leqslant 9$ (no more than 9 drivers are available)
$48x + 60y \geqslant 360$ (at least 360 tonnes of coal must be carried).

The region satisfying all these inequalities is shown unshaded in Figure 5. Since x and y must be positive integers, only the ten points marked with dots correspond to possible solutions. The contractor therefore has the choice of the following combinations of lorries:

3 six-tonne lorries and 4 ten-tonne lorries;
4 six-tonne lorries and 3 or 4 ten-tonne lorries;
5 six-tonne lorries and 2, 3, or 4 ten-tonne lorries;
6 six-tonne lorries and 2 or 3 ten-tonne lorries;
7 six-tonne lorries and 1 or 2 ten-tonne lorries.

Exercise C

*1 Plot the sets
$$\{(x, y): 2x + 5y < 10\} \quad \text{and} \quad \{(x, y): 5x + 4y > 10\}$$
together with
$$\{(x, y): x > 0\} \quad \text{and} \quad \{(x, y): y > 0\},$$
on one diagram, shading the areas not required. Name the point in the unshaded region with integral coordinates and two with non-integral coordinates.

2 Define six sets to specify the area left unshaded in Figure 6. If none of the sets contains its boundaries state which of the following points satisfy exactly five of the required conditions:
$$(3, 7), \quad (13, -1), \quad (6, 12), \quad (15, 7).$$

*3 The unshaded region in Figure 7 is given by the orderings $x \leqslant 0$, $y \leqslant 2$ and $y \geqslant x$. Say whether each of the following lines does or does not intersect the region.
     (a) $y = 1$.   (b) $x = 2$.   (c) $y = x + 2$.   (d) $x + y = 2$.   (SMP O-level)

*4 Write the following statements in symbols as inequalities:
     (a) The cost of 5 grapefruit (x pence each) and 6 oranges (y pence each) is at least £1.20.
     (b) Running at 8 m/s for p seconds and walking at 1.5 m/s for q seconds, Paul covers more than 400 m.
     (c) Less than 50 people are carried by x 12-seater minibuses and y 4-seater cars.
     (d) A piano-teacher gives f 40-minute lessons and p 30-minute lessons, starting at 9 a.m. and finishing before 1 p.m.

5 A pop singer is going to sing x folk-songs and y country-and-westerns at a concert. Each of the former takes 3 minutes and each of the latter 2 minutes to sing. Illustrate his possible programmes on a graph assuming that he can sing for (a) 20, (b) 40, (c) 60 minutes. In the event, he is told he may sing for between 20 and 40 minutes and must sing 8 country-and westerns; what are the limits to the number of folk-songs he can sing?

Linear programming 165

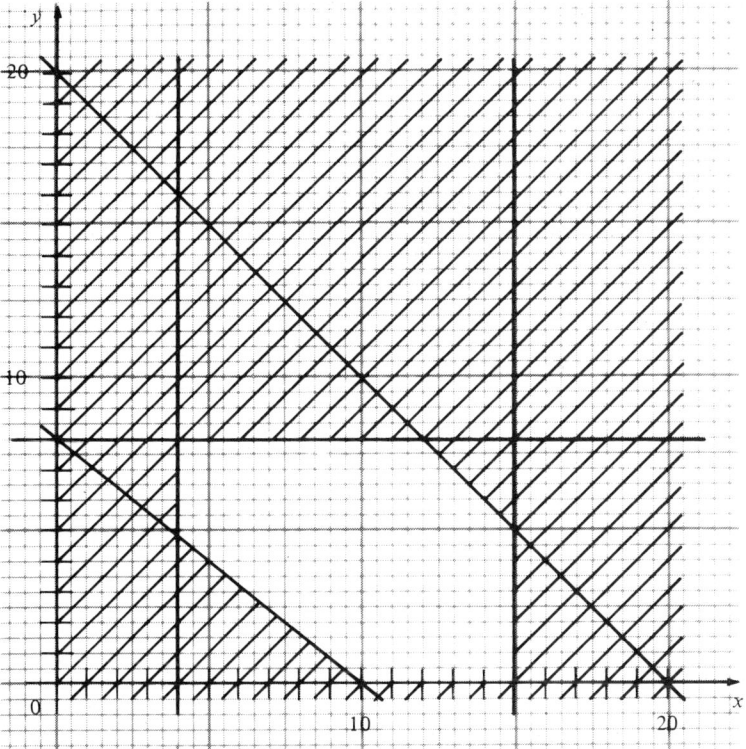

Figure 6

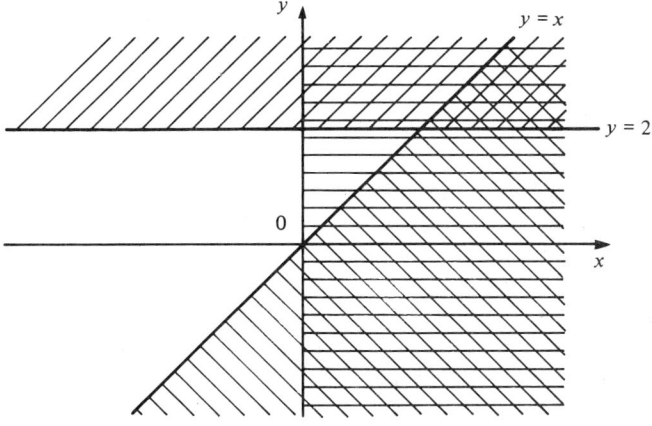

Figure 7

4. OPTIMISATION

Figure 8 shows the possible solutions to the haulage contractor's problem, as given in Example 5. Which of the possible solutions is the best? There are various answers to this question, depending on the criterion chosen.

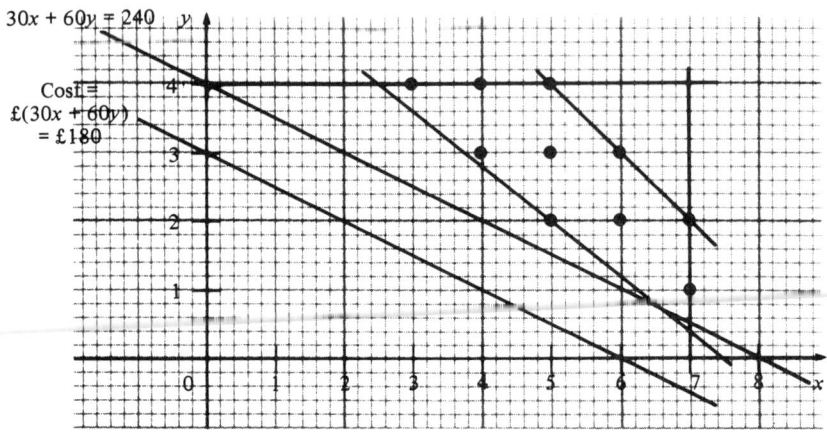

Figure 8

For example, the point $(5, 2)$ corresponds to using 5 six-tonne lorries and 2 ten-tonne lorries. This solution uses the smallest number of drivers, and 360 tonnes of coal are carried. On the other hand, more coal (384 tonnes) is carried (and the same number of drivers employed) if $x = 3$ and $y = 4$. Full employment of the drivers, and the maximum amount of coal carried, is achieved if the solution with $x = 5$ and $y = 4$ is used.

Lines of equal cost

Suppose that the contractor reckons that it costs him £30 to run a six-tonner for a day and £60 for a ten-tonner. Then the cost of using x six-tonners and y ten-tonners is £$(30x+60y)$. Perhaps he tries to use a combination of lorries that would only cost £180. There are several ways of doing this – for example, $(6, 0)$, $(4, 1)$, $(2, 2)$ or $(0, 3)$. These points all lie on the line $30x+60y = 180$, which has been drawn in Figure 3.

Similarly, points on the line $30x+60y = 240$ give solutions which cost £240: for example, $(8, 0)$, $(6, 1)$ and $(0, 4)$. This line is parallel to $30x+60y = 180$, but further from the origin. To make the cost as small as possible we find a parallel line (another line of equal cost) which goes through one of the possible solutions and which is as near to the origin as possible. The line which satisfies these conditions passes through $(5, 2)$ and $(7, 1)$; both these solutions cost £270, the minimum cost.

Example 6

A farmer wants to enclose a rectangular area for sheep. They require at least 480 m². For one side she will use a straight fence and for the other three she can use hurdles, each 2 m long, of which she has 40. What is the smallest number of hurdles she can use?

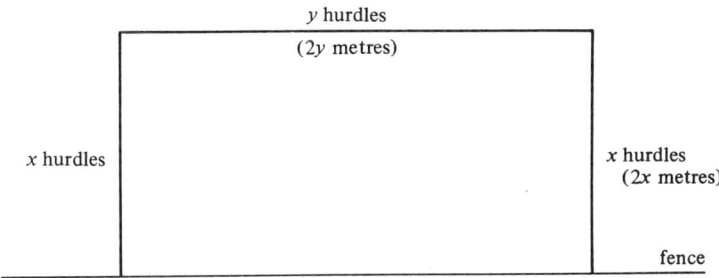

Figure 9

Let us suppose that she uses x hurdles for each of the two equal sides and y hurdles for the other as shown in Figure 9. Altogether she will require $2x+y$ hurdles. Since she has only 40 this gives rise to the inequality: $2x+y \leqslant 40$.

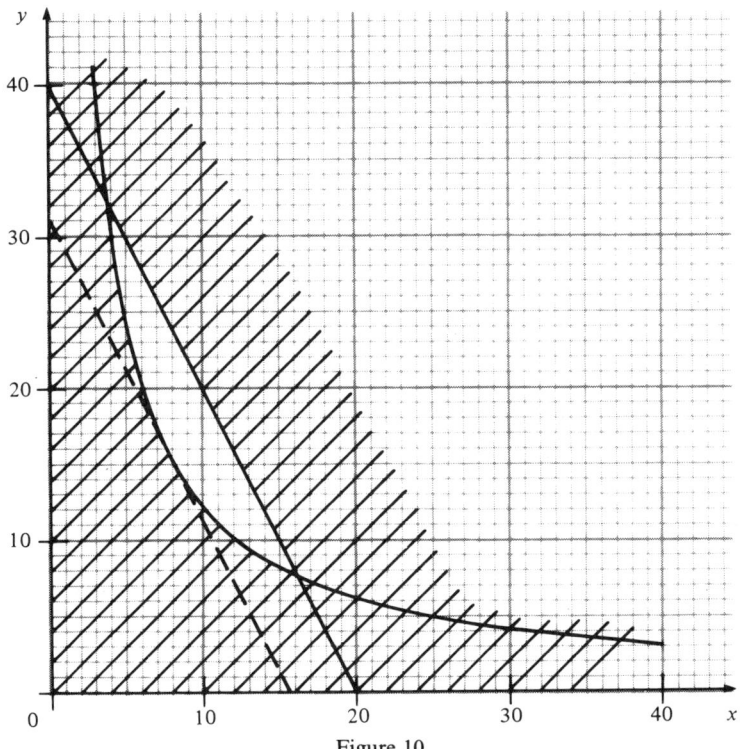

Figure 10

Each hurdle is 2 m long. The area enclosed will comprise $4xy$ m². This must cover 480 m² at least, so:
$$4xy \geq 480$$
$$\Leftrightarrow xy \geq 120$$

To graph this we must first plot a set of pairs (x, y) satisfying $xy = 120$ and then decide which side of the curve is appropriate. It is wise to set out a table of values.

x	30	20	15	11.0	8	6	4	3
y	4	6	8	11.0	15	20	30	40

These have been plotted in Figure 10. Now we test the origin $(0, 0)$. Is $0 \times 0 \geq 120$? No, so shade out the side containing it.

Identify the region satisfying the inequality $2x + y \leq 40$. Feasible solutions are integral (why?) pairs in the unshaded region.

To find the minimum number of hurdles we remember that any line parallel to $2x + y = 40$ passes through a set of values of (x, y) representing equal total numbers of hurdles. For instance, $(6, 20), (10, 12), (12, 8)$ all lie on $2x + y = 32$ and so represent the use of 32 hurdles. We need to find the line parallel to $2x + y = 40$ and nearest to the origin. This has been drawn as a broken line in Figure 10. It appears to pass through $(8, 15)$. Testing this combination reveals that $xy = 120$ and $2x + y = 31$. No other feasible solution uses so few hurdles and this is indeed the minimum arrangement.

Lines of equal profit

A similar technique is used when we want to maximise profit rather than minimise costs. In such a case we shall look for the line of equal profit that is furthest from the origin.

Exercise D

*1 All coordinates in this question are positive or zero.
   (a) Show graphically on one diagram the inequalities $x + y \leq 5$, $x \leq 2y$, shading the unwanted regions.
   (b) S is the set of points whose coordinates are whole numbers satisfying both these inequalities. H and K are points of S such that $x + 2y$ has its greatest value at H and $2x + y$ has its greatest value at K. Mark H and K on your diagram and state their coordinates. (SMP O-level)

2 (a) On a single diagram on squared paper show, by shading the unwanted regions, the set of points (x, y) satisfying the following inequalities:
$$x + y \geq 6, \quad 2x + 5y > 20, \quad x \leq 4, \quad y < 5.$$
   (b) State the coordinates of the point (x, y) giving the least value of $4x + y$, subject to these restrictions, if x and y are integers, and state this value. (SMP O-level)

3 The shaded region U in Figure 11 includes all its boundaries. The diagram is not drawn to scale. The maximum value of $(y - x)$ in U is 2.
Which are true and which are false?

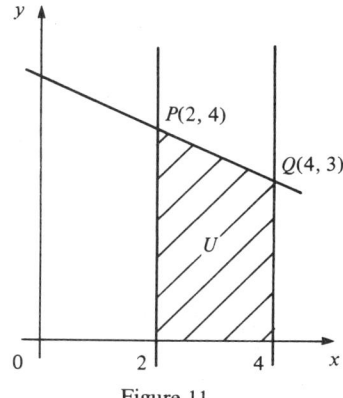

Figure 11

(a) The equation of PQ is $y = 5 - x$.
(b) The minimum value of $(y - x)$ in U is -4.
(c) The maximum value of $(x + y)$ in U is 7.
(d) If the set V is formed from U by excluding all its boundary lines, then the maximum value of $(x + y)$ in V is 6. (SMP O-level)

4 (a) Draw the graphs of $y = \frac{1}{2}x(3 - x)$ and $x + y = 2$ for values of x from -1 to 4, using the same axes with scales of 2 cm for 1 unit.
(b) (i) State the values of x at which your graphs cross.
(ii) State an equation in x which is satisfied by these values.
(c) On your graph shade the set
$$S = \{(x, y) : 0 \leqslant y \leqslant \tfrac{1}{2}x(3 - x)\}.$$
Mark the point P of S for which you estimate that $x + y$ has the greatest value. (SMP O-level)

*5 A builder has a 2-hectare plot on which to build houses. She will build the Dorset, which costs £40 000, or the Somerset which costs £20 000 to build. The former takes half a hectare, the latter only one-eighth. She cannot raise more than £200 000. Express the information in a table. If she decides to build x Dorsets and y Somersets write down two inequalities. If she makes a profit of £8000 on a Dorset and £3000 on a Somerset write down the equations of some lines of equal profit in as simple a form as possible and by plotting find out what feasible combination of houses will give her the greatest profit.

6 Part of a farm is to be planted with wheat and kale. The restrictions are shown in the following table:

	Wheat	Kale	Maximum available
Number of hectares planted	w	k	—
Number of days labour per hectare	2	1	10
Cost of labour per hectare in £	35	30	210
Cost of fertilisers per hectare in £	15	20	120

Write down the three restrictions on the variables w and k (both, of course, positive). Show them on a graph.

(a) Express the total number of hectares in terms of w and k. Is it necessary for w and k to be integers? Find the greatest possible area that can be planted.
(b) The profit is £40 per hectare of wheat and £30 per hectare of kale. What area should be planted for maximum profit?

7 Fred and Bill are the only porters available to unload packages, at least 1000 of which arrive at their factory every day. Bill unloads twice as fast as Fred who can manage 80 packages per hour. Fred always starts work at 7.00 a.m., Bill at 8.00 a.m. Fred likes to finish work later than Bill, too. If Fred is paid £2.00 per hour and Bill £2.75 per hour and they are employed so that the cost to the factory is least, find their hours of work per day. Bill is given a rise in wages and it becomes economical to ask him to decrease his hours of work and to increase Fred's. What was the least amount that his increase could have been per hour?

8 Vitamin extract X costs 75p per gram and vitamin extract Y costs 375p per gram. One gram of each contains:

Vitamin	Extract X (units)	Extract Y (units)
A	12	6
B	1	10
C	20	30
D	1	3
E	2	2

A pharmaceutical firm wishes to mix x g of X and y g of extract Y in such a proportion that every $(x+y)$ g of the mixture contains at least:

Vitamin	Mixture (units)
A	84
B	70
C	240
D	30
E	15

In what proportion should the extracts be mixed in order to minimise the cost of the mixture?

*9 A colliery manager works a number of faces and has two different types of machine available which have the following characteristics.

	Output per day (tonnes)	No. of face men required	Ash (%)	Production cost per tonne (£)
Machine A	400	20	10	13.50
Machine B	200	15	7	15.00

He has to meet the following conditions. The total output needed is from 2500 to 3000 tonnes. He has available less than 180 face men. The ash content must be less than 9% and coal with such an ash content would yield him £18 per tonne. How many machines of each type should he use to obtain maximum profit?

10 To make one Launceston Cake requires 275 g of flour, 170 g of butter and 3 eggs. One Sydney Cake requires 330 g of flour, 170 g of butter and 2 eggs. (Other ingredients are required as well, of course.) A cook has 3.3 kg of flour, 1.7 kg of butter and 24 eggs with which to make as many of these cakes as possible.
   (a) If x Launceston Cakes and y Sydney Cakes are made, explain why the mass of flour available means that $5x + 6y \leqslant 60$.
   (b) Write down (and simplify where possible) two other inequalities derived from the mass of butter and the number of eggs available.
   (c) Show these three inequalities graphically, taking values of x and y from 0 to 12, and using a scale of 1 cm to 1 cake.
   (d) State the maximum number of cakes that can be made under these conditions, and mark on your graph the point Z that represents the greatest number of Launceston Cakes possible if the maximum total number of cakes is made. (SMP O-level)

11 An outing is to be arranged for 40 members of a club. Transport is to be provided by cars hired from a self-drive hire company. This company owns two types of car, the 'small' four-seater saloon and the 'family' five-seater saloon. The respective costs of hire are £10.00 and £12.00.
   (a) Let x and y be the numbers of 'small' and 'family' cars hired respectively. Write down an inequality, other than $x \geqslant 0$ and $y \geqslant 0$, that must be satisfied by x and y, if the club outing is to take place.
   (b) The company makes it a condition of hire to the club that at least as many 'small' cars as 'family' cars must be hired.
       Ten non-drivers insist, for reasons of comfort, that they travel in 'family' saloons.
       Write down two further inequalities.
   (c) Using a scale of 1 cm to 1 unit on both axes, draw on one diagram graphs to illustrate all your inequalities. Shade the unwanted regions.
   (d) (i) Write down an expression for the total cost of hiring in terms of x and y.
       (ii) Find the number of cars of each type that should be used to minimise this cost.
       (iii) Calculate the total cost in this case. (SMP O-level)

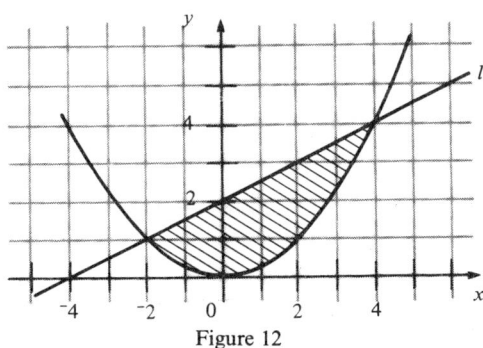

Figure 12

12 The equation of the curve in Figure 12 is $y = kx^2$, where k is a constant. Which of the following statements are true and which false?

(a) The equation of the line *l* is $x + 2y = 4$.
(b) $k = \frac{1}{4}$.
(c) Area of shaded region < 15.
(d) If (x, y) is in the shaded region, the greatest value of $x + y$ is 4.

(SMP O-level)

13 The distance *d* km that can be travelled by a motor boat at a steady speed of *v* km/h without refuelling is given by the formula
$$d \leqslant 12v - v^2.$$
Draw up a table of values and plot $d = 12v - v^2$ for the domain $0 \leqslant v \leqslant 12$.

Taking suitable scales, shade the area representing distances impossible at various speeds. What is special about 12 km/h? How do you account for this?

A trip round the bay is to last three hours. Express the relation between *d* and *v* for such a trip and plot it on your graph. What is the greatest distance that can be covered in this time and what will be the speed?

Find also the greatest distance that can be covered at any speed. How long will a trip of this distance take?

14 The maximum range of a radio station, *r* km, is given in terms of the angle $\theta°$ measured anticlockwise from north by the formula
$$r = \frac{60}{1 + \cos \theta°}.$$
Calculate the range of *r* for $\theta = 0, 30, 60, 90, 120, 150$ and plot your results (polar

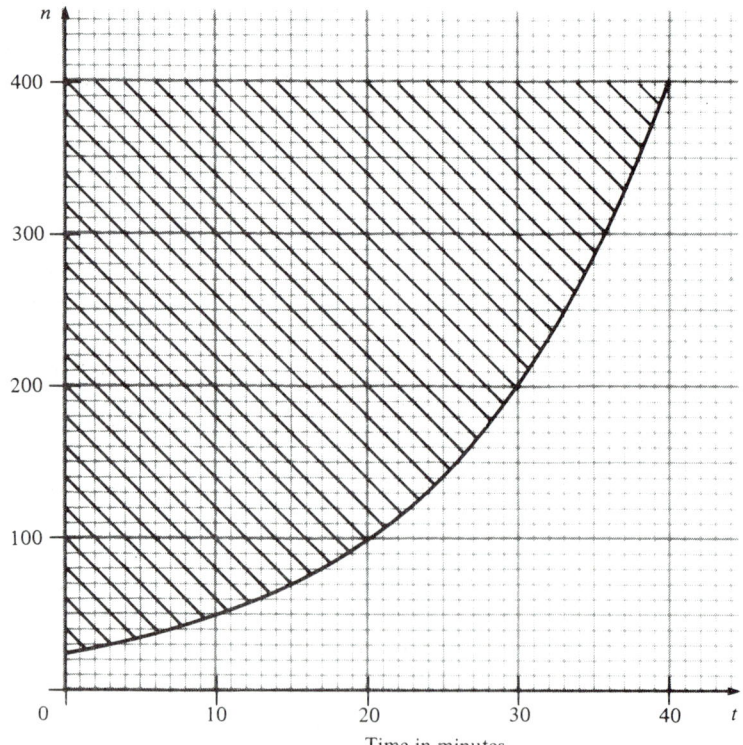

Figure 13

coordinates) as far as $\theta = 120$. Explain why the formula must be increasingly in error for angles of 150° and more. Is it proper to join up with a smooth curve? How can you complete the graph for the other two quadrants with least effort? Try to identify the curve. Which region represents points that cannot receive the station?

A repeater station with a range of 20 km all round is planned to give increased coverage. There are two possible sites, (a) at (50, 20°); (b) at (110, 130°). Which would give the greatest increase in area?

15 The unshaded region of the graph in Figure 13 shows the number of bacteria theoretically possible in a colony at certain times. Describe the law of growth. An inhibitor is supposed to be functioning, however, which restricts the number present, n, at time t minutes according to the relation
$$n < 2t + 100.$$
Use a transparent ruler or tracing paper to add this information to the graph. At about what time should the inhibitor have produced a reduction of more than 50% in the number of bacteria present?

5. COMPUTER-BASED MODELS AND SIMULATION

Particular commercial, industrial or scientific situations can, with appropriate simplification, be modelled by sets of equations or inequalities and/or simple sets of numerical data. When the model is relatively complicated, computers are used to investigate it. The object of the investigation may, fairly rarely, be to find a unique solution to a set of equations involved. More often there will be a solution set from which an 'optimum' (best) solution may be extracted. More often still, the defining relations do no more than place certain limits on possible outcomes of the situation. For example:

In a mathematical model for the siting and design of a steelworks, say, there might be 30 inequalities or equations involving 40 variables and, hence, a large number of possible solutions. The only way to deal with a situation of this sort is to guess values for some of the variables and let a computer substitute them in and work out the consequent steel output figures, etc. This process is known as *simulation*.

It could be an expensive error to build a steelworks of the wrong capacity in the wrong place. If the model is a good one, experimenting with the proposed design specifications can produce a simulation of the resulting financial disaster and so lead to suitable modifications.

The computer can be programmed to 'guess' values randomly within an appropriate range, and also probabilities (which can be varied) can be attached to certain events.

Listed below are a few of the areas in which computer-based mathematical models and simulations have been used in recent years.

Simulation of demands on nursing staff in a hospital ward.
The reaction of consumers to advertising.
The behaviour of small groups, for example, committees.
Planning systems of defence against nuclear attack.
The process of memorising and recalling learnt facts.

Simulation of changes in demand on a tyre manufacturing company.
Flight simulation for training pilots.
Forecasting numbers of applications for further education.
Simulation of queues in take-away fish and chip shops.
Simulation of moon landing.
Analysis of effectiveness of various swimming strokes.
The process of decision-making in various business situations.
Determination of likely effects of family planning clinics on population control in Costa Rica.
Effects of air traffic control systems.
Simulation of the agricultural economy of Southern Nigeria.
Simulation of predator–prey relationships.
Planning of bus routes.
Simulation of the growth of a new town.
Economic policy simulation for Czechoslovakia.
Simulation of traffic flow at road junctions.

From this fairly randomly selected list you will see that the range of applications is enormous. How useful and trustworthy the results are must depend of course on the assumptions and simplifications made in the modelling process.

There have been attempts, notably at the Massachusetts Institute of Technology, to produce an effective 'World Model' based on variables such as birth rate, death rate, extent of overcrowding, food availability, pollution, natural resources, capital investment, standards of living, and 'quality of life'.

If you have access to a computer software library, find out what simulation programs are available to you. Simulation games, ranging from moon landings to business games, and simulations of experiments in the sciences have been written for school use: a listing of the program for one of these will give you some feel for the challenge which programmers face when trying to produce a realistic computer-based model of even a relatively simple situation.

SUMMARY

An equation of the form $f(x) = k$ can be solved by:
(a) an algebraic method if $f(x)$ is simple enough;
(b) drawing the graph of $y = f(x)$ and finding where it crosses the line $y = k$;
(c) decimal search;
(d) rearranging the equation into the form $x = g(x)$ and trying the iteration $x_{new} = g(x)$. (Sections 1, 2)

A pair of simultaneous equations in two unknowns can be solved by drawing the graphs of the equations and finding the coordinates of the point, or points, of intersection. (Section 1)

Solution sets for simultaneous inequalities in two variables can be found from the corresponding regions on a graph. When these inequalities are modelling some situation, other factors, such as minimum cost, can be used to select one (or more) of the feasible solutions. (Sections 3, 4)

Summary

Summary exercise

1. Solve the equation $x^3 + 2x = 7$ to an accuracy of one decimal place by drawing the graph of $y = x^3 + 2x$ for $0 \leq x \leq 2$. Use decimal search to find the solution to two decimal places.

2. Show that the equation $x^3 - x^2 = 5$ can be rearranged to give $x = \sqrt{\left(\dfrac{5}{x} + x\right)}$ given that $x > 0$). Use the iteration $x_{\text{new}} = \sqrt{\left(\dfrac{5}{x} + x\right)}$, starting with $x = 2$, to solve the equation to an accuracy of four significant figures.

3. A small lake is to be stocked with two types of ornamental fish – fantails and shubunkins. The fish are obtainable only in two collections, the 'popular' which contains 5 fantails and 10 shubunkins, and the 'thoroughbred' which contains 6 fantails and 4 shubunkins.
   (a) The owner of the lake buys x 'popular' collections and y 'throughbred' collections. How many of each type of fish does he obtain?
   (b) The owner requires a minimum of 150 fish with more fantails than shubunkins. Write down and simplify the two inequalities in x and y that express these conditions.
   (c) Show these two inequalities graphically, using scales of 1 cm to one collection on each axis and shading the unwanted regions.
   (d) £100 is available for stocking the lake, and each collection costs £7. Explain why £98 is the maximum amount that can actually be spent, and show from your graph that there are two ways of spending this sum to satisfy the conditions. Write down the number of each type of fish in the way that gives the larger total number of fish. (SMP O-level)

8

Probability

In this chapter we review the basic ideas of probability and their application to combined events. We are mainly concerned with the outcomes from a pair of events, but at the end of the chapter we explore probabilities for the outcomes from three or more events.

1. DEFINITIONS

Relative frequency

A 10p coin is 'twirled' (that is, spun about a vertical axis, as shown in Figure 1) and we note which way up it lands. The table is a record of the first ten twirls. We call each twirl a *trial* and the result (head or tail) the *outcome*.

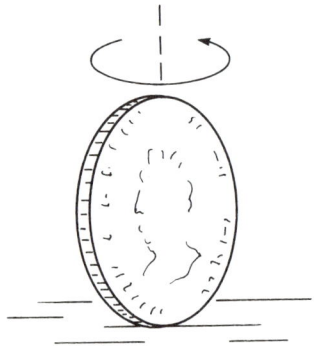

Figure 1

Number of twirl (N)	1	2	3	4	5	6	7	8	9	10
Outcome	T	T	H	H	T	T	H	H	H	H
Cumulative total of heads (r)	0	0	1	2	2	2	3	4	5	6
$\frac{r}{N}$ to 2 decimal places	0	0	0.33	0.5	0.4	0.33	0.43	0.5	0.55	0.6

The fraction $\frac{r}{N}$ is called the *relative frequency* of heads. It varies from twirl to twirl.

Probability

If this same experiment is continued for a long time it is found that the relative frequency 'settles down' to a number between 0 and 1, which is called the *probability* of the outcome being a head.

If the experiment is done fairly, and the coin is perfectly symmetrical, then we would expect approximately equal numbers of heads and tails, so we can argue that the probability of a head should be 0.5. This does not mean that there will ever be exactly the same number of heads as tails, but it means that in a long series the percentage difference between them will be very small and, the longer the series, the smaller the percentage difference. Ideas of symmetry such as this often help us to write down probabilities without conducting experiments.

If the experiment is repeated using a circular saucer, and a success consists of it coming down the 'right way up', there is no symmetry to help you and you might well be surprised by the result. It is wise to use an old saucer, and do it on a vinyl floor or a carpet with a close pile.

Where there is no likelihood of ambiguity, we can write $P(\text{head})$ or even $P(H)$ instead of 'the probability that the outcome is a head'.

The sum of the relative frequencies, and therefore of the probabilities, of all the possible outcomes must be 1. In particular, if we denote by $\sim A$ the outcome 'not A', we have

$$P(A) + P(\sim A) = 1 \quad \text{for any outcome } A.$$

Exercise A

*1 A card is drawn from a standard pack of 52 cards. Write down the probabilities of the following:
   (*a*) it is a club;
   (*b*) it is a 6;
   (*c*) it is the 6 of clubs;
   (*d*) it is not the 6 of clubs.

2 There are 14 boys and 16 girls in a mathematics set of 30. The teacher picks one at random to answer a question. What is the probability that it is not a girl?

3 The set of balls for snooker consists of 15 reds (R), 6 colours (C) and a white (W). A ball is chosen at random. Write down:
   (*a*) $P(W)$; (*b*) $P(C)$; (*c*) $P(\sim R)$.

4 Before you can start in the game of Ludo it is necessary to get a 'double' with the two dice that you throw. An experiment was carried out to see how many throws were needed. Here are the results of thirty trials. The figure 7 means that the 7th throw was a double, etc.

```
7   2   17   1    5   11   13    5    7    3
4   4    1   3    2    6    5    2    9    8
1   3    1   11   1   10    7   13    6    6
```

Calculate the relative frequency of doubles per throw for the distribution and compare what you find with the theoretical answer.

5 A bag contains green, blue and yellow balls and no others. The probability of drawing a green ball is $\frac{1}{3}$, of drawing a blue one is $\frac{1}{2}$. There are six yellow balls. How many balls are there in the bag?

6 A class does an experiment on the words in a paragraph of this book. They find that the probability of a word having less than five letters, $P(<5)$, is 0.64 and the probability of beginning with a consonant, $P(C)$, is 0.87 (to two decimal places). A boy says that there is something wrong because $P(<5)+P(C) = 0.64+0.87 > 1$. Answer him.

2. PROBABILITY OF COMBINED EVENTS

There are a number of different methods for finding the probabilities of outcomes from combinations of trials. We illustrate each with a different example.

Possibility space diagram

Example 1

Two dice are thrown. What is the probability that neither of them shows a 5?

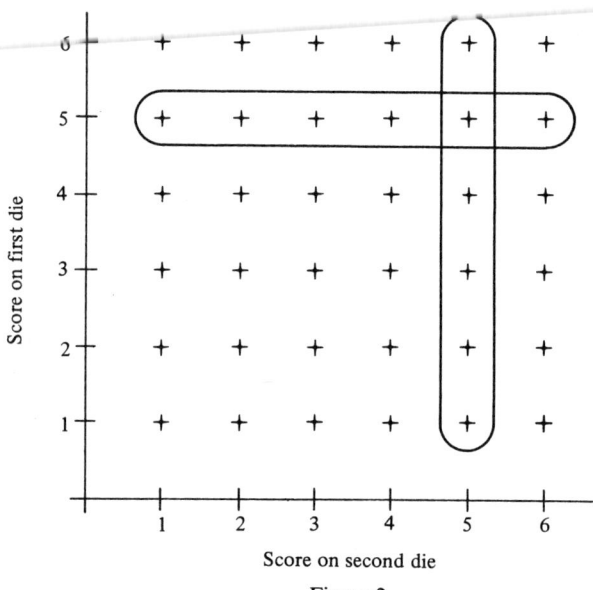

Figure 2

Figure 2 illustrates all the possible outcomes, which are equally probable. From the ringed crosses we see that

$$P \text{ (one or both dice show 5)} = \tfrac{11}{36}$$

and so $P \text{ (neither die shows 5)} = 1 - \tfrac{11}{36} = \tfrac{25}{36}$.

Listing ordered pairs

Example 2

A card is chosen at random from the following set: { ♣ 2, ♥ 3, ♦ 4, ♥ 5}. The chosen card is then replaced, and a second card chosen. What is the probability that both cards are hearts?

All the possible choices are listed below.

(♣2, ♣2) (♣2, ♥3) (♣2, ♦4) (♣2, ♥5)
(♥3, ♣2) (♥3, ♥3) (♥3, ♦4) (♥3, ♥5)
(♦4, ♣2) (♦4, ♥3) (♦4, ♦4) (♦4, ♥5)
(♥5, ♣2) (♥5, ♥3) (♥5, ♦4) (♥5, ♥5)

There are 16 possible outcomes, all equally probable, of which 4 are both hearts. The probability of choosing two hearts is therefore $\frac{4}{16} = \frac{1}{4}$.

Venn diagram

Example 3
A number is chosen at random from the first 12 natural numbers. Find the probability that it is:
(a) greater than 4; (b) a prime; (c) a prime greater than 4.

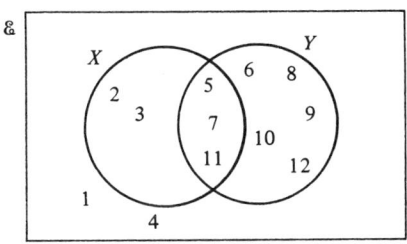

Figure 3

The Venn diagram in Figure 3 shows the set X of primes and the set Y of numbers greater than 4.
(a) $n(\mathscr{E}) = 12$ and $n(Y) = 8$ so $P(Y) = \frac{8}{12} = \frac{2}{3}$.
(b) $n(\mathscr{E}) = 12$ and $n(X) = 5$ so $P(X) = \frac{5}{12}$.
(c) $n(\mathscr{E}) = 12$ and $n(X \cap Y) = 3$ so $P(X \cap Y) = \frac{3}{12} = \frac{1}{4}$.

Tree diagram

The previous methods depend on breaking down a combined event into separate equally probable outcomes. Tree diagrams are particularly useful when dealing with outcomes which are not equally probable.

Example 4
On wet days, the probability that Emma is late for school is 0.2; on other days the probability is 0.1. If 30% of the days in one school year are wet, what is the probability on a randomly chosen day that Emma is late?

Figure 4 shows the relevant tree diagram. From it we see that
  P(wet day and Emma is late) $= 0.3 \times 0.2 = 0.06$,
  P(day is not wet and Emma is late) $= 0.7 \times 0.1 = 0.07$,
so P(Emma is late) $= 0.06 + 0.07 = 0.13$.

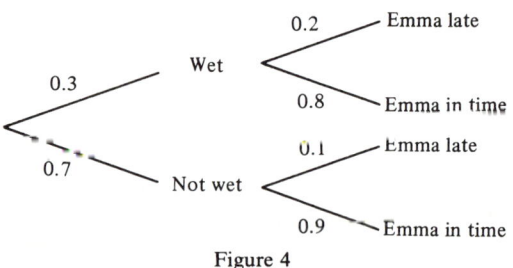

Figure 4

Sum of probabilities

If a die is thrown the probability of scoring an odd number is $\frac{1}{2}$, since three of the six possible outcomes (which are equally probable) are odd numbers. Similarly the probability of scoring 2 or 4 is $\frac{1}{3}$.

P(odd number or 2 or 4) $= P(1, 2, 3, 4$ or $5) = \frac{5}{6}$.
$\phantom{P\text{(odd number or 2 or 4)}} = \frac{1}{2} + \frac{1}{3}$
$\phantom{P\text{(odd number or 2 or 4)}} = P$(odd number)$+ P$(2 or 4)

In this case we are dealing with *exclusive* events – if one event occurs, the other cannot – and for exclusive events A and B,

$$P(A \text{ or } B) = P(A) + P(B).$$

When events are not exclusive, we have to take account of $P(A$ and $B)$. For example, when throwing a die,

P(odd score) $= \frac{1}{2}$
P(prime score) $= P(2, 3$ or $5) = \frac{3}{6} = \frac{1}{2}$
P(odd or prime score) $= P(1, 2, 3,$ or $5) = \frac{4}{6} = \frac{2}{3}$
but P(odd score)$+ P$(prime score) $= \frac{1}{2} + \frac{1}{2} = 1$.

In this case, an odd score and a prime score are not exclusive events, so in adding P(odd score) and P(prime score) we have allowed for the outcome 'odd prime score' twice. This is illustrated by the Venn diagram in Figure 5.

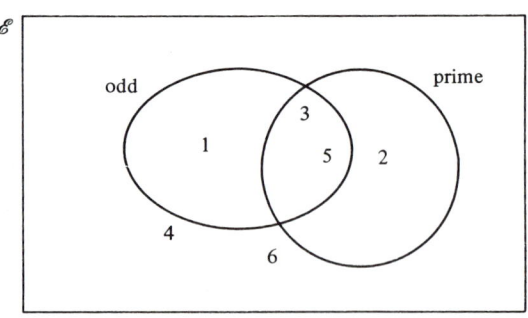

Figure 5

To allow for this 'double-counting', we must subtract P(odd prime score), so we have

P(odd or prime score) $= P$(odd score)$+ P$(prime score)$- P$(odd prime score)
$\phantom{P\text{(odd or prime score)}} \frac{2}{3} = \frac{1}{2} + \frac{1}{2} - \frac{1}{3}$

and in general,

$$P(A \text{ or } B) = P(A) + P(B) - P(A \text{ and } B).$$

Probability of combined events

Exercise B

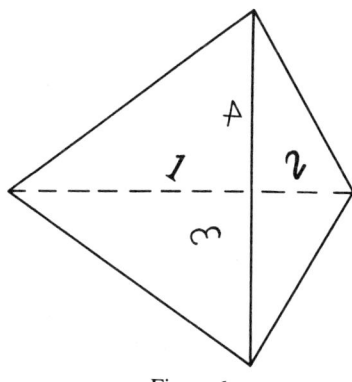

Figure 6

*1 Figure 6 illustrates a tetrahedral die. It is transparent and has four triangular faces, the one coming to rest on the table being the one that scores. Make a table of the possible outcomes if two such dice are thrown together and use it to calculate the following.
   (a) P(a 2 and a 3)
   (b) P(at least one 3)
   (c) P(a total of 4)
   (d) P(a double)
   (e) P(either a double or a total of 4)
   (f) P(a total of less than 2)

2 Two tetrahedral dice are thrown together. Draw a tree diagram for the probability of getting a 3 followed by a 4.

3 Calculate the probability of getting four 4s with four throws of a tetrahedral die.

*4 A card is selected at random from a pack of 52 playing cards.
   Write down the probabilities that it is:
   (a) a diamond; (b) a queen or a diamond (or both).

5 I throw two dice, each numbered 1 to 6, simultaneously.
   Which of the following statements are true and which false?
   (a) Throwing two sixes is less probable than throwing two fours.
   (b) The probability that both dice show the same score is $\frac{1}{6}$.
   (c) The most likely total score is 6.   (SMP O-level)

6 A bag contains 30 discs: 10 red, 10 green, 10 yellow.
   (a) If three are drawn out in succession and not replaced, what is the probability of drawing 2 reds and 1 yellow in that order?
   (b) If each disc is replaced after drawing what would the answer be now?
                                                                           (SMP O-level)

7 From a Youth Club consisting of ten girls and twelve boys a Chairman and a Secretary are to be chosen at random. (No one person may hold both offices.)
   (a) State the probability that a particular girl, Anne, will be chosen as Chairman.
   (b) Copy and complete the tree diagram in Figure 7, inserting in the brackets the probability for that particular stage (N.B. *not* the combined probability).

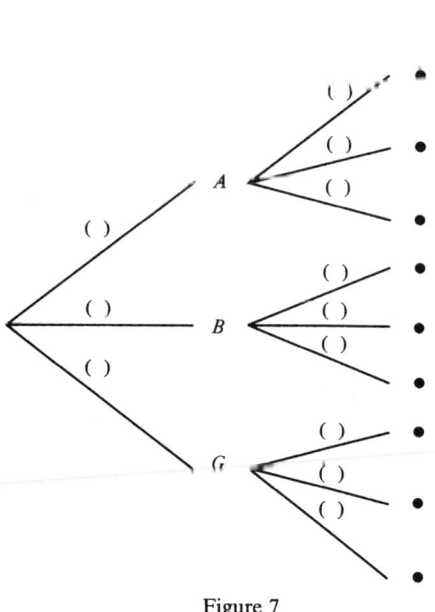

Figure 7

(*A* stands for Anne being chosen, *B* for a boy, and *G* for a girl other than Anne. Some probabilities may be zero.)

(c) What are the probabilities, before any selections are made, that Anne
  (i) will not be chosen as Secretary;
  (ii) will not be chosen for either office?

(d) A further rule is introduced to the effect that the Chairman and Secretary must be of opposite sexes. If the two names are chosen by drawing pieces of paper out of a hat, what is the probability that the second piece drawn will be invalid under this rule? (SMP O-level)

8 A policeman has a beat of four streets to walk every night. The streets form a square *ABCD*. When he comes to the end of a street he tosses a coin. If it comes down heads, then he doubles back on his tracks, if it comes down tails, then he walks down the other street.

(a) If he starts at *A*, draw a tree diagram to illustrate all the possible routes he could take in his first hour if it takes him 20 minutes to walk down one street.

(b) Write down the probabilities that he will not visit *AB*, *BC*, *CD*, *DA* at all during the hour.

(c) What is the probability that a crime committed at a random time in *BC* will be detected?

(The idea of a policeman tossing a coin at each intersection sounds stupid, but it is not so at all. If the policeman has a regular beat, then it is easy to anticipate his movements, and arrange crime accordingly. Even if he thinks he is varying his movements according to whim, he will almost certainly reveal a pattern over a longer period of time. The only way his movements can be made completely unpredictable is by using some such device as a coin.)

9 Roman candles come in boxes which cost 30p for a box of 12. Sixty boxes are tested, and the number of duds per box is found to be:

No of duds	0	1	2	3	4	5
No. of boxes	12	25	11	7	3	2

(a) What is the probability that there are exactly four duds in a box?
(b) What is the effective cost per working Roman candle?
(c) What is the probability that all the candles in two consecutive boxes will work?

10 The organisers of a fête are considering hiring a marquee for £250. They would like to avoid this expense, but are fearful of rain. On past experience, they expect that the takings at the fête will be down £500 if it rains and there is no marquee, but will be down only £50 if it rains and there is a marquee. If they hire a marquee, the organisers can take out insurance for £100 whereby the cost of hiring the marquee is refunded if there is rain on the day of the fête. They therefore have three possible strategies:
(1) not to hire a marquee;
(2) to hire a marquee and insure against rain;
(3) to hire a marquee and not to insure against rain.
What would you advise them to do if they estimate the probability of rain on the day of the fête to be:
(a) 0.25; (b) 0.4; (c) 0.6; (d) 0.7?

3. BINOMIAL PROBABILITIES

A tetrahedral die, with faces numbered 1, 2, 3 and 4, is thrown twice. (The face on the bottom of the die is the one which scores.) The number of threes scored is counted. Figure 8 shows the appropriate tree diagram.

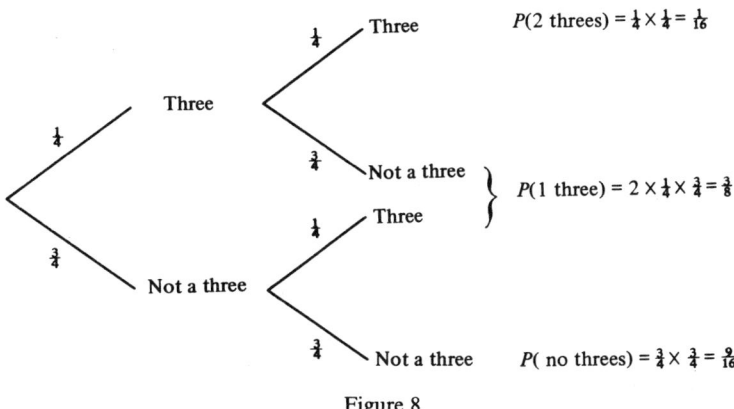

Figure 8

What happens if the die is thrown three times? Before drawing the tree diagram we notice that, since we are just counting the number of threes and are not concerned about the order in which they occur, we can amalgamate the two central 'twigs' of the tree diagram in Figure 8 to obtain the network in Figure 9. We must remember to allow for the two routes through the network to the point corresponding to the outcome of '1 three'.

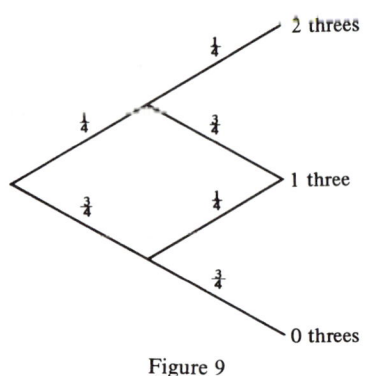

Figure 9

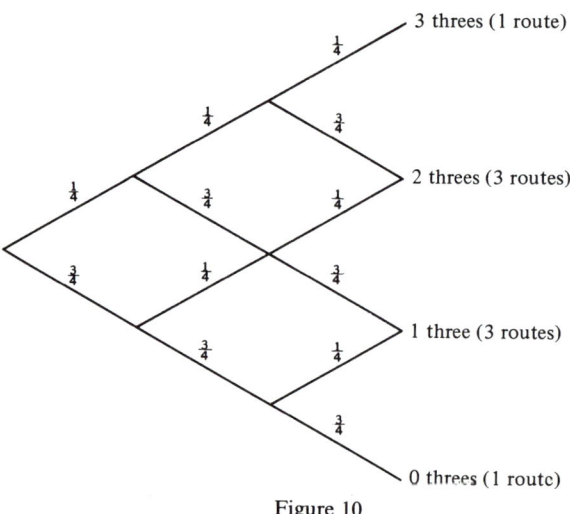

Figure 10

We then extend this network to deal with three throws of the die (see Figure 10). From this we deduce that

$$P(3 \text{ threes}) = (\tfrac{1}{4})^3 = \tfrac{1}{64}$$
$$P(2 \text{ threes}) = 3(\tfrac{1}{4})^2(\tfrac{3}{4}) = \tfrac{9}{64}$$
$$P(1 \text{ three}) = 3(\tfrac{1}{4})(\tfrac{3}{4})^2 = \tfrac{27}{64}$$
$$P(0 \text{ threes}) = (\tfrac{3}{4})^3 = \tfrac{27}{64}$$

The 3 routes through the network to the '2 threes' point correspond to the outcomes

three, three, not a three
three, not a three, three
not a three, three, three

each of which has probability $(\frac{1}{4})^2(\frac{3}{4})$. So the expression for each probability is of the form

number of routes $\times (\frac{1}{4})^{\text{number of threes}} \times (\frac{3}{4})^{\text{number of non-threes}}$

The network can clearly be extended to deal with any number of throws of the die. We just need to count the relevant number of routes for any particular case. Figure 11 shows the number of routes to series of points in the network.

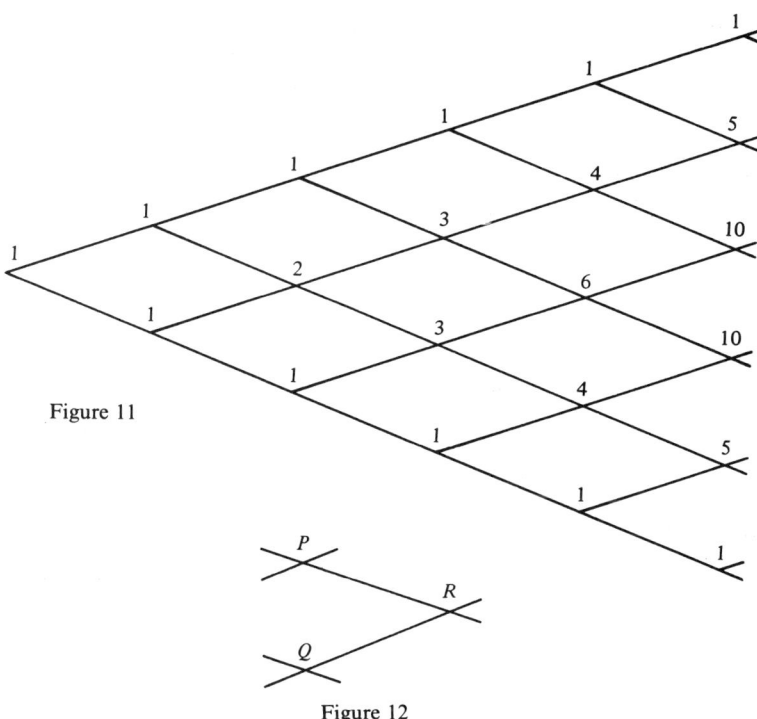

Figure 11

Figure 12

Notice how the numbers build up. In Figure 12:

$$\begin{aligned}\text{number of routes to } R &= \text{number of routes via } P + \text{number of routes via } Q \\ &= \text{number of routes to } P + \text{number of routes to } Q\end{aligned}$$

The numbers obtained constitute *Pascal's triangle*, which is usually written in rows, rather than columns, as follows:

```
              1
            1   1
          1   2   1
        1   3   3   1
      1   4   6   4   1
    1   5  10  10   5   1
  1   6  15  20  15   6   1
            etc.
```

So we can deduce, for example, that the probability of obtaining 2 threes in 6 throws of the die is

$$15(\tfrac{1}{6})^2(\tfrac{5}{6})^4 = \frac{1215}{4096} = 0.30 \text{ to 2 s.f.}$$

The word *binomial* is used to describe this sort of situation. The essential features are: a series of trials in which there are just two outcomes (a 'three' or 'not a three') and in which the probabilities of each outcome are the same for each trial.

Example 5

It is estimated that 5% of the pupils in a school are left-handed. What is the probability that of 5 pupils chosen at random just two are left-handed?

The appropriate row of Pascal's triangle is
$$1, 5, 10, 10, 5, 1$$
corresponding to 0, 1, 2, 3, 4, 5 left-handers.

So $P(2 \text{ left handers in } 5) = 10 \times 0.05^2 \times 0.95^3$
$$= 0.021 \text{ to 2 s.f.}$$

Exercise C

*1 The probability that a certain type of drawing-pin lands point up when tossed is 0.4. If four drawing-pins are tossed, what are the probabilities that the number landing point up is:
(*a*) 0;   (*b*) 1;   (*c*) 2;   (*d*) 3;   (*e*) 4?

2 It is estimated that 10% of the remould tyres leaving a factory are defective. Five tyres are selected at random. What are the probabilities of:
(*a*) no defective tyres;
(*b*) four defective tyres;
(*c*) at least one defective tyre?

3 It is estimated that 30% of the voters in Transylvania are supporters of the Vampire Party. If five voters are chosen at random, what is the probability that just two of them are Vampire Party supporters?

4 In a multiple choice test, 4 marks are awarded for giving the correct answer to a question and 1 mark is subtracted for giving any one of the four incorrect answers. Peter just guesses at the answers, so he has a chance of $\tfrac{1}{5}$ of choosing the correct answer. In answering five questions what are the probabilities that Peter scores:
(*a*) 20 marks;   (*b*) 15 marks;   (*c*) 10 marks;
(*d*) 5 marks;   (*e*) 0 marks;   (*f*) ⁻5 marks?

Suppose that 100 candidates used similar tactics. How many (to the nearest whole number) would you expect to obtain each of the possible scores from ⁻5 to 20? Use your answers to calculate the expected average mark for the 100 candidates.

5 Extend Pascal's triangle as far as the row beginning 1, 10, ...

*6 A particular commuter train runs to time on 90% of weekdays.
(*a*) What is the probability that in one week (Monday to Friday) it was on time on every day except one?
(*b*) What is the probability that it is not on time just twice in ten days?

7 A mail-order company has nine incoming telephone lines. If the probability that any one is in use is 0.8, find the probability that:
   (a) no lines are free;
   (b) two lines are free;
   (c) at least one line is free.
8 It is claimed that 60% of the seeds of a certain plant will germinate. What is the probability that exactly 6 out of 10 randomly chosen seeds of the plant will germinate?
9 The study of probability began with a correspondence between a French gambler, the Chevalier de Méré, and the mathematician Blaise Pascal. One of the Chevalier's questions was: Is it safe to bet that you will get at least one six in 4 throws of a die? Answer him.
10 Another of the Chevalier's questions was: Is it worth betting that in 24 throws of two dice there will be at least one double six? Answer his question.

SUMMARY

If, in N trials, an event has occurred r times, then the relative frequency of that event is $\dfrac{r}{N}$.

Probabilities may be found from arguments of symmetry or from investigating how the relative frequency settles down as N increases. (Section 1)

The probabilities of combined events can be found by drawing a possibility space diagram, by listing the ordered pairs, by drawing a Venn diagram, or by drawing a tree diagram. (Section 2)

When a trial is repeated and there are just two outcomes with the same probabilities on every occasion, Pascal's triangle can be used to obtain the relevant binomial probabilities. (Section 3)

Summary exercise

1 (a) Two unbiased coins are tossed together. State the probability that they will both (i) be heads, (ii) be the same (that is, either both heads or both tails).
   (b) One unbiased coin is tossed together with a 'loaded' coin which has a probability of $\frac{2}{5}$ of landing heads, $\frac{3}{5}$ of landing tails. State the probability that they will both (i) be heads, (ii) be the same.
   (c) Two coins, one with probability p, the other with probability q of landing heads, are tossed together. Obtain an expression for the probability r that they will be the same. By multiplying out show that $2(p-\frac{1}{2})(q-\frac{1}{2})+\frac{1}{2}$ is equal to your expression for r.
   If r is equal to $\frac{1}{2}$ state the value of $2(p-\frac{1}{2})(q-\frac{1}{2})$. What does this tell you about the coins? (SMP O-level)

2 A game is played with counters and a die on a board marked as in Figure 13.

Counters are placed on 0. Each player throws the die in turn. If the die shows 1 or 5, the counter is moved five squares towards 10 (move F); if 2, 3, 4 or 6, it is moved two squares towards 0 (move T). Each time, the counter is moved as far as possible without actually moving off the board. The winner is the player whose counter first reaches 10.

0	1	2	3	4	5	6	7	8	9	10

Figure 13

(a) State the probabilities, at a single throw, of (i) F, (ii) T, and calculate the probability that the first player wins on his second throw.

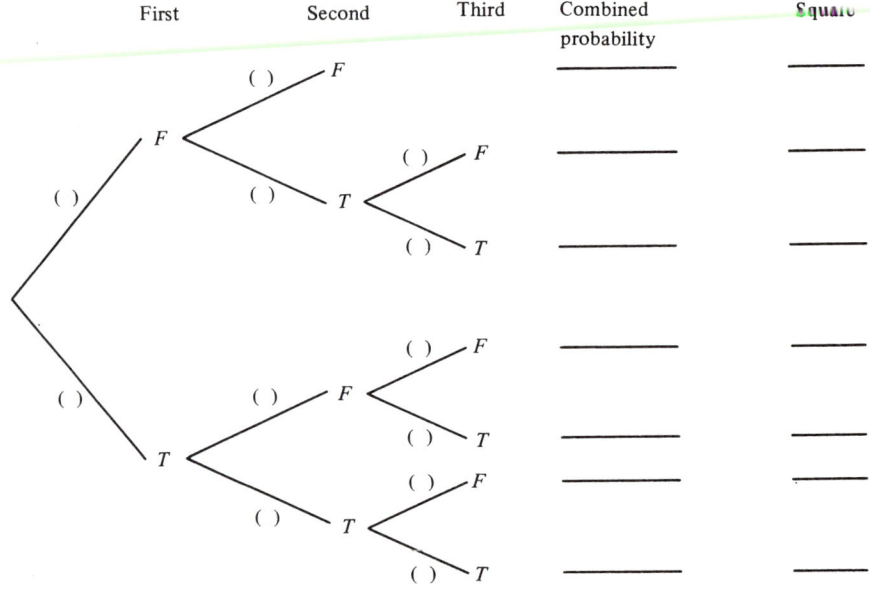

Figure 14

(b) Copy the tree diagram in Figure 14 relating to successive throws by one player and mark (in the brackets) the probabilities for each branch. Calculate and mark the combined probabilities and state which square is occupied by the counter after the three (or fewer) throws in each case.

(c) Calculate the probabilities that, after three throws by one player, the counter
   (i) has reached 10; (ii) is not then beyond 4.   (SMP O-level)

3 About 7.5% of men are colour-blind. In a group of 10 men chosen at random, what are the probabilities that:
   (a) none is colour-blind;
   (b) at least two are colour-blind?

What are the corresponding probabilities for a group of 10 women? (About 0.1% of women are colour-blind.)

9

Vectors applied

In this chapter we review our earlier work on vectors and trigonometry in a geometrical context. We then look at other vector quantities, such as velocities and forces.

1. POSITION AND DISPLACEMENT VECTORS

Translations have been specified by displacement vectors which are conveniently given by column matrices.

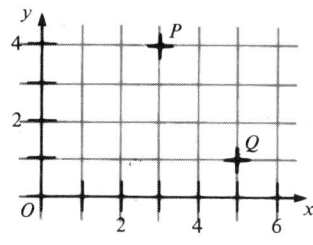

Figure 1

In Figure 1, the point $P(3, 4)$ is said to have position vector $\underline{OP} = \begin{bmatrix} 3 \\ 4 \end{bmatrix}$. The translation represented by $\begin{bmatrix} 3 \\ 4 \end{bmatrix}$ maps O onto P.

A translation from P to Q is described by the displacement vector $\underline{PQ} = \begin{bmatrix} 2 \\ -3 \end{bmatrix}$.

The position vector of the point Q is $\underline{OQ} = \begin{bmatrix} 5 \\ 1 \end{bmatrix}$.

A translation from O to Q is described by the displacement vector $\underline{OQ} = \begin{bmatrix} 5 \\ 1 \end{bmatrix}$.

A displacement from Q to O is described by $\underline{QO} = \begin{bmatrix} -5 \\ -1 \end{bmatrix}$.

Displacement vectors can be added or subtracted.
In Figure 1, $\underline{OP} = \underline{OQ} + \underline{QP}$.

As a check: $\underline{OP} = \begin{bmatrix} 3 \\ 4 \end{bmatrix}$ and $\underline{OQ} + \underline{QP} = \begin{bmatrix} 5 \\ 1 \end{bmatrix} + \begin{bmatrix} -2 \\ 3 \end{bmatrix} = \begin{bmatrix} 3 \\ 4 \end{bmatrix}$.

In general, as in Figure 2, $\underline{AB} = \underline{AO} + \underline{OB}$
$$= {}^{-}\underline{OA} + \underline{OB}$$
$$= \underline{OB} - \underline{OA}.$$

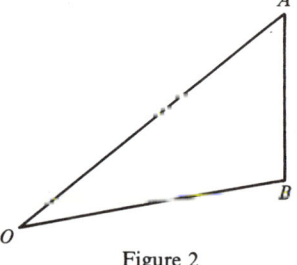

Figure 2

So for points $A\ (3, {}^{-}5)$, $B\ (4, {}^{-}7)$, for instance,
$$\underline{AB} = \begin{bmatrix} 4 \\ -7 \end{bmatrix} - \begin{bmatrix} 3 \\ -5 \end{bmatrix} = \begin{bmatrix} 1 \\ -2 \end{bmatrix}.$$

$OPQR$ is a parallelogram so that RQ is equal in length to OP and parallel to it (see Figure 3).

So we can write $\quad \underline{OP} = \underline{RQ} = \underline{a}$,
Similarly $\qquad\qquad \underline{PQ} = \underline{QR} = \underline{b}$,
then $\qquad\qquad\quad \underline{OQ} = \underline{OP} + \underline{PQ} = \underline{a} + \underline{b}$,
and $\qquad\qquad\quad \underline{PR} = \underline{PO} + \underline{OR} = {}^{-}\underline{a} + \underline{b} = \underline{b} - \underline{a}$.

Also, since G is the centre of half-turn symmetry of the parallelogram, it is the midpoint of OQ.

So $\underline{QG} = \tfrac{1}{2}\underline{OQ} = \tfrac{1}{2}(\underline{a} + \underline{b})$.

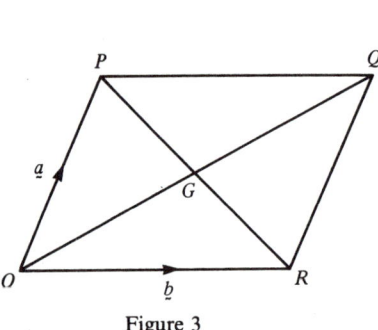

Figure 3

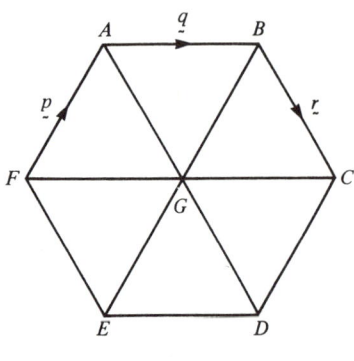

Figure 4

In Figure 4, which consists of equilateral triangles, a translation from F to A, written $\underline{FA}$, is the same distance and direction as a translation from D to C, written $\underline{DC}$.

So $\quad \underline{FA} = \underline{DC} = \underline{p}$
also $\quad \underline{EB} = 2\underline{FA} = 2\underline{p}$
and $\quad \underline{AF} = {}^{-}\underline{FA} = {}^{-}\underline{p}$.
$AB = FA$ in length only, not direction, so $\underline{AB} \neq \underline{FA}$.
It is true that $\underline{AB} = \underline{FG} = \underline{GC} = \underline{ED} = \underline{q}$
and $\underline{CB} = \underline{EF} = \tfrac{1}{2}\underline{DA} = {}^{-}\underline{r}$.

Position and displacement vectors

Exercise A

(All questions are taken from SMP O-level papers.)

*1 $OA = \begin{bmatrix} 3 \\ 4 \end{bmatrix}, OB = \begin{bmatrix} 2 \\ 3 \end{bmatrix}$.

Write as column vectors (a) AO; (b) AB.

2 a and b are the vectors represented by the line segments in Figure 5. Write down as column vectors:
(i) b; (ii) $a + 2b$.

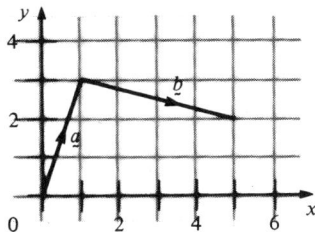

Figure 5

3 The position vectors of two points A and B are
$$\begin{bmatrix} 2 \\ -1 \end{bmatrix} \text{ and } \begin{bmatrix} -4 \\ 2 \end{bmatrix}$$
respectively. Write down the vector $2AB$.

4 If $a = \begin{bmatrix} 3 \\ 4 \end{bmatrix}$ and $b = \begin{bmatrix} -2 \\ 1 \end{bmatrix}$ find the vectors $\tfrac{1}{2}a$ and $a - b$.

*5 If $\begin{bmatrix} 2 \\ 3 \end{bmatrix} - \begin{bmatrix} c \\ d \end{bmatrix} = \begin{bmatrix} -1 \\ y \end{bmatrix}$, find c and d when $y = 2$.

6 (5, 3) is mapped on to (7, −1) by a translation. What is the image of (−2, 1) under the same translation?

7 (a) The translation given by the vector
$$a = \begin{bmatrix} -1 \\ 2 \end{bmatrix}$$
maps (1, 3) onto the point P. Find P.
(b) The translation which maps (0, 5) onto (1, 3) is given by the vector b. Find b.

8 Which of the following is equal to the vector EF in Figure 6?
(a) $p + q + r + s$; (b) $p - q - r - s$;
(c) $s + r + q - p$; (d) $s + r - q - p$.

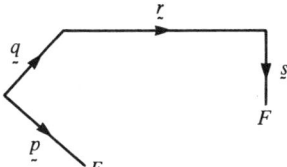

Figure 6

*9 $ABCDEF$ is a regular hexagon with centre O. Vector $OA = a$ and vector $OB = b$ (see Figure 7).
(a) Express the following vectors in terms of a and b:
DO, AF, AB, DB.
(b) Points L, M, N are given by $OL = a + b$, $OM = b - 2a$, $ON = a - 2b$. Find the vectors NF and FL. What does this tell you about the points N, F and L?
(c) Find the vector LM.
(d) What sort of triangle is LMN?

10 $ABCDEF$ is a regular octahedron. Vectors p, q, r, s are defined by the edges as shown in Figure 8. Which of the following statements are true and which are false?
   (a) $p+q = CE$. (b) $BF = r+p$. (c) $FE = p+q+r$. (d) $q = r+s$.
   ($EBFD$ and $ABCD$ are squares.)

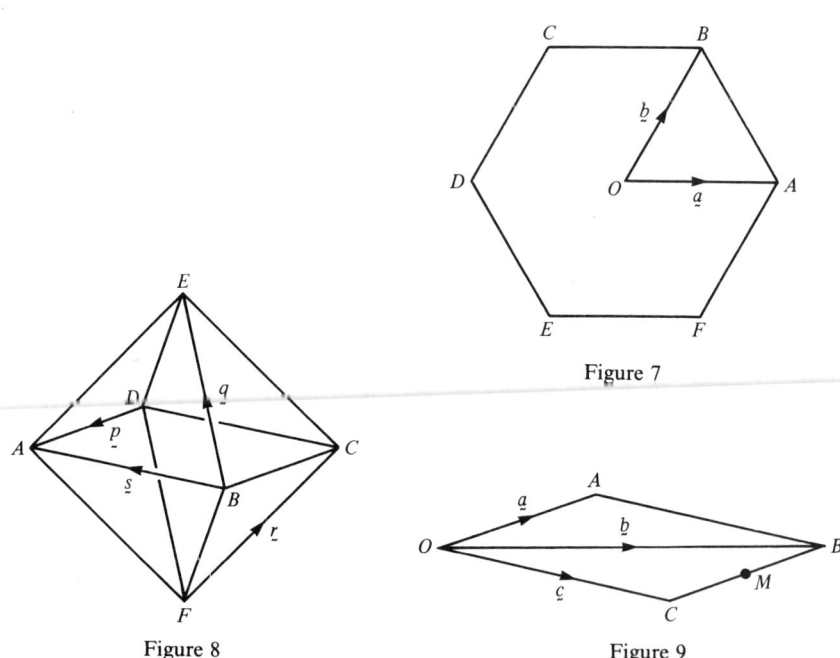

Figure 7

Figure 8

Figure 9

11 $OABC$ is a parallelogram. M is the midpoint of BC. The position vectors of A, B, C referred to the origin O are a, b, c (see Figure 9).
   (a) Write down, in terms of b and c, expressions for the following vectors: CB, CM, OM.
   (b) (i) Express AM in terms of a, b and c.
       (ii) P is a point (not shown on the diagram), with position vector p, such that $AP = \frac{2}{3}AM$. Express AP in terms of a and p, and show that p can be expressed in the form $\frac{1}{n}(a+b+c)$ where n is an integer.
   (c) Use the fact that $b = a+c$ to find p in terms of b only. Deduce a result about the position of P.

12 A, B, C have position vectors a, b, c, respectively, relative to an origin O.
   (a) Write in terms of a, b, c the vectors (i) CB, (ii) AC, (iii) $\frac{1}{2}AC$.
   (b) State the position vectors of the midpoints of (i) OB, (ii) AC.
   (c) If OA is parallel and equal to CB, find an equation connecting a, b, c. Deduce a connection between your answers to (b).
   (d) State which property of a parallelogram this demonstrates.

2. COMPONENTS AND RESULTANTS

In Figure 10, P is the point with cartesian coordinates (3, 4).
$$OP^2 = OA^2 + AP^2 \text{ (by Pythagoras' theorem)}$$
$$= 3^2 + 4^2 = 25$$
so $OP = 5$.
Also $\tan \angle AOP = \tfrac{4}{3}$
so $\angle AOP \approx 53°$.
The polar coordinates of P are $(5, 53°)$.

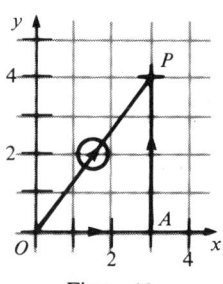

Figure 10

The vector $\underline{OP}$ can therefore be described either by writing $\underline{OP} = \begin{bmatrix} 3 \\ 4 \end{bmatrix}$ or by saying that its magnitude is 5 and that it makes an angle of 53° with the x-axis. The magnitude of $\underline{OP}$ can be written as $|\underline{OP}|$, or simply as OP.

$\underline{OP}$ is said to have a *component*, $\underline{QA}$, of magnitude 3 parallel to the x-axis and a component, $\underline{AP}$, of magnitude 4 parallel to the y-axis.
$$\underline{OP} = \underline{OA} + \underline{AP}$$
$$\begin{bmatrix} 3 \\ 4 \end{bmatrix} = \begin{bmatrix} 3 \\ 0 \end{bmatrix} + \begin{bmatrix} 0 \\ 4 \end{bmatrix}$$

$\underline{OP}$ is the sum of the vectors $\underline{OA}$ and $\underline{AP}$. The sum of two vectors is also called their *resultant* and denoted by ——⊖—— as shown in Figure 10.

In general, a vector $\underline{r}$, of magnitude r and making an angle of $\theta°$ with the x-axis, has a component of magnitude $r \cos \theta°$ parallel to the x-axis and a component of magnitude $r \sin \theta°$ parallel to the y-axis. (See Figure 11.) So we can write
$$\underline{r} = \begin{bmatrix} r \cos \theta° \\ r \sin \theta° \end{bmatrix} \quad \text{or} \quad \underline{r} = r \begin{bmatrix} \cos \theta° \\ \sin \theta° \end{bmatrix}.$$

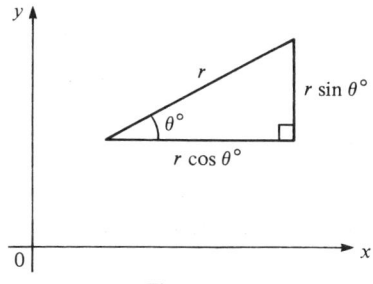

Figure 11

Example 1

Describe in column matrix form a displacement of magnitude 7 units in a direction making an angle of 201° with the x-axis, as shown in Figure 12(a).

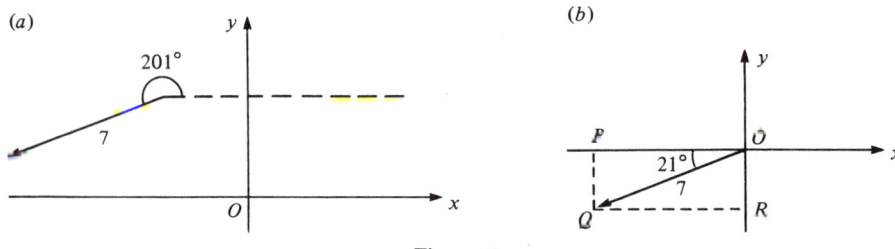

Figure 12

Solution (1): Consider an equal vector as in Figure 12(b).
$$OP = 7\cos 21° = 6.5 \text{ to 2 s.f.}$$
$$OR = PQ = 7\sin 21° = 2.5 \text{ to 2 s.f.}$$
so $O\underset{\sim}{Q} = \begin{bmatrix} -6.5 \\ -2.5 \end{bmatrix}$.

Solution (2): Using the result given above this example, the displacement is
$$\begin{bmatrix} 7\cos 201° \\ 7\sin 201° \end{bmatrix} \approx \begin{bmatrix} -6.5 \\ -2.5 \end{bmatrix}.$$

Use of bearings

Example 2

A ship travels 17 miles on a bearing 032°. What is the component of this journey in an easterly direction?

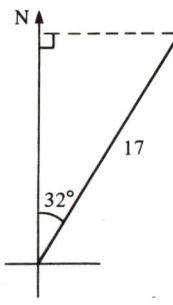

Figure 13

From Figure 13, the easterly component has magnitude $17 \sin 32° \approx 9.0$ miles.

Note that since geographical bearings are clockwise, from north, which does not fit in with the mathematics convention, column vectors should never be used without a clear description of what they are intended to mean. It is usually safest to avoid column vector notation with this type of problem.

Example 3

Leaving Portham a ship travels 21 miles on a bearing 137° and then 35 miles on a bearing 228°. Calculate its distance from Portham and the bearing of Portham from the ship.

Method (1)

A reasonably accurate sketch of the journey is helpful: see Figure 14(a).
(We shall work to an accuracy of three significant figures with a view to obtaining an answer likely to be accurate to the nearest mile and nearest degree.)

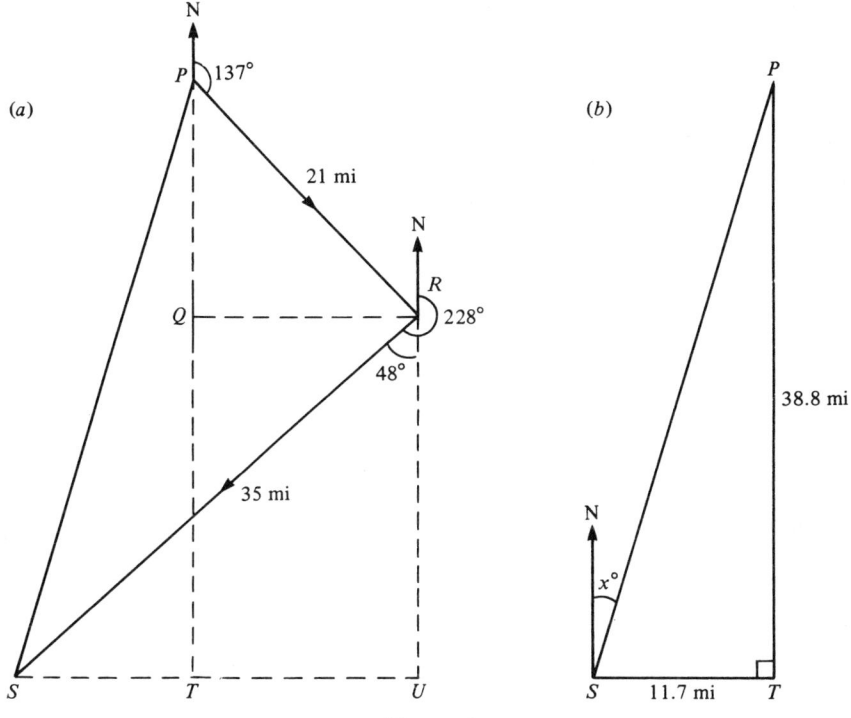

Figure 14

From the diagram, $PQ = 21 \cos 43°$ mi ≈ 15.4 mi,
$$QT = RU = 35 \cos 48° \text{ mi} \approx 23.4 \text{ mi}.$$
So the total distance travelled southwards, PT, is $(15.4 + 23.4)$ mi $= 38.8$ mi.
Also $QR = 21 \sin 43°$ mi ≈ 14.3 mi
and $SU = 35 \sin 48°$ mi ≈ 26.0 mi.
So the total distance travelled westwards, ST, is $(26.0 - 14.3)$ mi $= 11.7$ mi.
The distance from Portham, SP, is
$\sqrt{(38.8^2 + 11.7^2)} \approx 41$ mi (by Pythagoras' theorem; see Figure 14(b)).
Also, in Figure 14(b), $x° = \angle SPT$
$$\tan \angle SPT = \frac{11.7}{38.8} \Leftarrow SPT \approx 17°.$$
The bearing of Portham from the ship $\approx 017°$.

Method (2)

This method is for use, particularly, with calculators having trigonometric functions.

In general, consider a ship which travels a distance, d, on a bearing $\phi°$. (See Figure 15.)

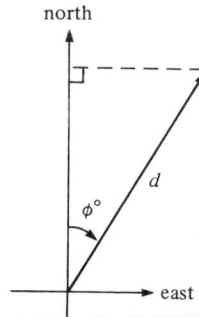

Figure 15

The northwards component of its journey is $d\cos\phi°$, and the eastwards component is $d\sin\phi°$.

This will be true whatever the size of ϕ so that our ship travels
northwards, a distance $(21\cos 137° + 35\cos 228°)$ mi and
eastwards, a distance $(21\sin 137° + 35\sin 228°)$ mi.

These two distances can be worked out directly on a calculator which has trigonometric functions and come to:
$^-38.8$ mi northwards and $^-11.7$ mi eastwards.

At this stage a sketch is again wise and produces Figure 14(b). The final part of the calculation is as before.

Exercise B

*1 $a = \begin{bmatrix} 12 \\ -5 \end{bmatrix}$, $b = \begin{bmatrix} -8 \\ 15 \end{bmatrix}$.

(a) Calculate the magnitudes of a and b.

(b) Calculate the angles between a and the x-axis, b and the x-axis, and between a and b.

2 Give the position vectors of the points A, B, C, D, having polar coordinates $A(2, 34°)$, $B(2, 100°)$, $C(2, 222°)$, $D(2, 345°)$. Hence write down the cartesian coordinates of these points. Describe the locus of all points having polar coordinates $(2, \theta°)$ as θ varies.

3 Find the polar coordinates of the points P, Q, R, S, having cartesian coordinates, $P(1, 2)$, $Q(3, ^-4)$, $R(^-5, 6)$, $S(^-7, ^-8)$.

4 If $y = mx$ is the equation of the locus of all points having polar coordinates $(r, 120°)$, where r can vary, what is the value of m?

5 The point P, with polar coordinates $(3, 0°)$, is reflected in the line $\theta = 20°$ to give P', which is then reflected in the line $\theta = 50°$ to give P''. State the polar coordinates of P' and P''. (See Figure 16.)

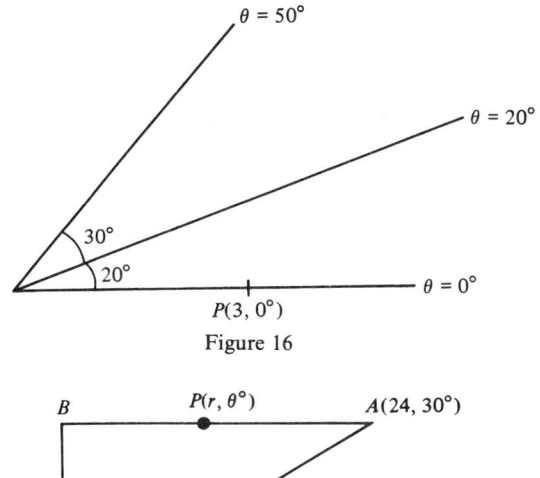

Figure 16

Figure 17

*6 The polar coordinates of the point A in Figure 17 are (24, 30°), BPA is a straight line parallel to the central direction Ox and OB is perpendicular to Ox.
   (a) What are the polar coordinates of B?
   (b) If $BP = 9$ units, what are the values of r and θ? (SMP O-level)

7 A vector of magnitude 5 makes angle 28° with the x-axis.
   Find (a) the component of this vector parallel to Ox,
        (b) the component parallel to Oy.

8 Find the magnitude and direction of the resultant (sum) of the vectors
$$\begin{bmatrix}1\\3\end{bmatrix}, \begin{bmatrix}2\\-4\end{bmatrix}, \begin{bmatrix}4\\4\end{bmatrix}.$$

9 Find the distance between points X and Y with polar coordinates (17, 250°) and (22, 136°) respectively.

10 (a) A ship sails a distance m miles on a bearing $\alpha°$. Write down a formula for
       (i) the northerly component, and
       (ii) the easterly component of its journey.
   (b) If the ship travels 17 miles on a bearing 029°, how far is it
       (i) north, (ii) east of its starting point?

11 Answer this problem by an accurate scale drawing, then check your answer by calculation.
   A yacht sails 4.2 km on a bearing 135° and then 5.9 km on a bearing 304°. On what bearing should it sail in order to return, on a straight course, to its starting point? How far will it have to sail?

12 After being lost in a storm overnight, a pirate makes various observations and reckons he is 12 miles north and 9 miles east of his base on Ras Sinku. What is the bearing of Ras Sinku from the pirate ship?

To avoid a reef, he has to sail due west 6 miles and then south-west 2 miles before he can set a straight course for base. What will then be the course he should set and how far will he then have to sail?

3. SOME OTHER VECTOR QUANTITIES

Vectors are used to represent other physical quantities which have magnitude and direction, for example velocities and forces. Like displacements, velocities or forces can conveniently be split into components in two perpendicular directions, or can be added together to find a resultant.

Example 4

A ship is sailing at 15 knots (that is, 15 nautical miles per hour) in the direction NNE. How far east and how far north does it travel in three hours?

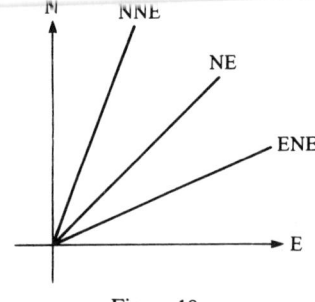

Figure 18

NNE is $\dfrac{45°}{2} = 22\tfrac{1}{2}°$ east of north (see Figure 18), so is equivalent to a bearing of 022.5°.

A velocity vector of 15 knots NNE therefore has:
  a northerly component of magnitude 15 cos 22.5° knots ≈ 13.9 knots
  an easterly component of magnitude 15 sin 22.5° knots ≈ 5.7 knots.
In three hours the ship travels
    3 × 13.9 nautical miles = 42 nautical miles north to 2 s.f.
    3 × 5.7 nautical miles = 17 nautical miles east to 2 s.f.

The unit of force is the *newton*, abbreviated to N, named after Sir Isaac Newton (1642–1727). Forces are also vectors.

Example 5

Spiro and his son Nikos are attempting to move their donkey into its shed (see Figure 19(*a*)). Spiro pulls with a force of 500 N and Nikos with a force of 400 N, in the directions shown. What is the magnitude and direction of the resultant force on the donkey?

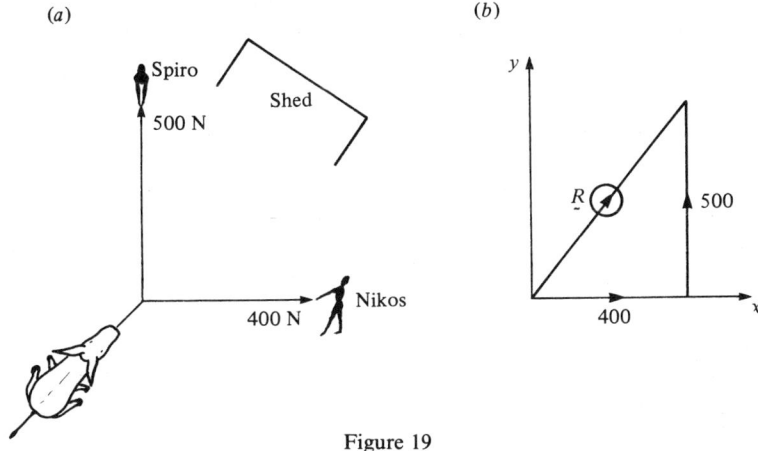

Figure 19

With x- and y-axes as shown in Figure 19(b), Spiro exerts a force of $\begin{bmatrix} 0 \\ 500 \end{bmatrix}$ N and Nikos a force of $\begin{bmatrix} 400 \\ 0 \end{bmatrix}$ N.

The total force on the donkey is $\begin{bmatrix} 0 \\ 500 \end{bmatrix}$ N $+ \begin{bmatrix} 400 \\ 0 \end{bmatrix}$ N $= \begin{bmatrix} 400 \\ 500 \end{bmatrix}$ N.

So the resultant, R, has magnitude $\sqrt{(400^2 + 500^2)}$ N $= 640$ N to 2 s.f. and its direction makes an angle $\theta°$ with the x-axis where $\theta° = \tan^{-1}\left(\dfrac{500}{400}\right) = 51°$ to the nearest degree.

Exercise C

*1 A ship sails at 18 knots on a course 072° for $2\frac{1}{2}$ hours. How far north and how far east of its starting point is it at the end of this time?

2 A ship leaves port sailing at 12 knots on a bearing 210° for 45 minutes and then continues at 9 knots on a bearing 308° for 90 minutes. By calculation, find on what bearing it should sail in order to return directly to port. If its maximum speed is 22 knots, how long will it take to get back to port?

3 A very small spider, situated at (0, 2) on Myfanwy's graph, (which she has drawn for homework with a scale in centimetres), gallops across the paper with velocity $\begin{bmatrix} 0.25 \\ 0.5 \end{bmatrix}$ cm/s for 10 seconds, and then makes a nasty little bright yellow mark on which Myfanwy's rubber has no effect. Where is the mark? What is the equation of the straight line along which the spider has progressed?

4 Find the magnitude and direction of the resultant (sum) of

  (a) forces $\begin{bmatrix} 0 \\ 30 \end{bmatrix}$ N and $\begin{bmatrix} 40 \\ 0 \end{bmatrix}$ N;

  (b) forces $\begin{bmatrix} -37 \\ 0 \end{bmatrix}$ N and $\begin{bmatrix} 0 \\ 54 \end{bmatrix}$ N;

(c) forces $\begin{bmatrix} 2 \\ 5 \end{bmatrix}$ N and $\begin{bmatrix} 4 \\ 3 \end{bmatrix}$ N;

(d) forces $\begin{bmatrix} 1 \\ 1 \end{bmatrix}$ N, $\begin{bmatrix} -2 \\ 5 \end{bmatrix}$ N and $\begin{bmatrix} 1 \\ -6 \end{bmatrix}$ N.

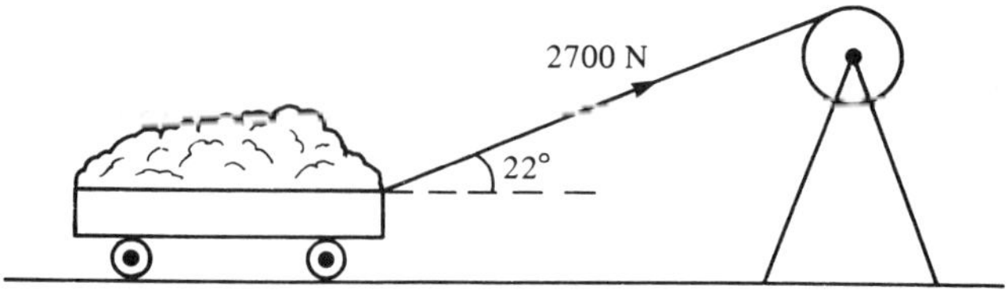

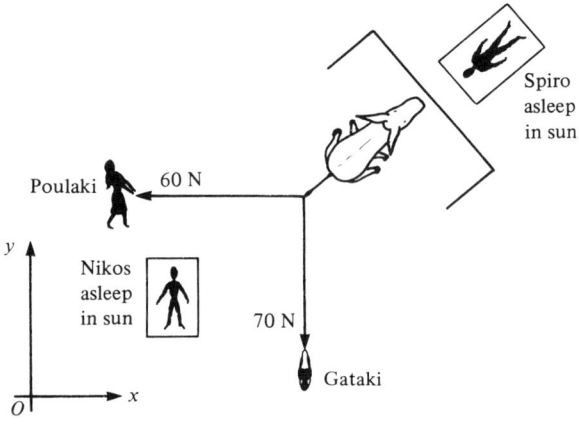

Figure 20

*5 In order to pull a loaded trolley along a track, a rope is connected to the front of the trolley and wound onto a drum as shown in Figure 20.

Find the horizontal component of the tension in the rope. If the horizontal resistances to motion add up to 2400 N, will the trolley move? What is the vertical component of the tension in the rope?

Figure 21

6 Nikos (see Example 5) has two younger sisters known as Poulaki and Gataki (which, in English, would be Chick and Kitten). Seeing the donkey in the shed, they decide to try to get it out by pulling on its tail, to the end of which they attach two pieces of string. (See Figure 21.) Poulaki pulls with a force of 60 N and Gataki with a force of 70 N in the directions shown.

Taking x- and y-axes as shown, find as a column matrix the resultant (sum) of these two forces.

If the resultant (sum) of the forces is more than 90 N the donkey will complain so loudly that Spiro will wake from his siesta and beat his daughters. Will this happen?

7 Express each of the forces shown in Figure 22 in column matrix form.

Hence find the sum (resultant) of these forces in column matrix form and calculate its magnitude and direction.

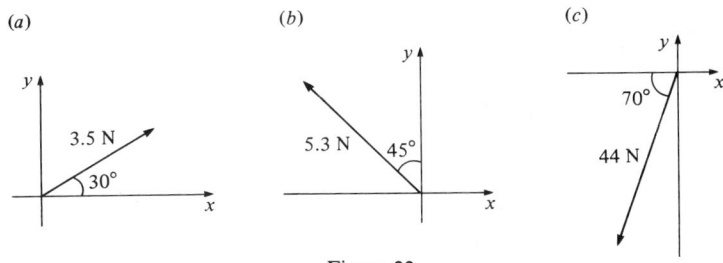

Figure 22

4. RELATIVE VELOCITY

When you walk from the front to the back of a ship, which is sailing forwards, you may, in fact, still be moving, relative to the sea, in the same direction as the boat, though more slowly!

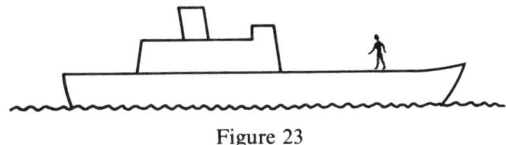

Figure 23

When you sit in a railway carriage in a station and the train next to you pulls out from the station, you often feel that you must be moving and that the other train is really standing still.

When you watch the sun setting, you imagine the sun moving while the earth stands still – in fact, the earth is spinning on its axis causing you to move relative to the sun.

Vectors can help us to understand relative velocity.

Example 6
Duncan swims (relative to the water) at about 1.5 m/s and wants to cross a river which is flowing with an average mid-stream speed of about 1.0 m/s. Neglecting the fact that the speed of the river is less near the banks, find the direction he will move relative to the bank if he 'aims' perpendicular to the bank. (See Figure 24(*a*).)

Figure 24

There are two velocities we know:
Duncan's velocity relative to the water: 1.5 m/s perpendicular to the bank.
The velocity of the water relative to the earth: 1.0 m/s parallel to the bank.
Adding these, in Figure 24(b), we see that the resultant velocity of Duncan relative to the earth makes angle $\theta°$ with the direction of flow of the river where

$$\theta° = \tan^{-1}\left(\frac{1.5}{1.0}\right) \approx 56°.$$

Example 7

Suppose we want to find in what direction Duncan must aim so as to reach a point on the opposite bank immediately opposite his starting point.

The velocity of water relative to earth is unchanged, and we need to add the velocity of Duncan relative to the water, of magnitude 1.5, in a direction such that the resultant of these velocities is perpendicular to the river bank.

The first stage is shown in Figure 25(a).

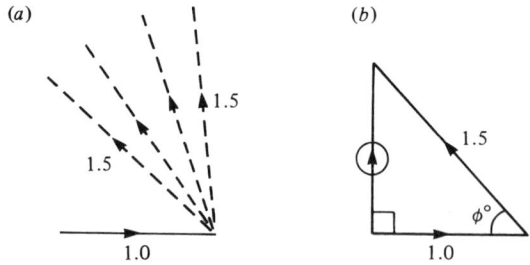

Figure 25

The locus of the end of the velocity vector of length 1.5 is an arc of a circle of radius 1.5. But the resultant sum of these velocities must be straight across the river.

The final picture is shown in Figure 25(b).

The direction he must aim makes angle $\phi°$ with the (upstream) direction of the river bank where

$$\phi° = \cos^{-1}\left(\frac{1.0}{1.5}\right) \approx 48°.$$

Exercise D

*1 An ant attempts to cross a conveyor belt moving at 7.5 cm/s. The ant walks in a direction perpendicular to the edge of the belt at 4.5 cm/s. Find by calculation, in what direction, relative to the earth, the ant will move as it crosses the belt. If the belt is 25 cm wide, how far will the ant be carried in the direction of the motion of the belt before it gets across?

2 A boat is travelling at 12 knots relative to the sea on a bearing of 235° but there is a steady current of velocity 4 knots from the east. Add these vectors together in an accurate scale drawing. By taking measurements from the drawing state the speed and direction of motion of the boat relative to the earth.

3 Two dodgems, one travelling at 6 m/s, the other at 4 m/s, meet in head-on collision. What is the relative velocity of impact? If the cars had been travelling at right angles to one another, what would have been the relative velocity of impact?

4 The River Fludde flows at 1.2 m/s between straight parallel banks 48 m apart.

Sarah, who swims at 1.6 m/s (relative to the water) aims in a direction such that her resultant velocity carries her straight across the river.

Calculate the direction in which she aims and the time she takes to cross.

Clare, who also swims at 1.6 m/s, aims straight across the river and so is carried some distance downstream while she crosses. How far is her landing place from Sarah's? How long does she take to cross?

If Sarah and Clare both start at the same time, how fast will Clare have to run up the river bank in order to arrive at Sarah's landing place at the same time as Sarah does?

5 A ferry, which travels at about 1.2 m/s relative to the water, has to cross a shallow river 140 m wide which flows at about 0.8 m/s between the parallel banks. In order to dock successfully at a point straight opposite the starting point, the captain steers a course so that he arrives at a point 20 m upstream and then disengages the engine and drifts into the harbour area. From a scale drawing find the course the captain must steer.

5. FORCES IN EQUILIBRIUM

Sir Isaac Newton, in the *Principia* (1687), gave three laws of motion which form the basis of 'Newtonian mechanics', a mathematical model for the study of the motion of objects when acted on by forces. His first law of motion stated (but in Latin) that 'every body continues in its state of rest or of moving uniformly in a straight line, except in so far as it is made to change that state by external forces'.

If the sum of the forces acting on an object is zero, it is said to be in *equilibrium*. It will then either be stationary or will be moving with constant velocity. Conversely, if an object is stationary, or moving with constant velocity, the sum of the forces acting on it must be zero.

Objects on the earth are attracted, by gravitation, towards the centre of the earth. This force of attraction is called the *weight* of the object concerned. A mass of m kg has a weight on the earth of about $10m$ newton (and a weight of about $2m$ newton on the moon). A donkey of mass 150 kg has a weight of about 1500 N.

A simplified model of the forces acting on a donkey at rest on a road is as in Figure 26.

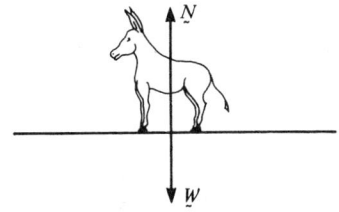

Figure 26

W represents the weight of the donkey and N represents the *normal reaction* of the road on the donkey, preventing the donkey accelerating downwards towards the earth's centre. In this simple model the forces are shown as if they acted through the centre of the donkey. Really, the weight, for example, acts all over the donkey and there are four lots of normal reaction at its four hooves.

Example 8

In the case of Nikos and the donkey, Nikos pulls with a force of 400 N, but fails to shift the donkey. The donkey's mass is 150 kg and they happen to be standing on a bridge as in Figure 27.

Find the reaction between the bridge and the donkey.

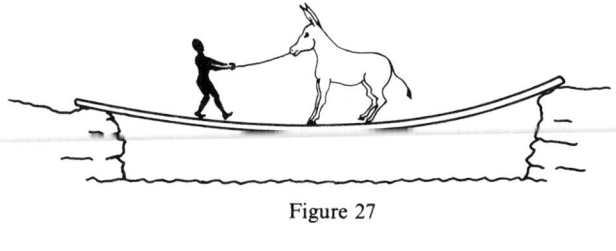

Figure 27

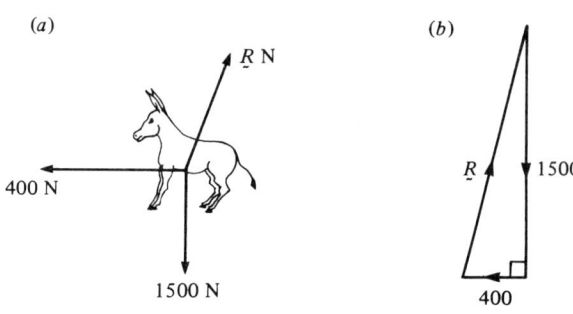

Figure 28

The forces acting on the donkey may be modelled by Figure 28(*a*). Notice that the reaction of the bridge on the donkey has tilted over a bit away from the pull because there is some friction between the donkey's hooves and the bridge preventing it sliding along. The sum of the three force vectors is zero because the donkey is not accelerating, that is, it is in equilibrium (until the bridge collapses). So the force vectors may be added as in Figure 28(*b*). The reaction has magnitude $\sqrt{(400^2 + 1500^2)}$ N = 1550 N to 3 s.f.

Example 9

Nikos now has the donkey (mass 150 kg – and so weight 1500 N) loaded onto the ferry to be taken to his grandfather in Ithaca. The donkey is temporarily in equilibrium as shown in Figure 29(*a*). What are the forces in:

(*a*) the wire from the top of the crane;
(*b*) the sailors' rope?

Forces in equilibrium

(a)

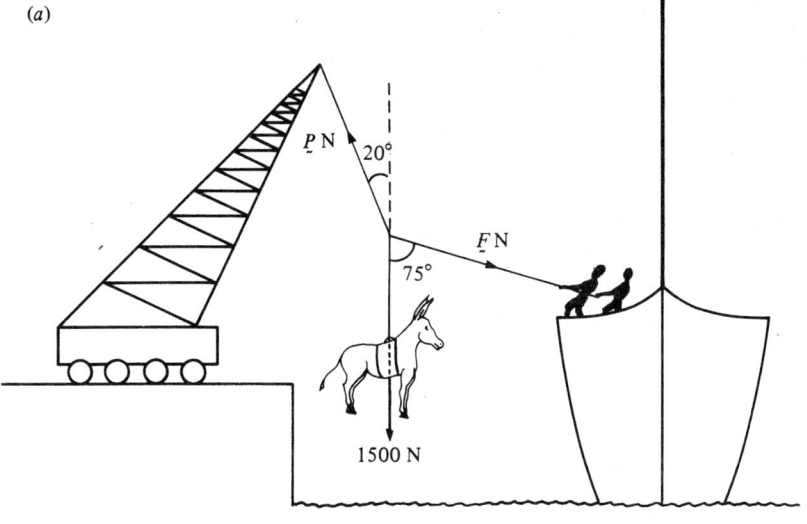

(b)

(c)

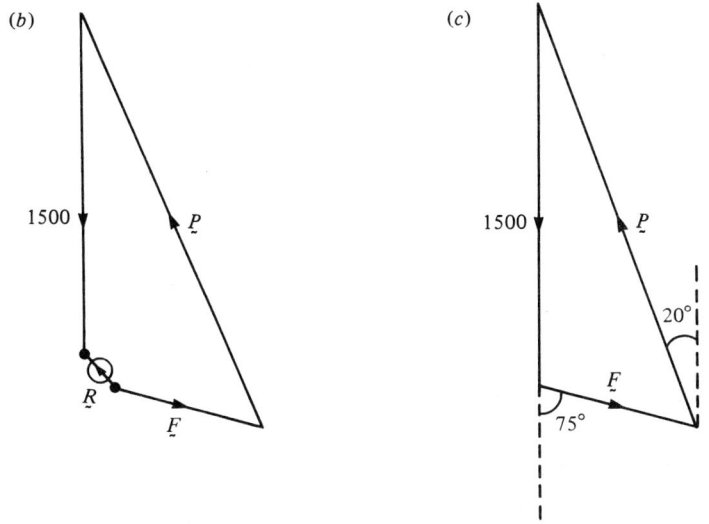

Figure 29

The forces acting on the donkey are shown in Figure 29(a):
  the weight of 1500 N,
  the tension in the crane wire, P newton, and
  the pull of the sailors' rope, F newton.
Since the donkey is in equilibrium, the sum of these forces must be zero. Figure 29(b) represents an attempt to find the sum of the forces – R represents the resultant. But R must be zero, so the force vectors must form a triangle as in

Figure 29(c). This triangle can then be drawn to scale: we find that $F \approx 630$ and $P \approx 1770$.

The force in the crane wire is 1770 newton and the force in the sailor's rope is 630 newton.

Example 10

An object is in equilibrium under forces $\begin{bmatrix} 300 \\ 500 \end{bmatrix}$ N, $\begin{bmatrix} -400 \\ -100 \end{bmatrix}$ N, and a third unknown force $\underset{\sim}{F}$ N. Find the unknown force as a column matrix.

Since the forces are in equilibrium, their vector sum is zero.

$$\begin{bmatrix} 300 \\ 500 \end{bmatrix} + \begin{bmatrix} -400 \\ -100 \end{bmatrix} + \underset{\sim}{F} = \underset{\sim}{0} \Rightarrow \begin{bmatrix} -100 \\ 400 \end{bmatrix} + \underset{\sim}{F} = \underset{\sim}{0}$$

$$\Rightarrow \underset{\sim}{F} = \begin{bmatrix} 100 \\ -400 \end{bmatrix}$$

The unknown force is $\begin{bmatrix} 100 \\ -400 \end{bmatrix}$ N.

Exercise E

*1 Find as a column matrix the sum (resultant) of the forces $\begin{bmatrix} 35 \\ 22 \end{bmatrix}$ N and $\begin{bmatrix} -17 \\ -32 \end{bmatrix}$ N.

What third force must be added so that the resultant of the three is zero?

2 Just before landing on the deck of the ferry, the donkey (weight 1500 N) is in the position shown in Figure 30 with Nikos and Spiro pulling horizontally, and is in equilibrium.
   (a) Sketch a triangle showing that the sum of the forces is zero, and calculate $\underset{\sim}{P}$ and $\underset{\sim}{F}$.
   (b) Draw this triangle accurately, to scale, and so confirm your calculated answers by measurement.
   (c) What is the vertical component of the force $\underset{\sim}{P}$? What is the horizontal component of the force $\underset{\sim}{P}$?

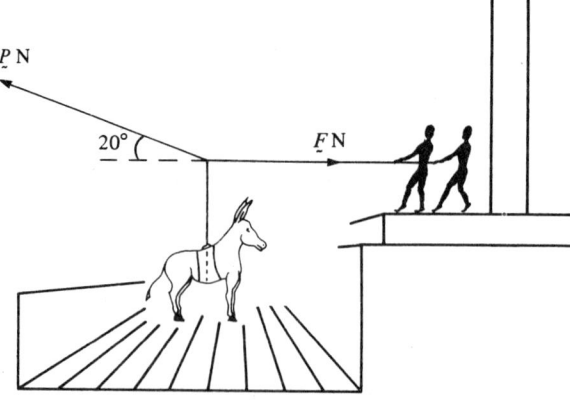

Figure 30

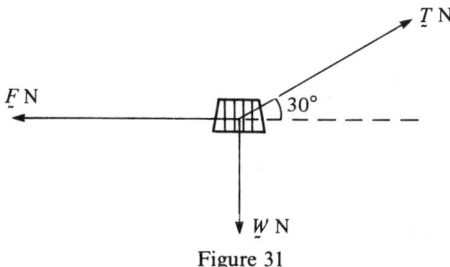

Figure 31

3 Figure 31 shows a block of mass 12 kg under the action of three forces.
   (a) State the approximate weight, W newton, of the block.
   (b) Write down the horizontal and vertical components of the force T and hence write it as a column matrix.
   (c) Write down an equation, in column matrix form, which states that the three forces are in equilibrium.
   (d) From the bottom row of the equation, find T.
   (e) From the top row of the equation, find F.

4 A microphone of mass 0.6 kg is suspended from the ceiling of a concert hall by a wire and held in position over the violins by a horizontal string so that the wire from the ceiling makes an angle of 15° with the vertical. Calculate the tension in the string and the tension in the wire.

*5 A hot-air balloon is tethered to the ground by a cable which makes an angle of 70° with the horizontal. The resultant of the vertical upthrust on the balloon and the weight of the balloon is a vertical upward force of 7500 N. Find from a scale drawing the horizontal force of the wind on the balloon. Check your result by calculation.

6 A man pushes horizontally, with a force of 500 N, on a packing case of mass 160 kg which refuses to move (that is, remains in equilibrium). What is the magnitude of the reaction of the ground on the packing case?

   The man attaches a rope around the case, climbs some steps and pulls on the rope so that he is exerting a force of 500 N in a direction which makes an angle of 35° with the horizontal. The case still will not budge: what is now the reaction of the ground on the case?

7 Find the magnitude and direction of the resultant of these forces:
   (a) 52 N making 109° with the x-axis and 84 N making 237° with the x-axis;
   (b) three forces each of magnitude 10 N making, respectively, angles of 27°, 147°, 267° with the x-axis.

6. FORCE AND ACCELERATION

Isaac Newton's second law of motion states that 'change of motion is proportional to the force acting and takes place in the direction of the force'.

Change of motion is measured by mass × acceleration, so this law can be written
$$\text{mass} \times \text{acceleration} \propto \text{force}$$

and the acceleration is in the direction of the force. The unit of force (the newton) is chosen so that the constant of proportionality is 1 when the mass is measured

in kilograms and the acceleration is metres per second per second. So we have
$$F = ma$$
where a m/s² is the acceleration given to an object of mass m kg by a force F N. A force of 1 N gives a mass of 1 kg an acceleration of 1 m/s² in the direction of the force.

Example 11

What force would give a mass of 5 kg an acceleration of 12 m/s² south-west?
Substituting in $F = ma$, we have
$$F = 5 \times 12 \text{ N south-west} = 60 \text{ N south-west}.$$

Example 12

If a force $\begin{bmatrix} 10 \\ 20 \end{bmatrix}$ N is applied to a mass of 5 kg, find the acceleration.
$$F = ma \Rightarrow a = \frac{1}{m} F$$
The acceleration is $\frac{1}{5}\begin{bmatrix} 10 \\ 20 \end{bmatrix} = \begin{bmatrix} 2 \\ 4 \end{bmatrix}$ m/s².

Example 13

A trolley of mass 110 kg which runs along horizontal rails is pulled steadily by a wire inclined at 30° to the horizontal (see Figure 32).

If the tension in the wire is 990 N and the resistances to motion are small enough to be neglected, find the acceleration of the trolley and its velocity after 5 seconds if the tension remains unchanged.

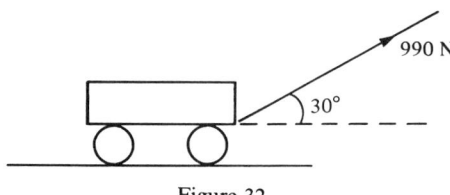

Figure 32

The horizontal component of the tension is $990 \cos 30°$ N ≈ 857 N.
$a = \frac{1}{m} F$ so the acceleration is $\frac{857}{100} = 8.57$ m/s² in the directon of the force.

Every second the trolley gains in velocity by 8.57 m/s. After 5 seconds its velocity is $8.57 \times 5 = 43$ m/s to 2 s.f.

Exercise F

*1 Calculate the forces which will give:
   (a) a mass of 3 kg an acceleration of 2 m/s²;
   (b) a mass of 2 kg an acceleration of 3 m/s²;
   (c) a mass of 2 mg an acceleration of 30 m/s².

2 Calculate the magnitudes of the acceleration of a mass of 5 kg under the action of
   (a) a force of 20 N;
   (b) forces of 30 N and 40 N at right angles to one another.
3 A bullet of mass 0.35 g is acted on by an average force of 100 N for 0.4 s while it is in the barrel of the gun. What is its acceleration? How fast will it be going at the end of this time?

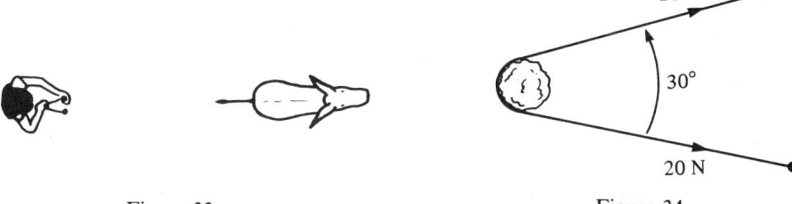

Figure 33   Figure 34

4 Figure 33 shows an aerial view of the donkey and Gataki who is now armed with a catapult loaded with a stone of mass 100 g.
  Gataki draws back the elastic until the tension in each arm is 20 N and the angle between the two pieces of elastic is 30° (see Figure 34).
  What is the acceleration of the stone at the instant that Gataki releases it?
  Shortly after this, the donkey (mass 150 kg) accelerates suddenly at about 15 m/s². With what force must it be pushing backwards on the ground with its hooves in order to do this (assuming it does not slip)?

*5 A spherical spaceship travelling at 250 m/s accelerates for 10 seconds, in a direction perpendicular to its original path, at a steady rate of 18 m/s². What is the magnitude of its final velocity? Through what angle has it changed direction? If its mass is 2200 kg, what force was exerted while it was accelerating?

6 An object of mass 0.20 kg is in equilibrium under the action of three forces: its weight, a force of magnitude 1.5 N making an angle of 17° with the upwards vertical and another force $\underline{T}$, being the tension in a string attached to the body (see Figure 35). Find the direction and magnitude of $\underline{T}$.
  If the string suddenly breaks, find the magnitude and direction of the acceleration of the body.

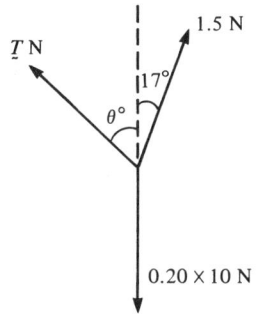

Figure 35

SUMMARY

Some examples of displacement vectors

$OP = p = \begin{bmatrix} 1 \\ 3 \end{bmatrix}$ is the position vector of $P(1, 3)$ in Figure 36.

$$OP + OQ = p + q = OR$$
$$\begin{bmatrix} 1 \\ 3 \end{bmatrix} + \begin{bmatrix} 5 \\ 4 \end{bmatrix} = \begin{bmatrix} 6 \\ 7 \end{bmatrix}$$

$$PQ = {}^-p + q = -\begin{bmatrix} 1 \\ 3 \end{bmatrix} + \begin{bmatrix} 5 \\ 4 \end{bmatrix} = \begin{bmatrix} 4 \\ 1 \end{bmatrix}$$ (Section 1)

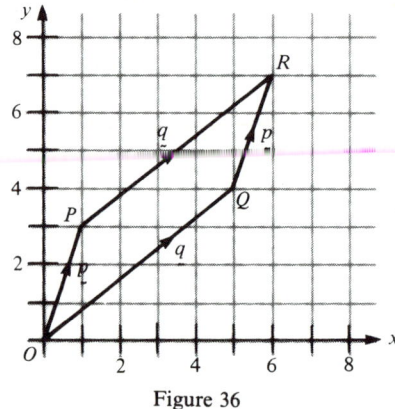
Figure 36

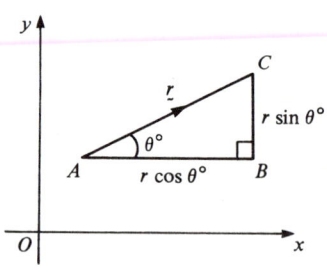
Figure 37

Components and resultants

In Figure 37:
  r has components: of magnitude $r\cos\theta°$ parallel to Ox;
                     of magnitude $r\sin\theta°$ parallel to Oy.
  r is the resultant of AB and BC. (Section 2)

Vector quantities

Displacement, velocity, acceleration, and force are examples of vector quantities, having magnitude and direction. A diagram like Figure 37 could represent addition of velocities, or addition of forces, for instance. (Section 3)

Bearings

When dealing with problems involving bearings, one must remember that they are measured clockwise from the north. It is safer, therefore, to avoid use of column matrices. (Section 2)

Summary

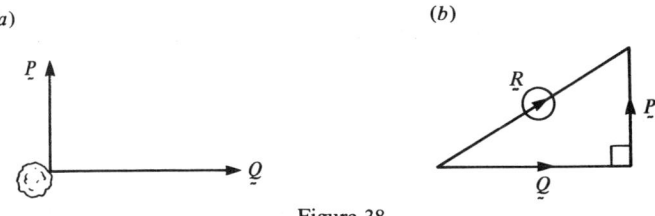

Figure 38

Forces

Forces can be added, like other vector quantities, or split into components.

In Figure 38(a), forces P and Q can be added, as in Figure 38(b), to give resultant R.

P and Q are then the components of R. (Section 3)

Forces in equilibrium

Newton's first law: Every body continues in a state of rest or of constant velocity unless the total force acting on the body is non-zero.

For an object in equilibrium, the vector sum of the forces acting on it is zero, as in Figures 39(a) and (b). (Section 5)

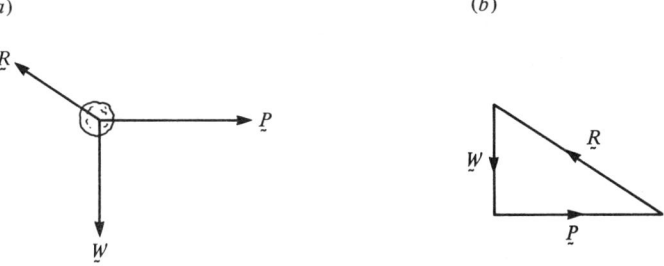

Figure 39

Force and acceleration

If the total force acting on an object is F newton then its acceleration, a m/s², is given by Newton's second law which is equivalent to
$$F = ma$$
where m kg is the mass of the object. (Section 6)

Summary exercise

1. If $p = \begin{bmatrix} 3 \\ -1 \end{bmatrix}$ and $q = \begin{bmatrix} 2 \\ 5 \end{bmatrix}$, find:
   (a) $p+q$;
   (b) $p-q$.

   If P is the point $(3, {}^-1)$ and Q the point $(2, 5)$, and $OPRQ$ is a parallelogram, state the coordinates of R.
   Find also the magnitude and direction of PQ.

2. (a) (i) Find the polar coordinates of the point having cartesian coordinates $(3, {}^-5)$.
   (ii) State the magnitude and direction of a force $\begin{bmatrix} 3 \\ -5 \end{bmatrix}$ N.
   (b) (i) Find the cartesian coordinates of the point having polar coordinates $(2, 235°)$.
   (ii) What is the magnitude of the component, parallel to Oy, of a force of 4 N making an angle of 235° with Ox?

3. Starting from camp, a scout walks 2.6 km on a bearing 035° and then 3.5 km on a bearing 325°.
   What is the bearing of camp from his final position and how far is he away from camp?

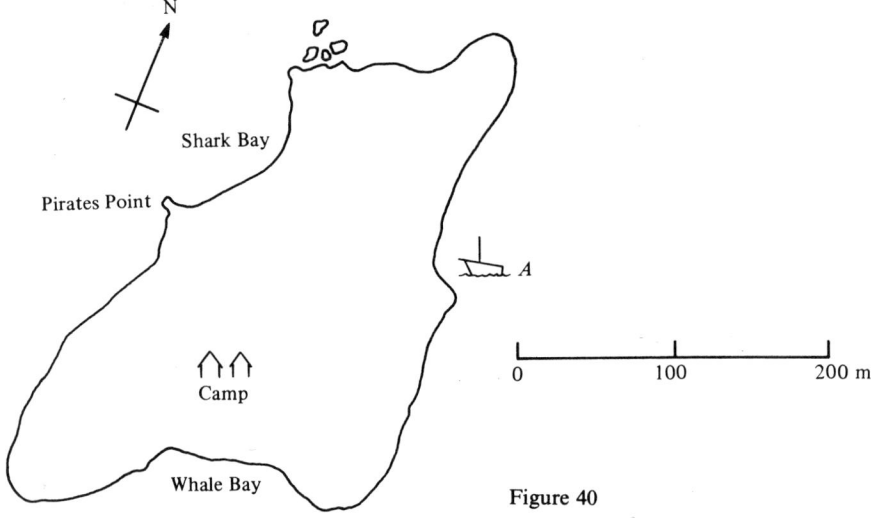

Figure 40

4. An expedition's supplies, dropped by parachute, are falling vertically, relative to the air, at a steady speed of 20 km/h, while the wind is blowing steadily from the east at 30 km/h. With what speed will the supplies hit the ground? If the parachute opened at a height of 140 m above the boat at A in Figure 40, describe roughly where the supplies will land.

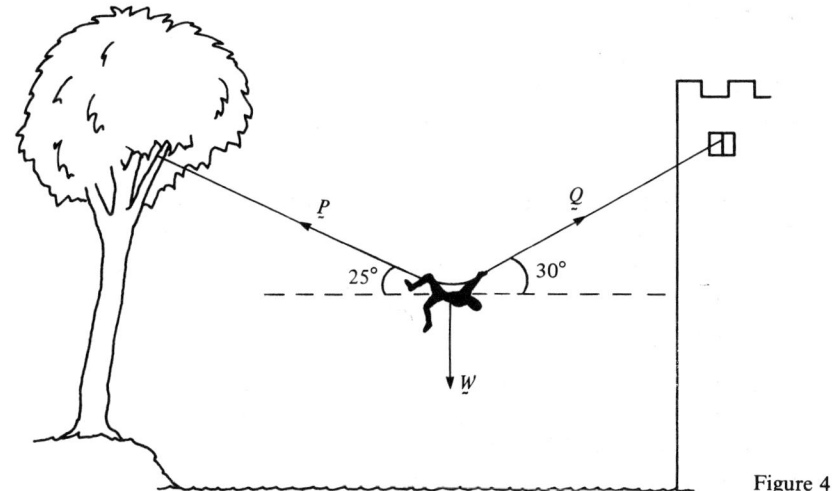

Figure 41

5 Figure 41 shows Lance-Corporal Peabody crossing the River Gunge by means of a rope. (Neither his, nor yours, to reason why.) Lance-Corporal Peabody 'weighs' (that is, has a mass of) 82 kg. Draw to scale a triangle representing the three force vectors, $P, Q,$ and W, in equilibrium and hence find the magnitude of P and Q.

10

Geometry

1. WHAT IS GEOMETRY?

Geometry is the study of space. All our activities concerning area and volume, trigonometry, graphs have contributed to a feel for geometry. Some chapters in these books have been more obviously geometrical – the sequence gradually extending the repertoire of transformations, for example. We have viewed space from a variety of standpoints, using locus ideas one moment, vectors at another, concentrating on specific special shapes like quadrilaterals for a time then looking at more general properties. Ultimately, this diversity works to our advantage but in the short term it may be confusing. This chapter attempts to weave some of these strands together and incidentally to strengthen each one.

Exercise A contains some questions that will form the background of the discussions in later sections.

Exercise A

1 Figure 1 shows an up-and-over garage door partially opened. Slots ensure that A moves horizontally and B moves vertically. $AB = 120$ cm, $BR = 80$ cm.

Using a scale of 1:20, draw a diagram showing the door in several positions from completely closed to completely open. Then draw the locus of R and also the locus of Q, the midpoint of AB.

Can you describe the two curves you have obtained?

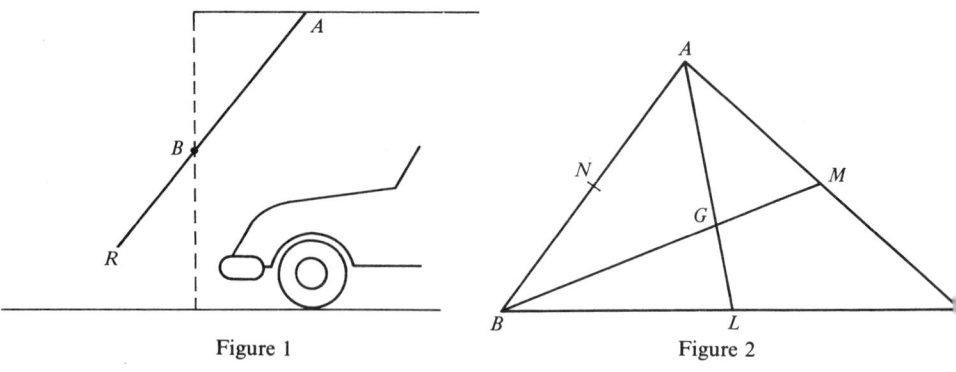

Figure 1   Figure 2

2 Draw a large triangle ABC (not isosceles). Join A to the midpoint L of BC, and B to the midpoint M of CA. (AL and BM are called *medians* of triangle ABC; they do

What is geometry? 215

not bisect the angles of the triangle and they should not be confused with the perpendicular bisectors of the sides. See Figure 2.)

AL intersects *BM* at *G*. Measure as accurately as you can *AG*, *GL*, *BG*, *GM*. Comment on your answers.

Draw the third median *CN*. What do you find?

3 Draw a large triangle and its medians on cardboard or fairly stiff paper. Cut the triangle out. Make a hole at one point on a median and let the triangle dangle from a pin through this hole. (See Figure 3.) What do you notice? Repeat with the pin through a point on one of the other medians and with the pin through the point where the medians meet.

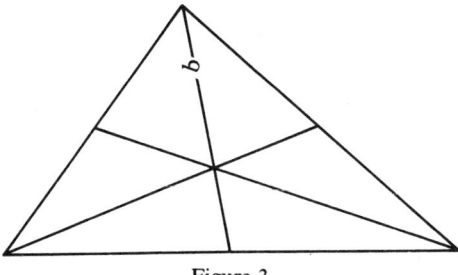

Figure 3

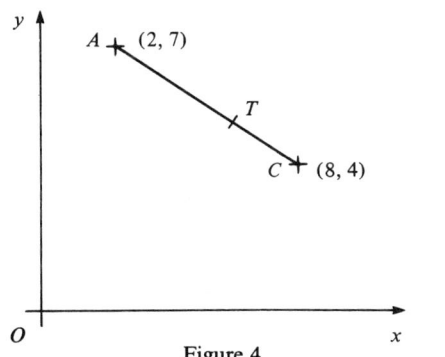

Figure 4

4 (a) Write down the coordinates of the midpoint of *AC* in Figure 4.
(b) *T* is the point of trisection of *AC* nearer *C*, that is, $CT = \frac{1}{3}AC$, $AT = \frac{2}{3}AC$. Write down in turn the vectors $\underline{AC}$ and $\underline{AT}$ and hence the coordinates of *T*.
(c) Repeat (a) and (b) if *A* is the point (a, b) and *C* is (c, d). Show that the coordinates of *T* can be written
$$\left(\frac{a+2c}{3}, \frac{b+2d}{3}\right).$$

5 Draw a triangle *ABC* with $AB = 4$ cm, $AC = 8$ cm. The angle at *A* can be any size you choose. Draw the bisector of the angle at *A*, and let it meet *BC* at *D*. Measure *BD* and *DC*.

Repeat with a different triangle but keeping $AB = 4$ cm, $AC = 8$ cm. Are your answers connected in any way?

6 Repeat question 5 with $AB = 6$ cm, $AC = 9$ cm.

7 (a) Find the area of a triangle ABC in which $AB = 6.3$ cm, $AC = 8.3$ cm, and angle $BAC = 44.6°$.
   (b) Find a formula for the area of a triangle ABC with $AB = p$ cm, $AC = q$ cm, and angle $BAC = \alpha°$.

8 Draw $AB = 6$ cm (towards the left side of the page). Construct the locus of P such that $AP = 2\ BP$. Two points on the locus can be found with $AP = 7$ cm, $BP = 3.5$ cm, for example (see Figure 5), and you can choose other suitable pairs of lengths.

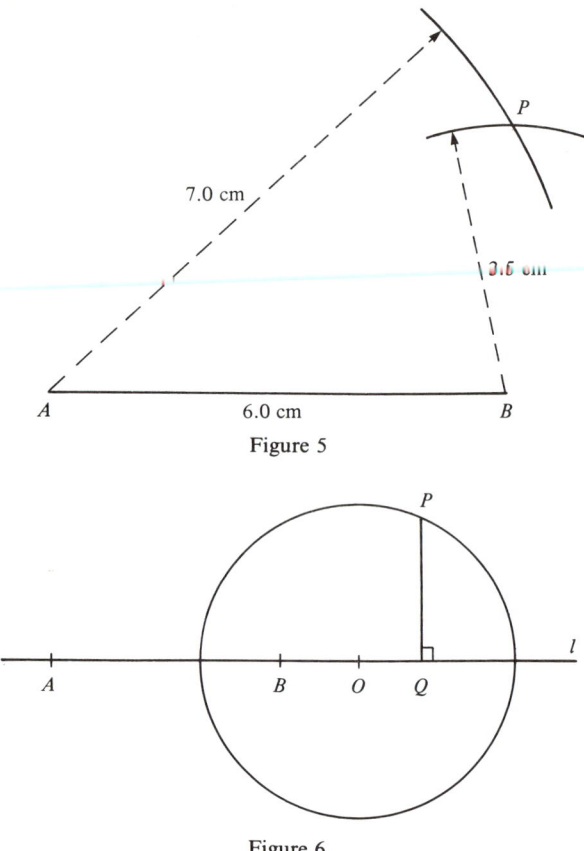

Figure 5

Figure 6

9 In Figure 6, the line l passes through the centre O of the circle. $OA = 8$ cm, $OB = 2$ cm, and the circle has radius 4 cm. Calculate PQ^2, AP^2, BP^2 when OQ is: (a) 1 cm, (b) 2 cm, (c) 3 cm.

2. PROOF

The locus of the point Q in question 1 seems to be circular. You may suspect also that the locus in question 8 is a circle. From a drawing, however, accurate, one can only guess at such results. You should remain sceptical until conclusive arguments have been advanced. Proofs may use any knowledge you have

Proof

acquired in the past and any method at your disposal. The following examples have been chosen to illustrate the rich choice we have even at this stage.

Example 1

Show that the locus of Q (Exercise A, question 1) is a circle.

Method (1)

Join OQ and draw the line QL perpendicular to OA. (See Figure 7.)

Now $OL = LA$ since $AQ = QB$ and QL is parallel to OB (similar triangles; enlargement, centre A).

It follows that triangle OQL is a reflection in QL of triangle AQL and hence OQ and QA are equal. So $OQ = 60$ cm in whichever position the garage door is. The locus of Q is a circle with centre O and radius 60 cm.

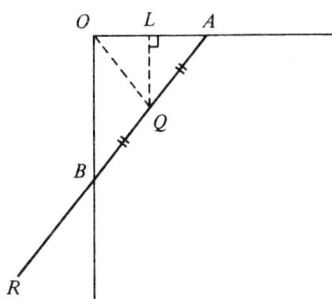

Figure 7

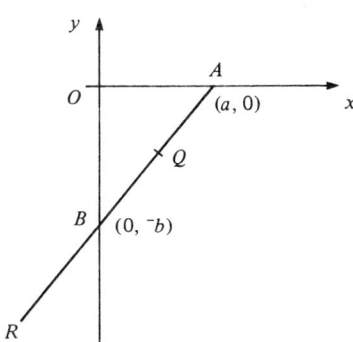

Figure 8

Method (2)

Draw coordinate axes with O as the origin as shown in Figure 8. Call the points A $(a, 0)$ and B $(0, ^-b)$. Then by Pythagoras' theorem,
$$a^2 + b^2 = 120^2 = 14400.$$
Now Q is the midpoint of AB and so has coordinates $(\tfrac{1}{2}a, ^-\tfrac{1}{2}b)$.
So, using Pythagoras' theorem again,
$$\begin{aligned}OQ^2 &= (\tfrac{1}{2}a)^2 + (^-\tfrac{1}{2}b)^2 \\ &= \tfrac{1}{4}a^2 + \tfrac{1}{4}b^2 \\ &= \tfrac{1}{4} \times 14400 = 3600.\end{aligned}$$
$OQ = 60$ cm and we see as before that Q lies on the circle with centre O and radius 60 cm.

Example 2

Show that the locus of the bottom of the garage door (Example 1) is elliptical.

First of all we must be clear what an ellipse is. It is an oval, but there are many different kinds of oval and an ellipse is one special type. The simplest definition is that it is the image of a circle under a one-way stretch.

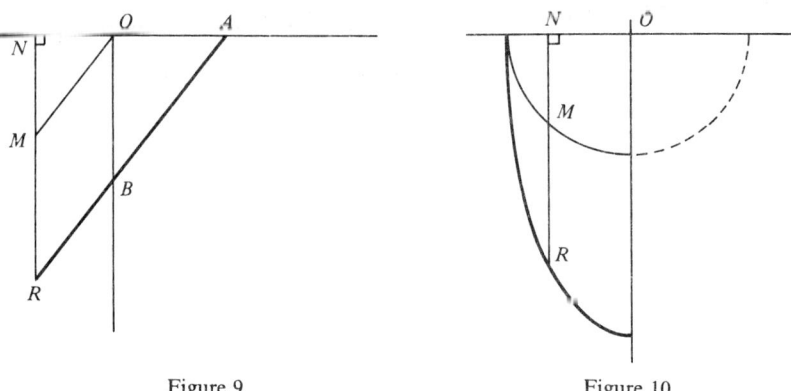

Figure 9   Figure 10

In Figure 9, RN has been drawn perpendicular to OA, and OM is parallel to AR.

Now $OMRB$ is a parallelogram and hence $OM = BR = 80$ cm. Consequently, as the door opens and closes, M moves on a circle with centre O and radius 80 cm.

Also ONM and ANR are similar triangles and $\dfrac{NR}{NM} = \dfrac{AR}{OM} = \dfrac{200}{80} = \dfrac{5}{2}$. We see that R is the image of M under a one-way stretch with invariant line OA and scale factor $2\frac{1}{2}$. The locus of M is an elliptical arc (see Figure 10).

Example 3

One might wonder whether the bisector of an angle of a triangle will divide the opposite side into equal segments. In fact the ratio of BD to DC in Figure 11 turns out to be the ratio of the two other sides of the original triangle – AB and AC. We prove this in two ways.

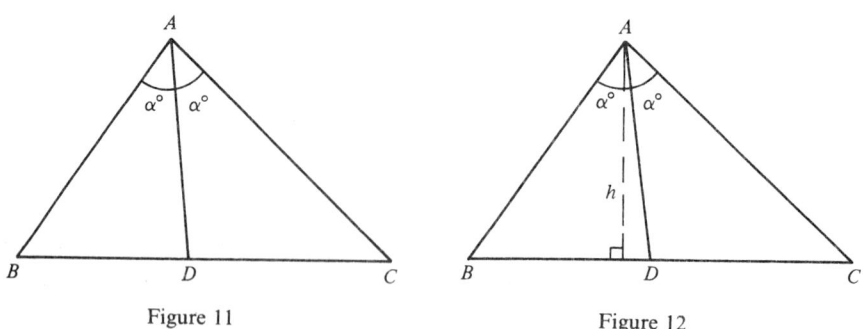

Figure 11   Figure 12

Method (1)

If BD and DC are regarded as the bases of the triangles ABD and ADC, both triangles have the same height h. (See Figure 12.)

So $$\frac{\text{Area of } ABD}{\text{Area of } ADC} = \frac{\frac{1}{2} \times BD \times h}{\frac{1}{2} \times DC \times h} = \frac{BD}{DC}.$$

Starting afresh:
$$\frac{\text{Area of } ABD}{\text{Area of } ADC} = \frac{\frac{1}{2} \times AD \times AB \times \sin \alpha°}{\frac{1}{2} \times AD \times AC \times \sin \alpha°} = \frac{AB}{AC}.$$

(This is equivalent to treating AD as the base of each triangle.)

Hence $\dfrac{BD}{DC} = \dfrac{AB}{AC}$.

Method (2)

Reflect triangle ABC in AD to give Figure 13.

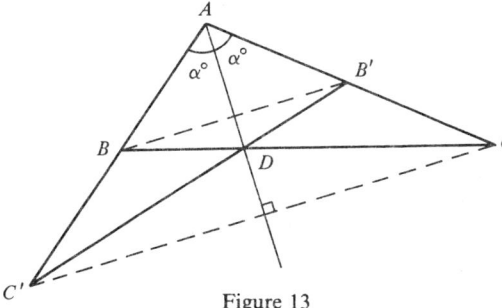

Figure 13

Because of the equal angles at A, B' lies on AC and C' on AB. BB' and CC' are parallel, both being perpendicular to the axis of reflection AD.

From the similar triangles DBB', DCC', $\dfrac{BD}{DC} = \dfrac{BB'}{CC'}$.

There is another pair of similar triangles, ABB' and $AC'C$. The scale factor for these $= \dfrac{BB'}{C'C} = \dfrac{AB}{AC'}$.

Hence $\dfrac{BD}{DC} = \dfrac{AB}{AC'} = \dfrac{AB}{AC}$, since $AC' = AC$.

Example 4

Prove that the medians of a triangle always meet in a point and this point (called the *centroid*) is a point of trisection of each median.

Again we employ two of the many methods available.

Method (1)

Shear Figure 14(*a*) (in which L, M, N are the midpoints of the sides of triangle ABC) so that the image is isosceles with $A'B = A'C$. For clarity the image is drawn separately as Figure 14(*b*). Now, in any shear, straight lines remain

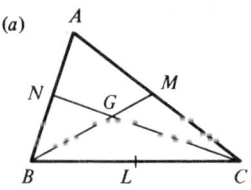 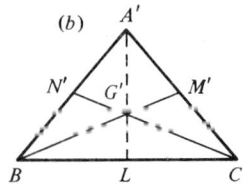 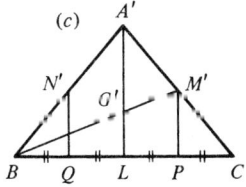

Figure 14

straight, midpoints remain midpoints; so BM' and CN' are medians of the image triangle, and the point G' where they intersect is on $A'L$ because of the symmetry of this figure. Shearing back, this means that AL, BM, CN, meet in a point in Figure 14(a).

Furthermore, lines through M' and N' parallel to $A'L$ clearly bisect BL and LC, and so BC is divided into four equal segments. It follows that $BG' = 2\,G'M'$ and similarly G' is a point of trisection of CN' and $A'L$ also. But points of trisection remain points of trisection under a shear, so in the original diagram the medians trisect each other at G.

Method (2)

This time we imagine the triangle drawn on graph paper. In order that our conclusions should apply to a triangle of any shape or size, we use letters rather than particular numbers for the coordinates of the points as shown in Figure 15.

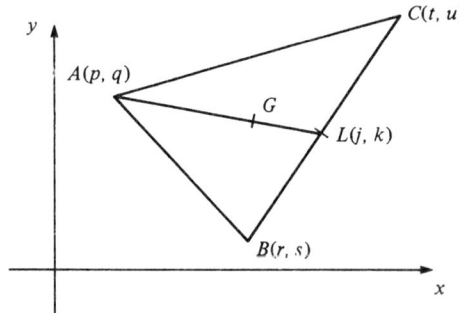

Figure 15

Now if G is two-thirds of the way along AL, then G is $\left(\dfrac{p+2j}{3}, \dfrac{q+2k}{3}\right)$.

Since L is the midpoint of BC, $j = \dfrac{r+t}{2}$, $k = \dfrac{s+u}{2}$, giving $2j = r+t$, $2k = s+u$.

Hence G is $\left(\dfrac{p+r+t}{3}, \dfrac{q+s+u}{3}\right)$.

Repeating this working with each of the other medians in turn, we find that $\left(\dfrac{p+r+t}{3}, \dfrac{q+s+u}{3}\right)$ is two-thirds of the way from B to M and also two-thirds of the way from C to N. This is because of the 'algebraic symmetry' of the coordinates of G; if p and r are interchanged, for example, the x-coordinate of G is unchanged.

Notice that, for some proofs, transformations may provide the explanation we find simplest; for others, coordinates and algebra may serve us best. The endless variety provides both the fascination and the difficulty of the study.

Exercise B

1 O is the centre of the circle in Figure 16. Prove that angle ACB is a right angle.

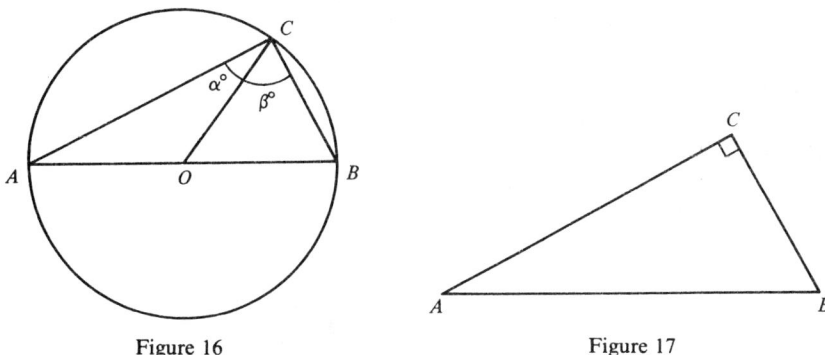

Figure 16   Figure 17

2 In Figure 17, angle ACB is a right angle. Show that the centre of the circle through A, B and C is the midpoint of AB.

3 O is the centre of the circle in Figure 18. Obtain expressions (in terms of α, β) for the angles OAC, AOD, BOD, AOB, and deduce that
$$\text{angle } AOB = 2 \times \text{angle } ACB.$$

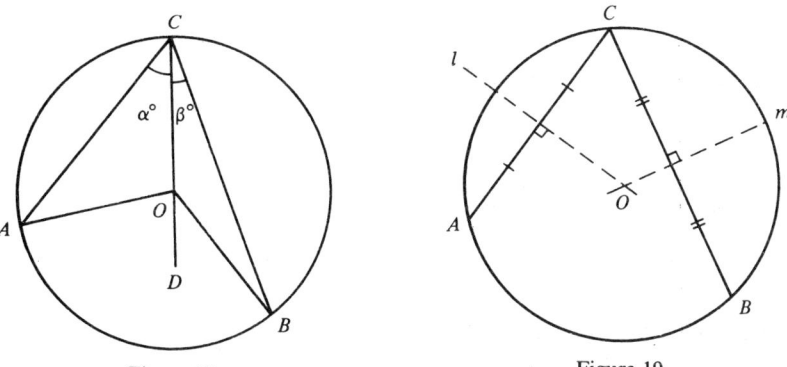

Figure 18   Figure 19

4 In Figure 19, *l* and *m* are the perpendicular bisectors of AC and CB. They meet at O.
   (a) Explain why the angle between *l* and *m* equals angle ACB.
   (b) What is the image of A under reflection in *l* followed by reflection in *m*?

(c) What is the centre of the single rotation equivalent to the combination of the reflections in (b)?

(d) How can you deduce from the previous facts that angle $AOB = 2 \times$ angle ACB?

5 In Figure 20, each of the sides of triangle ABC has been trisected.
   (a) Explain why PS and QR are parallel to AB.
   (b) If M is the midpoint of CA, show that G lies on the median BM and that $BG = 2\ GM$.
   (c) Show similarly that G lies on the other two medians.

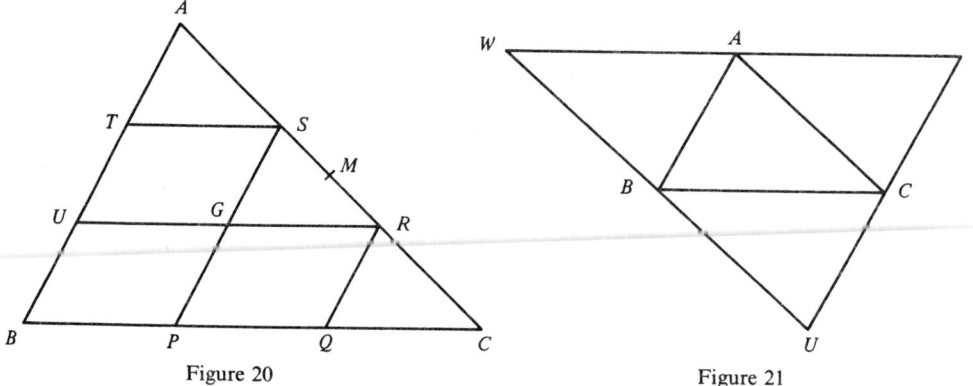

Figure 20   Figure 21

6. In Figure 21, the sides of $\triangle UVW$ are parallel to the sides of $\triangle ABC$.
   (a) What is the scale factor of the enlargement that will map $\triangle ABC$ onto $\triangle UVW$?
   (b) What is the image of A under this enlargement and what point maps onto A?
   (c) What can you tell about the centre of this enlargement from (b)?
   (d) Use the enlargement to show that the medians of $\triangle ABC$ meet in a point and trisect each other.

7 Draw a large triangle ABC (neither right-angled nor isosceles) and construct the circumcentre O (where the perpendicular bisectors of the sides meet), the centroid G (where the medians meet) and the orthocentre H (where the altitudes meet). What do you notice?

8 G is the centroid of $\triangle ABC$ and l is the perpendicular bisector of BC. What is the image of l under the enlargement with centre G and scale factor -2? Explain why the orthocentre is the image of the circumcentre.

9 Give an explanation why the three perpendicular bisectors of the sides of a triangle ABC meet in a point. Explain also the fact that the three altitudes meet in a point.

3. LINKS WITH ALGEBRA

Geometry and algebra help each other. This takes place all the time and all we shall do in this section is to draw attention to some of the different ways this happens.

Graphs

Our work on, for example, proportion, simultaneous equations and inequalities, quadratic equations, rates of change, is made more memorable and intelligible through seeing the graphical interpretations alongside the more abstract algebra.

Equally valuable is the use of algebra to assist in solving geometrical problems. Example 1, method (2) and Example 4, method (2) illustrate this point. We give one more instance, extending the work of Exercise A, questions 8 and 9.

Example 5
A and B are fixed points 8 cm apart.
Prove that the locus $\{P: AP = 3BP\}$ is a circle.

You might like to start by constructing some points on the locus given by the following table of values.

AP	6	$7\frac{1}{2}$	9	$10\frac{1}{2}$	12
BP	2	$2\frac{1}{2}$	3	$3\frac{1}{2}$	4

You soon see that AP and BP can be neither too small nor too large – $AP = 4\frac{1}{2}$, $BP = 1\frac{1}{2}$ is impossible, so also is $AP = 15$, $BP = 3$. The first and last pairs of numbers in the table give the points P_1 and P_2 on the line AB itself. (See Figure 22.) If the locus is indeed a circle, it has diameter $= P_1B + BP_2 = 2 + 4 = 6$ cm, and its centre must be 3 cm to the right of P_1, that is, 1 cm to the right of B.

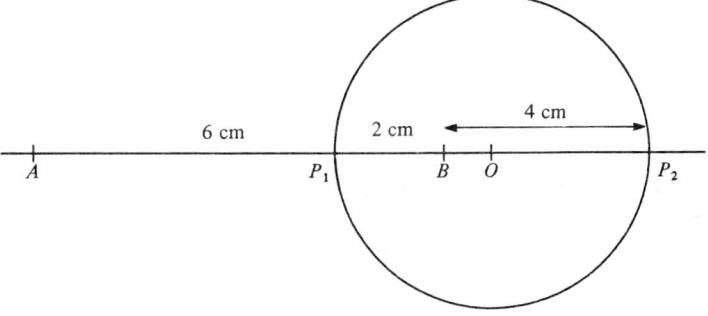

Figure 22

Now consider a general point P of the locus and suppose that it is p cm to the right of O (along AB) and q cm above AB. (See Figure 23.)
All we know about P initially is that $AP = 3 BP$. By Pythagoras' theorem:
$$BP^2 = (1+p)^2 + q^2 \text{ and } AP^2 = (9+p)^2 + q^2.$$
Let us see what this information tells us most simply about p and q.

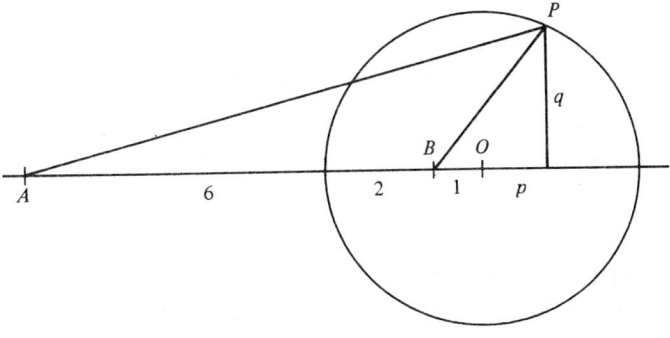

Figure 23

$$AP = 3BP \Rightarrow \quad AP^2 = 9BP^2$$
$$\Rightarrow \quad (9+p)^2 + q^2 = 9[(1+p)^2 + q^2]$$
$$\Rightarrow \quad 81 + 18p + p^2 + q^2 = 9[(1 + 2p + p^2) + q^2]$$
$$\Rightarrow \quad 81 + 18p + p^2 + q^2 = 9 + 18p + 9p^2 + 9q^2$$
$$\therefore \quad 72 = 8p^2 + 8q^2$$
$$\Rightarrow \quad p^2 + q^2 = 9$$

Check that you agree with each stage of the algebraic manipulation. Then look at the diagram and interpret our conclusion. It shows that:
$$OP^2 = 9$$
that is,
$$OP = 3.$$

Every point of the locus is therefore 3 cm from O. The locus is a circle, centre O, radius 3 cm.

Matrices

A quite separate link between geometry and algebra arises from our use of matrices to represent transformations and of transformations to illustrate matrices. We have seen that combinations of transformations correspond to multiplication of their matrices. Once we have discussed stretches and shears, we could interpret any 2×2 matrix as a combination of reflection, rotation, stretch and shear. The only snag is that

$$\begin{bmatrix} x \\ y \end{bmatrix} \rightarrow \begin{bmatrix} a & b \\ c & d \end{bmatrix} \begin{bmatrix} x \\ y \end{bmatrix}$$

maps (0, 0) onto itself whatever the values of a, b, c, d, so we can only represent in this way transformations which leave the origin invariant. We shall now indicate briefly how this restriction can be overcome.

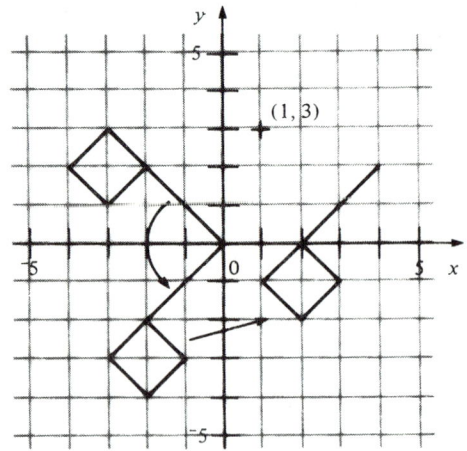

Figure 24

$$\begin{bmatrix} x \\ y \end{bmatrix} \rightarrow \begin{bmatrix} x \\ y \end{bmatrix} + \begin{bmatrix} 4 \\ 2 \end{bmatrix}$$

is an algebraic way of representing the translation $\begin{bmatrix} 4 \\ 2 \end{bmatrix}$. Since $\begin{bmatrix} 0 & -1 \\ 1 & 0 \end{bmatrix}$ is the matrix of a quarter-turn about the origin,

$$\begin{bmatrix} x' \\ y' \end{bmatrix} = \begin{bmatrix} 0 & -1 \\ 1 & 0 \end{bmatrix} \begin{bmatrix} x \\ y \end{bmatrix} + \begin{bmatrix} 4 \\ 2 \end{bmatrix}$$

represents this quarter-turn followed by the translation. Now this is clearly equivalent to a single quarter-turn about some other centre. Our usual methods soon identify this point as (1, 3).

As a check, work out the image of (1, 3) itself.

$$\begin{bmatrix} x' \\ y' \end{bmatrix} = \begin{bmatrix} 0 & -1 \\ 1 & 0 \end{bmatrix} \begin{bmatrix} 1 \\ 3 \end{bmatrix} + \begin{bmatrix} 4 \\ 2 \end{bmatrix}$$

$$= \begin{bmatrix} -3 \\ 1 \end{bmatrix} + \begin{bmatrix} 4 \\ 2 \end{bmatrix}$$

$$= \begin{bmatrix} 1 \\ 3 \end{bmatrix}.$$

So (1, 3) maps onto itself. The only invariant point is the centre of rotation, so we have indeed found the centre correctly.

We can reverse the above process and find in the form

$$\begin{bmatrix} x' \\ y' \end{bmatrix} = \begin{bmatrix} a & b \\ c & d \end{bmatrix} \begin{bmatrix} x \\ y \end{bmatrix} + \begin{bmatrix} e \\ f \end{bmatrix}$$

an algebraic representation of a more general transformation. Note that (e, f) is the image of the origin.

Example 6

Find an algebraic description for reflection in $y = x + 2$.

The transformation is equivalent to a reflection in the parallel line through the origin, followed by a translation $\begin{bmatrix} -2 \\ 2 \end{bmatrix}$. This gives

$$\begin{bmatrix} x' \\ y' \end{bmatrix} = \begin{bmatrix} 0 & 1 \\ 1 & 0 \end{bmatrix} \begin{bmatrix} x \\ y \end{bmatrix} + \begin{bmatrix} -2 \\ 2 \end{bmatrix}.$$

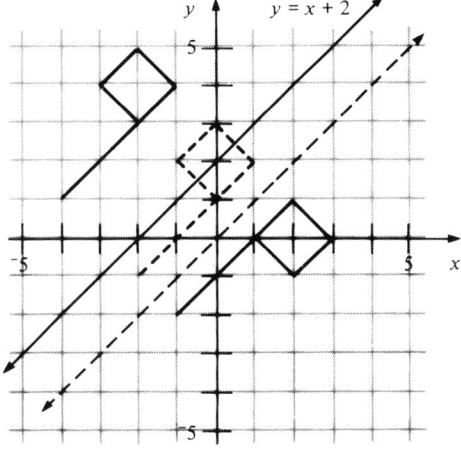

Figure 25

Example 7

Find the single transformation equivalent to a quarter-turn about (1, 3) followed by reflection in $y = x+2$.

From our previous examples we have,

$$\begin{bmatrix} x''' \\ y'' \end{bmatrix} = \begin{bmatrix} 0 & 1 \\ 1 & 0 \end{bmatrix} \begin{bmatrix} x' \\ y' \end{bmatrix} + \begin{bmatrix} -2 \\ 2 \end{bmatrix} \quad \text{and} \quad \begin{bmatrix} x' \\ y' \end{bmatrix} = \begin{bmatrix} 0 & -1 \\ 1 & 0 \end{bmatrix} \begin{bmatrix} x \\ y \end{bmatrix} + \begin{bmatrix} 4 \\ 2 \end{bmatrix}.$$

Hence

$$\begin{bmatrix} x' \\ y' \end{bmatrix} = \begin{bmatrix} -y+4 \\ x+2 \end{bmatrix}$$

and

$$\begin{bmatrix} x'' \\ y'' \end{bmatrix} = \begin{bmatrix} 0 & 1 \\ 1 & 0 \end{bmatrix} \begin{bmatrix} -y+4 \\ x+2 \end{bmatrix} + \begin{bmatrix} -2 \\ 2 \end{bmatrix}$$

$$= \begin{bmatrix} x+2 \\ -y+4 \end{bmatrix} + \begin{bmatrix} -2 \\ 2 \end{bmatrix}$$

$$= \begin{bmatrix} x \\ -y \end{bmatrix} + \begin{bmatrix} 0 \\ 6 \end{bmatrix}$$

$$= \begin{bmatrix} 1 & 0 \\ 0 & -1 \end{bmatrix} \begin{bmatrix} x \\ y \end{bmatrix} + \begin{bmatrix} 0 \\ 6 \end{bmatrix}.$$

Now $\begin{bmatrix} 1 & 0 \\ 0 & -1 \end{bmatrix}$ represents a reflection in the x-axis, so we have a reflection in a line parallel to the x-axis. Moreover the origin maps onto (0, 6) so the axis of reflection is $y = 3$.

Exercise C

1 Two discs, centres P and Q, fit exactly into a box with a square of side 10 cm as base. Their radii are r cm and 2 cm. (See Figure 26.)
   Show that $AP = r\sqrt{2}$ cm. Write down expressions for PQ, QC and AC.
   Form an equation for r and solve it.

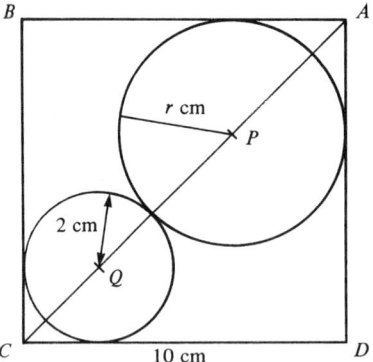

Figure 26

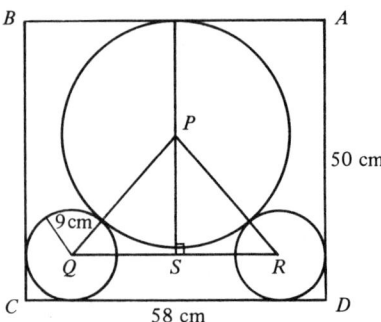

Figure 27

2 In Figure 27, each of the small circles has radius 9 cm. If the large circle has radius x cm, show that $PS = (41-x)$ cm. What are the lengths of PQ and QS?
Form an equation for x and solve it. Find whether three discs of these radii will fit in the box with the small circles in the corners B and C.

3 Construct the locus of a point P equidistant from $F(0, 4)$ and the x-axis.
(Figure 28(a) shows one possible point, where both distances are 6 units.)
If P is the point (a, b), obtain an equation connecting a and b, and hence show that the locus is the graph of $y = \tfrac{1}{8}x^2 + 2$.
What is the name of this type of curve?

(a) 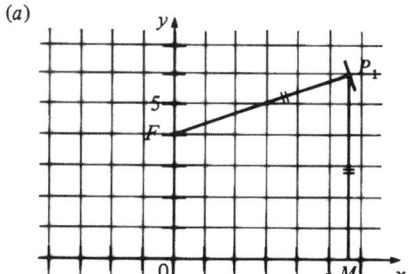   (b)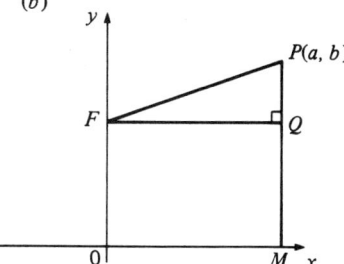

Figure 28

4 Draw the locus of the point whose distance from $(0, 2)$ is half its distance from the line $y = 8$. Prove that this is the graph of $4x^2 + 3y^2 = 48$. What is the name of this type of curve?

5 For what values of x (positive and negative) is
(a) $x^2 < x+6$;
(b) $\dfrac{12}{x} < x-4$?

Solve these inequalities algebraically if you can.
Then, for (a), draw the graphs of $y = x^2$ and $y = x+6$ with the same axes. Also use a graphical method to solve (b).

(a) 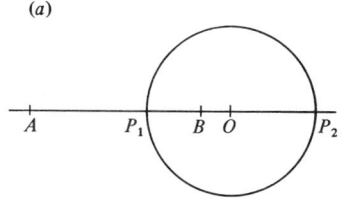   (b)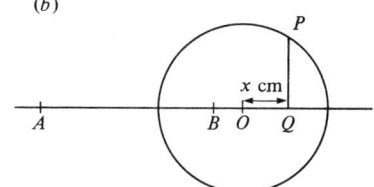

Figure 29

6 In Figure 29(a), A and B are fixed points and $AB = 6$ cm. The locus $\{P: AP = 2PB\}$ is shown, and P_1, P_2 are the points of the locus on AB. Find BP_1 and BP_2; and show that $OB = 2$ cm, O being the midpoint of $P_1 P_2$.
In Figure 29(b), the circle has radius 4 cm and centre O. $AB = 6$ cm, $BO = 2$ cm, $OQ = x$ cm. Find PQ^2, AP^2 and BP^2 in terms of x and deduce that $AP = 2PB$.

7 A and B are fixed points with $AB = 6$ cm. Prove (as in Example 5) that all points of the locus $\{R: AR = 4RB\}$ lie on a circle.

*8 The mapping $\begin{bmatrix} x \\ y \end{bmatrix} \to \begin{bmatrix} 0 & 1 \\ -1 & 0 \end{bmatrix} \begin{bmatrix} x \\ y \end{bmatrix} + \begin{bmatrix} 3 \\ 7 \end{bmatrix}$ describes a rotation through 270°.

Find the coordinates of the centre of rotation by finding the invariant point of the mapping.

9 An enlargement E is described by the mapping
$$\begin{bmatrix} x \\ y \end{bmatrix} \to \begin{bmatrix} -2 & 0 \\ 0 & -2 \end{bmatrix} \begin{bmatrix} x \\ y \end{bmatrix} + \begin{bmatrix} 9 \\ 6 \end{bmatrix}.$$

(a) Find the effect of E on the triangle $A(2, 0)$, $B(7, 0)$, $C(0, 4)$ and draw the triangle and its image on graph paper.

Use your drawing to find the scale factor and the position of the centre of enlargement.

(b) Calculate the invariant point of the mapping algebraically and check that it coincides with the centre of enlargement.

*10 Find the invariant point for each of the following transformations and give the geometric significance of the point in each case:

(a) $\begin{bmatrix} x \\ y \end{bmatrix} \to \begin{bmatrix} -3 & 0 \\ 0 & -3 \end{bmatrix} \begin{bmatrix} x \\ y \end{bmatrix} + \begin{bmatrix} -20 \\ 12 \end{bmatrix}$ (an enlargement);

(b) $\begin{bmatrix} x \\ y \end{bmatrix} \to \begin{bmatrix} 0 & -1 \\ 1 & 0 \end{bmatrix} \begin{bmatrix} x \\ y \end{bmatrix} + \begin{bmatrix} -5 \\ 2 \end{bmatrix}$ (a rotation);

(c) $\begin{bmatrix} x \\ y \end{bmatrix} \to \begin{bmatrix} 3 & 0 \\ 0 & 6 \end{bmatrix} \begin{bmatrix} x \\ y \end{bmatrix} + \begin{bmatrix} 4 \\ -10 \end{bmatrix}$ (a two-way stretch).

11 The diagrams in Figure 30 show the effect of different rotations on triangle ABC. By considering each transformation as a combination of a rotation about the origin followed by a translation, write down the matrix description and hence find the centre of rotation in each case. Check that the mediators of AA', BB' and CC' meet at these points, by using a ruler on the figure.

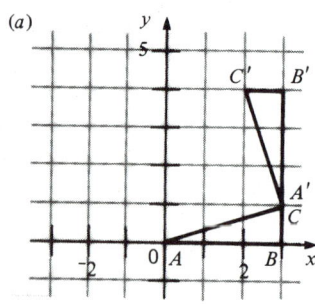
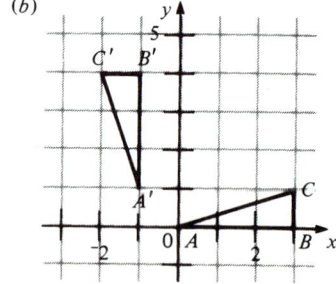
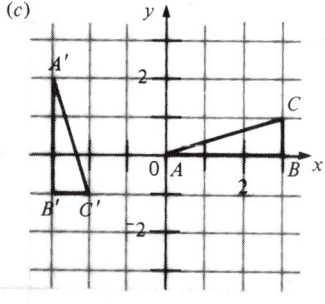
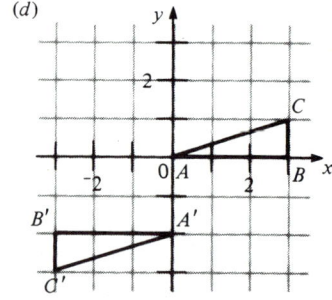

Figure 30

12 Find the matrix description of the following transformations:
   (a) a half-turn about the point (5, 3);
   (b) an enlargement from (2, ⁻7) with linear scale factor 2;
   (c) a 90° rotation about (⁻4, 1);
   (d) a two-way stretch with scale factor 5 from the line $x = 2$ and with scale factor 2 from the line $y = 4$.

4. THE ALGEBRA OF TRANSFORMATIONS

We have frequently investigated the single transformation equivalent to a given transformation followed by another. You may recollect, for example, that reflection **L** in *l* followed by reflection **M** in *m* (see Figure 31) is equivalent to a rotation $\mathbf{R}_{O,\,2\alpha°}$ about O through an angle of $2\alpha°$.

We write this $\mathbf{ML} = \mathbf{R}_{O,\,2\alpha°}$.

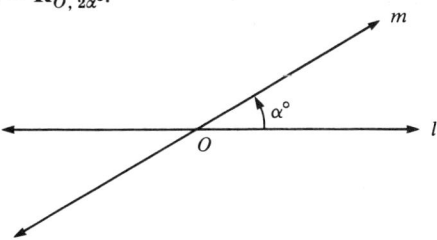

Figure 31

In Section 3, we noted how 'ordinary algebra', in which letters stand for numbers, plays a part in geometry. The above statement is an example from the algebra of transformations in which each symbol stands for a transformation. Once we know the rules of this algebra, we can use it to establish further results (see, for example, Exercise B, question 4). We start by considering how to discover precisely the transformation equivalent to the combination of any two isometries.

Our first method has been by drawing, finding the effect on any simple motif in any chosen position. This is straightforward and effective – but imprecise. In the case above, with $\alpha° = 40°$, drawing might suggest that **ML** is a rotation about O (or a point close to it) through about 79°.

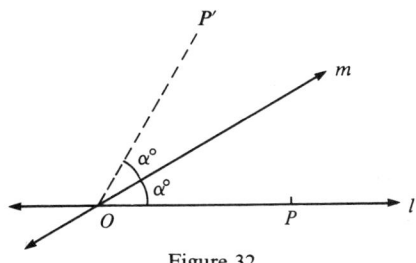

Figure 32

A proof might proceed as follows:
   (i) An indirect isometry followed by another indirect isometry is equivalent to a direct isometry.

(ii) $O \xrightarrow{L} O \xrightarrow{M} O$. Since O is an invariant point, the answer is a rotation about O (the other kind of direct isometry, a translation, has no invariant point).

(iii) See what happens to one other special point. Choose a point P on l. It does not move in the first stage; it then maps onto P' under the reflection M. The required angle of rotation equals angle $POP' = 2\alpha°$.

It is an interesting exercise to consider in similar fashion the combination of all possible pairs of isometries – rotation followed by translation, reflection followed by rotation, etc. We give one more example here.

Example 8

Find the single transformation equivalent to a rotation **R** about A through $\alpha°$, followed by a translation **T** represented by the vector v.

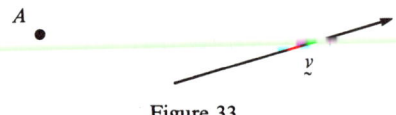

Figure 33

Since both transformations are direct isometries, the answer is a direct isometry, too. Any line in an image figure will make an angle of $\alpha°$ with the corresponding line in the object figure, so we are looking for a rotation **S** of $\alpha°$ about some point C.

Now $\mathbf{S}(A) = \mathbf{TR}(A) = \mathbf{T}(A) = A'$, so A is rotated to A' (see Figure 34) and this shows that C must be the third vertex of an isosceles triangle as shown.

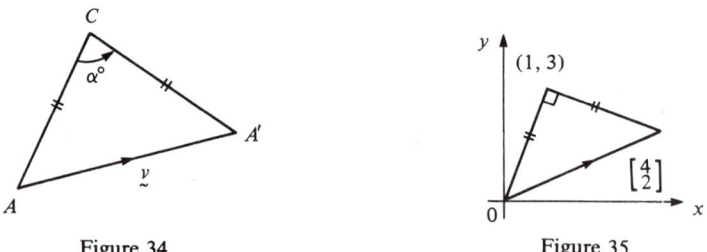

Figure 34   Figure 35

Notice that this is a generalisation of the result in Section 3 (p. 225), where a quarter-turn about O followed by a translation $\begin{bmatrix} 4 \\ 2 \end{bmatrix}$ was found to be equivalent to a quarter-turn about $(1, 3)$.

Using the algebra of transformations

We shall now illustrate a new and elegant method of proof.
The first result of Section 4 was $\mathbf{ML} = \mathbf{R}_{O,\,2\alpha°}$.
This allows us to replace the pair of reflections by the rotation. But we could

also reverse this process and replace a rotation by a pair of reflections, if this would serve a useful purpose. And the axes of reflection can be any two lines through O separated by half the angle of rotation. Thus in Figure 36, $\mathbf{R}_{O, 2\alpha°}$ can be replaced by **QP** just as well as **ML**.

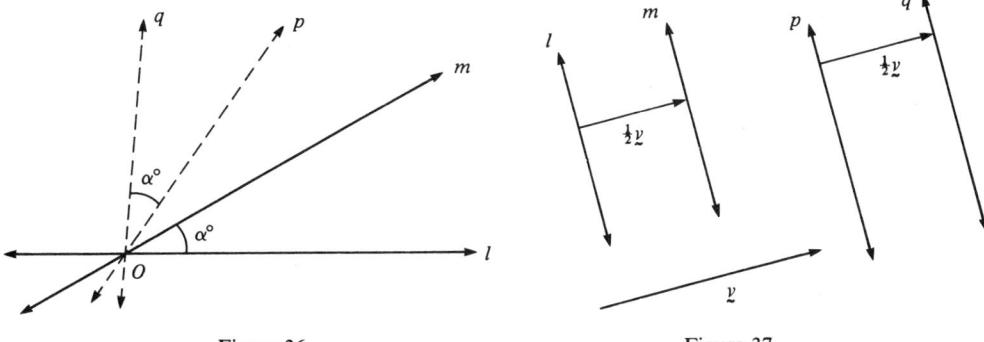

Figure 36   Figure 37

Similarly, in Figure 37, a translation through the vector v can be replaced by **ML** or **QP** (the four axes of reflection now being all perpendicular to v and spaced as shown).

Example 8, re-worked

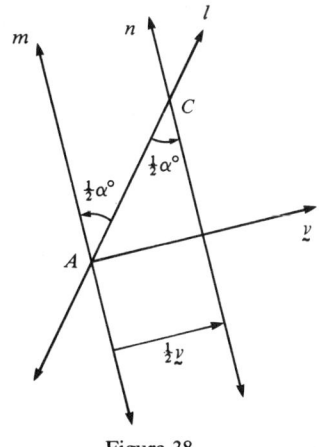

Figure 38

Referring to Figure 38, we can now write
$$\mathbf{TR} = (\mathbf{NM})(\mathbf{ML})$$
$$= \mathbf{NMML}.$$
The algebra of transformations is associative, meaning that brackets are unnecessary. The rotation **R** followed by the translation **T** is equivalent to reflecting first in l, then in m, then in m again, and finally in n.

You will say that reflecting in m twice in succession is a waste of time, since **MM** = **I**, the identity transformation.

The full working is $\mathbf{TR} = \text{NMML}$
$= \text{NIL}$
$= \text{NL}$
$= \mathbf{R}_{C, \alpha°}.$

The final rotation is about the point where n and l meet, and the angle is double the angle between these lines. We have identified the same point C as we did before.

Exercise D

1 $\mathbf{T}_1$ is the translation with vector v_1, and $\mathbf{T}_2$ is the translation with vector v_2. What is the single transformation equivalent to $\mathbf{T}_2 \mathbf{T}_1$?

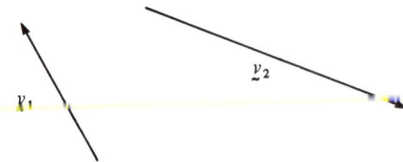

Figure 39

*2 $\mathbf{H}_1$ is the half-turn about $(1, 2)$ and $\mathbf{H}_2$ is the half-turn about $(8, 7)$. Describe exactly the single transformation equivalent to $\mathbf{H}_2 \mathbf{H}_1$ and prove your answer correct.

3 In Figure 40, the half-turn about A ($\mathbf{H}_A$) is equal to ML. If $\mathbf{H}_B = \text{NM}$, where is the line n? Describe the single transformation equivalent to $\mathbf{H}_B \mathbf{H}_A$ by simplifying NMML.

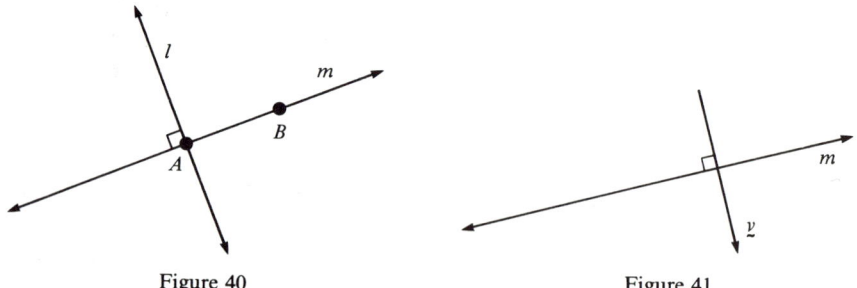

Figure 40 Figure 41

4 In Figure 41, v is perpendicular to m; $\mathbf{M}$ is the reflection in m; $\mathbf{T}$ is the translation with vector v. Find the single transformation $\mathbf{MT}$ by one or more of the following methods:
  (a) by drawing, showing what happens to a single motif of your own choice;
  (b) by considering the images of points on m under $\mathbf{MT}$;
  (c) by looking for points which are invariant under $\mathbf{MT}$;
  (d) by replacing $\mathbf{T}$ by a combination of reflections.

5 For the transformations of question 4, find the single transformation equivalent to $\mathbf{TM}$.

*6 Simplify $R_{A, 20°} M$ and $MR_{A, 70°}$ where A lies on m as in Figure 42.

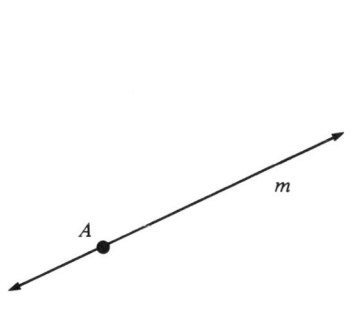

Figure 42   Figure 43

7   (a) In Figure 43 state several possibilities for the centres of two half-turns equivalent to the translation $ABCD \to GDEF$.
    (b) Comment on your answers in the light of questions 2 and 3.
8   (a) In Figure 43 state several possibilities for the centres of two anticlockwise quarter-turns equivalent to the half-turn which maps $ABCD$ onto $EFGD$.
    (b) If the first centre is called X and the second centre Y, what can you say about the angles of triangle XYD?
9   Let Q_1 be the quarter-turn about O (0, 0), Q_2 be the quarter-turn about A (8, 2), and H_2 be the half-turn about A (8, 2).
    Let B and C be the centres of single rotations equivalent to $Q_2 Q_1$ and $H_2 Q_1$. Locate B and C and comment on the angles of triangles OAB, OAC.
10 For the transformations of question 9, find $Q_1 Q_2$ (3, 5) and $Q_1 H_2$ (6, 10). Where are the centres of the single rotations equivalent to $Q_1 Q_2$ and $Q_1 H_2$?
11 Start a diagram by marking two points and labelling them A and B. If now $R_{A, 100°}(C) = C'$ and also $R_{B, 70°}(C') = C$, construct the points C and C'.
12 Start a new diagram and mark two points A and B. Construct the point P such that $R_{B, 70°} R_{A, 100°}(A) = P$. What does this tell you about the centre C of the single rotation $R_{C, \gamma°}$ equivalent to $R_{B, 70°} R_{A, 100°}$?
    Construct the point Q such that $R_{B, 70°} R_{A, 100°}(Q) = B$. What does this tell you about C?
13 Copy Figure 44. Given $R_{A, 100°} = ML$, draw the line l; given $R_{B, 70°} = NM$, draw the line n.
    What can you deduce from the fact that $NMML = NL$?
    What is the angle of the single rotation equivalent to $R_{B, 70°} R_{A, 100°}$?

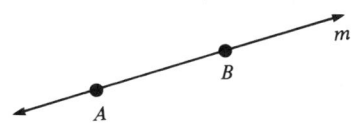

Figure 44

14 In Figure 45, O is the circumcentre of triangle ABC. Show that $\mathbf{NML}(B) = B$ and that $\mathbf{NML} = \mathbf{Q}$.

Deduce that $\mathbf{NM} = \mathbf{QL}$ and say what that implies about the angles in the diagram.

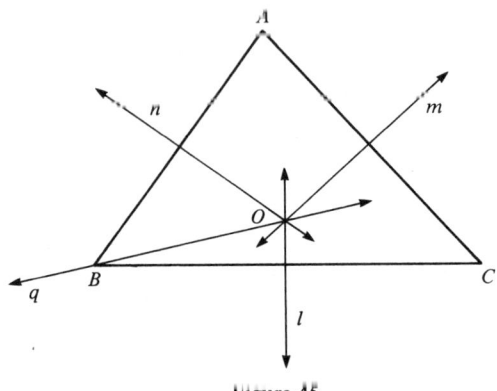

Figure 45

Express $\mathbf{MLN}$ and $\mathbf{LMN}$ as single reflections.
($\mathbf{L}$ denotes reflection in the line l, etc.)

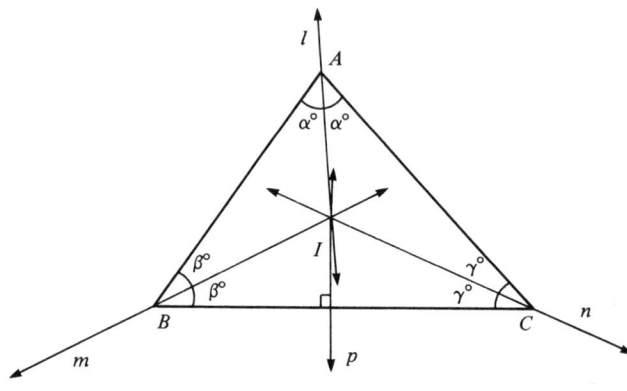

Figure 46

15 In Figure 46, I is the in-centre of triangle ABC.

Show that $\mathbf{MLN} = \mathbf{P}$ and that $\mathbf{NL} = \mathbf{PM}$. What can you deduce about the angles in the diagram?

($\mathbf{L}$ denotes reflection in the line l, etc.)

16 $\mathbf{R}_A, \mathbf{R}_B, \mathbf{R}_C$ denote $60°$ rotations about the vertices of a triangle labelled anticlockwise as in Figure 47.

Find $\mathbf{R}_A \mathbf{R}_B \mathbf{R}_C \mathbf{R}_A \mathbf{R}_B \mathbf{R}_C(B)$ and state the centre and angle of the single rotation equivalent to $\mathbf{R}_A \mathbf{R}_B \mathbf{R}_C$.

Show that $\mathbf{R}_A(C)$, $\mathbf{R}_A \mathbf{R}_B(C)$, B and C are the vertices of a parallelogram.

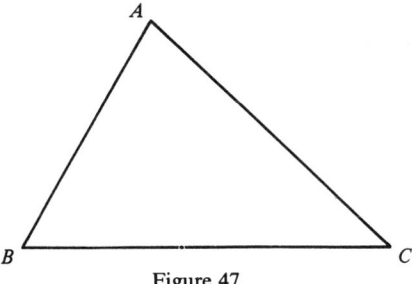

Figure 47

17 In Figure 48, *BCU*, *CAV*, *ABW* are equilateral triangles. *BV* meets *CW* at *Z*.

Show by rotation that angle $BZW = 60°$. Does this mean that a circle can be drawn through *U*, *B*, *Z*, *C*? Explain why angle $UZC = 60°$ and why *AU* passes through *Z*.

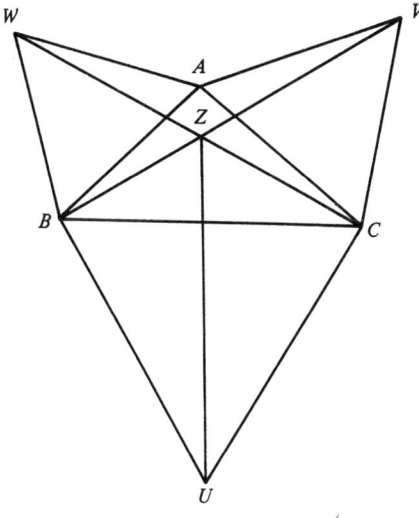

Figure 48

REVISION PAPER 1

Matrices

1. $A = \begin{bmatrix} 1 & 0 \\ 1 & -3 \\ 1 & 2 \end{bmatrix}$, $B = \begin{bmatrix} -1 & 0 \\ 1 & 2 \\ 0 & 4 \\ -3 & 0 \end{bmatrix}$, $C = \begin{bmatrix} 2 & 0 \\ 3 & 3 \\ 3 & -4 \\ -1 & -1 \end{bmatrix}$, $D = \begin{bmatrix} -1 & 0 & 2 \\ 0 & 2 & -1 \\ 2 & -1 & 0 \\ 0 & 0 & 1 \end{bmatrix}$.

   (a) Only two of these matrices may be added. State which two they are, and evaluate their sum.

   (b) Only two of these matrices may be multiplied. Write them down in the correct order for multiplication, and evaluate their product. (SMP O-level)

2. The Trans-Can Airline has eight Viscounts, six Tridents and two Caravelles. East Atlantic Airways have nine Viscounts, one Trident and seven Caravelles, and the Il-Oil Company has two Viscounts, eleven Tridents and no Caravelles.

   (a) Express this information as a 3×3 matrix **A**.

   (b) The Viscount carries 50 passengers, the Trident carries 140 and the Caravelle 80. Write down a suitable product of two matrices which when evaluated will determine the number of passengers that each airline is able to carry when all its aircraft are full.

   (c) Evaluate this product.

   (d) Describe what information would be given by pre-multiplying your matrix **A** by the row matrix [1 1 1]. (SMP O-level)

3. The average number of passengers per day travelling by rail from London to three towns, A, B and C is given by the matrix **P**.

   $$\mathbf{P} = \begin{bmatrix} 170 & 120 & 200 \\ 880 & 480 & 700 \end{bmatrix} \begin{matrix} \text{First class} \\ \text{Second class} \end{matrix}$$

   The distances are respectively 200 km, 300 km and 400 km.

   (a) Express these distances as a suitable vector **M** and calculate **PM**.

   (b) First-class fares are calculated at the rate of 1.4 pence per km, second-class at 0.9 pence per km. Express these rates as a suitable vector **F**, calculate **FPM** and say what information is conveyed by the product.

   (c) It is proposed to abolish the two classes and charge all passengers at the same rate. Find this rate, in pence per km, if the total revenue is to remain the same as before. (SMP O-level)

4. $A = \begin{bmatrix} 1 & 2 \\ 0 & 3 \end{bmatrix}$, $B = \begin{bmatrix} 1 & -\frac{2}{3} \\ 0 & \frac{1}{3} \end{bmatrix}$, $C = \begin{bmatrix} 2 & 0 \\ 4 & 1 \end{bmatrix}$, $D = \begin{bmatrix} \frac{1}{2} & 0 \\ k & 1 \end{bmatrix}$.

   (a) Evaluate **AB**.

   (b) Find the value of k which makes **CD** the unit matrix.

   (c) Simplify **CABD** with the value of k found above. What does this show about the inverse of **CA**?

   (d) What is the inverse of **AC**? (SMP O-level)

5. The matrix $\mathbf{M} = \begin{bmatrix} p & q \\ 0 & s \end{bmatrix}$ is such that

   (i) $\mathbf{M}\begin{bmatrix} 3 \\ 1 \end{bmatrix} = \begin{bmatrix} 5 \\ 2 \end{bmatrix}$ and (ii) $\mathbf{M}\begin{bmatrix} 5 \\ 2 \end{bmatrix} = \begin{bmatrix} 7 \\ 4 \end{bmatrix}$.

   (a) Write down an equation for p and q using equation (i).
   Write down an equation for p and q using equation (ii).
   From these two equations find p and q.

(b) State the matrix **M**.

(c) If $\mathbf{M}^n \begin{bmatrix} 3 \\ 1 \end{bmatrix} = \begin{bmatrix} 7 \\ 4 \end{bmatrix}$, write down the value of *n*. (SMP O-level)

REVISION PAPER 2

Transformations

1. △ is the arrowhead whose vertices are *P*(1, 2), *Q*(5, 1), *R*(4, 2) and *S*(5, 3). (See Figure 1.)
   E is the enlargement from the origin of scale factor 3.
   F is the enlargement from the point (5, 5) of scale factor −2.

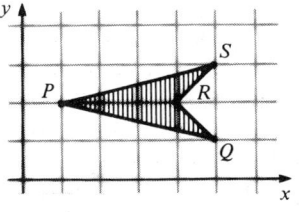

Figure 1

   (a) Draw accurately, on a single diagram, △, **E**(△) and **F**(△), labelling each vertex with its coordinates. (Use squared paper and take values 0 to 14 on each axis.)
   (b) Use your diagram to state as fully as possible the transformation that maps **E**(△) onto **F**(△).
   (c) Comment briefly on your result. (SMP O-level)

2. (a) On squared paper, with a scale of 1 cm to a unit, draw axes to show values of *x* from 0 to 16 and values of *y* from 0 to 12. Draw the triangle whose vertices are (6, 3), (6, 4) and (8, 3) and label it △.
   (b) The transformation **P** is the enlargement with centre (0, 0) and scale factor 2, **Q** the enlargement with centre (16, 0) and scale factor 1.5. Draw and label the triangles **P**(△) and **QP**(△) and hence express **QP** as a single transformation as fully as possible.
   (c) By further drawing or by reasoning, determine what kind of transformation **U** satisfies the equation
   $$\mathbf{QP} = \mathbf{UPQ}.$$ (SMP O-level)

3. In Figure 2 *AE* bisects ∠*A*, *AB* = *AD* and *FD* is parallel to *BC*.
   (a) State a single transformation that maps *B* onto *D* and *E* onto *F*. Name a line segment equal to *BE*.
   (b) State a single transformation that maps *D* onto *C* and *F* onto *E*. Copy and complete the statement
   $$\overline{EC} = \overline{AC}.$$
   (c) Given that *AB* = 5 cm, *AC* = 7 cm and *BC* = 6 cm, calculate *EC*.
   (SMP O-level)

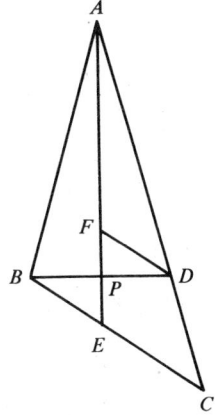

Figure 2

4 The rectangle $OABC$ can be transformed into the rectangle $OCED$, where the order shows corresponding vertices, by an enlargement with centre O followed by a reflection. (See Figure 3.)

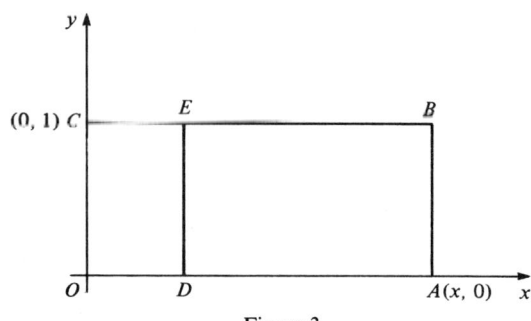

Figure 3

(a) For the case $x = 2$,
  (i) draw the figure on squared paper and show the position of the image of $OABC$ after the enlargement.
  (ii) state the scale factor of the enlargement and the equation of the mirror-line for the reflection.
(b) If, now, $x = k$,
  (i) state the scale factor and the length of OD;
  (ii) if, also, $AD = 1$ unit, write down another expression for the length of OD and hence show that
  $$k^2 - k - 1 = 0.$$
  (SMP O-level)

5 A, B, C are three points on a circle centre O. R is the image of O under reflection in AC. (See Figure 4.)

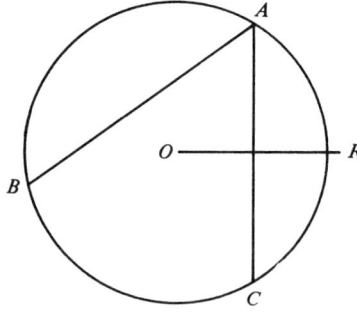

Figure 4

(a) Explain why $AOCR$ is a rhombus.
(b) State a relation between the sizes of angles OAC and OAR.
(c) Q is the image of O under reflection in AB. State a similar relation between angles OAB and OAQ, and hence obtain a relation between angles BAC and QAR.
(d) If **T** is the translation which maps A onto O name, with reasons, the images of R and Q under **T**.
(e) Deduce a relation between angles BAC and BOC. (SMP O-level)

REVISION PAPER 3

Matrices and transformations

1 A triangle has vertices at $A(1, 0)$, $B(7, 4)$ and $C(1.5, 1)$. The points A', B' and C' are the images of A, B and C under the transformation **S** whose matrix is
$$\begin{bmatrix} 1 & -1.5 \\ 0 & 1 \end{bmatrix}$$
   (a) Find the coordinates of A', B' and C', and show the triangles ABC and $A'B'C'$ on one diagram.
   (b) Describe **S** in words as fully as possible.
   (c) Find the area of each of the triangles $A'B'C'$ and ABC. (SMP O-level)

2 The transformations **P** and **R** are defined by:
$$\mathbf{P}: \begin{bmatrix} x \\ y \end{bmatrix} \to \begin{bmatrix} 1 & 2 \\ 0 & 1 \end{bmatrix} \begin{bmatrix} x \\ y \end{bmatrix} \qquad \mathbf{R}: \begin{bmatrix} x \\ y \end{bmatrix} \to \begin{bmatrix} x \\ y \end{bmatrix} + \begin{bmatrix} 1 \\ 2 \end{bmatrix}.$$
   (a) Find the image of $(-1, 2)$ under (i) **PR**, (ii) **RP**.
   (b) Find u and v if
$$\mathbf{PR}: \begin{bmatrix} x \\ y \end{bmatrix} \to \begin{bmatrix} 1 & 2 \\ 0 & 1 \end{bmatrix} \begin{bmatrix} x \\ y \end{bmatrix} + \begin{bmatrix} u \\ v \end{bmatrix}.$$
   (**PR** means **R** followed by **P**.) (SMP O-level)

3 A transformation **T** is given by
$$\mathbf{T}: \begin{bmatrix} x \\ y \end{bmatrix} \to \begin{bmatrix} 0 & -1 \\ 1 & 0 \end{bmatrix} \begin{bmatrix} x \\ y \end{bmatrix} + \begin{bmatrix} 0 \\ 4 \end{bmatrix}.$$
   (a) Find the images under **T** of the points $A(1, 0)$, $B(4, 0)$ and $C(3, 2)$.
   (b) On squared paper draw the triangle ABC and its image under **T**. Hence describe geometrically the single transformation given by **T**.
   (c) Describe fully
      (i) the transformation **P** whose matrix is $\begin{bmatrix} 0 & -1 \\ 1 & 0 \end{bmatrix}$;
      (ii) the translation **V** such that **P** followed by **V** is equivalent to **T**;
      (iii) the translation **W** such that **W** followed by **P** is equivalent to **T**. (SMP O-level)

4 On a sheet of squared paper draw axes of x and y and graduate them on a scale of 2 cm to a unit to show values of x and y from -2 to 4. Label the point $(2, 1)$ as A, label $(1, 2)$ as B and label $(-1, 1)$ as C.
   The transformation **H** is given by pre-multiplication of column vectors by
$$\begin{bmatrix} 0.5 & 1 \\ -0.25 & 1.5 \end{bmatrix}.$$
   This transformation maps A, B and C onto A', B' and C' respectively. Calculate the coordinates of these points, and mark the points in your diagram. Shade in different ways the quadrilaterals $OABC$, $OA'B'C'$, O being the origin.
   What type of transformation is **H**?
   Using a property of this type of transformation, or otherwise, calculate the area of triangle $A'B'C'$. (SMP O-level)

5 $\mathbf{U}: \begin{bmatrix} x \\ y \end{bmatrix} \to \begin{bmatrix} x \\ y \end{bmatrix} + \begin{bmatrix} 3 \\ 2 \end{bmatrix}. \qquad \mathbf{V}: \begin{bmatrix} x \\ y \end{bmatrix} \to \begin{bmatrix} 0 & -1 \\ 1 & 0 \end{bmatrix} \begin{bmatrix} x \\ y \end{bmatrix}.$

   (a) Describe the geometrical effect of the transformations **U** and **V**.

(b) Express in terms of **U** and **V** the transformations

$$\mathbf{P}: \begin{bmatrix} x \\ y \end{bmatrix} \to \begin{bmatrix} 0 & -1 \\ 1 & 0 \end{bmatrix} \left(\begin{bmatrix} x \\ y \end{bmatrix} + \begin{bmatrix} 3 \\ 2 \end{bmatrix} \right);$$

$$\mathbf{Q}: \begin{bmatrix} x \\ y \end{bmatrix} \to \begin{bmatrix} 0 & -1 \\ 1 & 0 \end{bmatrix} \begin{bmatrix} x \\ y \end{bmatrix} + \begin{bmatrix} 3 \\ 2 \end{bmatrix}.$$

(c) Find the image of (−2.5, 0.5) under **P**.

(d) Find the point (x, y) which is mapped onto itself by **Q**. (SMP O-level)

6 (a) Calculate the coordinates of the image of the point A(4, 3) obtained by pre-multiplying its column vector

$$\begin{bmatrix} 4 \\ 3 \end{bmatrix} \text{ by the matrix } \begin{bmatrix} 0.6 & -0.8 \\ 0.8 & 0.6 \end{bmatrix}.$$

(b) Show that this mapping is a rotation about the origin O and calculate its angle.

(c) Calculate the image of B(2, 5) under the same rotation and hence the area of triangle OAB. (SMP O-level)

7 (a) Describe the transformations whose matrices are

$$\mathbf{R} = \begin{bmatrix} -1 & 0 \\ 0 & 1 \end{bmatrix} \text{ and } \mathbf{S} = \begin{bmatrix} 0 & -1 \\ 1 & 0 \end{bmatrix}.$$

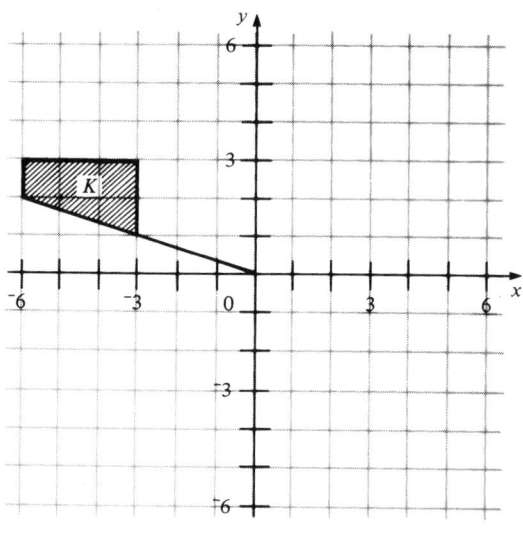

Figure 5

(b) Copy Figure 5 on squared paper and on it draw and label L and M, where L = R(K) and M = S(K).

N is another image of K such that the figure formed by K, L, M and N has just one line of symmetry. Draw and label N on your diagram.

(c) Describe the transformation that maps K onto N. If **T** is the matrix of this transformation, express **T** in terms of **R** and **S**, and compute **T**. (SMP O-level)

REVISION PAPER 4

Miscellaneous

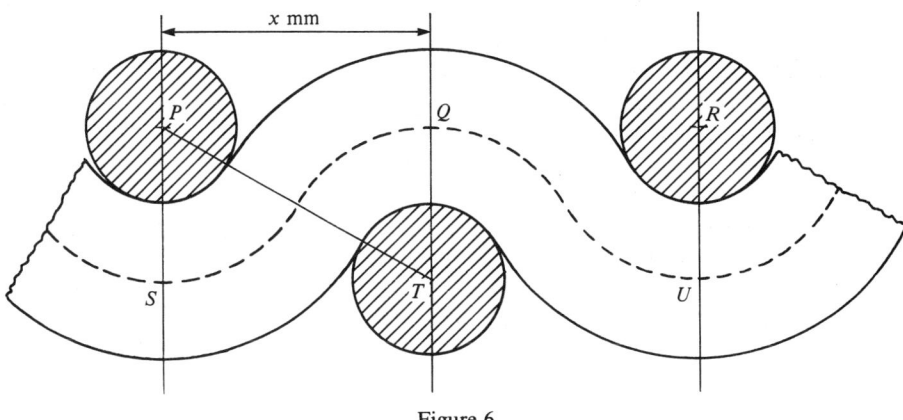

Figure 6

1 Figure 6 shows a magnified section across a piece of woven fabric. The shaded circles show threads running along the fabric. One thread running across is also shown. The diameter of each thread is 0.2 mm. *PQR* and *STU* are straight lines.
   (a) By considering the lengths *PT* and *QT* calculate *PTQ* and the distance x mm shown in the diagram.
   (b) Calculate the length of the arc *SQ*.
   (c) If the fabric is one metre wide, calculate the total length of a cross-thread.
   (SMP O-level)

2 The moon may be assumed to be a sphere of diameter 3480 km and to have a system of latitude and longitude like the earth. *P* and *Q* are points on the moon's surface at latitude 60° N; *P* has longitude 90° W and *Q* has longitude 90° E.
   (a) State the distance from *P* to *Q* along a straight line (that is, through the moon).
   (b) Calculate the length of the shortest route from *P* to *Q* on the moon's surface.
   (c) Calculate the length of the route from *P* to *Q* along the circle of latitude 60° N.
   (d) An astronomer *A* on earth can just see both *P* and *Q*. Taking the distance of the moon from the earth at this time to be 382 000 km, calculate the size of angle *PAQ*. (SMP O-level)

3 A reservoir is to be constructed to hold 3.2×10^7 m³ of water when full, and an accurate model of it is built to a scale of 1:200.
   (a) When the model is full of water the greatest depth is 18 cm. What will be the greatest depth in the reservoir when full?
   (b) If the surface area of the water in the model is 40 m², calculate the corresponding surface area of the water in the reservoir.
   (c) Write down the volume of water in the model, when full.
   (d) When the model is full, a decrease in the height of the water level of 1 cm produces a decrease in volume of 5×10^5 cm³. Calculate the corresponding decrease in volume for the reservoir (that is, when the water level drops 200 cm).
      Express the decrease in volume in the model as a percentage of the original volume. What will be the corresponding percentage decrease for the reservoir?
   (SMP O-level)

242 Revision papers

4 A lorry seen from above appears as a rectangle. The road surface of a roundabout is a ring between two concentric circles.
   (a) Sketch the roundabout and show a lorry which is just able to get round it without overstepping the roadway at any point. Draw in the line of symmetry of the whole figure.
   (b) The lorry is 3 m wide and 12 m long. The radius of the outer circle of the roundabout is 10 m. Calculate the radius of the inner circle if the lorry can just get round.
   (c) On another roundabout the roadway is 4.2 m wide and the same lorry can just get round. Write down an equation for the radius of the inner circle and hence calculate this radius. (SMP O-level)

5 (a) One pair of opposite faces of a red cube is marked with a 1, another pair is marked with a 6, the third pair with an 8. If the cube is thrown as a die, what is the probability of scoring 6 in one throw?
   (b) A blue cube similarly has 3, 5, and 7 on its pairs of opposite faces. Copy Figure 7 and ring those points which correspond to the score of the red cube being greater than the score of the blue one. If the two cubes are thrown together, what is the probability that the score of the red one will be greater?
   Which colour is more likely to have the higher score?

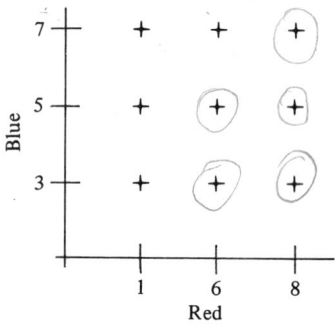

Figure 7

   (c) A yellow cube has 2, 4, 9 on its opposite faces. Draw diagrams similar to that given in Figure 7 for (i) blue and yellow, (ii) yellow and red; in each case state which colour is more likely to have the higher score if the two cubes are thrown together.
   Comment on your answers. (SMP O-level)

REVISION PAPER 5

Miscellaneous

1 A vertical flagpole ABC of height 9.0 m stands on a horizontal field, and is supported by guylines from B to pegs at P, Q and R. The guylines are of equal length and are inclined at 45° to the horizontal. P is 5.0 m due north of A and PQR is an equilateral triangle. (See Figure 8.)
   (a) Calculate the altitude (angle of elevation) of the sun when the shadow of C is at P.

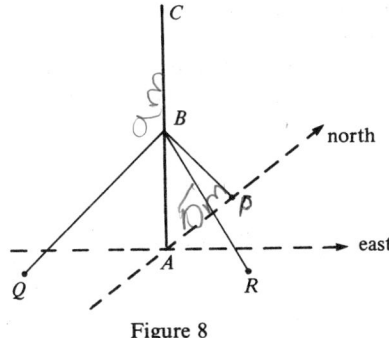

Figure 8

(b) When the sun is due west of the flagpole its altitude is 40°, and the shadow of C is at a point X. Calculate the distance AX.
(c) On squared paper draw and letter, to a scale of 1:100,
   (i) the plan,
   (ii) the side elevation from the east, of the flagpole and guylines. Show distinctly on your plan (for example, in a different colour) the point X and the shadow of the flagpole and guylines when the sun is due west.
(SMP O-level)

2 A forester can spend a maximum of £144 on buying young spruce and larch trees to plant a site of area one hectare. The trees are sold in multiples of 100, spruce costing £9 per hundred and larch £12 per hundred. Each hundred spruce require an area of at least 0.1 hectare; and each hundred larch an area of at least 0.05 hectare. To reduce monotony, neither type of tree may exceed three times the other in number.
   (a) If the forester buys x hundred spruce and y hundred larch, deduce four inequalities (other than $x \geq 0$ and $y \geq 0$) satisfied by x and y.
   (b) Show these inequalities graphically, using a scale of 1 cm to 100 trees on each axis.
   (c) When the trees are sold for timber the profit is equivalent to 60p on each tree originally planted. On your graph draw and label the line that corresponds to a total profit of £720. Hence find the smallest number of larch trees that can be bought initially to obtain this profit. (SMP O-level)

3 The rate of use of gas in a village during part of a typical winter day is given in the table:

Hours after 6 a.m.	0	$\frac{1}{2}$	1	$1\frac{1}{2}$	2	$2\frac{1}{2}$	3	$3\frac{1}{2}$	4
Rate of use in m³/hour	5.5	7	9	10.5	11	11	10	8	7

   (a) On squared paper, draw a graph to represent these figures.
   (b) Calculate the average hourly increase of the rate between 6 a.m. and 7.30 a.m.
   (c) Estimate the area under the graph, making your method clear, and state what the area represents.
   (d) From your answer to (c) calculate the average rate of use during the 4 hours.
(SMP O-level)

4 A water tank is 4 m deep. The depth, d metres, of water in the tank at time t seconds after the start of an experiment is represented by
$$d = 2 + \cos(30t)°.$$
   (a) With a scale of 2 cm to 1 second and 5 cm to 1 metre, draw a graph to show

the depth of water during the first 6 seconds of the experiment. Take 0, 1, 2, 3, 4, 5, 6 for values of t and plot corresponding values of d.

(b) From your graph find the length of time during the first 6 seconds for which the water is *less than* $1\frac{1}{2}$ m deep.

(c) A float, which slides freely on a vertical rod placed in the tank, stays on the water's surface. Read off, and write down, the depth of water at time 0 seconds and at time $4\frac{1}{2}$ seconds. Hence find the average speed of the float during the first $4\frac{1}{2}$ seconds of the experiment. Express your answer in centimetres per second.

(d) Find the number of times during the first *minute*, at which the water is exactly $1\frac{1}{2}$ m deep.
(SMP O-level)

5 A message is coded as follows:
   (1) A is coded as 11, B as 12, and so on, so that Z is coded as 36. The digits 0 to 9 are left unchanged; a space is coded as 10.
   (2) The numbers obtained from stage (1) are arranged as the columns of a 2-row matrix. (If the message has an odd number of letters, a space is added at the end.)
   (3) The matrix is pre-multiplied by the matrix
   $$\begin{bmatrix} 7 & 3 \\ 2 & 5 \end{bmatrix},$$
   all multiplications being carried out in arithmetic modulo 37.
   (4) The entries in the product matrix are interpreted as letters or digits according to the coding in (1).

For example, SMP NEW BOOK 5 would be coded as follows:
(1) S   M   P   N   E   W   B   O   O   K   5
    29 23 26 10 24 15 33 10 12 25 25 21 10   5

(2) $\begin{bmatrix} 29 & 26 & 24 & 33 & 12 & 25 & 10 \\ 23 & 10 & 15 & 10 & 25 & 21 & 5 \end{bmatrix}$

(3) $\begin{bmatrix} 7 & 3 \\ 2 & 5 \end{bmatrix} \begin{bmatrix} 29 & 26 & 24 & 33 & 12 & 25 & 10 \\ 23 & 10 & 15 & 10 & 25 & 21 & 5 \end{bmatrix} = \begin{bmatrix} 13 & 27 & 28 & 2 & 11 & 16 & 11 \\ 25 & 28 & 12 & 5 & 1 & 7 & 8 \end{bmatrix}$

(4) Completed coded message: COQRRB25A1F7A8.

(a) Encode the message: THE LAST PROBLEM.
(b) Show that the inverse of 29 for multiplication mod 37 is 23, and hence find the inverse of the coding matrix. (The entries in your matrix should be positive integers.)
(c) Decode the following
   1IRNSFJ 1 9QD1V6RQB2BLM0IJF4AXKO4KO7
(d) Complete the quotation.
   (If necessary, consult WK9O7QHIXM7QZO7GCB.)
(e) Write and use computer programs to encode and decode messages by this system.

Answers

Answers are given only to questions marked *, and when questions have parts (a), (b), (c) etc. answers are given to some of the parts only.

CHAPTER 1 PLANS AND ELEVATIONS

Exercise A (p. 2)

1 (a) 4 m by 5 m (into bay).
4 0.9 m.

Exercise C (p. 9)

8 $PQ = 2.7$ cm.

Exercise D (p. 19)

1 (a) $AE = 5.0$ cm.
4 56°.
7 78°.
10 34°.

CHAPTER 2 POLYNOMIALS

Exercise A (p. 27)

1 (a) $x < {}^-2$ or $x > 3$; (d) $x \leqslant {}^-2$ or $x \geqslant 3$.
3 (a) ${}^-4 < x < {}^-3$ or $x > 1$; (d) ${}^-4 < x < 1$ or $x > 3$:

Exercise B (p. 30)

1 (a) $x^2 + 10x + 21$; (e) $21 + 4x - x^2$; (i) $8x^2 + 22x + 15$.
2 (a) $(x+1)(x+3)$; (d) $(3-x)(2+x)$.
4 (a) $x^3 + 12x^2 + 41x + 42$; (e) $48x^3 + 188x^2 + 244x + 105$.

Exercise C (p. 33)

1 (a) $(x+4)^2 - 4$; vertex $({}^-4, {}^-4)$;
   (e) $(x+4.5)^2 - 2.25$; vertex $({}^-4.5, {}^-2.25)$.
2 (a) $(x+4)^2 - 4$; vertex $({}^-4, {}^-4)$;
   (e) $(x+4)^2 - 7$; vertex $({}^-4, {}^-7)$.

Exercise D (p. 35)

1 (a) $x = 1$ or ${}^-5$; (e) $x = 1$ or ${}^-6$; (i) $x \approx {}^-5.24$ or ${}^-0.76$.
2 (a) $x \approx {}^-4.35$ or 0.35; (c) $x = {}^-1$ or $\tfrac{1}{3}$.
6 (a) $x < {}^-5$ or $x > 1$.

CHAPTER 4 MATHEMATICAL MODELS

Exercise B (p. 86)

1 (a) 400 N.
5 0.75 m.
9 110 hesioseconds.
11 14.3 g.
14 21.5 hesiohours.

Exercise C (p. 94)

7 $y = 3x^2$.
11 $y = 2\sqrt{x}$.
15 Gradient $= 1.5$.
17 The graph is a straight line through the origin with gradient 3.14.
20 (b) $y = 0.9\sqrt{x}$.
23 (b) $y = \dfrac{1000}{x^2}$.
27 (a) and (c) may be true.
31 (b) $t \approx 23.3\sqrt{m}$.

Exercise D (p. 99)

1

x	-3	-2	-1	0	1	2	3
x^2	9	4	1	0	1	4	9
2^x	0.125	0.25	0.5	1	2	4	8
2.5^x	0.064	0.16	0.4	1	2.5	6.25	15.625

4 $y = 2^x$.
7 (a) and (c) are consistent with the data.

Exercise F (p. 106)

1 Volume without peel $= \tfrac{1}{6}\pi (D-2t)^3$ cm^3.
5 $\alpha = \dfrac{Kc^2}{h^2}$.
11 $x = 16(A+1)$.
14 $C = \pm\sqrt{(D^2 - T^2)}$.

Exercise G (p. 111)

1 (a) $\{p : 0 \leqslant p \leqslant 1\}$; (e) {non-negative real numbers}.
5 £60.
7 630 m² to 2 s.f.

CHAPTER 5 STATISTICS

Exercise C (p. 127)

1 (a) 4; (e) 5.04; (i) 1.
5 (a) Mean $= 3.2$; mode $= 3$; median $= 3$.

Answers 247

Exercise D (p. 132)

1 Time A: median = 12; inter-quartile range = 14−10 = 4.
3 (*a*) (i) Median = 12; (ii) mean = 12.3.

CHAPTER 6 STRUCTURE

Exercise A (p. 137)

1 (*a*) Identity transformation; (*c*) Identity.

3 (*a*) $\begin{bmatrix} -1 & 0 \\ 0 & -1 \end{bmatrix}$.

5 (*a*) 12; (*d*) 22.

7 (*a*) $\begin{bmatrix} 26 & 33 \\ 44 & 59 \end{bmatrix}$.

Exercise B (p. 139)

1

× mod 7	1	2	3	4	5	6
1	1	2	3	4	5	6
2	2	4	6	1	3	5
3	3	6	2	5	1	4
4	4	1	5	2	6	3
5	5	3	1	6	4	2
6	6	5	4	3	2	1

3 (*a*) (i) **H**; (iii) **Y**.

5

∩	∅	{a}	{b}	{a, b}
∅	∅	∅	∅	∅
{a}	∅	{a}	∅	{a}
{b}	∅	∅	{b}	{b}
{a, b}	∅	{a}	{b}	{a, b}

7 (*a*) **T**; no.

Exercise C (p. 142)

1 Identity = 1. Inverse pairs: (1, 1), (2, 4), (3, 5), (6, 6).
12 (*a*) $fg(x) = 3x-13$; $(fg)^{-1}(x) = \frac{1}{3}(x+13)$.
14 (*a*) $\begin{bmatrix} 1 & 1 \\ 5 & 3 \end{bmatrix}$; (*e*) $\begin{bmatrix} -1.5 & 0.5 \\ 2.5 & -0.5 \end{bmatrix}$.

Exercise D (p. 144)

1 (*a*) Yes.
4 (*a*) {translations}: closed, commutative and associative.

Exercise E (p. 145)

1 (*a*) 36; (*c*) 36.

5 (*a*) $\begin{bmatrix} 11 & -1 \\ 4 & 5 \end{bmatrix}$; (*c*) $\begin{bmatrix} 1 & 4 \\ 7 & 8 \end{bmatrix}$.

248   Answers

Exercise F (p. 147)

1 (*a*) (i) 3; (ii) 3; (iii) 3;   (*d*) (i) 2; (ii) 2, ⁻2; (iii) 2, 5.

CHAPTER 7   EQUATIONS, INEQUALITIES AND GRAPHS

Exercise A (p. 157)
1 (*a*) $x = 0$ or 5.
3 $x = 1$ or 1.9.
5 $x = 2, y = 1$.
7 $x = \frac{1}{2}, y = 2$ or $x = 3, y = \frac{1}{3}$.

Exercise C (p. 164)
1 (2, 1).
3 (*a*), (*c*) and (*d*) intersect the region.
4 (*a*) $5x + 6y \geqslant 120$.

Exercise D (p. 168)
1 $H(0, 5); K(3, 2)$.
5 3 Dorsets and 4 Somersets.
9 5 of each type of machine.

CHAPTER 8   PROBABILITY

Exercise A (p. 177)
1 (*a*) $\frac{1}{4}$;   (*c*) $\frac{1}{52}$.

Exercise B (p. 181)
1 (*a*) $\frac{1}{8}$;   (*c*) $\frac{3}{16}$.
4 (*a*) $\frac{1}{4}$.

Exercise C (p. 186)
1 (*a*) 0.1296;   (*c*) 0.3456.
6 (*a*) 0.328.

CHAPTER 9   VECTORS APPLIED

Exercise A (p. 191)

1 (*a*) $\begin{bmatrix} -3 \\ -4 \end{bmatrix}$.

5 $c = 3$.
9 (*a*) $\underset{\sim}{DO} = \underset{\sim}{a}$; $\underset{\sim}{AB} = \underset{\sim}{b} - \underset{\sim}{a}$;   (*c*) $\underset{\sim}{LM} = 3\underset{\sim}{a}$.

Exercise B (p. 196)

1 (*a*) Magnitude of $\underset{\sim}{a} = 13$;   (*b*) angle between $\underset{\sim}{a}$ and $\underset{\sim}{b} = 141°$.
6 (*a*) *B* has polar coordinates (12, 90°).

Exercise C (p. 199)

1 14 nautical miles north, 43 nautical miles east.
5 Horizontal component of tension has magnitude 2500 N.

Exercise D (p. 202)

1 The ant moves in a direction making an angle of 31° with the direction of motion of the belt.

Exercise E (p. 206)

1 The sum is $\begin{bmatrix} 18 \\ -10 \end{bmatrix}$ N.
5 2700 N.

Exercise F (p. 208)

1 (*a*) 6 N.
5 Final velocity is 310 m/s at an angle of 36° to its original direction.

CHAPTER 10 GEOMETRY

Exercise C (p. 226)

8 (5, 2).
10 (*a*) (⁻5, 3).

Exercise D (p. 232)

2 The translation with vector $\begin{bmatrix} 14 \\ 10 \end{bmatrix}$.
6 $\mathbf{R}_{A,\,20°}\,\mathbf{M}$ = reflection in the line through A making an angle of 10° with m.

FORMULAE AND NOTATION

Mensuration

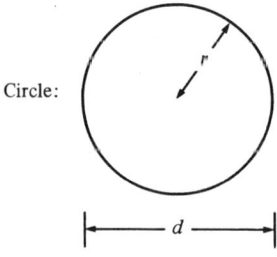

Circle:

Circumference = $2\pi r = \pi d$
Area = πr^2

Sphere:

Surface area = $4\pi r^2 = \pi d^2$
Volume = $\frac{4}{3}\pi r^3$
Surface area of zone bounded by parallel planes = $2\pi rh$

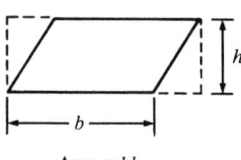

Parallelogram:

Area = bh

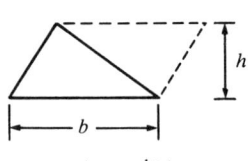

Triangle:

Area = $\frac{1}{2}bh$

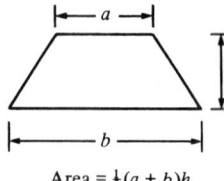

Trapezium:

Area = $\frac{1}{2}(a+b)h$

Prism, including cylinder:

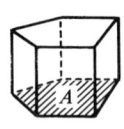

p = perimeter of base

Surface area (excluding ends) = ph
Volume = Ah

For the circular cylinder:
  Surface area (excluding ends) = $2\pi rh$
  Volume = $\pi r^2 h$

Pyramid, including cone:

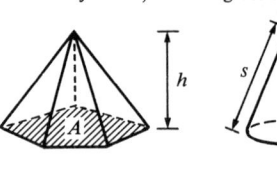

Volume = $\frac{1}{3}Ah$

For the circular cone:
  Surface area (excluding base) = πrs
  Volume = $\frac{1}{3}\pi r^2 h$

Trigonometry

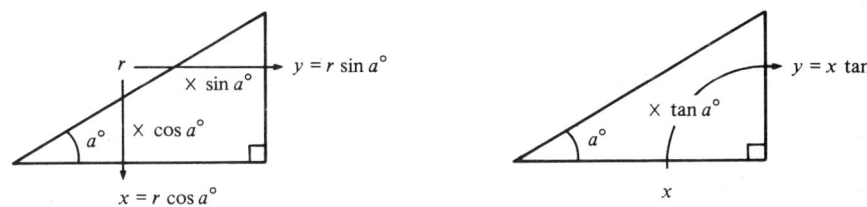

Pythagoras' theorem: $r^2 = x^2 + y^2$

Set Notation

$x \in A$: the element x is a member of the set A.
$A \subseteq B$: the set A is a subset of the set B.
$A \cup B$: the union of sets A and B; that is, the set of all elements which are members of set A or set B.
$A \cap B$: the intersection of sets A and B; that is, the set of all elements which are members of both set A and set B.
$\mathcal{E}$: the universal set; that is, the set of all elements under consideration.
ϕ: the empty set; that is, the set with no members.
A': the complement of the set A; that is, the set of all elements which are members of $\mathcal{E}$ but are not members of A.

Venn diagrams

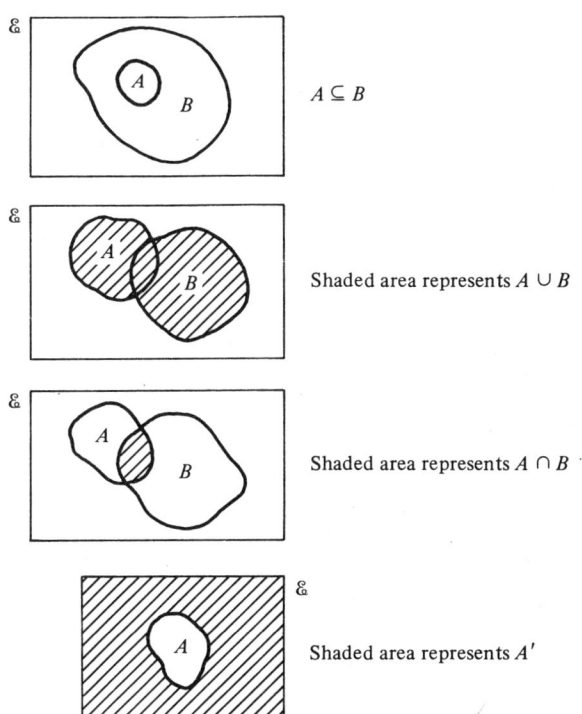

$A \subseteq B$

Shaded area represents $A \cup B$

Shaded area represents $A \cap B$

Shaded area represents A'

Index

acceleration 207–8
algebras 137
areas, formulae for 49
arithmetic modulo n 138
associative operation 143
averages 125–7

bearings 194
binomial probability 183–6
BS 1957 44

centroid of a triangle 219–20
'clock arithmetic' 138
coding 244
combination tables 138
combination of isometries 229–32
commutative operation 138
complex numbers 146
compound interest 45
cone, volume of 49
cubic polynomial 28
cumulative frequency 130–1
cylinder, volume and surface area of 49

degree of a polynomial 28
distributive law 145

Einstein's birthday 150
elevations 1
equations,
   decimal search method 159
   graphical solutions 155–7
   iterative method 159–60
   quadratic 33–4
   solving 142
   of straight line graphs 88
exclusive events 180

force
   and acceleration 207–8
   as a vector 198–9
   in equilibrium 203
   units 198, 207
formulae 105–6
   for areas and volumes 49
frequency diagram 122
FT index 70

gradient 88
graphs
   of inequalities 163–4

line graph for statistics 117
   of polynomial functions 25–7
   straight line 88
gravitation 203
grouped data 122, 125, 126
groups 143–4

hire purchase 77–9

identity elements 140
index numbers 64–8
inequalities, quadratic 25–6
integers 146
inter-quartile range 130
inverse elements 141
irrationality of $\sqrt{2}$ 150
iteration 159–60

linear programming 163–8
lines of equal cost 166
lines of equal profit 168
lowest common multiple 39

matrices
   and transformations 224–5, 239–40
   data storage 236
mean 125, 126
median 125, 126
medians of a triangle 214–5
mensuration 49
metric units 41
mode 125
Monge, Gaspard 6
mortgages 73–5
multipliers 86, 91–3

natural numbers 146
newton (unit of force) 198, 207
numbers, sets of 146

optimisation 163, 166–8

parallelogram, area of 49
Pascal's triangle 185
percentages 45
pictogram 114
pie chart 115–6
plan 1
polynomials 28
possibility space diagram 178
prism, volume of 49

Index

probability
  binomial   183–6
  definition   177
projections   6
proof in geometry   216–20
proportion   85, 88, 90
pyramid, volume of   49

quadratic equations   33–4
quadratic polynomial   28
  symmetric form   31–2
quartiles   130–1

range   129–30
rateable value and rates   46
ratio   44
rational numbers   146
real numbers   146
relative frequency   176
relative velocity   201
Retail Price Index   68
rounding of measurements   44

savings   71
scale factors   44, 85, 91–3
  for area and volume   52
scatter diagrams   102–3
scientific notation   40
self-inverse functions   141
similarity   51
simulation   173
sphere, volume of   49

spread, statistical   129–31
standard form   40
statistical diagrams   114–7
straight line graph, equation of   88

Third angle plan and elevation   6–7
transformations
  algebra of   229–32
  and matrices   224–5, 239–40
  geometrical   237–8
trapezium, area of   49
triangle
  area of   49
  centroid of   219–20
tree diagram   179–80

units, metric   41

vectors
  components of   193
  displacement   189
  force   198
  position   189
  relative velocity   201
  resultant   193
  velocity   198
Venn diagram, for probability   179
vertex of a parabola   32
volumes, formulae for   49

weight   203
weighted index numbers   67–8